PHOTOGRAPHING TRAVEL

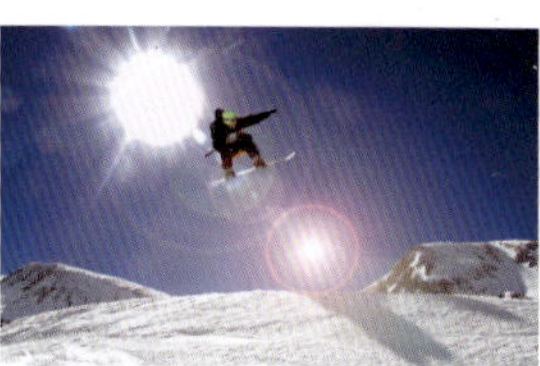

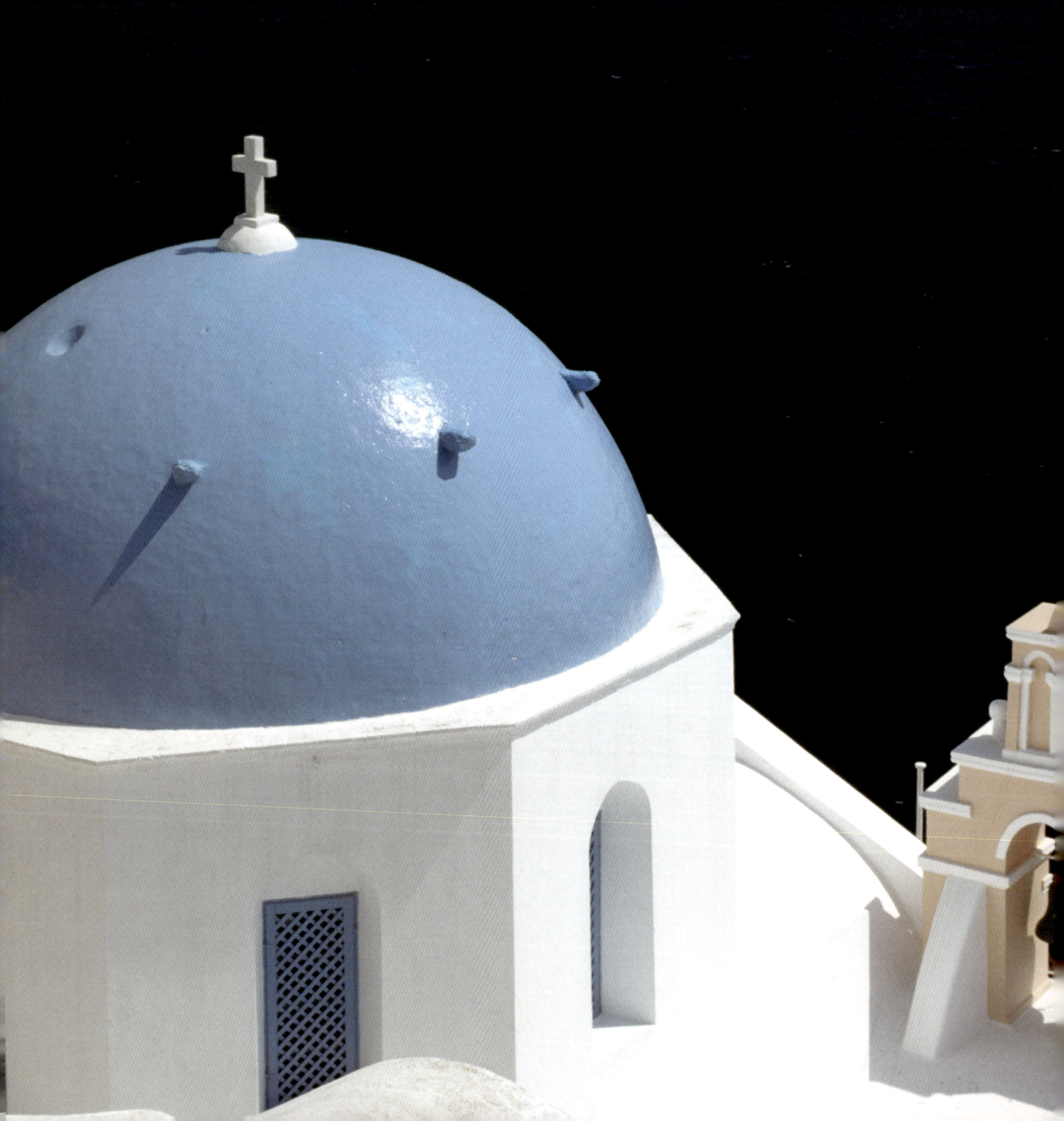

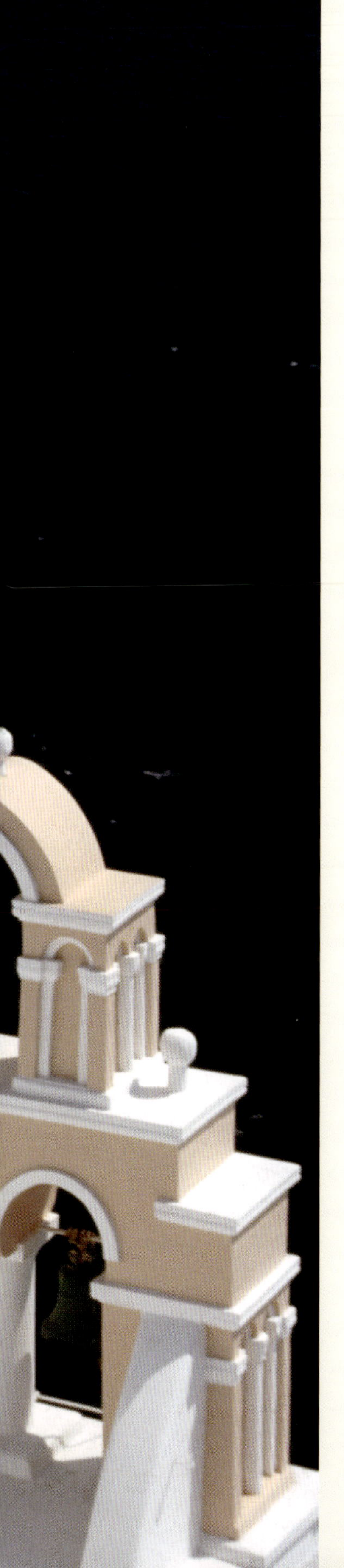

PHOTOGRAPHING TRAVEL

Alex Milovsky

VIVAYS PUBLISHING

Published by Vivays Publishing Ltd
www.vivays-publishing.com

English copyright © 2011 Vivays Publishing Ltd

© 'Art-Rodnik Publishing House' 2011
© Alex Milovsky, original text, 2011
© Alex Milovsky, pictures, 2011

A catalogue record for this book is available from the British Library

ISBN 978-1-908126-01-6

Publishing Director: Lee Ripley
Design: Andrew Shoolbred
English translation by Karen George in association with First Edition Translations Ltd., Cambridge, UK
Printed in China

CONTENTS

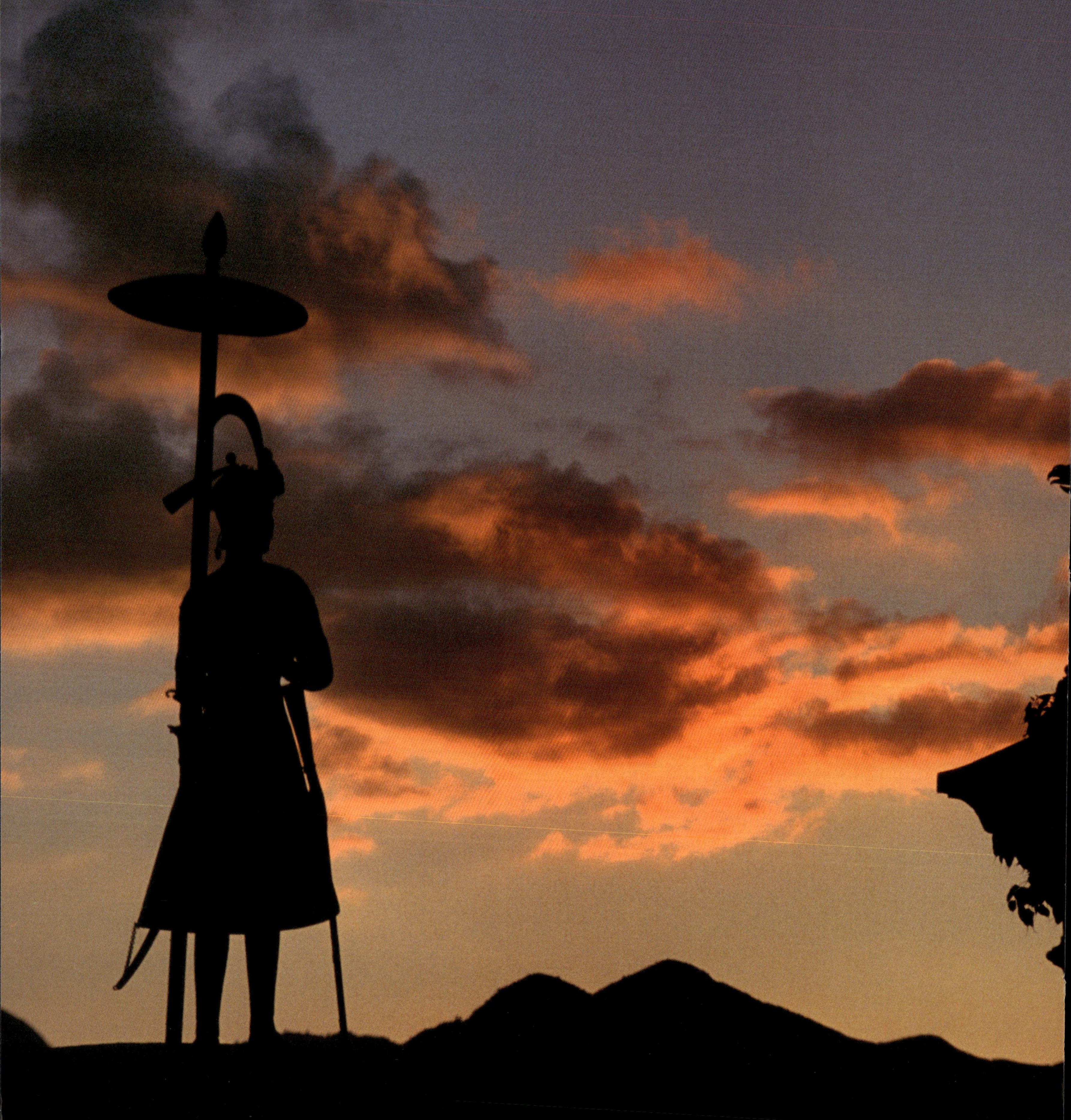

INTRODUCTION

Every traveller is a photographer and every photographer a traveller. The rapid development and accessibility of compact cameras, which now don't even need film, has brought these two roles much closer together. The automatic camera has dramatically simplified a process that used to be quite complex, reducing it to ordinary button-pressing. Now it costs nothing to take photos, even if you have no understanding of shutter speeds, apertures, guide numbers and other basic concepts that, until recently, had to be understood by the amateur photographer.

But what kind of photo you get is a different matter! No automatic camera frees you from the need to compose the frame and to position the light source – both of which will have a fundamental effect on the result. Just clicking away mindlessly with a point-and-shoot camera can only create a well-framed shot by accident. Of course, for the family album intended only for family and friends, photos where everything is sharp and recognisable will do. But if you feel the need for more, if you want to exhibit or take part in competitions, put out your own photographic magazine, post your pictures on photography websites, if you are drawn to creative photography, then forget about happy accident – and forget about the rules, for there is art too in breaking them. Always look for a solution that goes beyond the hackneyed!

Even when you set off on a journey through the most interesting, attractive countries, it would be naive to expect that the photos you take will all be masterpieces worthy of an award or a prize. Even the best photographers in the world can be left with just 'dry dust' after making a painstaking selection, like the few grains remaining on the bottom of a gold prospector's pan. A really great shot is always skill plus luck, so remember – keep expanding your portfolio all your life!

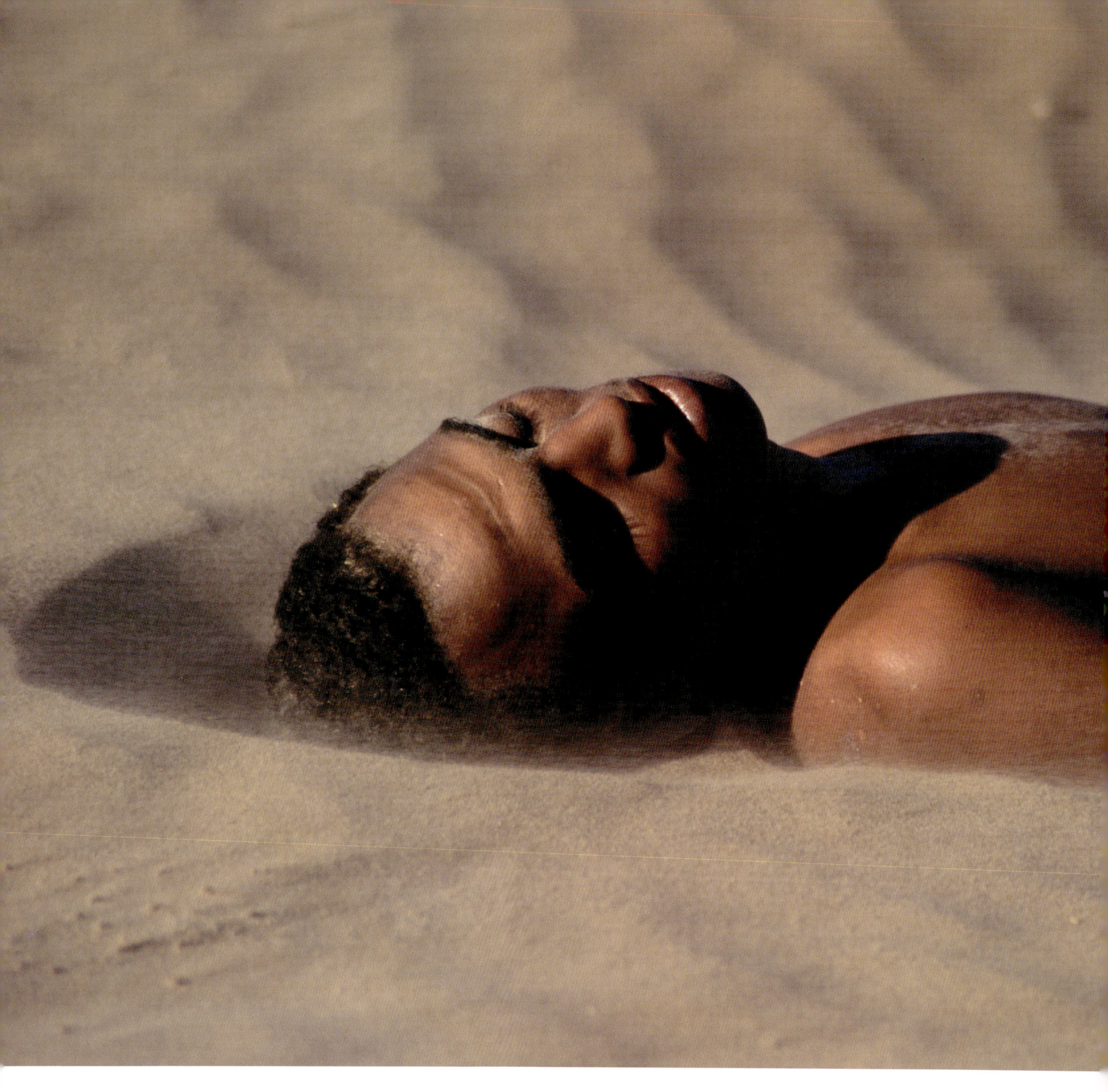

In praise of digital

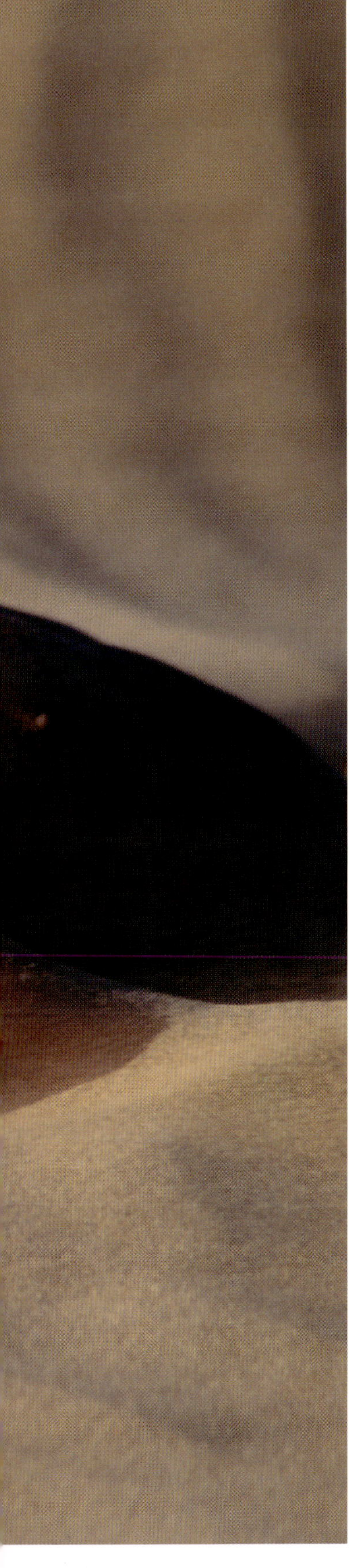

'Don't trust a friend with your wife, your car or your camera': Of course, this saying should be treated with a sense of humour. However, comparing your relationship with your camera to someone's relationship with his wife tells you something fundamental about the serious nature of choosing photographic equipment, especially for the travel photographer. When you are somewhere in the Amazon jungles or the Nubian Desert, it will be too late to complain that you haven't got the right lens or filter.

The choice of cameras for a visit to faraway lands (or even to the nearby environs of your own town) depends on the tasks you have set yourself, your skills, and your physical and financial resources. If you are going to be satisfied with a small album of photographs printed up quickly in a lab catering for amateurs, the choice is obvious – a fairly inexpensive compact camera with a 3x or 4x zoom. If you choose a camera that is super-light, easy to handle or very tiny, however, you will sacrifice image quality. Although here too, there are exceptions – for example, mini-cameras which, at the high end, have Leica lenses. But even they won't compensate for such severe drawbacks as the absence of a view-finder.

The market mainly offers the more serious travelling photographer variations on the sophisticated compact camera with 10x – 12x zoom, with view finder and with image stabilisation, that looks like – and even almost is – a reflex camera. The undoubted advantages of such cameras are their portability on any trip (even the most difficult), the huge range of focal lengths, the high resolution (12 or more megapixels), the fixed lens, which prevents any dust getting onto the sensor – and the fact that they work out at half or a third of the price of a reflex camera with a minimal set of lens assemblies. The minuses are the absence of a through-lens viewfinder and of a good wide-angle lens, the small size of the sensor (leading to noise at higher-than-minimal sensitivity), the low continuous drive speed and the general slowness in comparison with a fast reflex camera. However, taking into account rapid development and improvements in digital photo technology, these disadvantages will very soon be overcome.

The most serious photographer needs a reflex camera with a set of lenses that covers the range of focal lengths from 18 to 200 mm or even, ideally, from 10 or 12 to 300 mm when converted into full-format matrix.

The decisive factor, which has a radical impact on the size, weight and cost of lenses, is lens speed. The most popular telephoto zoom lens (with a focal length of 70–200 or 80–200 mm and a lens speed of 2.8) is twice the size, four times the weight and five times more expensive than a similar lens made by the same firm with a lens speed of 4–5.6. So what kind of crazy person lugs an unwieldy tube that costs about as much as a second-hand car with them over hills and dales?

There is no need to explain the value of a fast lens to people who use reflex cameras. They can work in low light conditions, achieving high impact images by blurring the background when taking a portrait – in other words, 'it's a must' for the professional. This is absolutely true when we are talking about advertising, glamour or portrait photography. When it comes to travel photography, we should not subscribe unreservedly to this view. There are a thousand situations where it is better for your own personal safety to look like a tourist and not a professional photographer: in an Eastern bazaar, in a place of worship or a museum, on the beach of a high-class hotel, in a private club, in Paris or Rome by night and – even in the daytime – in the South Bronx, Lagos or Rio de Janeiro. For the same reason, it's also better to reject the easily recognisable professional photo vest in favour of an ordinary jacket with big pockets.

Of course, I am talking primarily about digital technology, leaving the film camera aside, although there are people who argue strongly in favour of film – if only because with 'digital' photography, we do not have any tangible medium with the information on it (i.e. film), and this can prove fatal to the picture's fortunes. While this is true, the advantages of 'digital' for the travel photographer in particular are significant: you

The small country of Iceland delights
the travel photographer with its
variety of natural phenomena.
Dettifoss, one of dozens of picturesque
waterfalls, falls into a narrow canyon
(with a depth of around 300 metres).
The spray that hangs over it, pierced
by the sunlight, has a beneficial effect
on the photograph – but certainly not
on the camera.

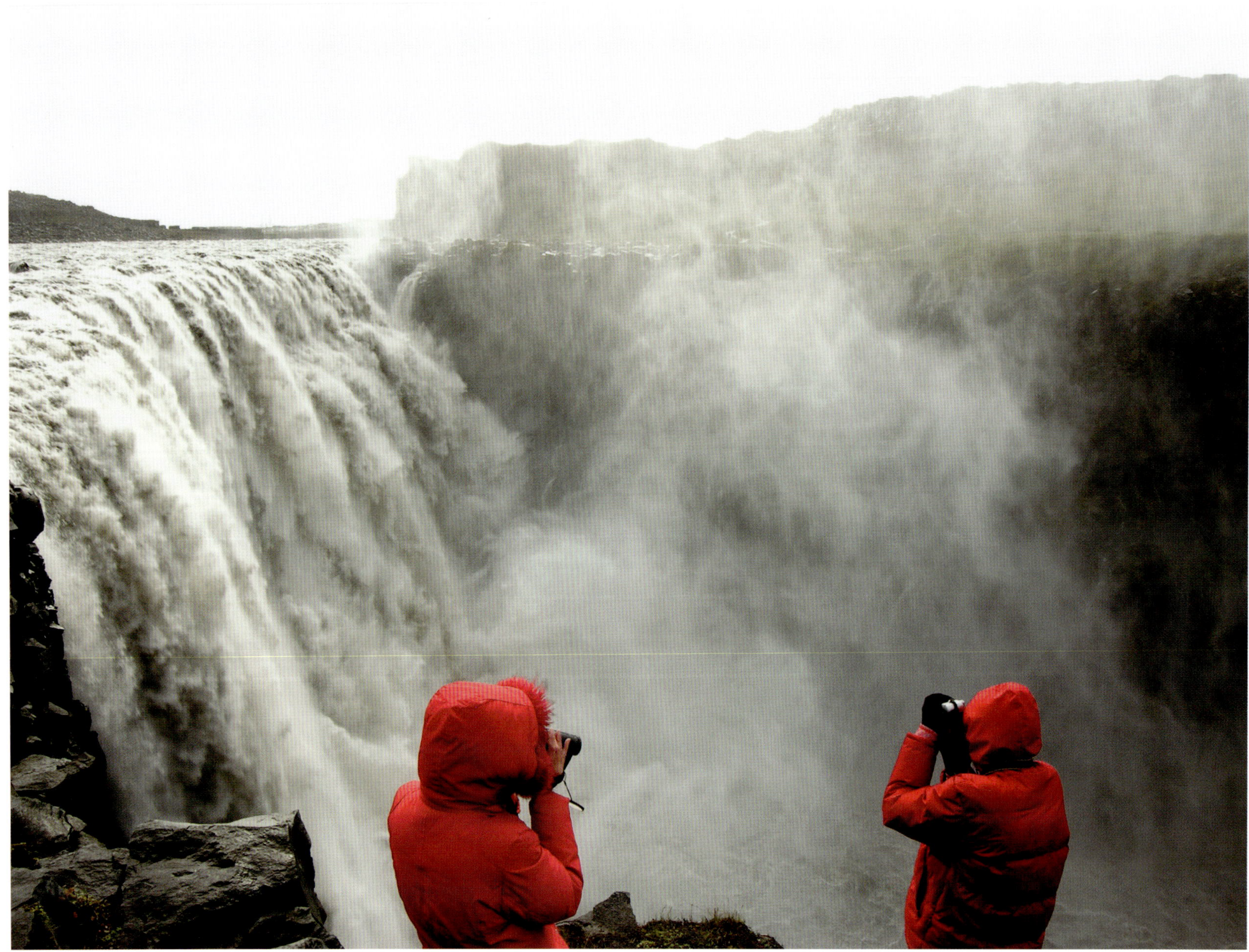

Bavaria, Germany. In the run-up to the Alpine skiing season, mountain resorts are always on tenterhooks: will there be enough snowfall? But here there has been gnomish magic at work: cars have been turned into enormous snow drifts, and very tall white hats, like those worn by guardsmen in a fairy tale, have piled up on top of the street lights.

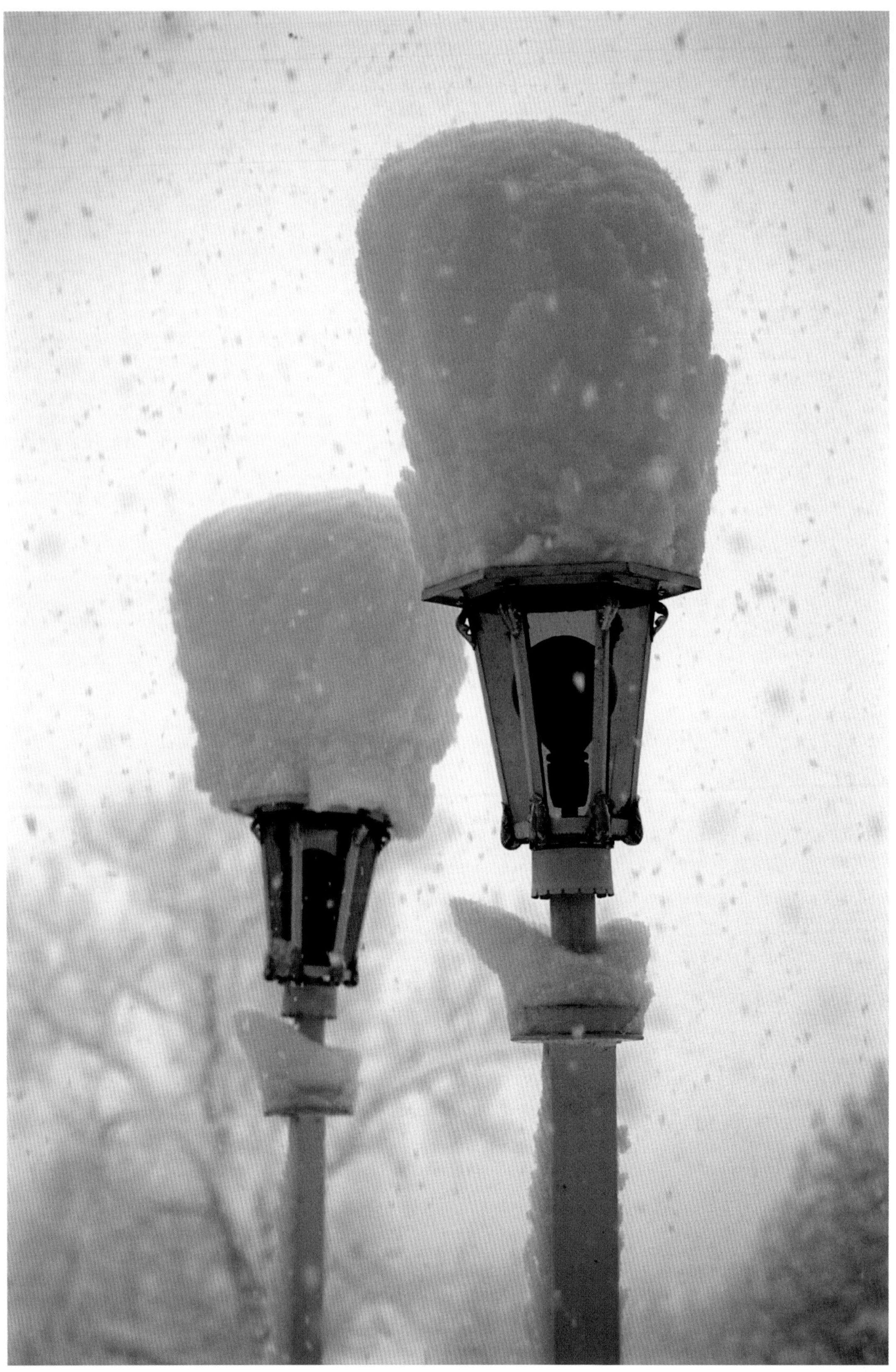

The quayside area of Bryggen in
Bergen, Norway, with its wooden
houses dating from the times of the
Hanseatic League. This group of
buildings looks wonderful taken from
any angle and in any light. However,
backlighting from the setting sun is
always especially striking.

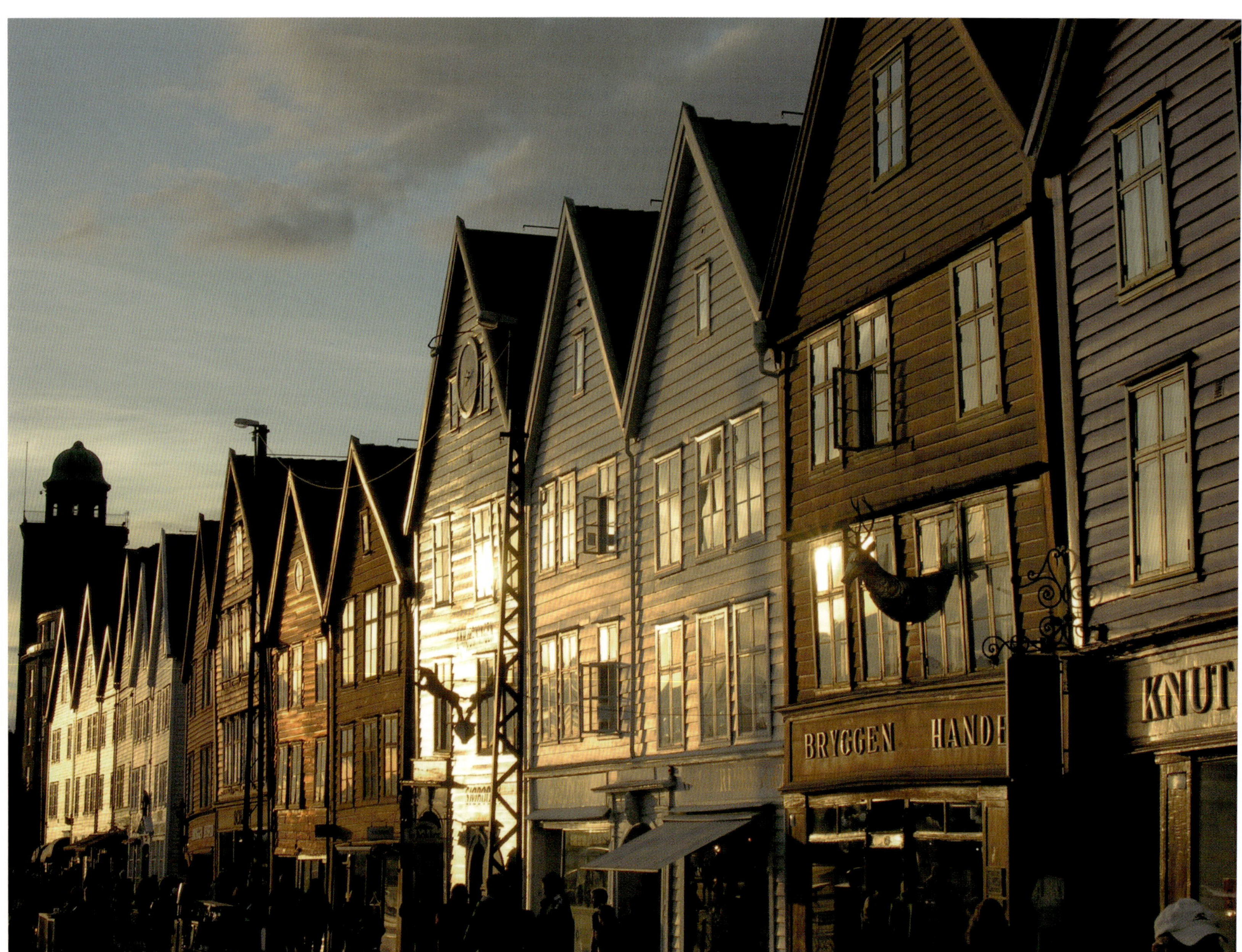

No obstacle can stand in the way of the true photographer's passion – it's only a question of the right equipment. This photographer dad, travelling in Carinthia (Austria) with his young son, has organised everything with the utmost common sense: his camera bag, sitting comfortably on his chest, partly balances out the weight of his son in the baby carrier on his back. His son is already learning about travel photography.

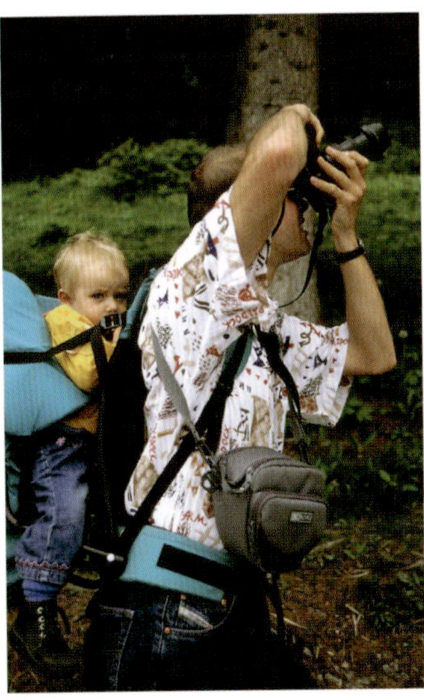

Photographers don't do dress codes. I photographed my colleague, Mihail Ovchinnikov, doing his Yasser Arafat imitation, with an Arab headdress on his head and embracing his Leica (right-hand photo), in the Eskimo settlement of Amassalik in Greenland. Normally, photographers travel alone, and then a mirror can come to their aid.

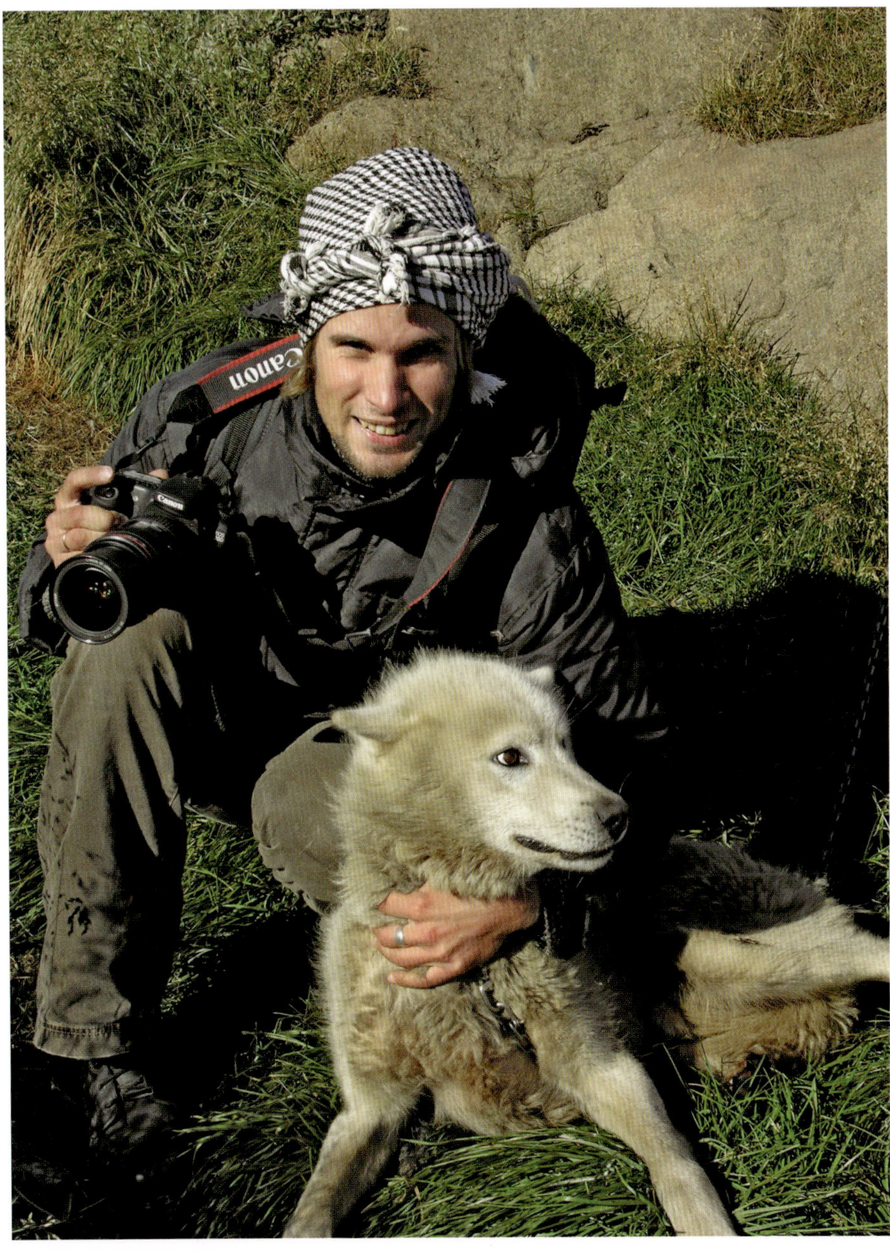

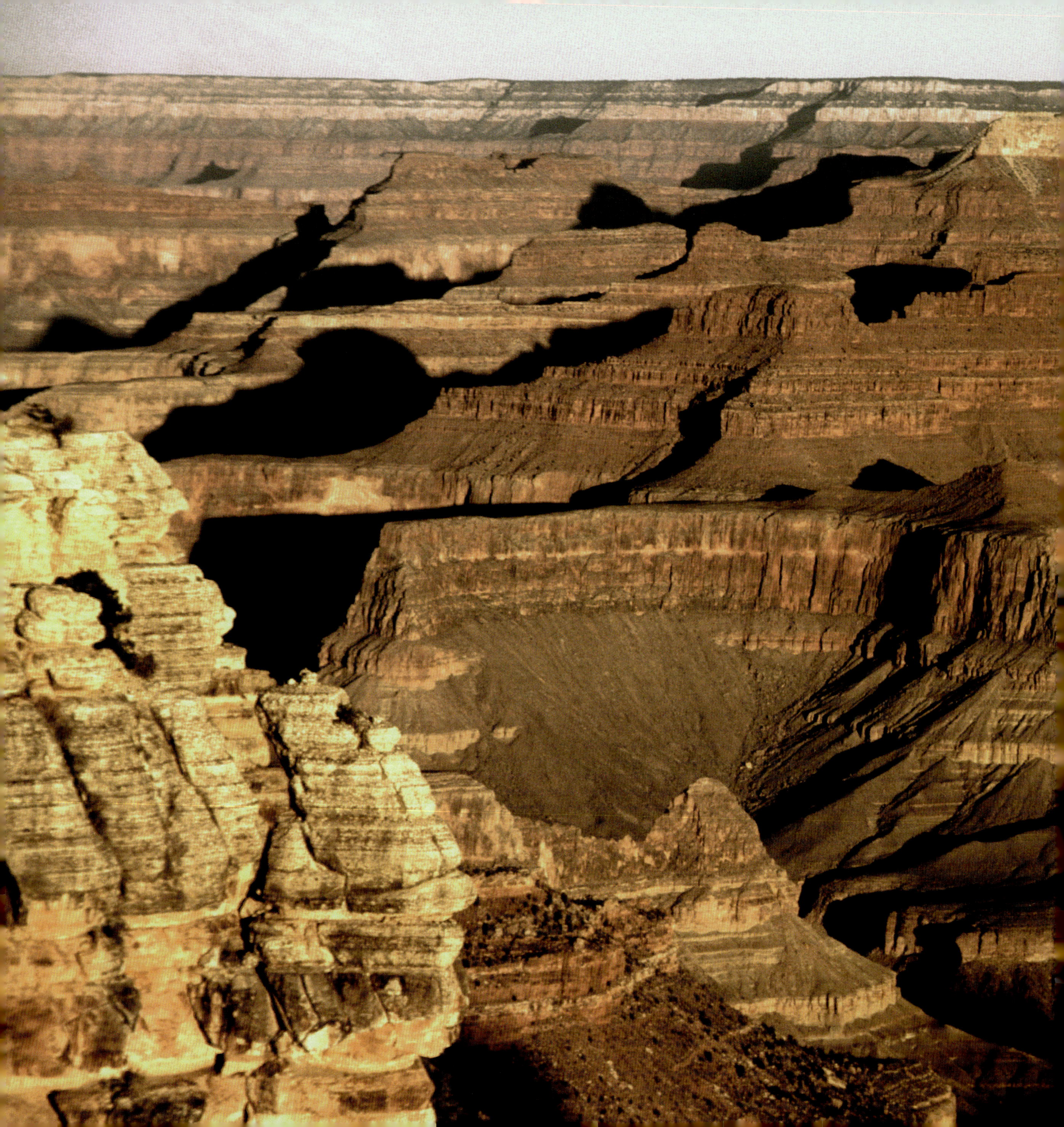

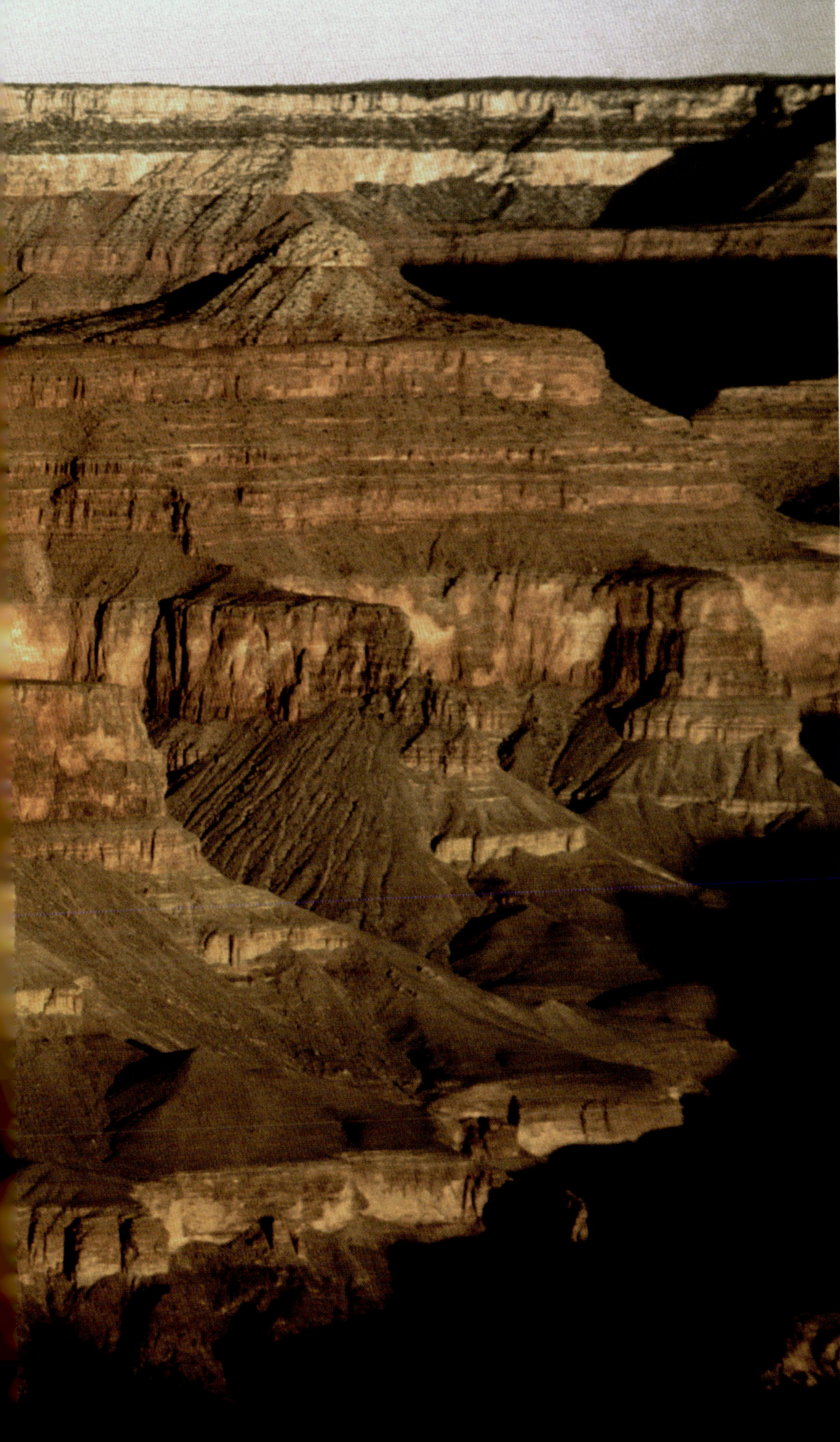

can see the results at once and wipe anything you don't need. Instead of a bag full of expensive film, you can just take a couple of lightweight flash drives, which are not sensitive to X-rays at airport security. You can also easily change film speed and colour temperature to a huge range of values – for all the situations you could ever think of photographing!

With digital photography, you can save your pictures using RAW format. The RAW file format is digital photography's equivalent of a negative in film photography: it contains untouched, 'raw' pixel information straight from the digital camera's sensors. This allows you to correct or compensate for even bad mistakes or blunders made when setting up the photo. This is especially important for unexpected situations, when you have to shoot at random, without managing to set the correct exposure, aperture and colour balance. In order to keep your photos safely, you need to have a portable hard drive and, for backup, copy the photo files to a CD or DVD. Even though this will involve you in extra costs, it can be many times cheaper than the cost of buying reversible film (for slides), developing it and framing the pictures.

With all its advantages, the digital lens also has some drawbacks. When the lenses in the matrix are changed, dust may get in, together with micro-particles of metal caused by the friction between the lens and the bayonet socket, which can not always be removed, even by the presence of a self-cleaning mechanism or by blowing them away. This results in spots and stains on the image. Cleaning a matrix is a difficult and rather expensive process, fraught with consequences for its protected lens, and replacement can cost a third of the price of the camera. For this reason, even for diehard adherents of 'fixes' – lenses with an unchanged focus distance, giving a crystal clear image with no distortion – it's better, when on a trip, to content oneself with high-quality zoom attachments

Professional zoom attachments, with an aperture ratio of 2.8, are of equal quality to 'fixes' and have focus distance ratios no greater than three, but even modern zoom attachments with ratios of five can easily be worn out by daily use. And in addition, completely acceptable quality can be attained by superzoom attachments such as the Nikon 18-200 for DX

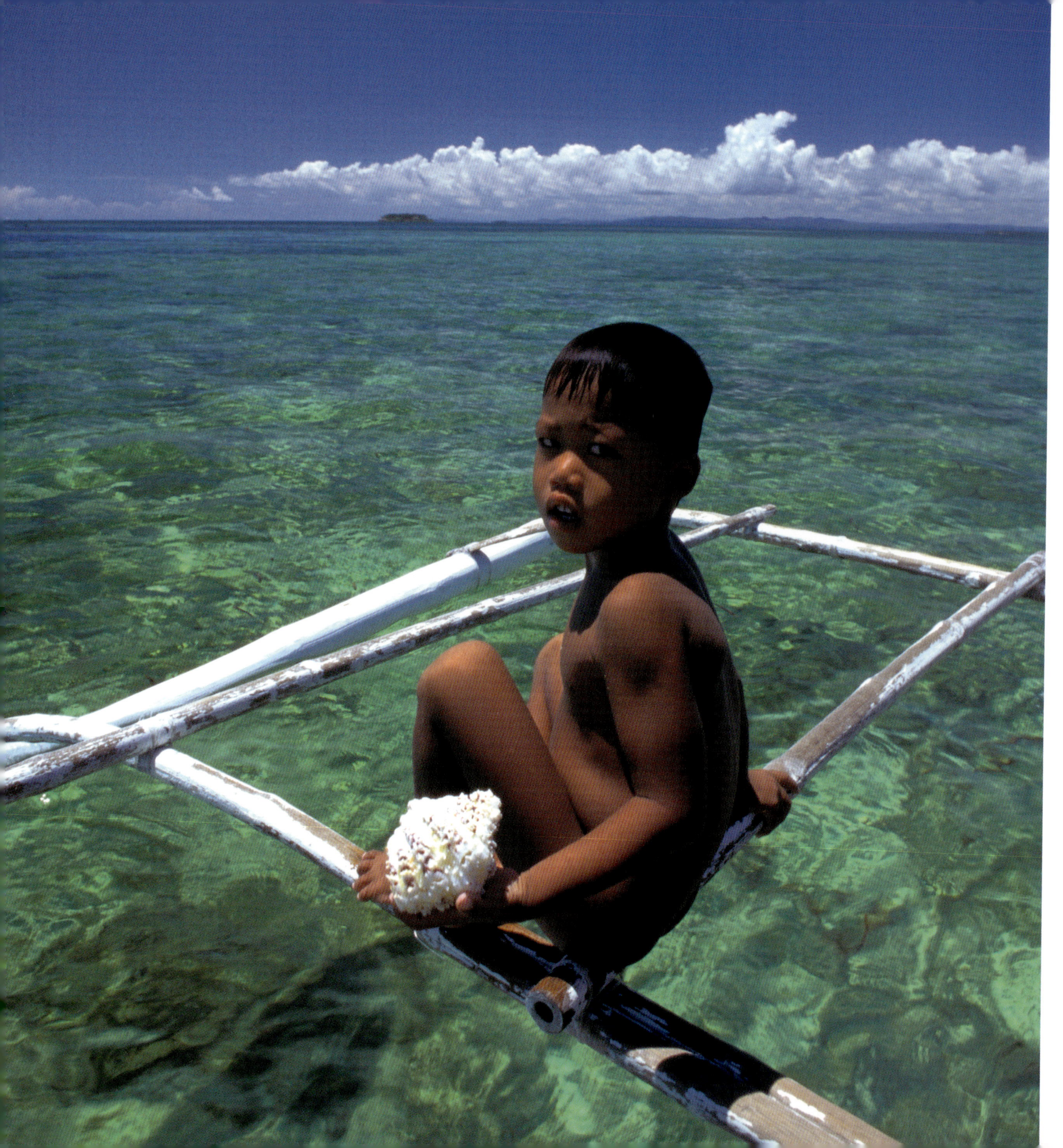

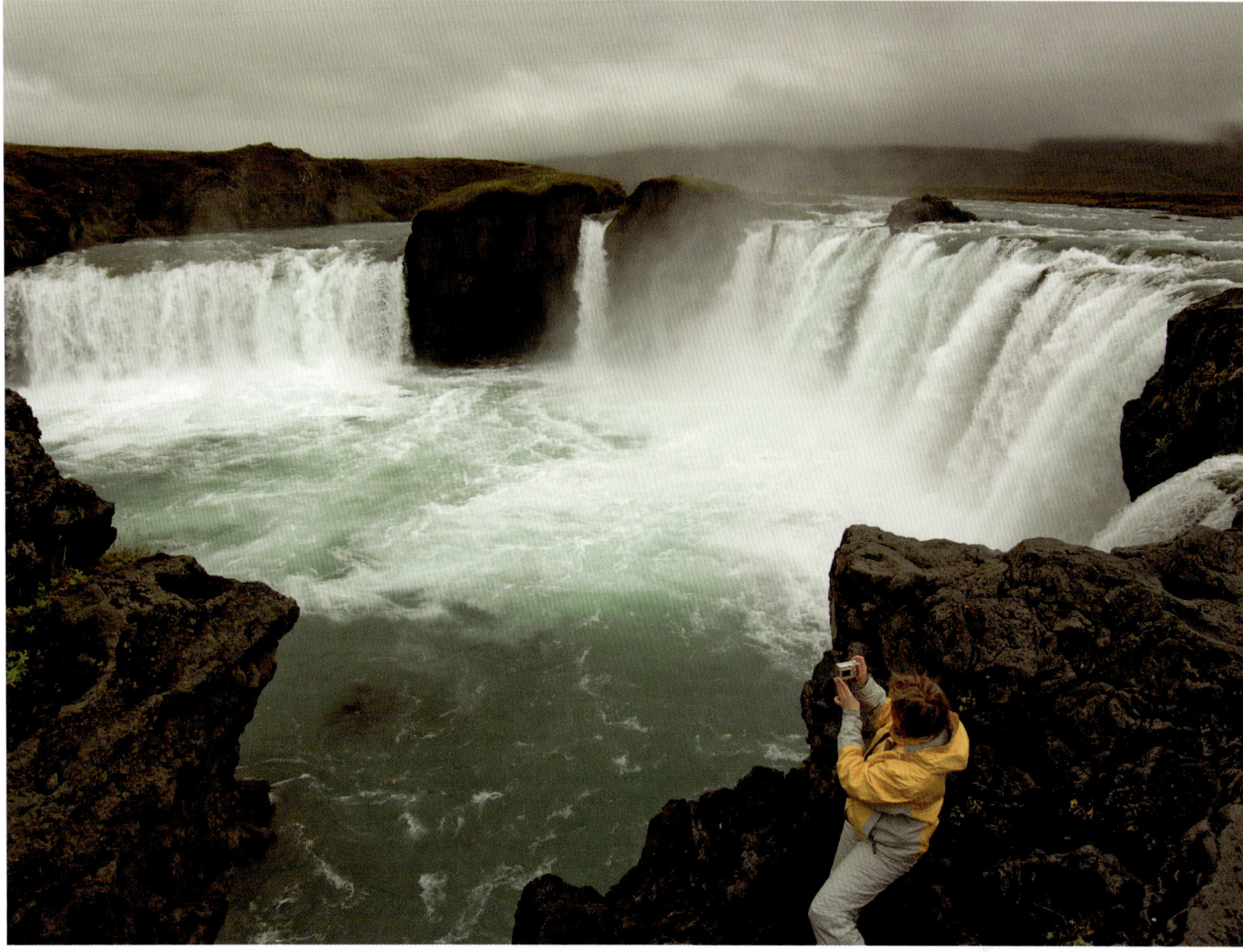

matrices and the 28-300 for FX matrices, which basically allow you to forget about changed lenses and to change the focus distance instantaneously from wide-angle to powerful tele-shots

The principle difference in travel photography from the point of view of the shot is that – for example, when taking a portrait – you sometimes have fractions of a second in which a face full of texture and expression is open to you. You won't have time to change the lens if you're taking a close-up, and to adjust the camera. But you can succeed by making a half-revolution of the superzoom and pressing the button. Moreover, if you're photographing people, it's better if they don't know you're doing it, so as to preserve the naturalness of their behaviour and their facial expression. A tele-zoom lens is good for this.

So it's extremely complicated to make recommendations as to the contents of a 'high-class tool kit' for travel photography, and we must all solve this problem for ourselves. Apart from three zooms, the usual contents of my photo-bag include a wide-angled lens with a high aperture ratio and a 'portrait lens'. Many years of experience have proved that the focal distance range which is currently most popular, the one most frequently called for, is 24–85 mm. (from the 'architectural' wide-angled lens to the 'portrait lens'). With a single lens like that, you can set out on your journey confident that you can take photos of the highest quality!

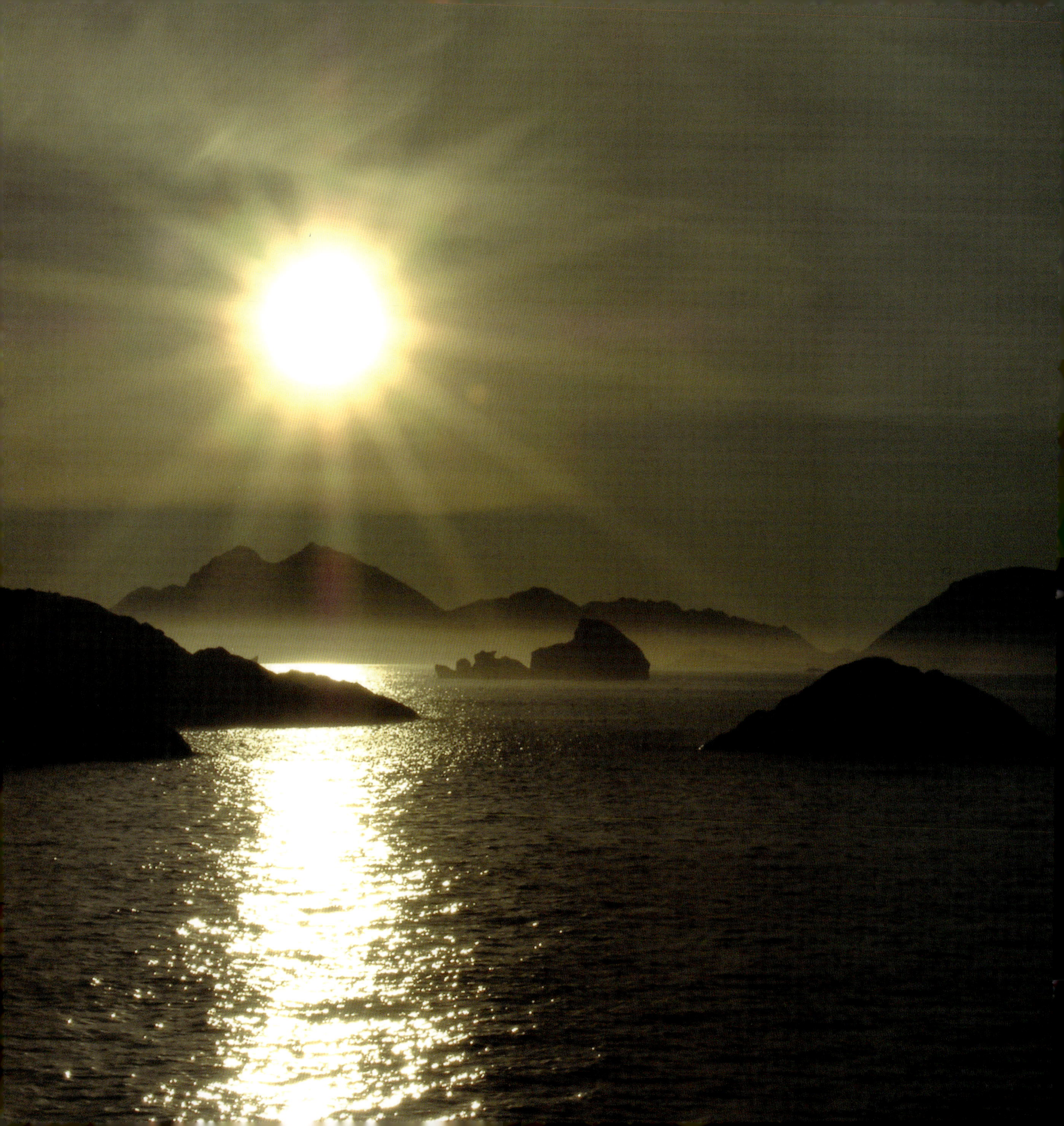

Rocks, islands and icebergs off the
shores of Greenland just after sunrise.
In a few minutes' time, the light
will change abruptly: colours will be
added, the sky will be revealed. But
the sense of mystery of this huge,
distant, glacier-covered land, whose
shores are rarely lucky enough to be
touched by the sea – since its straits
are blocked with ice all year round –
will fall away.

Quayside in the old Hanseatic City of
Lübeck, Germany – a UNESCO World
Heritage Centre. Taking this photo
before sunset – when the sky is not
yet dark but lights have already been
lit indoors – allows the photographer
to obtain a beautiful silhouette of the
old buildings, their windows reflected
in the water, against the background
of the glowing vault of heaven with
the clouds highlighted by the sunset.

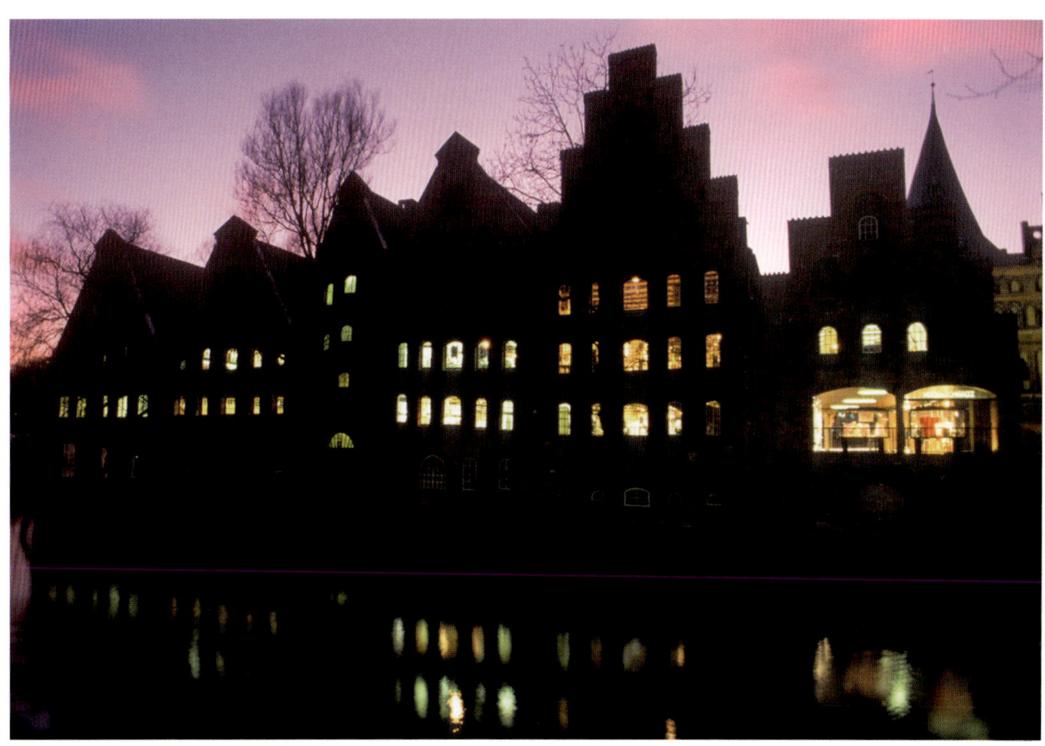

Photoshopping

In digital photography, there are currently three main, generally accepted image formats: JPG, TIFF and RAW. The first of these 'compresses' the information contained in the shot, so significantly more pictures can be recorded in the same size memory. The camera registers the pictures more quickly, and loss of quality by comparison with an uncompressed format is minimal – practically imperceptible, to be precise – if the picture is printed without corrections at postcard size. However, each time the picture is saved again on the computer, part of the information is lost. Therefore, before any processing, it is wise to re-save the picture in TIFF format, where there will be no loss of quality

In TIFF format, the camera records the full, uncompressed volume of information, guaranteeing better quality when large pictures are printed. It is true that the time needed to record the photograph increases and so fewer shots can be taken. In particular, advanced compact cameras 'go slow', taking a whole half-minute to 'digest' one shot!

The format used by professionals – RAW – is strongly recommended to anyone with a serious interest in the quality of the photograph. Using a smaller amount of memory than that needed for TIFF, it allows the more complex work involved in processing a photograph from a microelectronic camera to be transferred onto the shoulders or – to be more precise – to the brain of a powerful computer. And it charitably overlooks any errors and blunders that the photographer has made when setting up the shot. However, it does have its complications: whereas the first two formats are identical for all cameras, RAW has individual differences not only for each make of camera, but also for each model, and so it requires its own software. (This usually appears on the manufacturer's web site two or three weeks after a new model goes on sale, and it can be imported from there.) A dozen or so conversion programs for processing RAW files have been developed, the majority of which have to be paid for. But they are well worth the cost.

A special word must be reserved for the photographer's chief assistant – 'Photoshop'. Using this program allows you to literally transform any picture, whatever the format in which it was created. Any computer manipulation of photographs must be minimal and done correctly. You can frame the picture, level the line of the horizon, straighten 'sliding' buildings, delete building cranes that spoil the landscape, correct the colour, or the contrast. But this must be within sensible limits which every photographer sets for him or herself. Is it acceptable to 'glue' a few beautiful clouds or a flight of birds from another shot onto the sky of an attractive landscape – or not? While it may be very effective to superimpose one picture on another, this is not travel photography – it is something quite different. Even the most stylish montage cannot replace the sense of satisfaction derived from taking a good photograph.

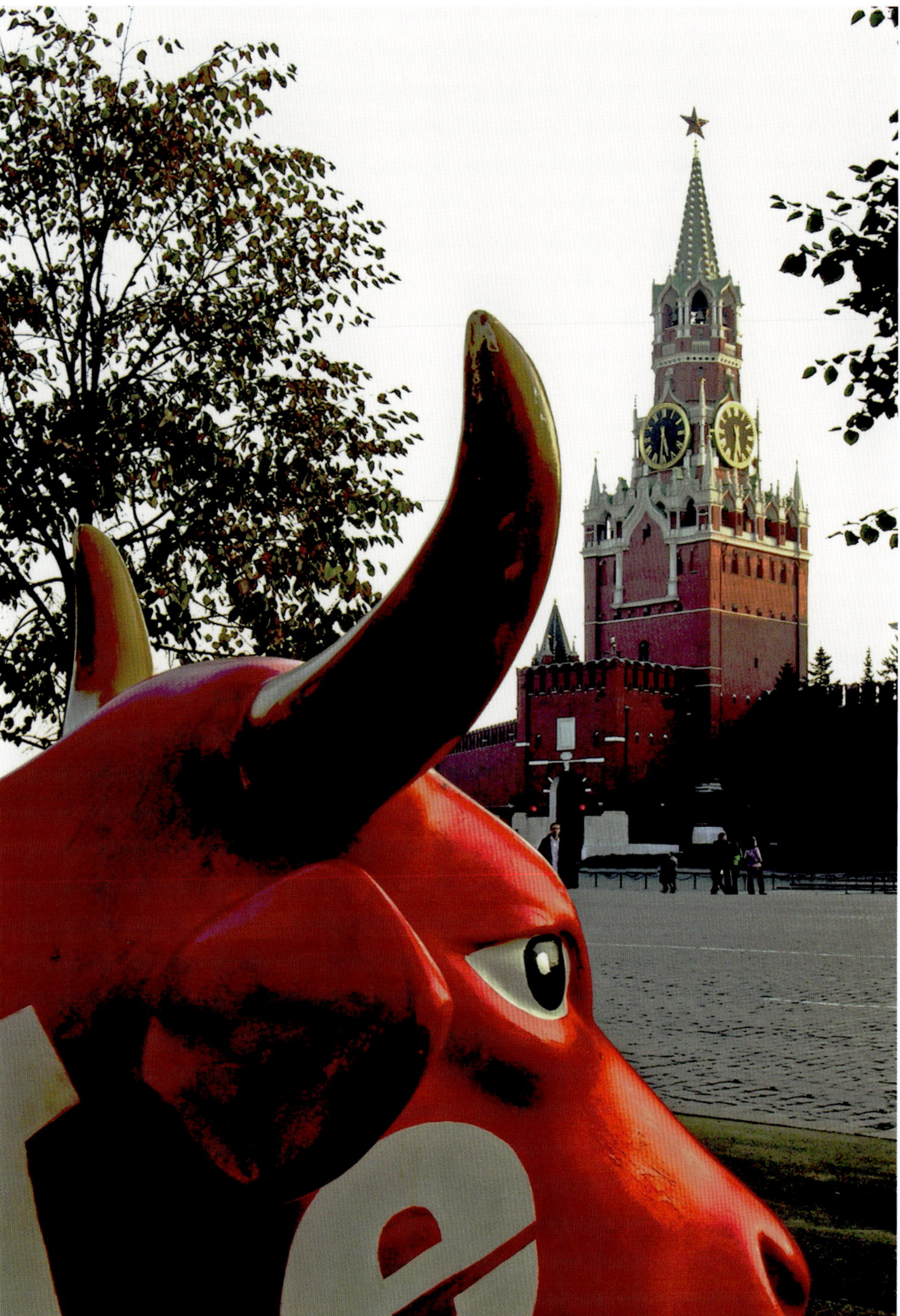

One fine evening, while walking in
Red Square with a compact camera,
I was astounded to see a herd of
cows, peacefully walking along in
front of GUM. It's true they were
made of papier maché, but they were
life size and beautifully drawn and
painted. Displays with cows like these
have become fashionable in European
cities. One of the heifers was quite
happily gazing at the Kremlin wall.
I made her colour a bit richer and
increased the contrast in Photoshop,
and this deepened the intensity of
the photo.

Three huge swords thrust into the
ground near Stavanger – a memorial
to battles that achieved the unification
of the principalities of Norway. Legend
has it that the first King of Norway
was roused to feats of arms by his
love for the ambitious daughter of one
of his princes, who desired to become
queen. The technical element of this
photo is extremely simple: it has been
'Photoshopped' to produce extreme
contrast.

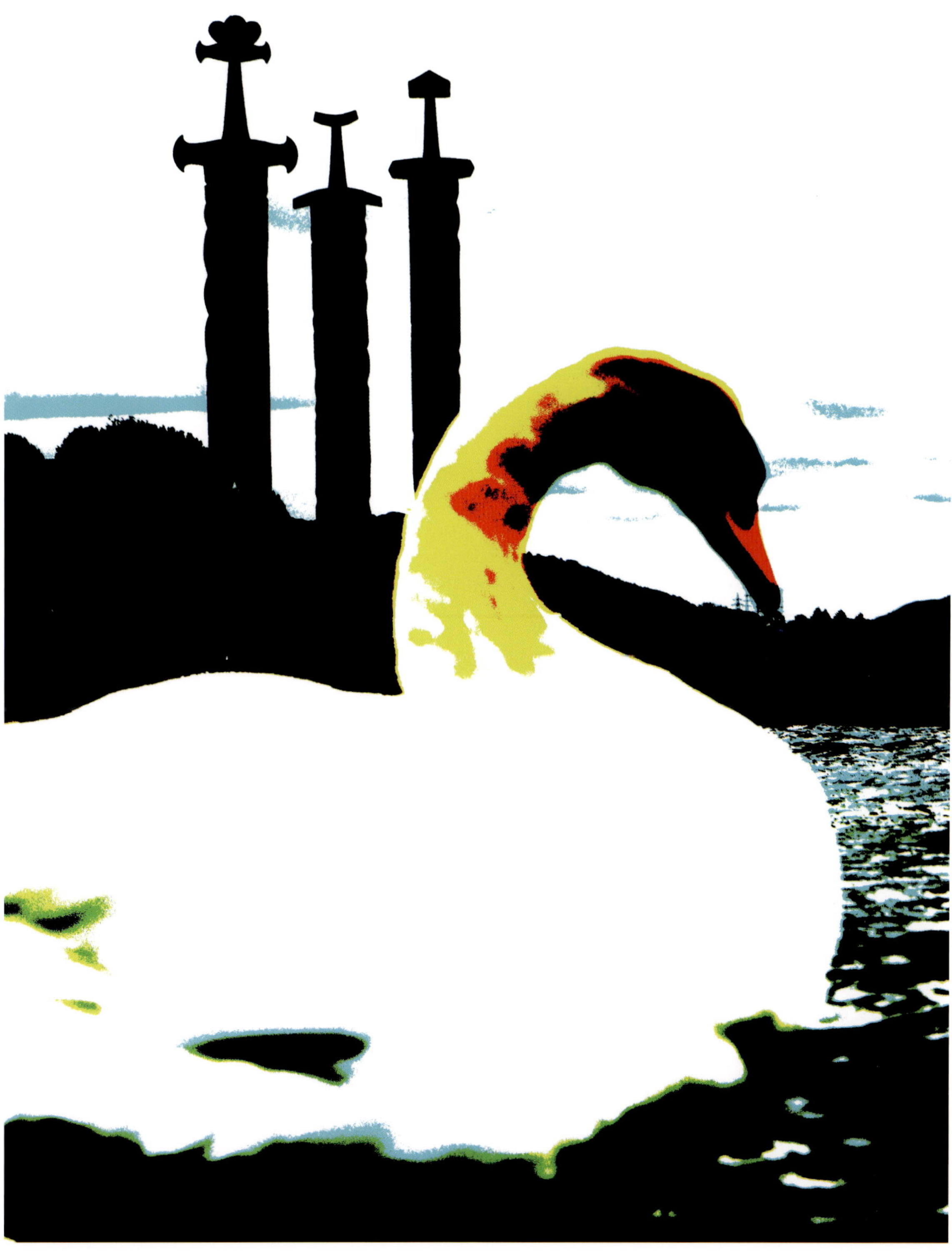

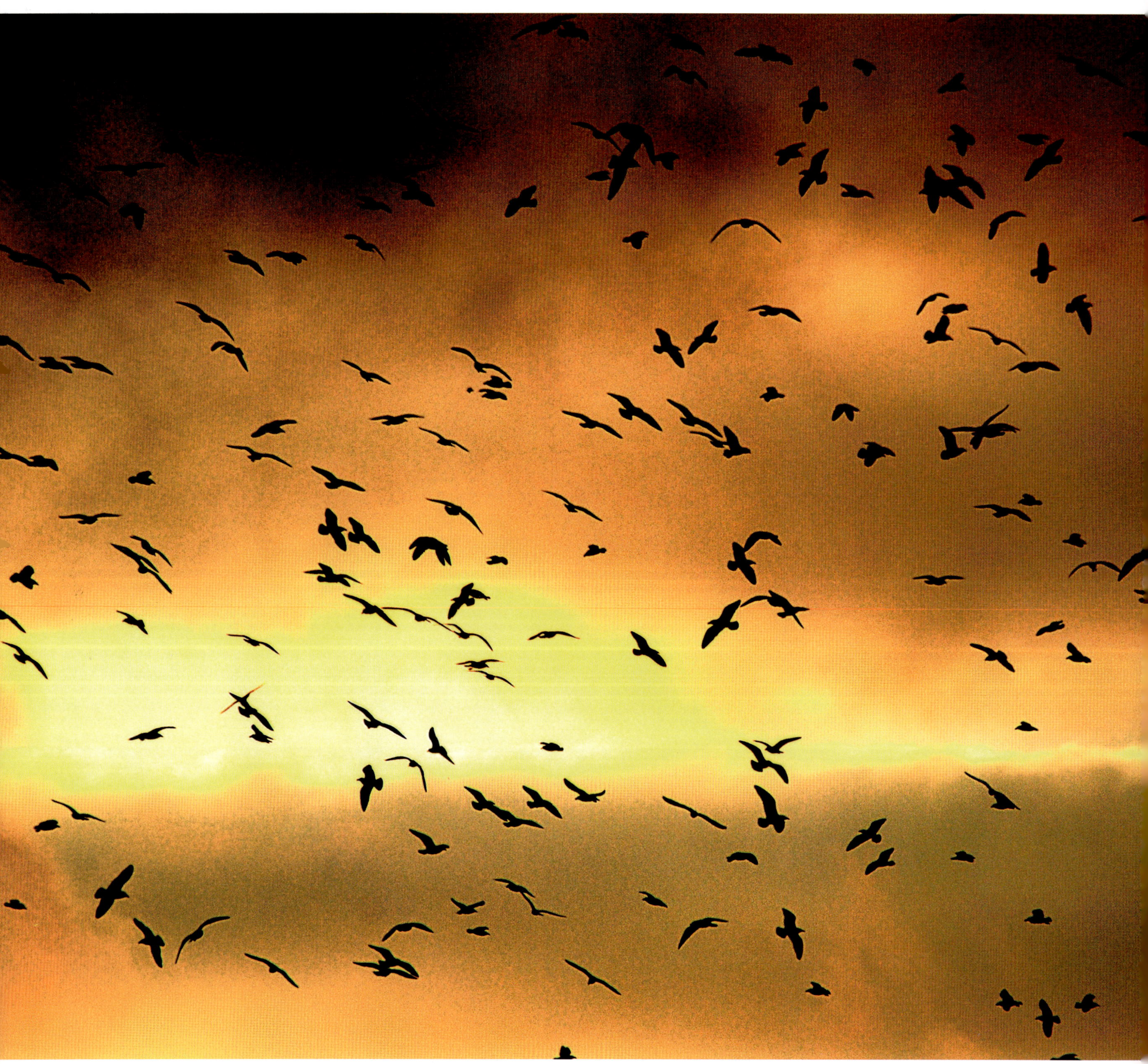

'Bird flu'. An extremely simple photo: a flock of birds in the Spanish port of Alicante, photographed in the evening against the background of an unremarkable sky and then given strong contrast using Photoshop. As a result, their flight has taken on a kind of feverishness: disquietingly, it forcibly recalls Alfred Hitchcock's famous thriller, 'The Birds'.

'Turbulence'. This photograph, too, conveys a sense of anxiety, as it was taken from an aeroplane landing in a strong wind. The shot was taken through a porthole, when it was almost dark, at 1600 ASA and then 'Photoshopped'.

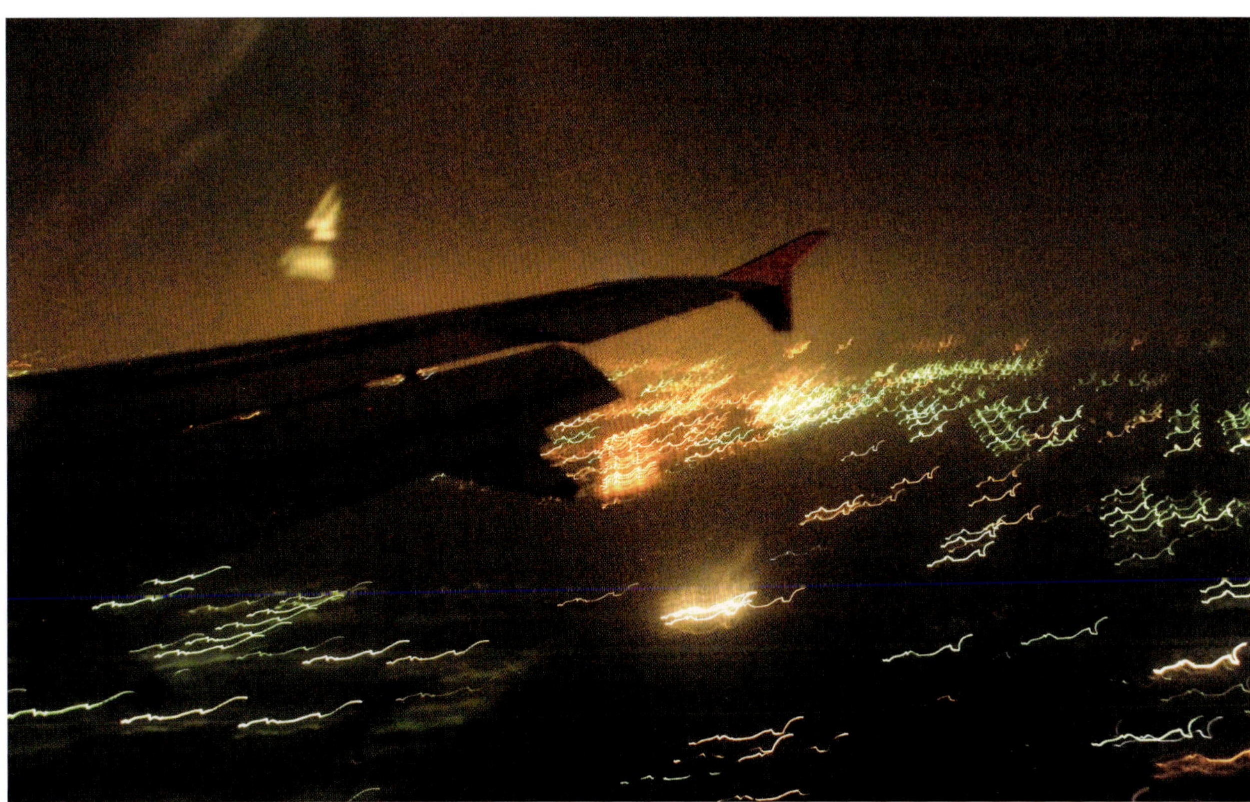

OVERLEAF
A bridge over a Norwegian fjord, photographed at sunset with the top deck of a motor ship, using a telezoom lens. I had to wait a long time for this silhouette shot to make sure the boat going under the bridge and the traffic going over it blended correctly. The zoom has been pulled out almost as far as possible. Because I'm so far away, the shot almost faded out, so I perfected it in Photoshop.

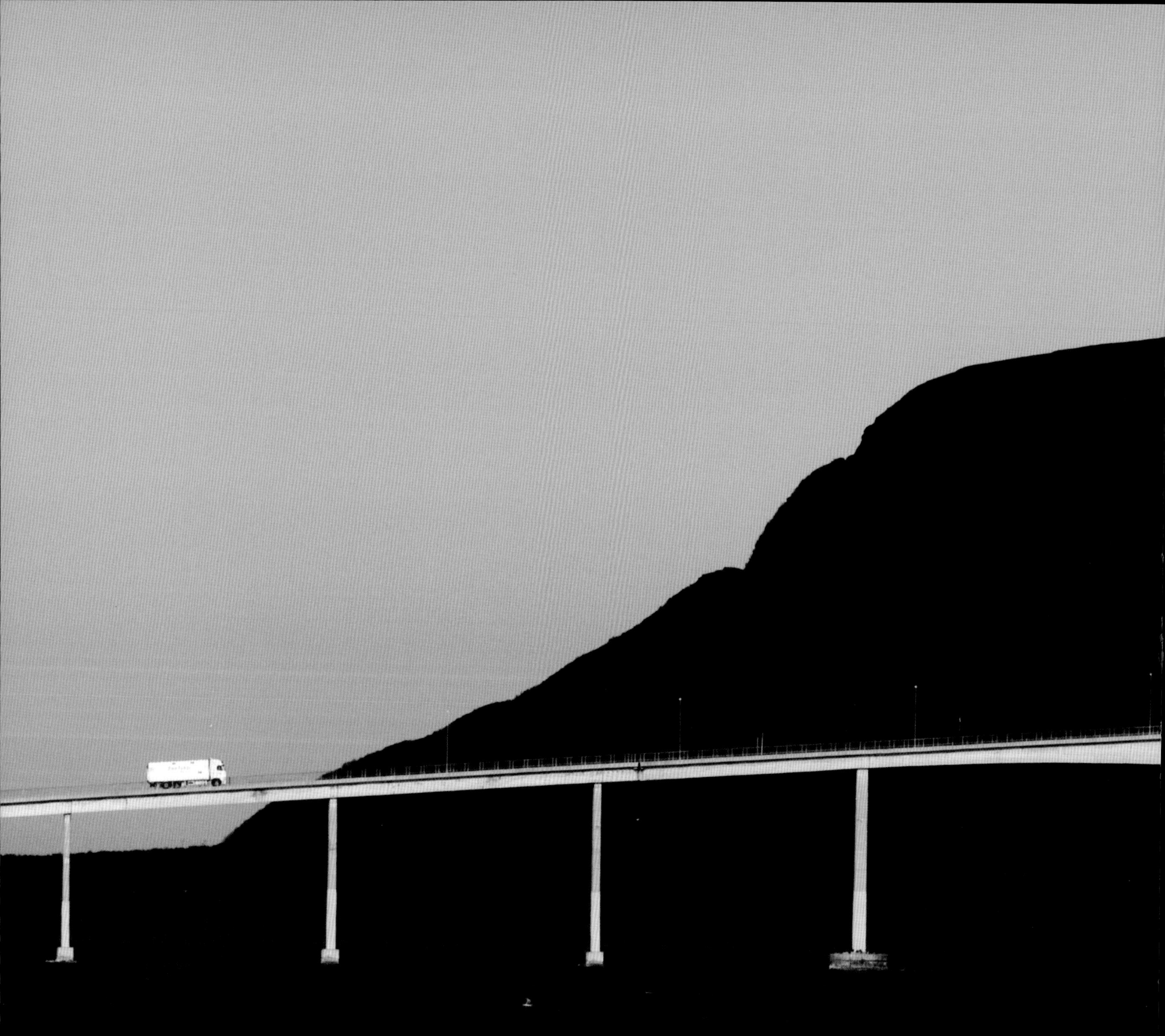

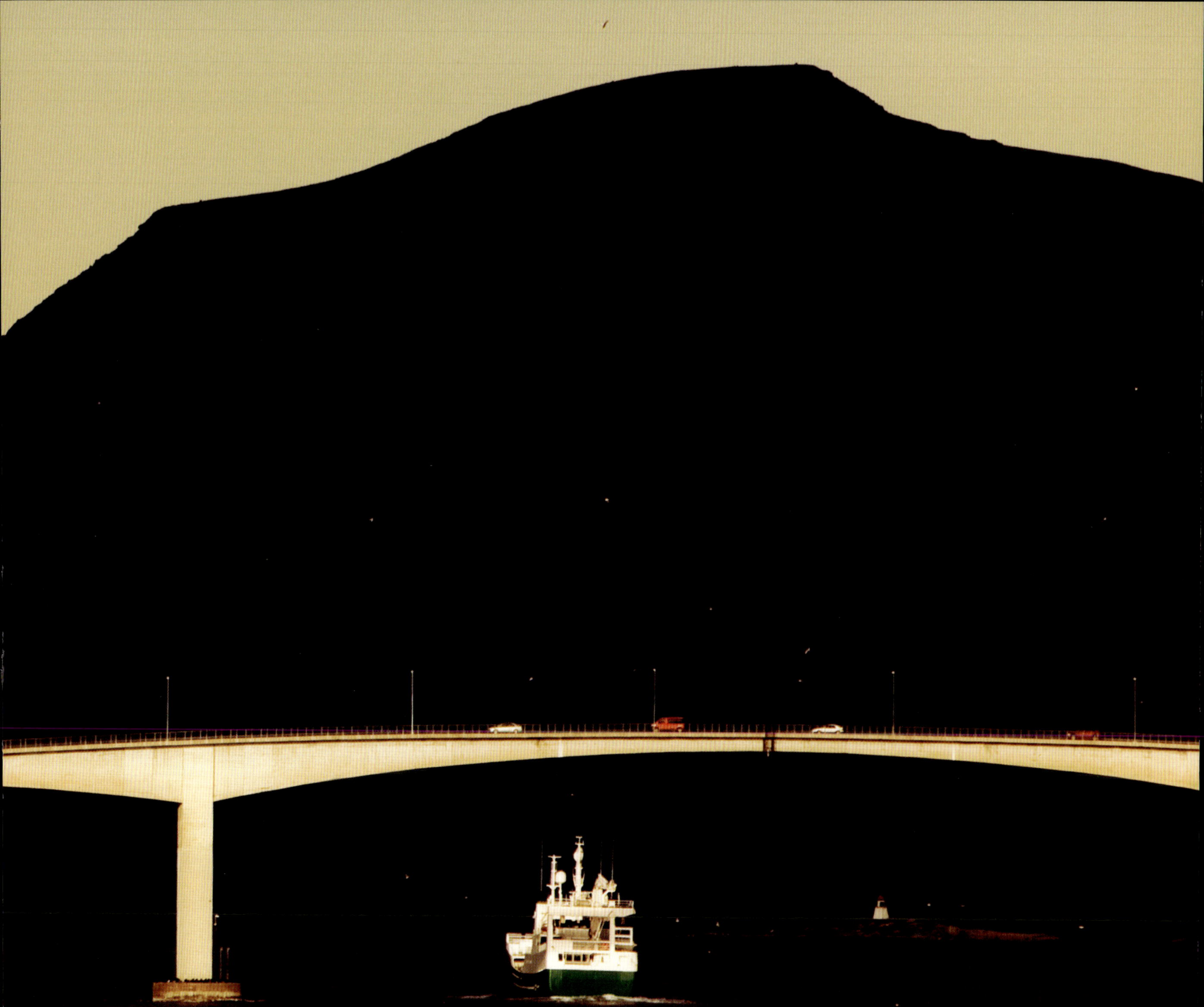

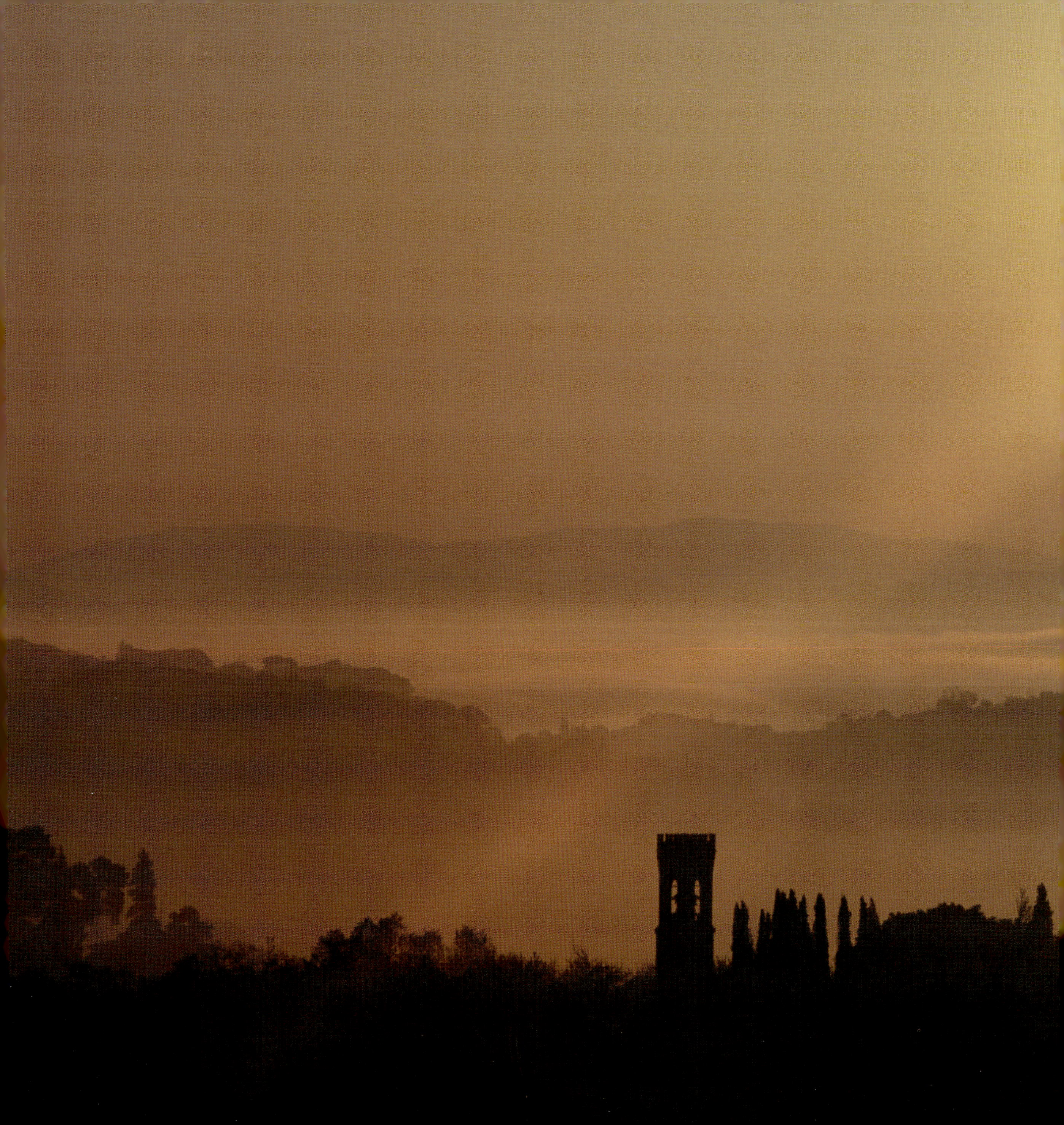

Shine a light

The first rule of photography is 'don't shoot into the sun'. What is there to argue with? If you take a photo into the sun of a smiling girl on a beach wearing a wide-brimmed hat, then you will only be photographing the hat – instead of her face, the photo will show a dark void. The face is there, but it is in deep shade and the camera sets the exposure according to the bright sunlight. If your camera has an exposure correction function, of course, you can increase the aperture by two f-stops or take an accurate light reading on the face, but then everything around it will simply be over-exposed. The same fate awaits the facade of an architectural monument of white stone if, as you stroll around Rome or Suzdal, you catch it with the sun behind it. And although you can use fill-in light on the girl's face, if you want to fill in the Colosseum you will need to set up half a dozen airport searchlights.

A balloon photo gives a good idea of
how the setting sun still has the same
colour temperature as when it rose,
the same golden shades of colour. And
the balloon itself is actually legendary.
It's the 55-metre Breitling Orbiter
3, in which the balloonists Bernard
Picard and Bryden Jones successfully
completed the first non-stop balloon
flight round the world in 1999.

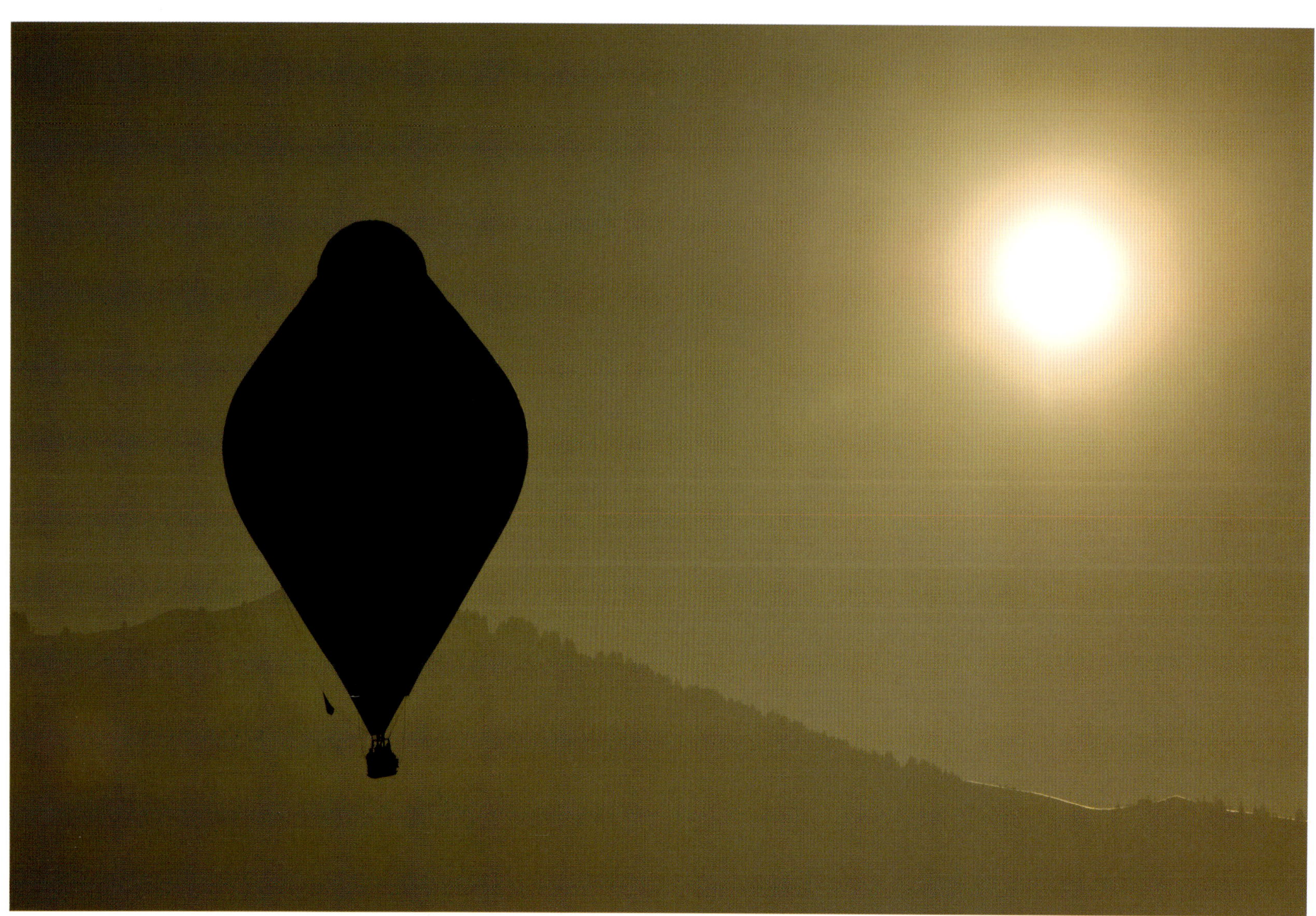

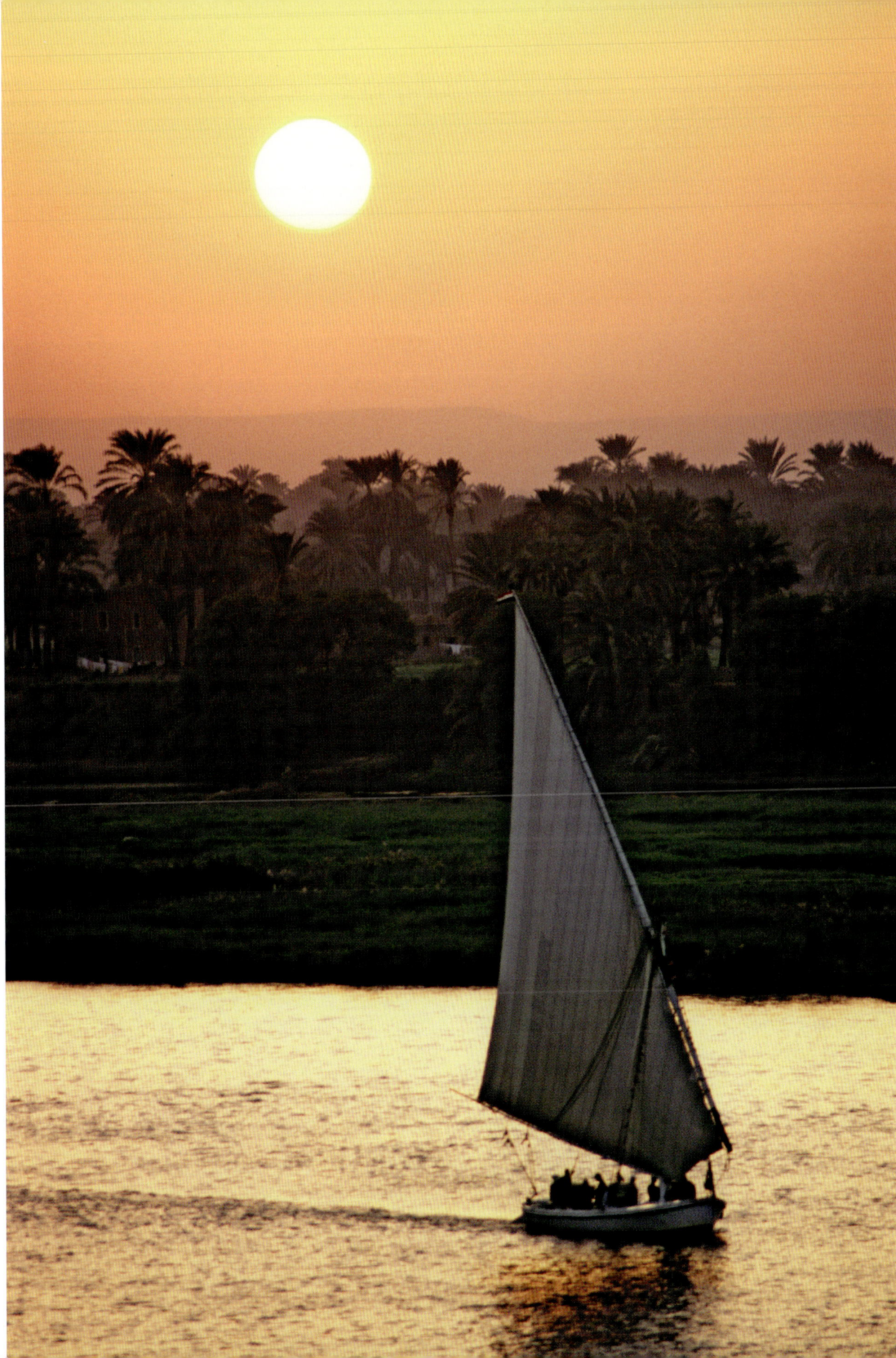

The sunsets over the Nile are very beautiful. This shot, which makes the sun look bigger, was taken with a 300-mm. telephoto lens, from the high right bank near Luxor. The sun in the top left-hand corner is balanced out by the *felucca*, the sailing boat at the bottom right.

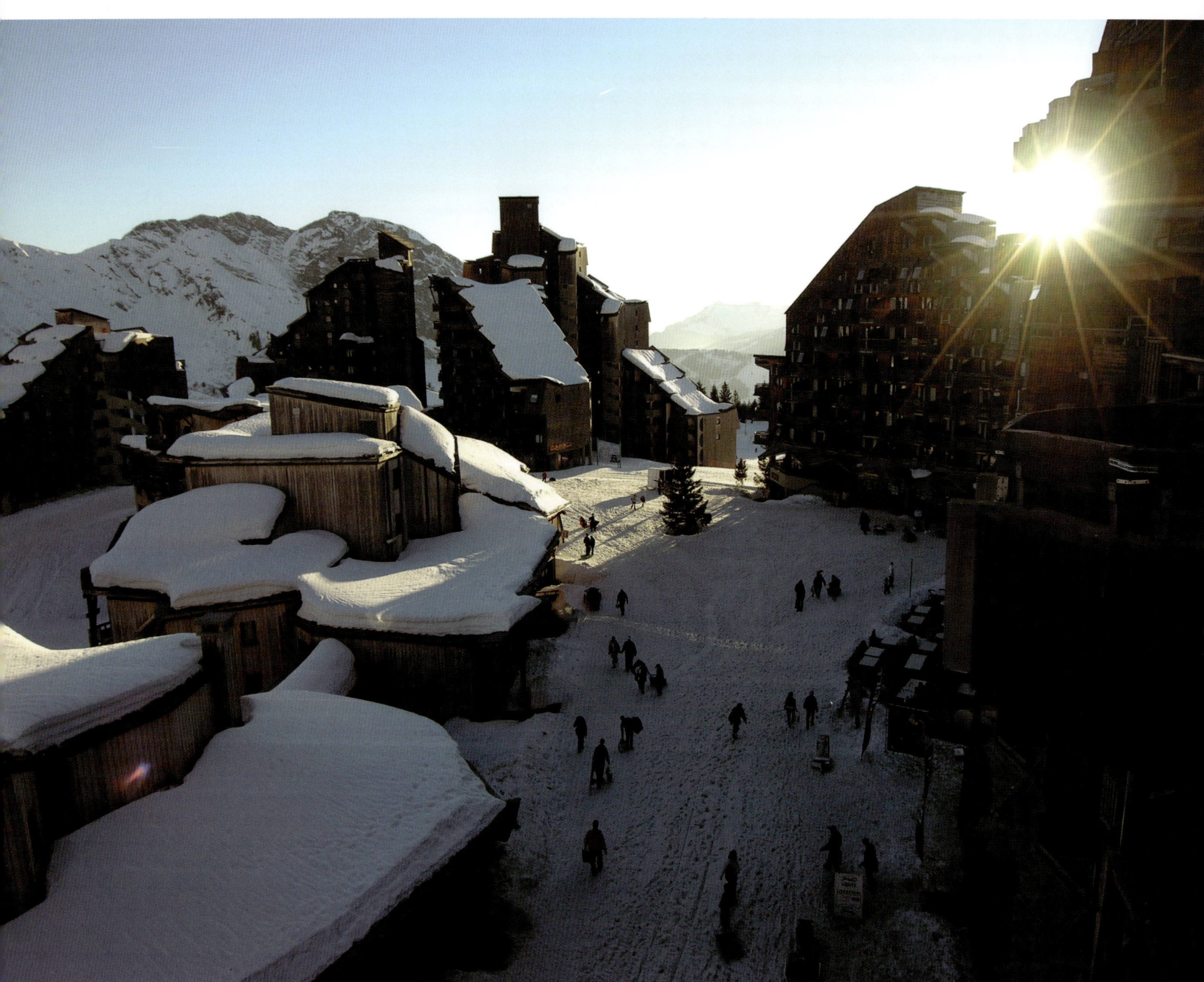

The Alpine ski resort of Avoriaz.
France. 'Head-on' sunlight can also
play an effective role if it is used
within the frame as light 'through
a sheltered window', or even, as in
this case, through just one window
pane. It is as if we are looking at an
unbearably bright light source through
protective goggles, thanks to which –
despite the back light – details of the
unusual architecture are revealed.

In the rocky wastes of Greenland, a
distant ancestor of cotton or of the
dandelion... . The main reason to let
the dazzling sun into the frame is that
this loose, translucent material acts
as a medium for its rays, like feathery
strands or a horse's mane.

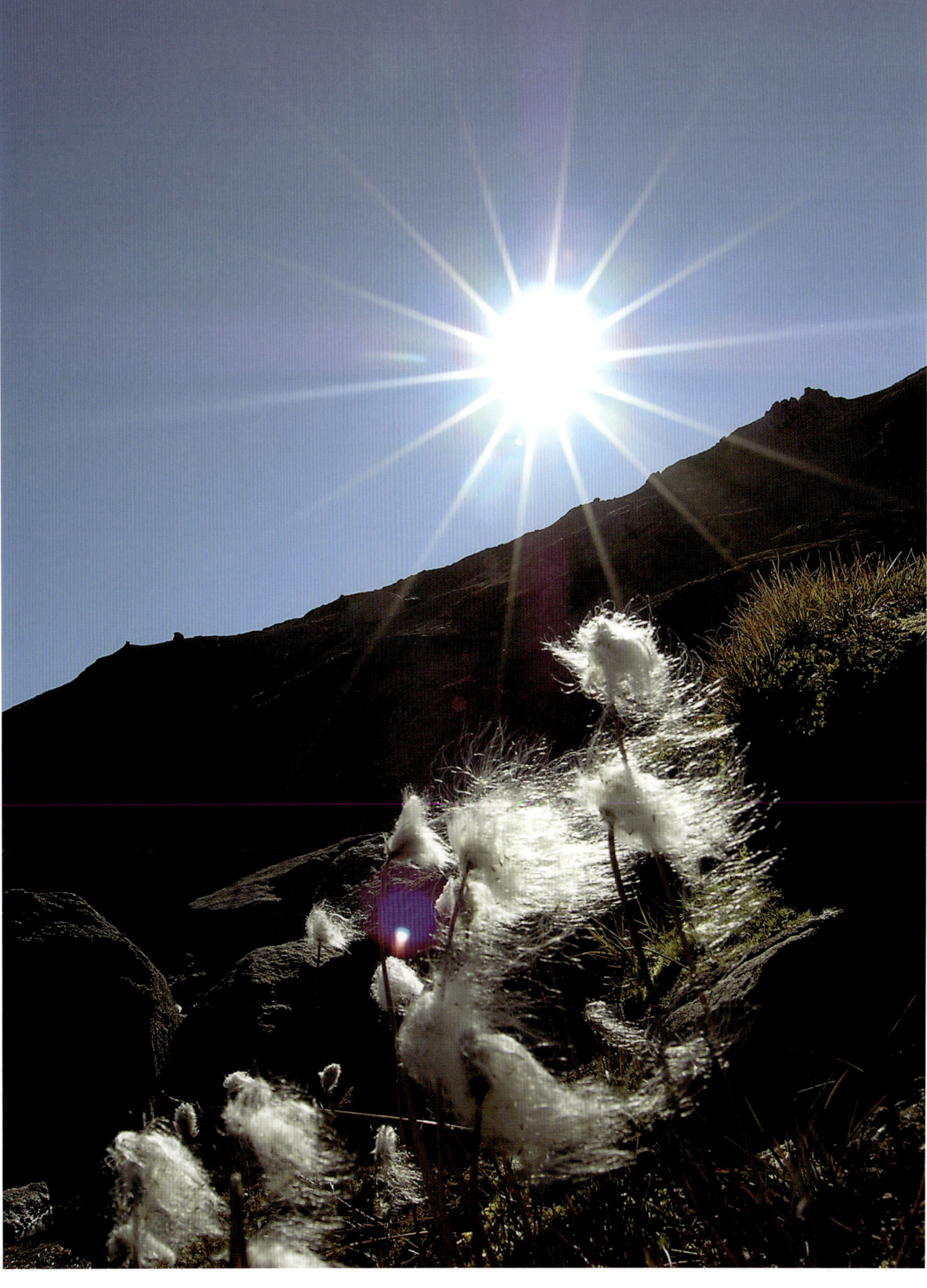

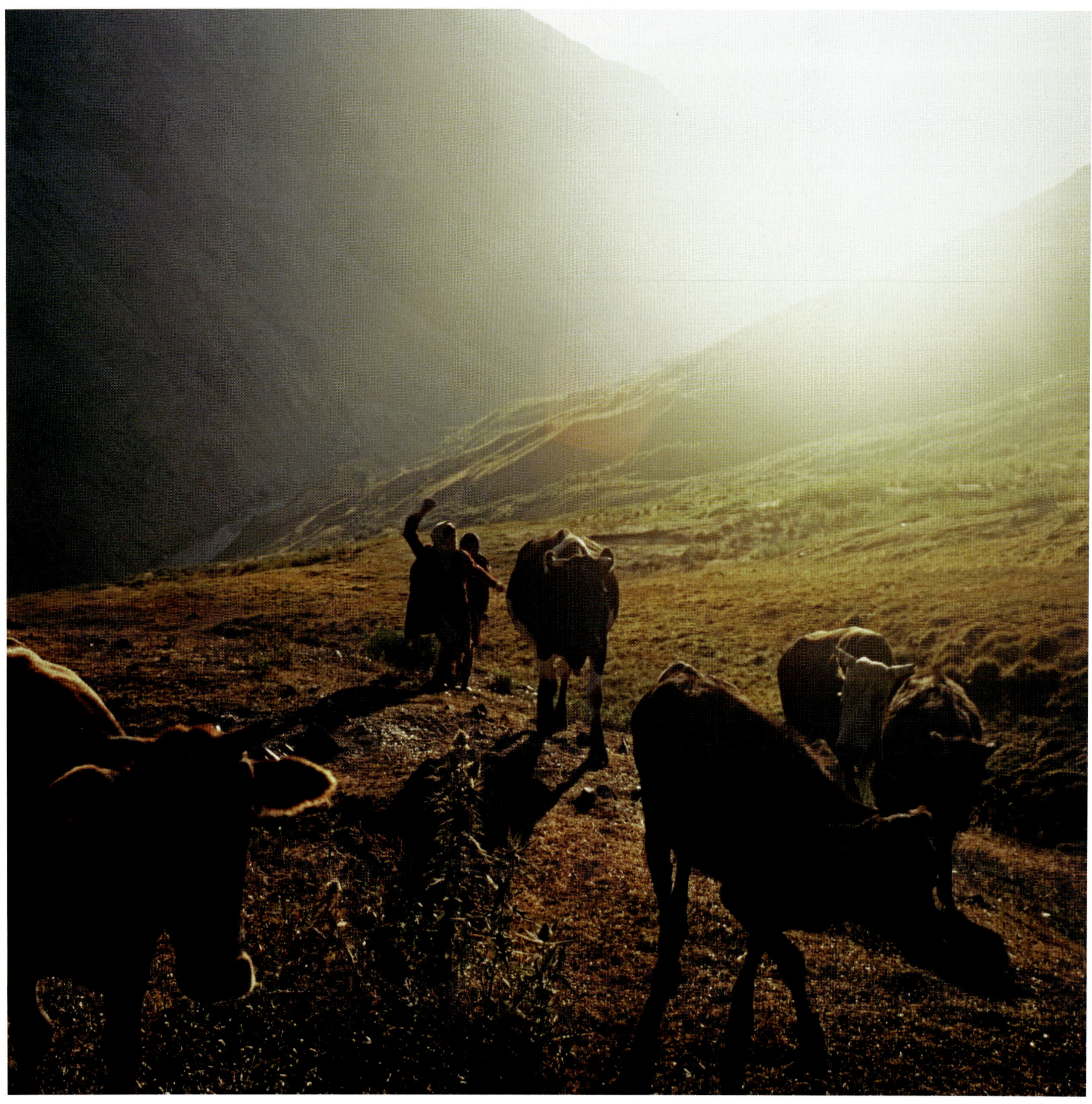

Mountainous Tadjikistan. A golden radiance has flared up in the stony depths of the ravine. The rising of the sun, which is invisible behind the mountains, has awoken the spirits of the ancestors with the age-old fiery call of Zarathustra, and the shepherds have driven their flock back into the village. The eternal and the transitory have revealed their most secret forms to the photographer.

A snowboarder makes a jump in Andorra. This is the first shot I took using a digital camera. They had only just made their appearance and they were still decidedly experimental and 'theoretical', so it was difficult for me to get the jumper into the shot. This was taken with the help of a 4-megapixel Olympus, the best available at the time. Many years were still to go by before I became converted to 'digitals'. This shot has been 'Photoshopped'.

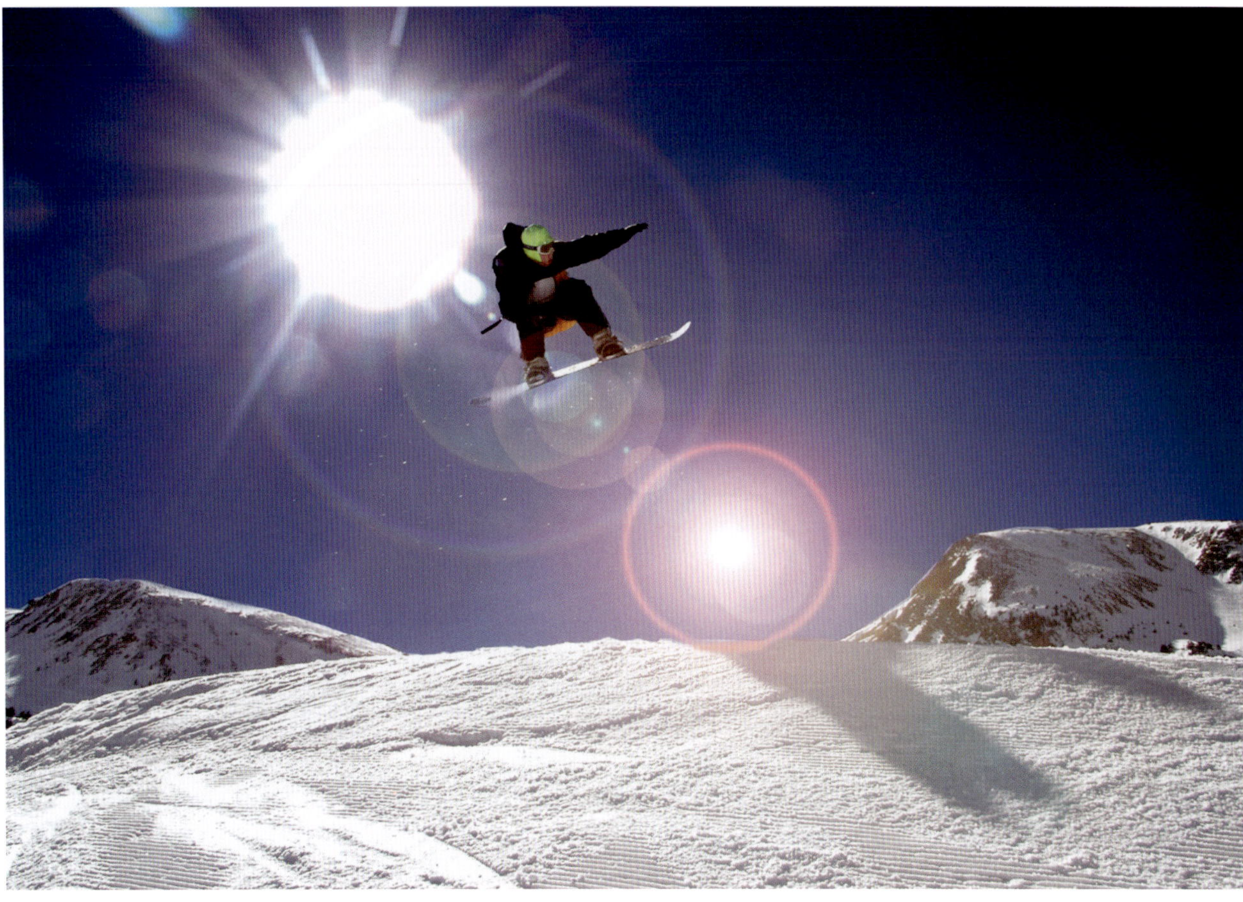

However, not everything is so simple and obvious. A shot taken into the sun is capable of conveying much more that is significant about nature, people's moods or the atmosphere of an event. The rays of the rising sun are exceptionally good for this. For example, pictures taken into the rising sun through a morning mist or steam rising from the ground are very beautiful and striking.

Every morning at dawn, the Buddhist monks in their saffron robes throng into the food market of Bangkok asking for donations for their monasteries – this is the only way they can get anything to eat. The traders will have prepared some little parcels containing various types of food, and staged scenes of 'charitable giving' are, of course, tempting for a photographer. After taking about twenty shots with flash in the semi-darkness of the covered market, I went out into an alley, hoping to take the same scene in natural light. I rapidly found someone selling various powdered spices, standing in the deep shadow of a niche. Even when photographing the 'correct' way – in sunlight – I would still have been obliged to light him with a flash, but the photo wouldn't have conveyed what time of day it was. So I turned my back to the sun, which was scarcely over the horizon, reset the flash to the 'fill in' setting, taking account of the general illumination, and stood waiting for a monk. One soon appeared and received his rations – and I took my photo, in which both participants in the scene are well lit, and it's clearly visible that the events are taking place in the early morning.

The most effective shots of a young woman photographed into the sun are achieved when the wind ruffles her hair and she appears to have a golden halo. But at midday too, at sunset or at any other time of day, it is worth looking first at the sun – and deciding whether or not to include it in your shot.

'Before the setting of the sun'

If you observe carefully how the light changes as the sun moves, then you will notice that early in the morning, after sunrise, everything around is tinged with warm yellow-golden tones. Then this warmth somehow falls away, and the higher the sun climbs, the colder and more lifeless the light becomes – until, when the sun is at its zenith, the light is a bright yet dead grey-blue. And so photos taken at that time will have the same quality. In the second half of the day, as the sun starts to descend towards sunset, the light again takes on pleasant yellowish tones and the shadows lengthen, bringing solidity back to the world around you. The early morning and just before the evening are the best time for photographs. On those rare days when neither cloud cover nor smoke prevents the sun from sinking to the furthest line of the horizon like a crimson ball, for a few minutes or even seconds just before sunset everything around you – white clouds, buildings, faces – takes on magical pink or orange tints.

If there are a few clouds – especially cirrus clouds – flitting across the sky, then the sun can spring a surprise even after it has set, filling them in with crimson. Nature does not often bestow its special favours on photographers by providing the circumstances to take a picture that is out of the ordinary –

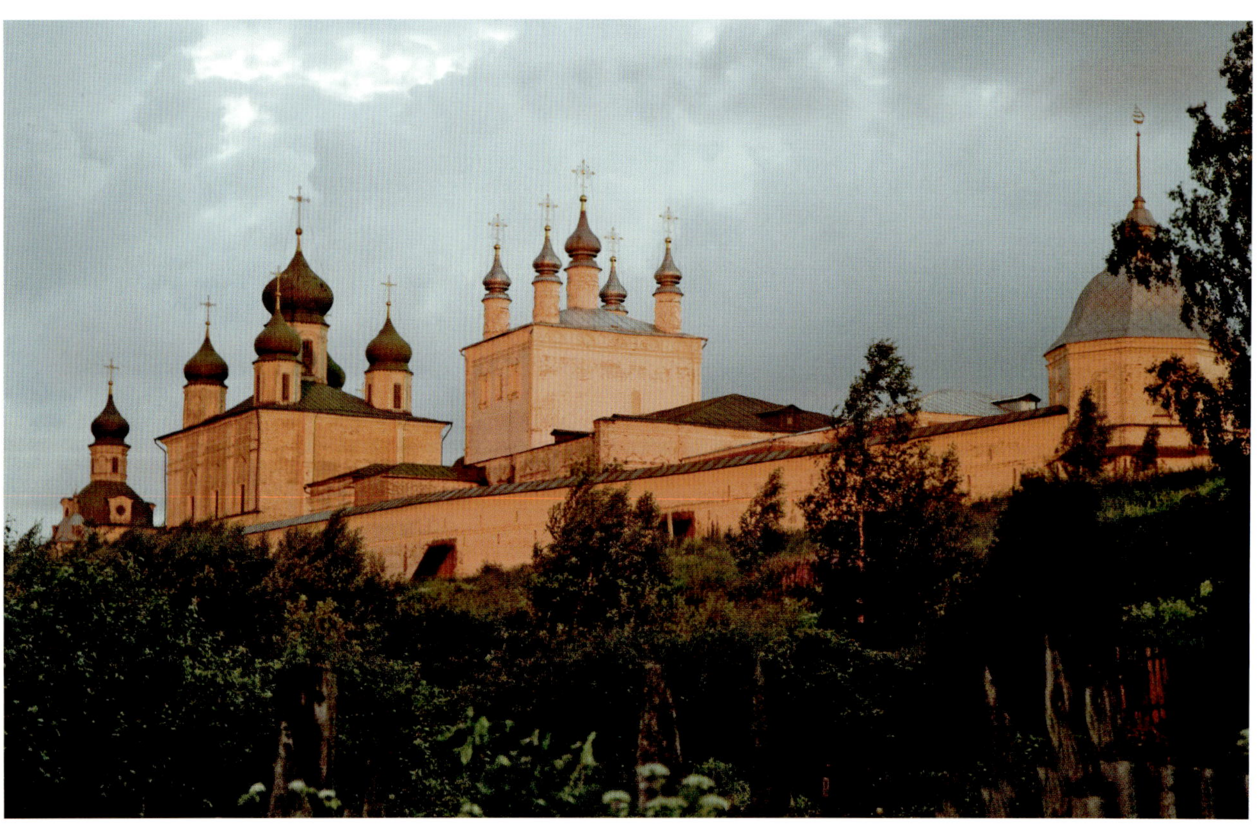

But Photoshop had nothing to do with this picture. The white walls and churches of the Goritski monastery in Pereslavl-Zalesskii have miraculously taken on the colour of red whortleber-ries under a rainy, leaden sky, thanks to the last rays of the sun, setting over the Pleshtyeyevoi Lake.

Custodians of Nepal. By struggling to balance on a high stone wall, the photographer has managed to snatch this shot of the silhouettes of a bronze guardsman and lion on the roof of a Hindu temple, just before the orange light faded from the clouds.

so you must learn how to make use of these fleeting moments.

As frequently occurs in travel photography, successful photos are connected with unusual, sometimes tragi-comic circumstances. Once, on the edge of the Nepalese capital, Kathmandu, I was returning to my hotel in the evening when I saw, against the darkening sky, the silhouette of some kind of bronze warrior or guard, which promised a decent photo. It was perfectly complemented by a lion on the roof of a temple. I couldn't get a full-length shot of the warrior, so I crawled onto a shaky wooden fence and waited until the clouds turned golden. I took all the shots I had left, packed away my camera in the rucksack, and then noticed that the clouds above me were taking on a lush orangey-pink colour, which grew stronger and stronger.

But I had no more film left! I went into a nearby shop, where I'd noticed some Fuji slide film on a shelf (who knows how it got there). I grabbed a roll of film and frantically re-set the camera. I crawled onto the fence with the agility of a monkey, succeeded in framing the shot and pressed the button once. But in a single moment, the clouds had darkened.

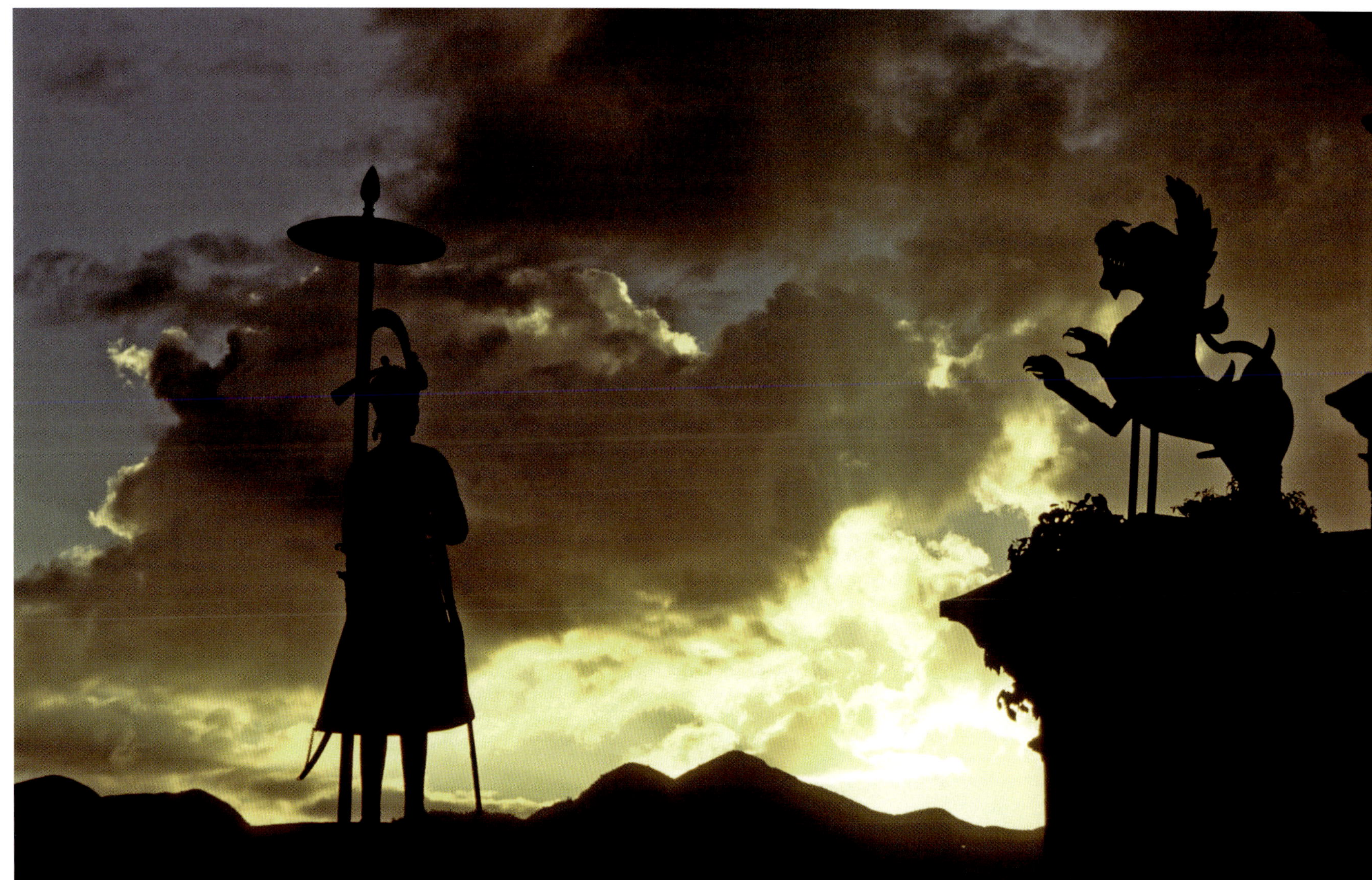

Architectural contrasts of Bangkok.
Even without the lovely clouds, the
South-East Asian sky just before
sunset is a gift to the photographer,
and in itself provides a striking decor
for the pagodas and skyscrapers

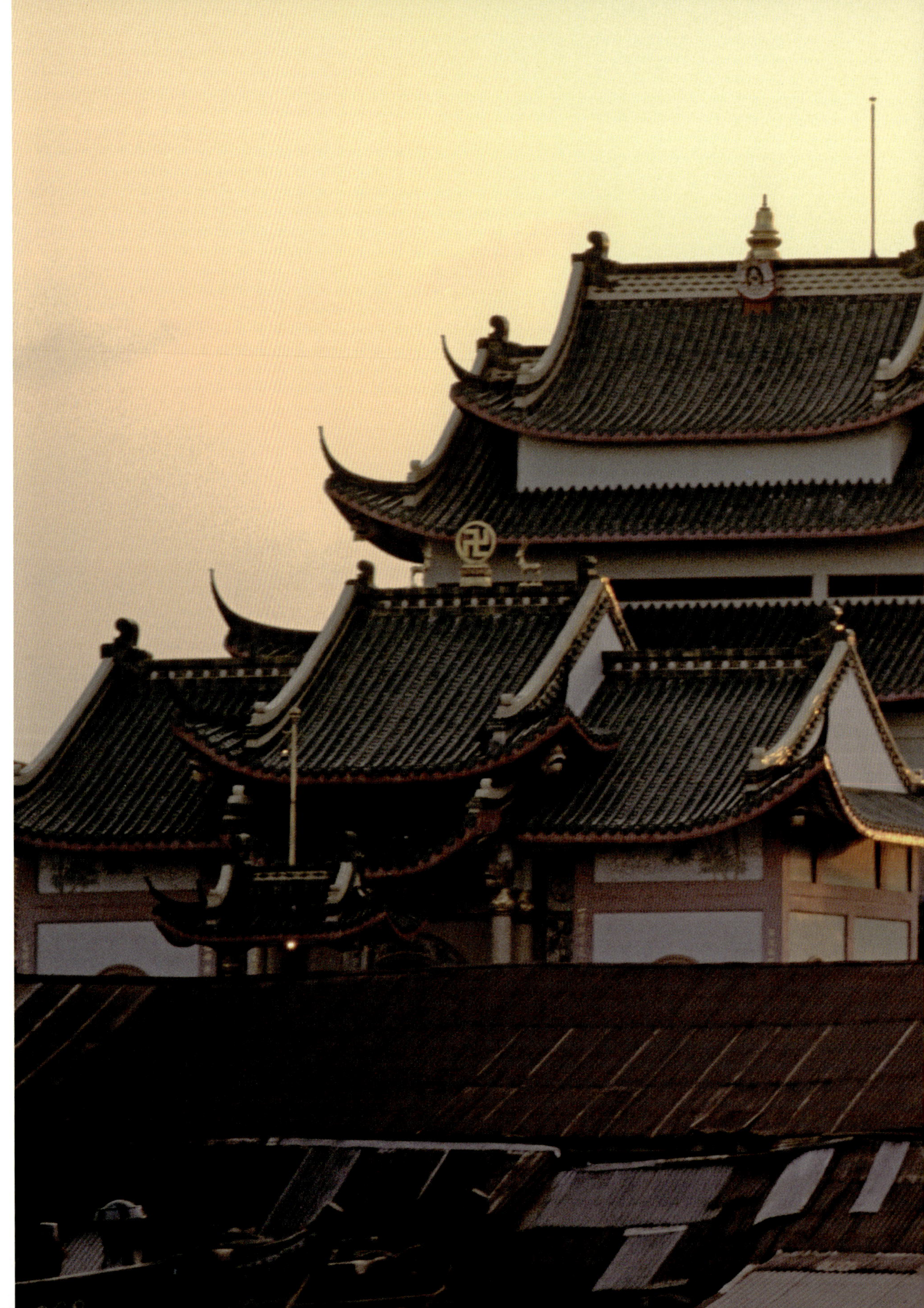

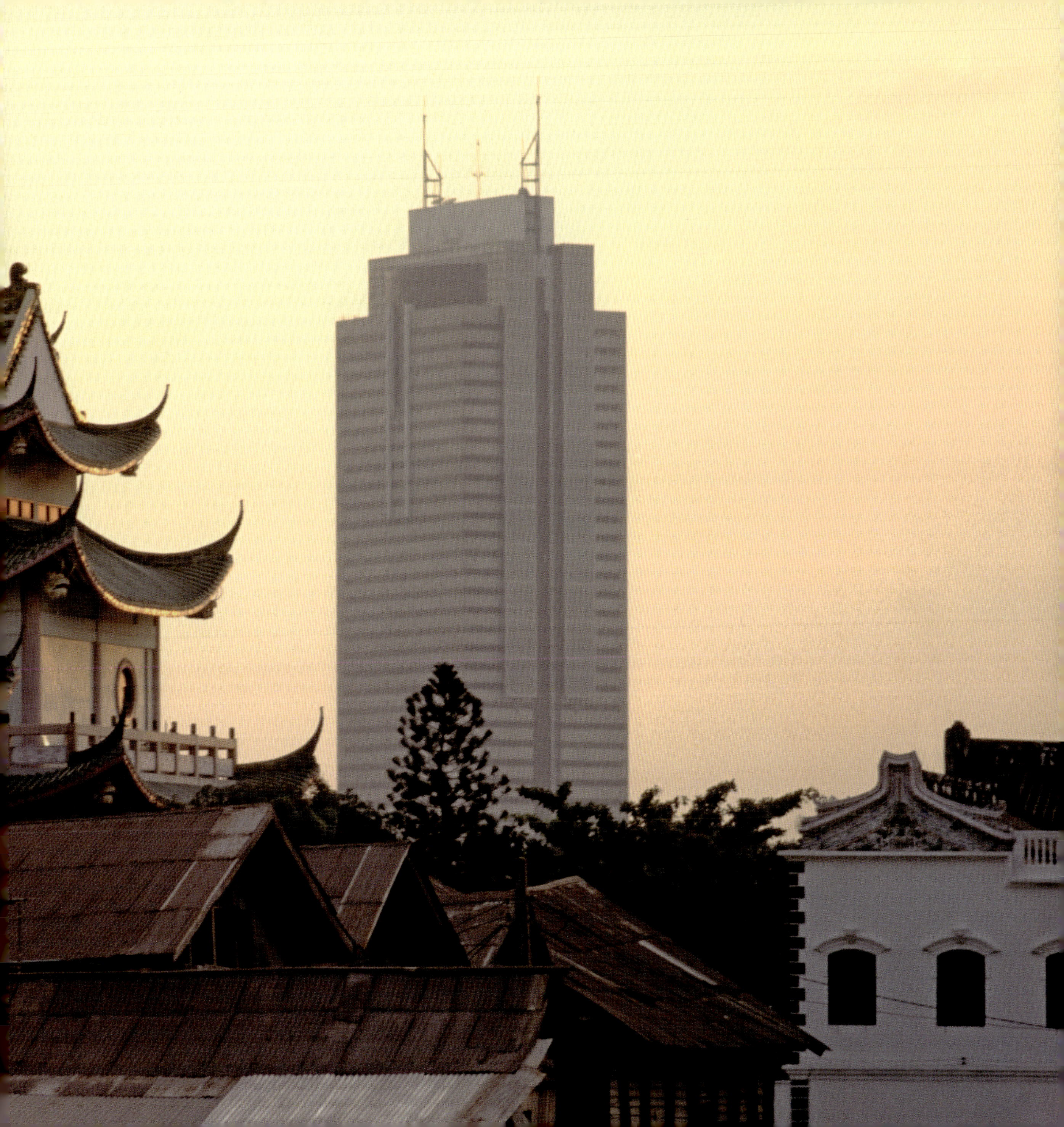

A sunset at the Lykia World Hotel in
Turkey. The reflection of the setting sun
in the pool creates a striking image.

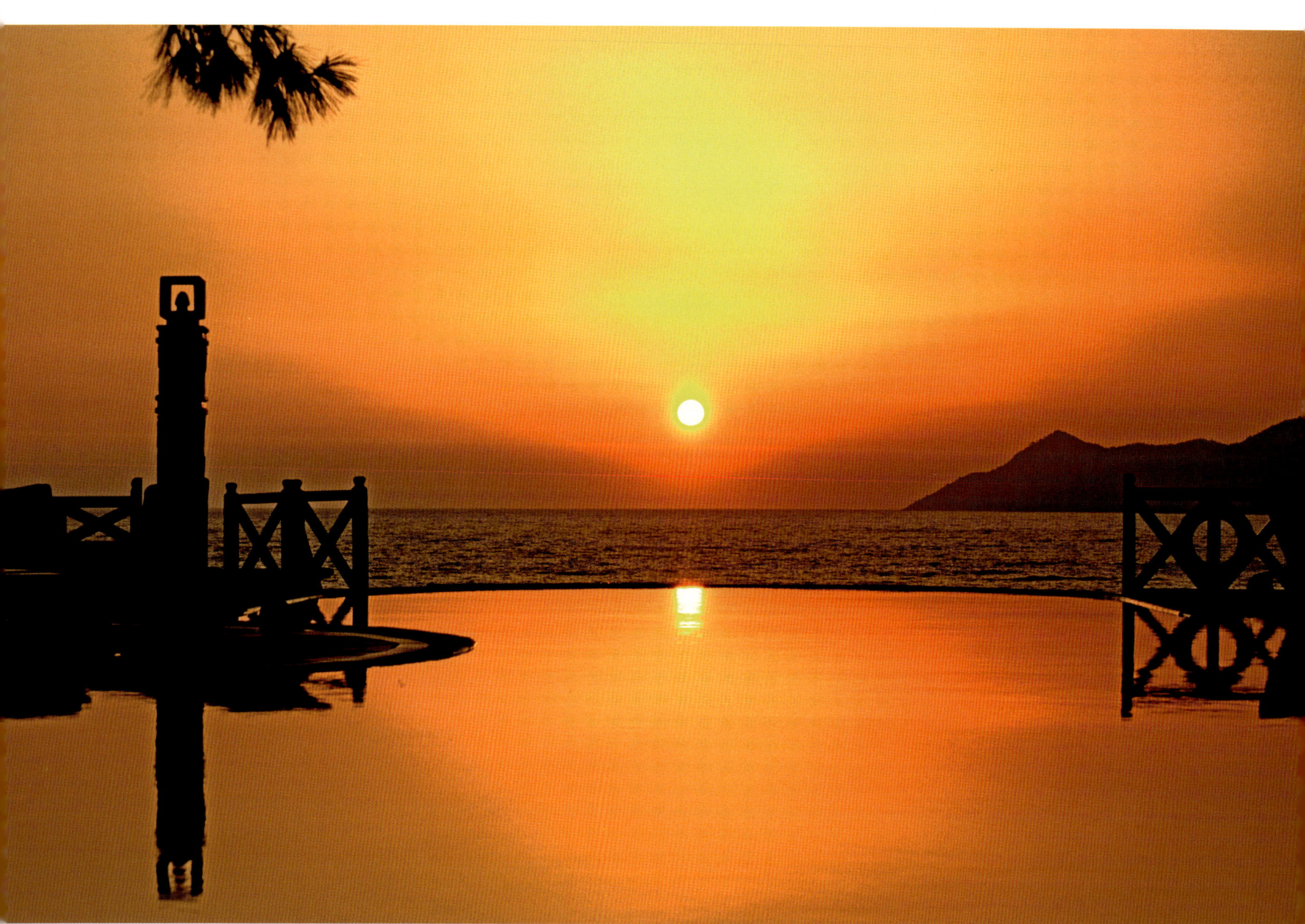

A beach in Goa. These gypsy–like
dandies, with huge rings in their ears
and noses, festooned with ornaments
made from silver, mother of pearl
and mirror fragments, are natives of
Gujarat peddling their treasures to
the tourists.

Warrior marionette in the market at
Djerba. Tunisia. This beautiful puppet
was photographed by the light of the
setting sun, displaying the deep rich
colours of his red full-dress uniform
and brass equipment. Well-dressed
wooden marionettes like this can also
be found in the bazaars of India and
other countries.

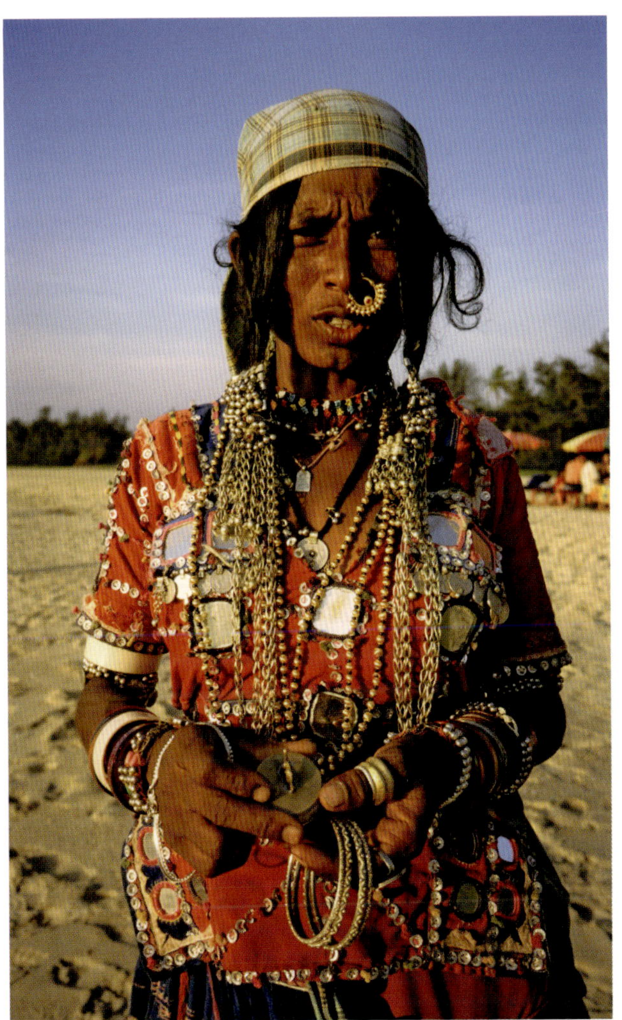

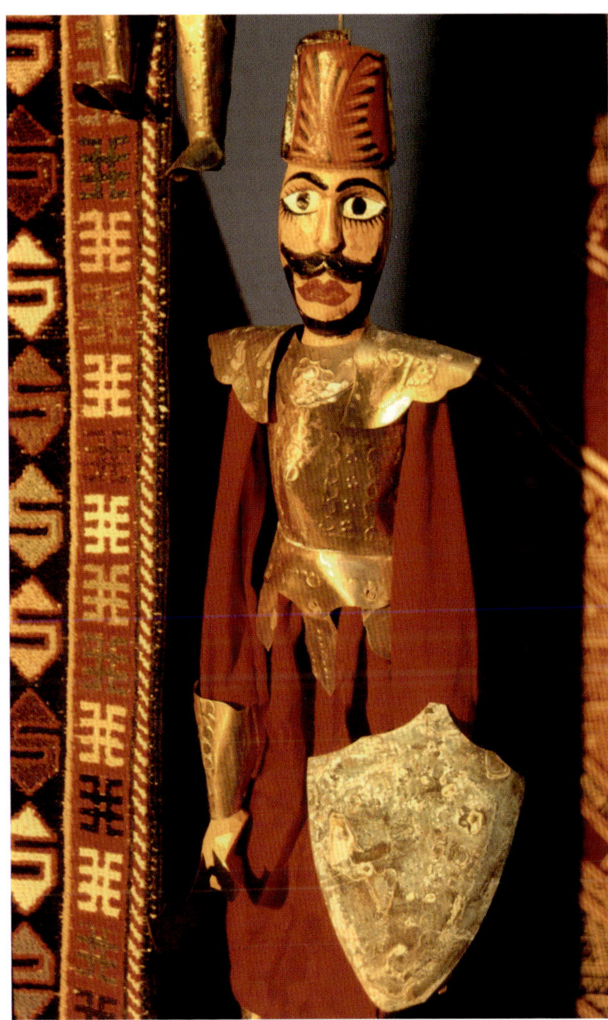

Silent night

You will need a reliable tripod, as without one, night-time photography will not be easy. And a park bench, a windowsill, the bonnet of a parked car or an asphalt pavement can all come to your rescue – in a word, any level, stable surface on which you can place your camera. It is true that, even then, without an articulating display you may not always manage to aim the camera accurately at the subject of your photo.

The technical element is fairly simple: Set your camera to automatic, take a test shot using a cable release or a self-timer, then make corrections according to the outcome. At shutter speeds of several seconds or more, a lightweight tripod must be set up somewhere that is protected from movement by the wind. For stability, you can hang your camera bag or some other heavy counterweight on it.

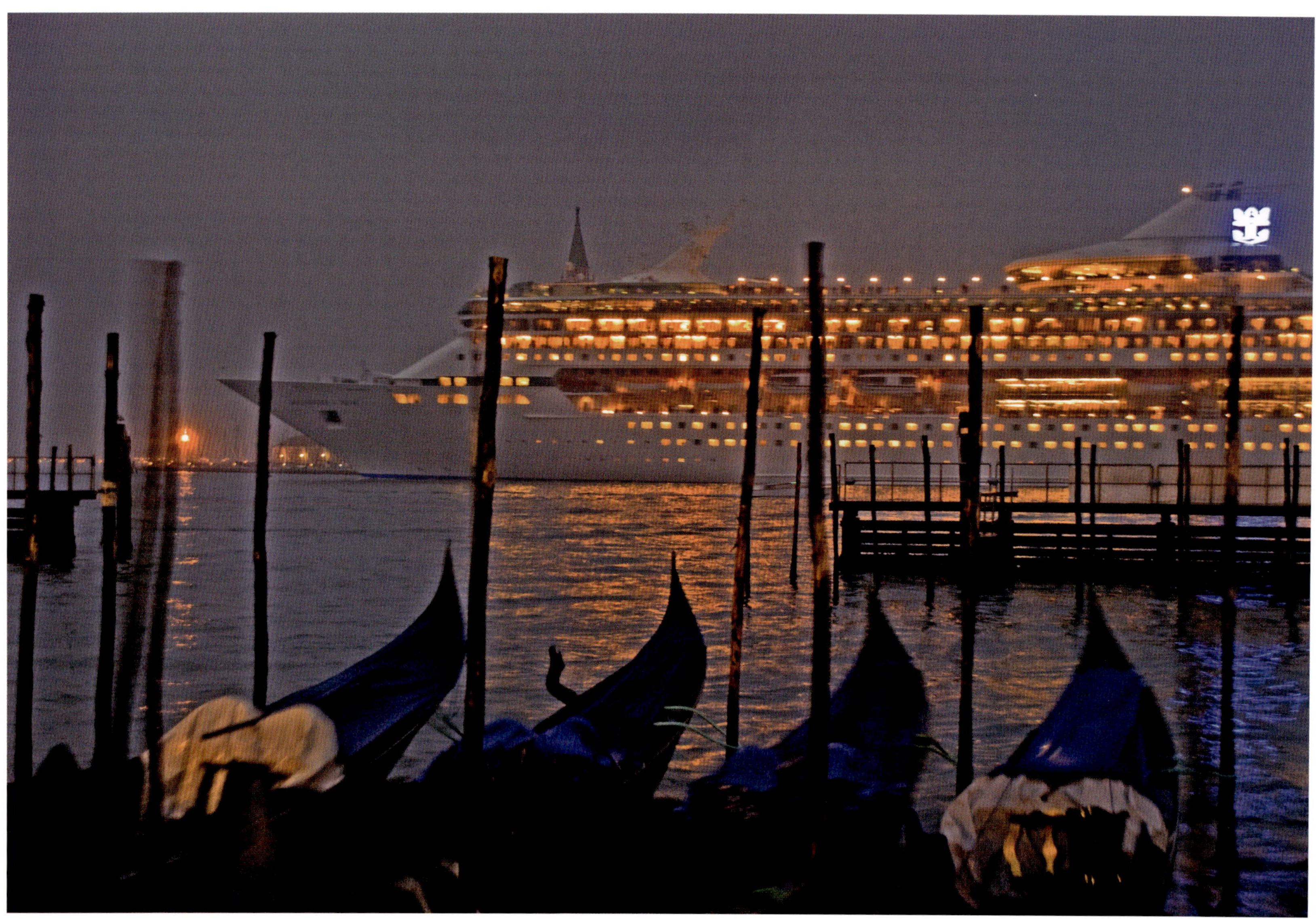

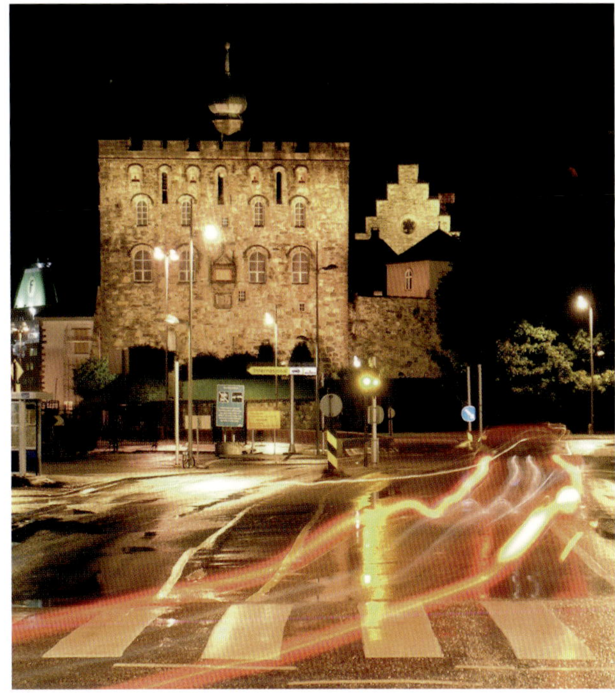

on one side were standing out of the water on piles of logs, with patches of brightness shining from those few windows where lights were on. What a pity I hadn't seen them before the sunset – what a shot I'd missed! Or maybe not yet? What could a 'little digital mirror' do? I considered the problem – to turn night into late evening, I needed an exposure of at least one-tenth of a second at 800 ASA. Night was falling quickly, but it had only just begun (even on photographic cameras, the auto-focus plays tricks in the dark).

I still hadn't decided how I was going to do this. I fitted the camera with an AF 20/2.8 lens, I framed the houses, set the focus for the gleaming lights, and selected the 'manual' position for enhanced focus. But how could I make the camera freeze for 10 – 15 seconds? Standing the tripod on rickety planks wouldn't work. I fitted a blind on the lens. Now the camera could take up a horizontal position. Lying flat on the cold, damp boards at the intersection of two little bridges, I positioned the camera with my right hand on the last plank of the two bridges before the water.

The Nikon flickered for a few seconds, then froze. I smoothly pressed the button, and this seemed to take for ever. The picture was completely out of focus. I altered the speed to 1600 and set the automatic release for 10 seconds. Once again I pressed the button, then lay completely still on the planks, not even breathing. Once I saw the picture on the screen, I didn't regret not having noticed these houses earlier – it was the darkness of the night which made the photo worthwhile!'

A very rewarding subject for night-time photography can be a well lit city with traces of light from the red tail lights of cars. Here, of course, a tripod is necessary, since a shutter speed of several seconds is required – anything shorter and you will have to set the film speed to maximum, which will inevitably have an effect on picture quality. There are a few other little tricks as well. Try waiting until there are several cars standing at the traffic lights, and then press the shutter as they move off.

Strictly speaking, taking photos in complete darkness is a thankless task, because there will be gaps between lighted objects. Luckily, between the twilight and the night, nature has provided the photographer with an extremely short space of time which is much better suited to taking photos - when the traffic lights have already come on, the windows in the houses are lit up, and the sky and the surrounding landscape have not yet merged in the gloom. This time is particularly good for photographing ski resorts framed by mountaintops. So, if you're trying to recover after making a few photographic errors, prescribe yourself a 'limited light diet'!

On a clear night with a full moon, visibility is no worse than at dusk, and the moonlight itself gives the landscape a romantic character, especially with its reflection in the water.

In Trondheim, while on my way to the Norwegian downhill skiing resorts, the sun came out at dusk from behind the clouds for the first time that day. Against the light, I photographed the sunset over a bay, with raindrops, which had lit up thousands of 'fireflies' on the calm surface of the water. I succeeded in photographing a very stylish, 'hi-tech' bridge made of stainless steel, but then the light over the town quickly faded. There were no quays as such – the houses just stopped right at the edge of the bay or the river. It was already dark as I walked along, and with difficulty I made out that the old-fashioned houses

Firework display above the Moscow
Kremlin – taken from a bridge using
a tripod, with a 15-second exposure.
With a longer exposure, another
firework would have been in the shot,
but the bridge was vibrating and the
shot might have been smudged.

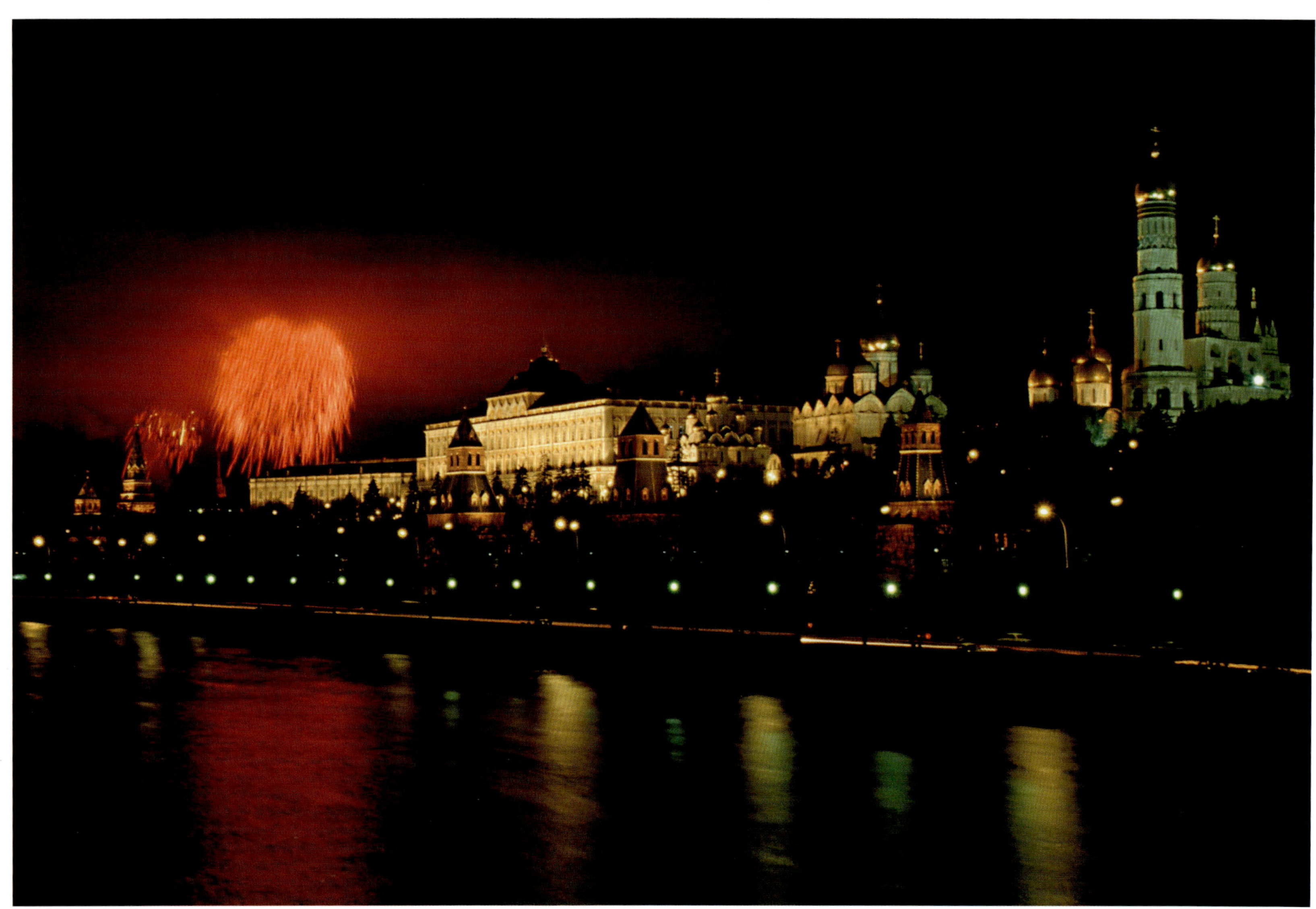

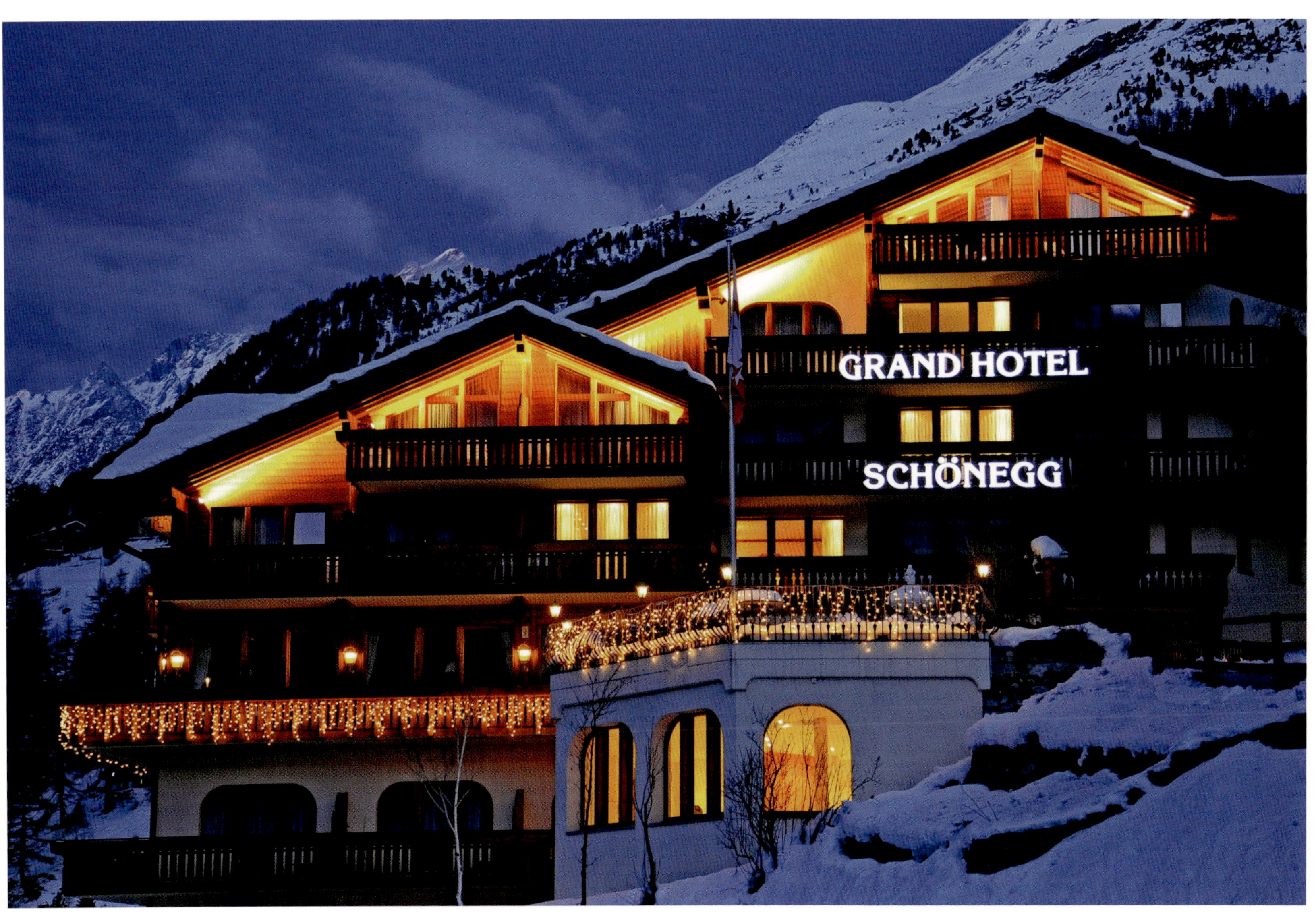

The Grand Hotel Schönegg glows against the background of the mountains and the darkening sky.

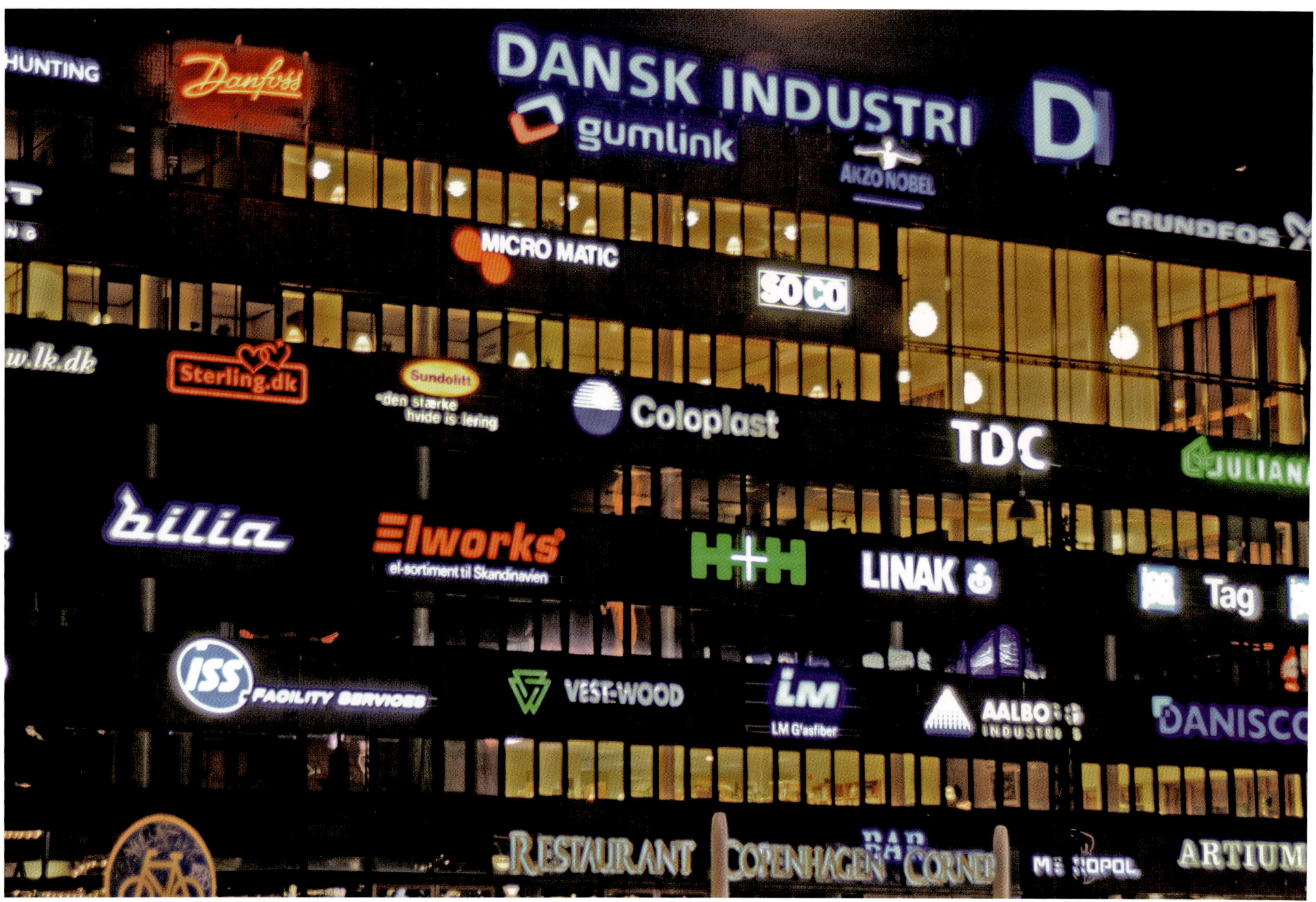

An illuminated advert 'rescues' a large building with an extremely uninspiring – not to say primitive – shape, erected (God knows why) opposite the Town Hall in the ancient surroundings of the very centre of Copenhagen, and 'makes' this nocturnal photo.

This annual summer music festival in
Estonia takes place in the middle of
a lake, with thousands of spectators
ranged along the shore. Bonfires and
a blaze of floating candles create a
magical glow.

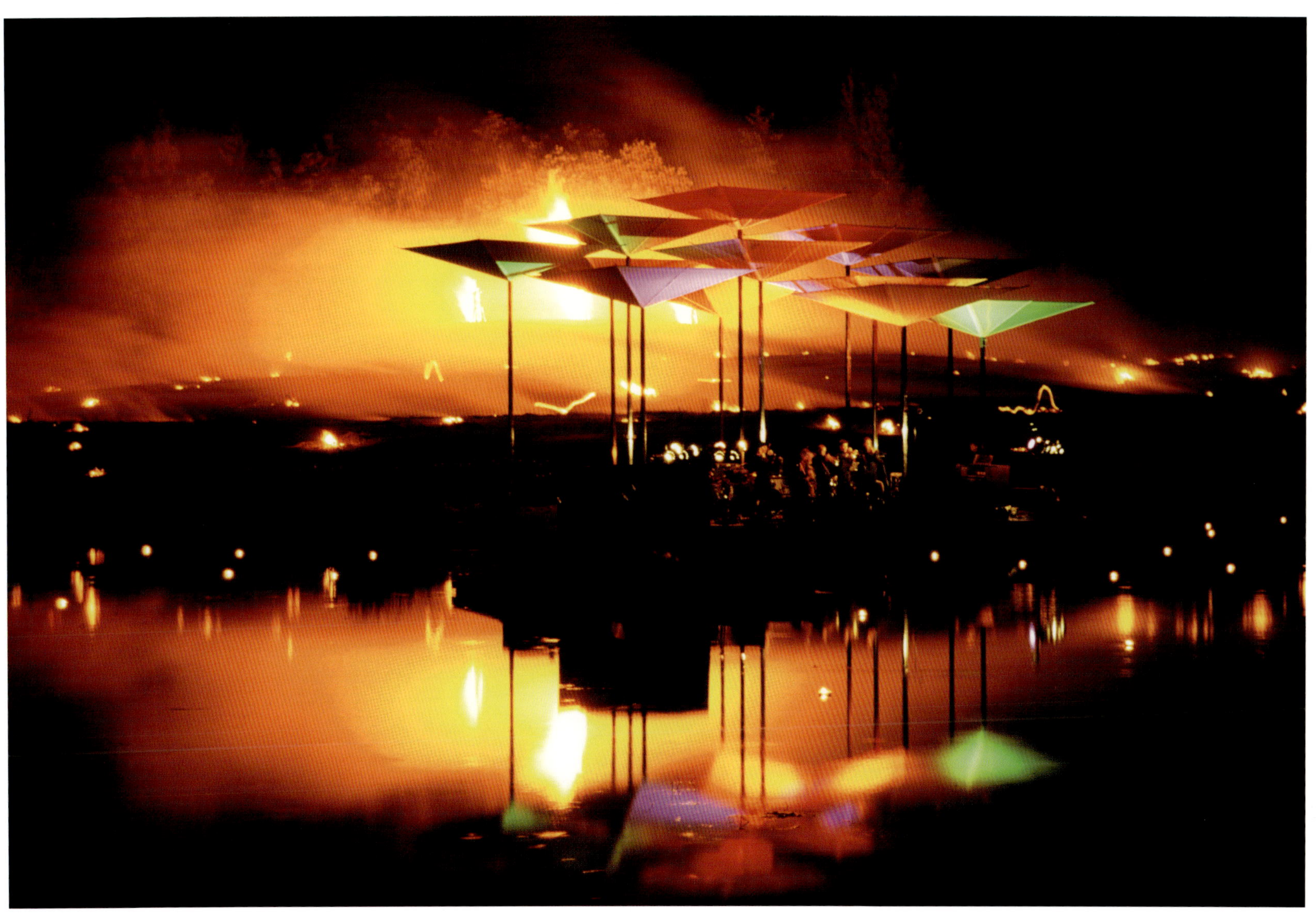

Seen through the mist

It can happen that you have travelled somewhere for the warm sunny weather, but it has turned out to be far from the holiday paradise that you desired. As a photographer, you don't have to get depressed: the exceptions to the rules are in our favour. The vicissitudes of the elements may be exactly what allows you take much more striking photos than you could on a clear sunny day! You can outwit the grey sky and the drizzle by taking your photographs in the evening when the buildings are lit up or – even better – spot lit, which is frequently the case, for as a rule we do not photograph ordinary buildings, but palaces, castles and mansions.

The minutes just before a thunderstorm are great – when thick black clouds have already slid across the sky and the atmosphere is full of anxious anticipation, but the low sun is still highlighting the tension that is hanging in the air. A chance shaft of sunlight unexpectedly breaking through a dense black storm cloud and lighting up a fragment of landscape can be particularly effective. It was just in this way that I was able to photograph the extremely beautiful Książ, near the Polish town of Walbrzych.

I had to take about 500 pictures at 110 sites throughout Poland for a photo-album on Polish architectural monuments.

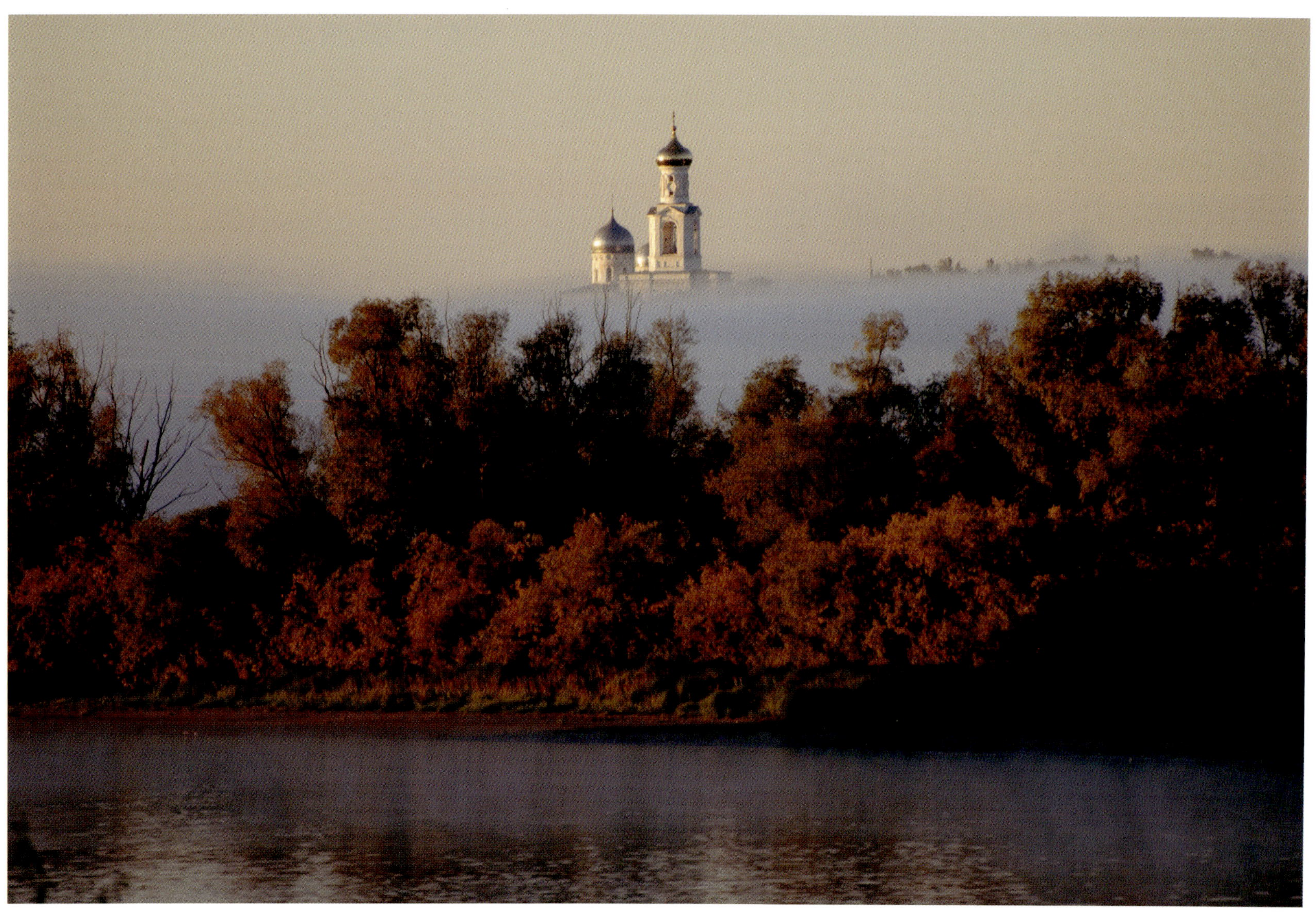

I covered 10,000 kilometres in a Polish Fiat over a month and a half. And that's how I got stuck for two days in the hotel at the castle, with my brutally tight schedule in danger of disruption due to the incessant rain. On the third day, the sky grew even darker, but in the evening as I was sorting out the photos I'd taken I suddenly I saw a ray of sun reflected on the wall. I dragged the Nikon out of its box, flew down the stairs and raced through the rain to the castle . It was standing like an illuminated decoration against a dark backdrop, like 'a ray of light in a kingdom of darkness'. Realising that I wouldn't get there in time, I opened the zoom lens up to maximum and pressed the button twice while on the move. The next minute, the fortress had been swallowed up by the grey murk once more. But I'd got my shot, and I could move on to Wroclaw.

Rain isn't a problem if you're taking photos with a professional camera and a lens which is suitably protected against moisture and dust – and, of course, if the shot is worth it. It's best to do this in a waterproof jacket with a hood, however! One evening, I was driving my car from Novgorod to Moscow under a really heavy downpour. There were black clouds all the way to the horizon. But to the left of the highway,

LEFT
A hotel balcony or window frequently offers a splendid position for a photographer. The Georgian cathedral of the Yuriev monastery in Novgorod, rising out of the mists of dawn, taken from the balcony of the 'Rossiya' hotel on the Alexander Nyevski Embankment. It's several kilometres away from the monastery, so the shot was taken using a lens with a focal distance of 300 mm.

RIGHT
In the Winter camp of the Chukchi, a line of sledges stands waiting for the time when the reindeer herders will lead the migration to the Summer pastures. The surrounding mist and the wan sunshine accurately convey the atmosphere of acute isolation, demonstrating how far removed from us this entire primeval world of the nomads of the tundra is, both in space and time.

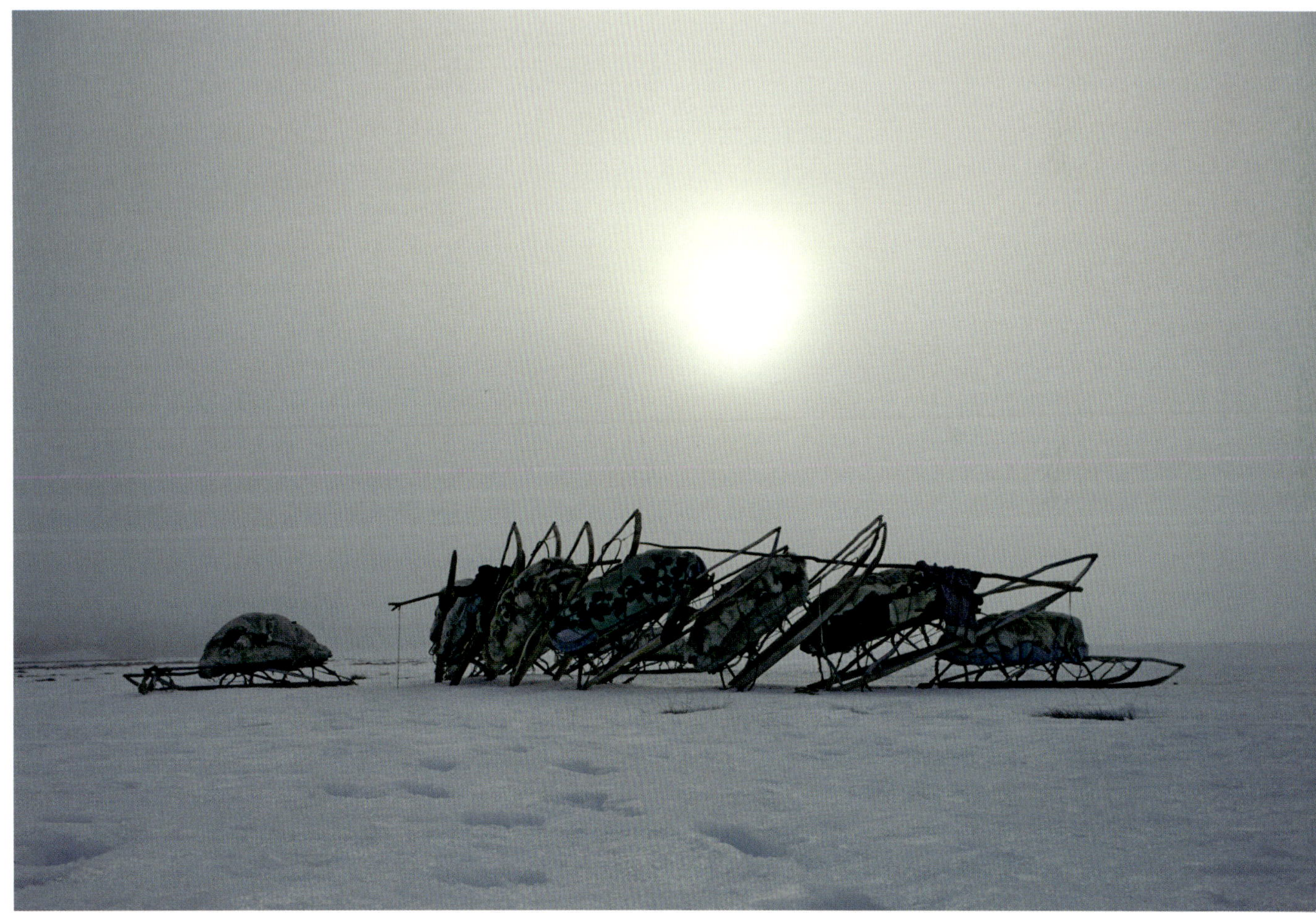

The mountain of Penken, near the Alpine ski resort of Mayrhofen, Austria. Natural light – no special effects. The unusual luminescence on an overcast, foggy day is explained by the play of a single ray of sunlight piercing the veil of storm clouds for just an instant.

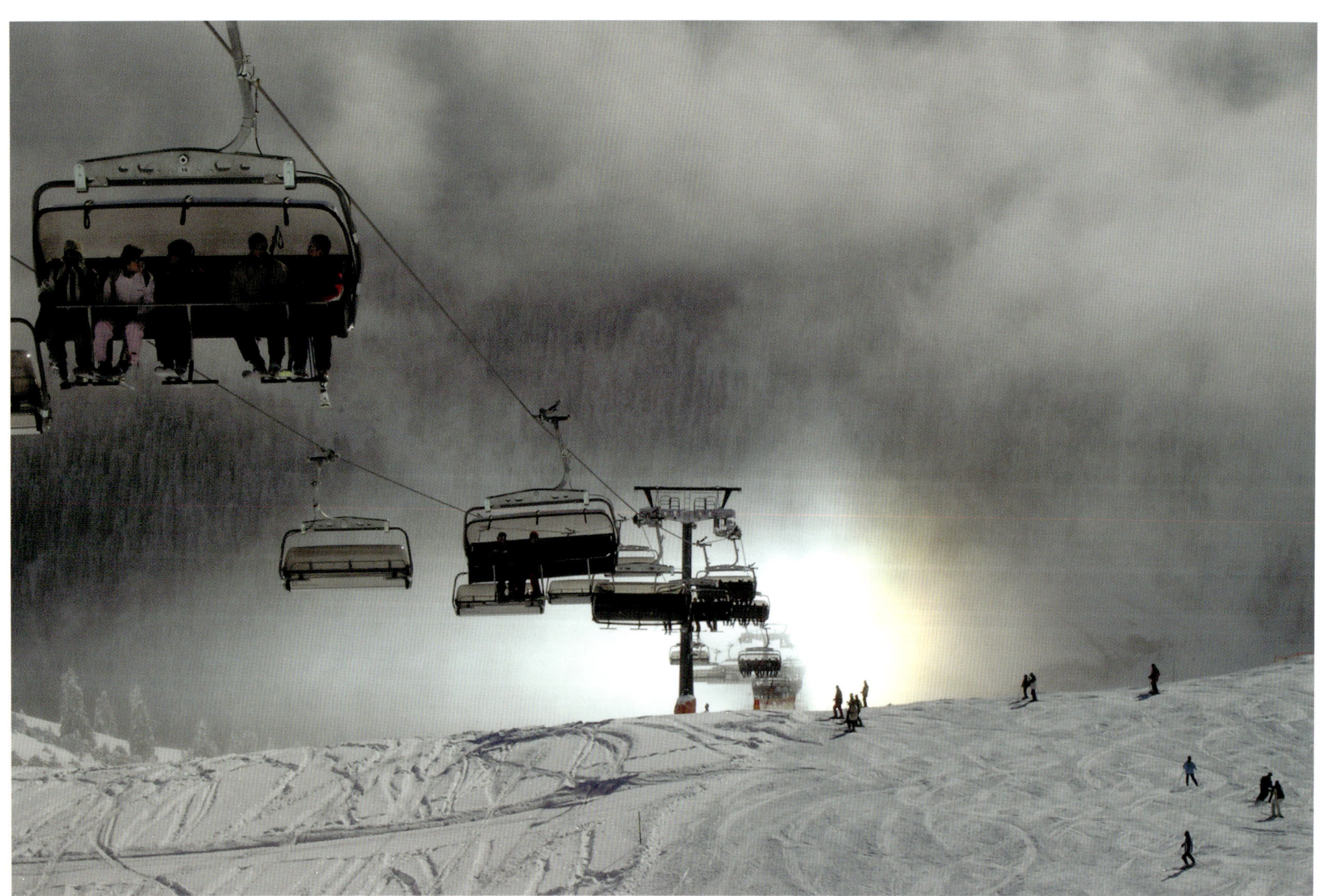

A solitary balloon hangs high above the mist which engulfs the valley below.

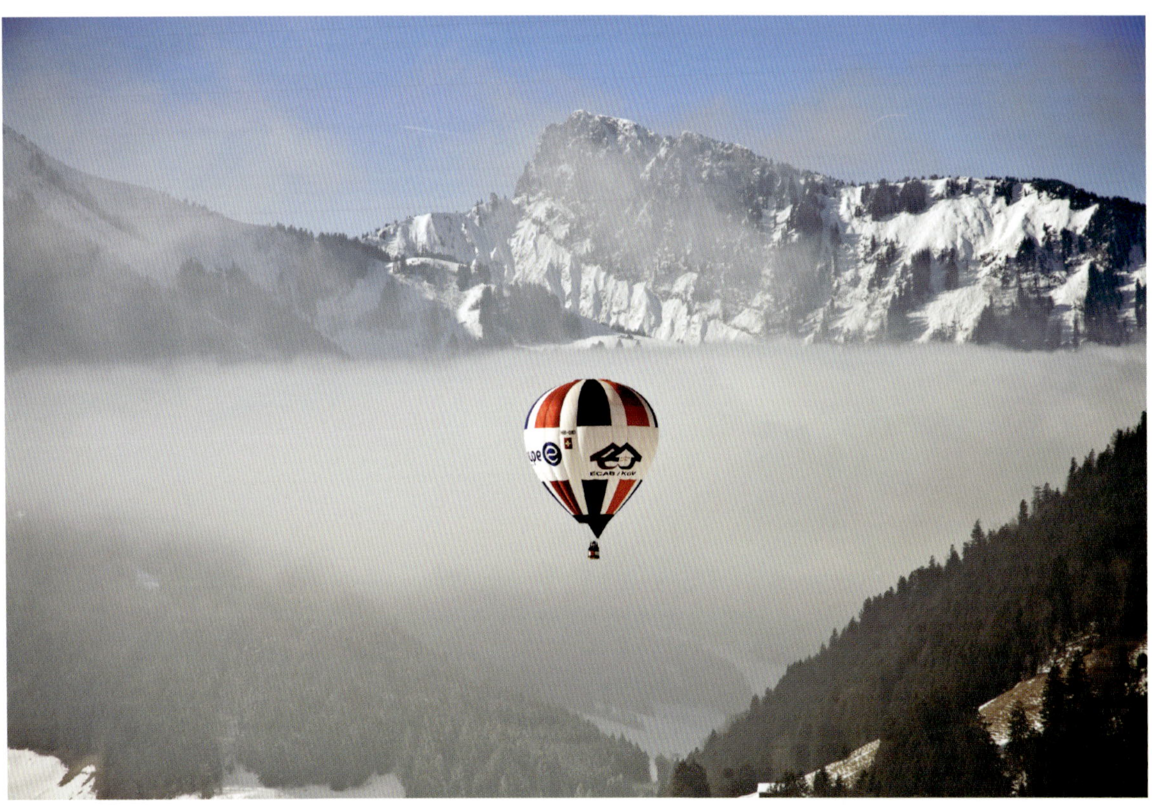

Church near Tver, taken with a wide-angled 24-mm. lens to get all of the rainbow into the shot. In itself, a rainbow doesn't 'make' the picture. There has to be something striking in the foreground, or a landscape of exceptional beauty.

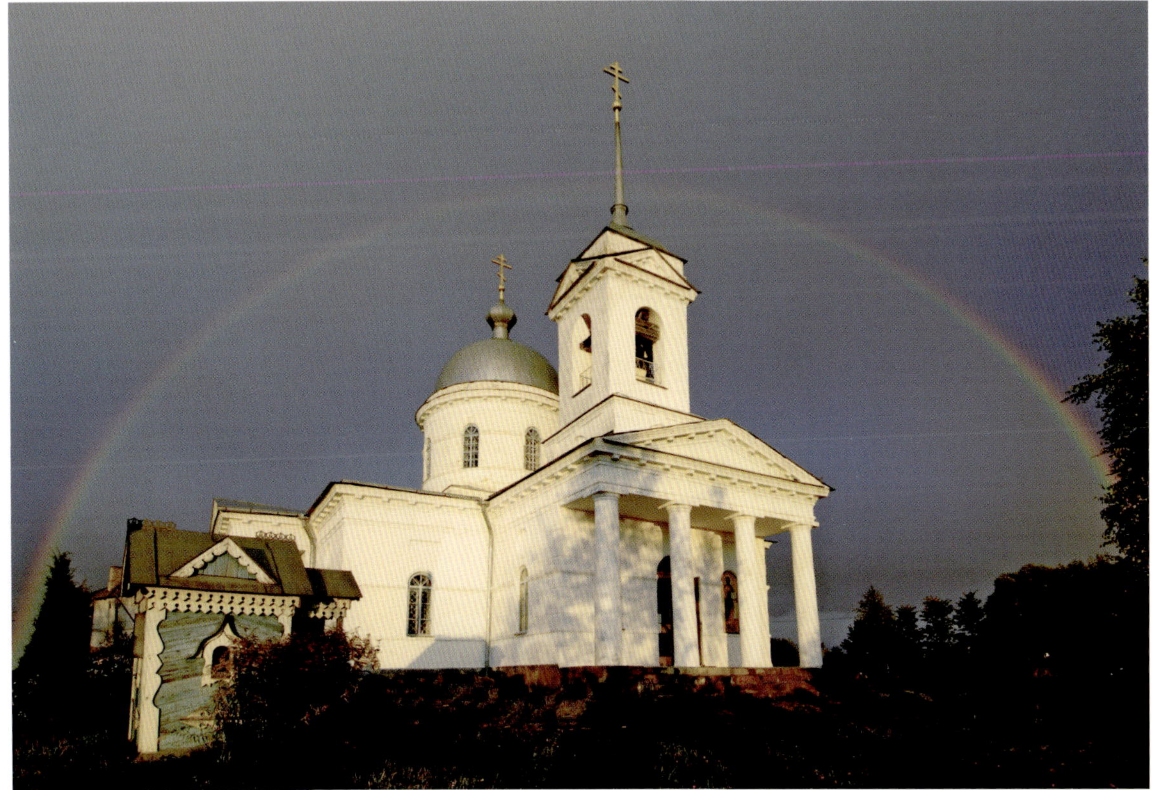

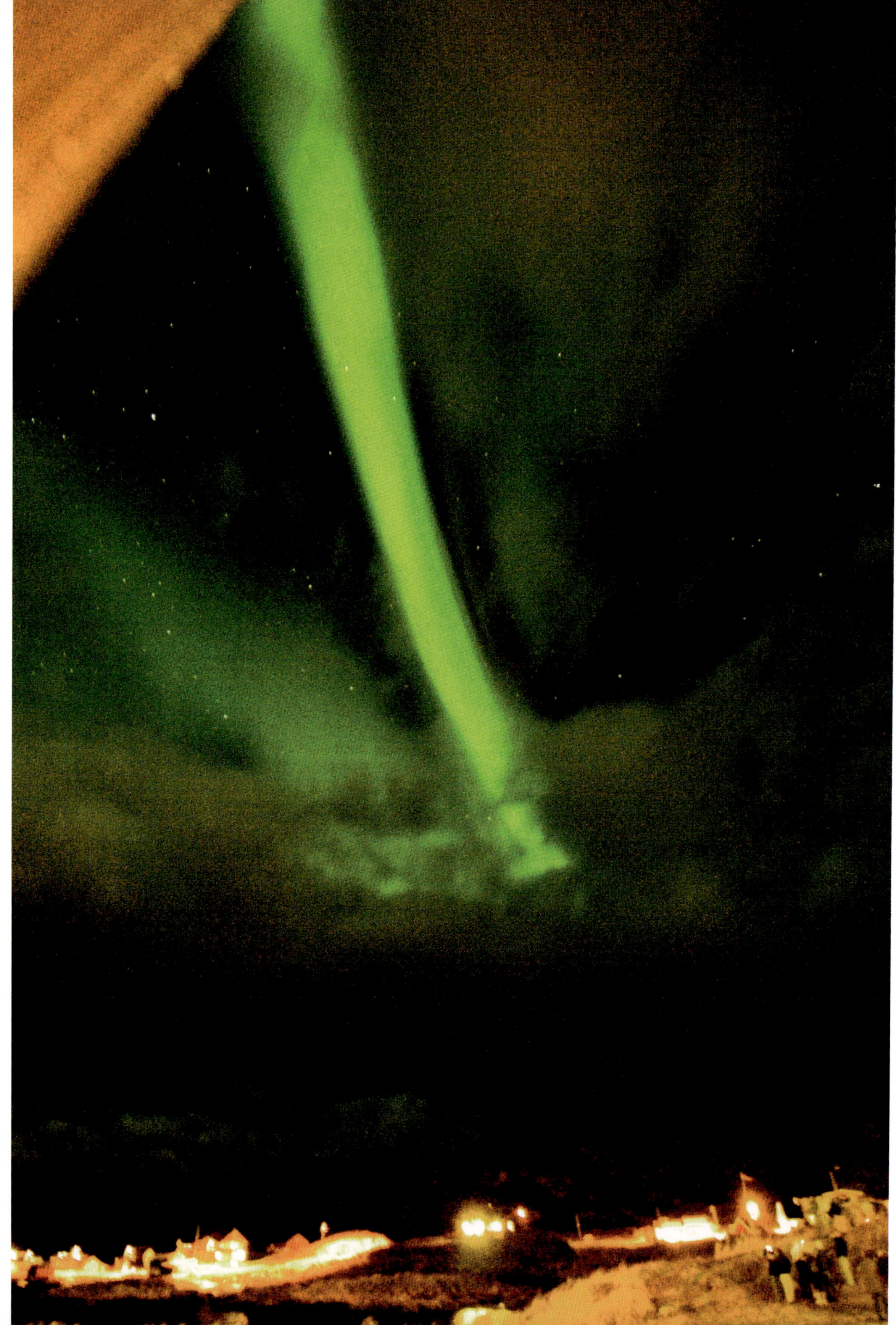

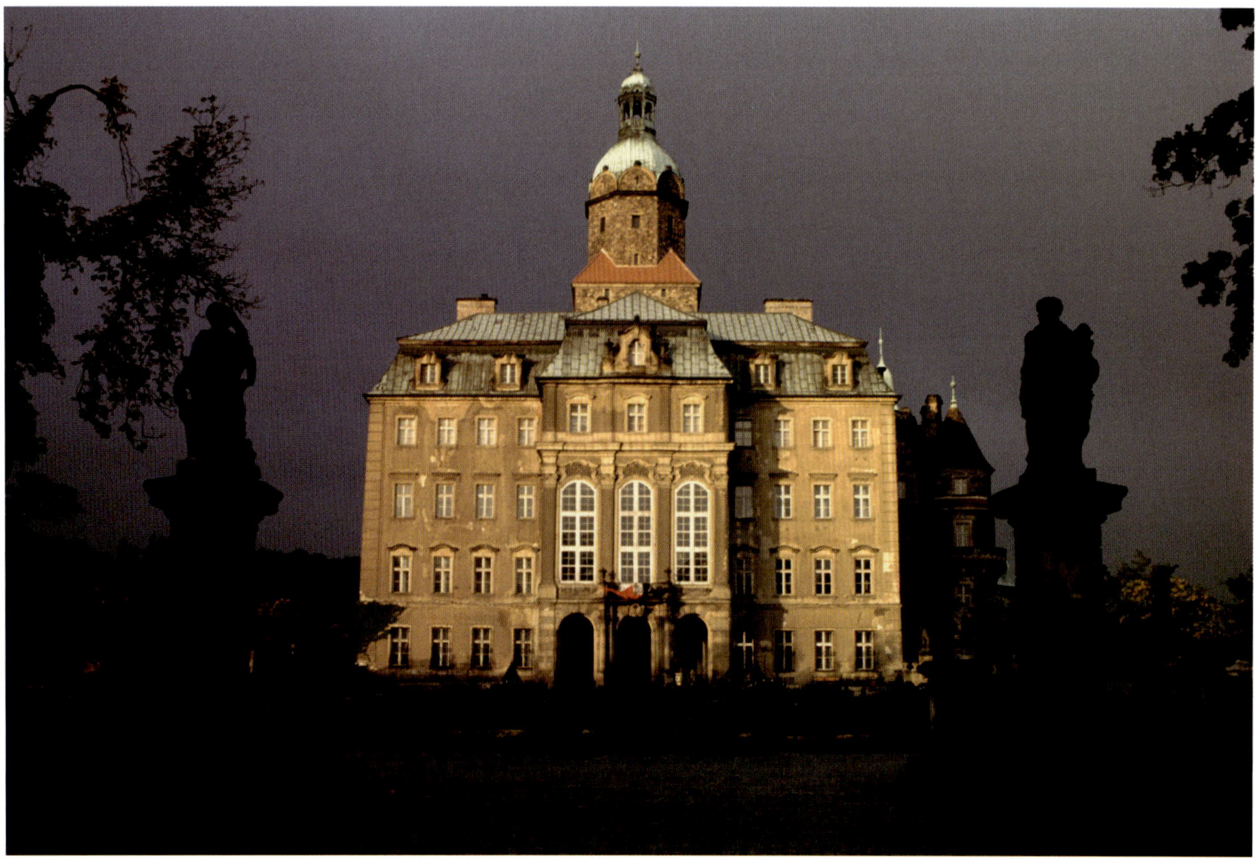

there was a complete rainbow which went right down to the
ground. It was an unbelievably beautiful sight, but in order to
make a really striking photo something was needed in the front
part of the composition. I drove on for many kilometres, praying
that the rainbow wouldn't fade away, and then a light-coloured
church came into view, clearly visible against the background
of the dark sky. The church was extremely appealing due to the
provincial classicism of its lines and proportions.

I got out of the car and found the spot from which the
church stood out best against the arch of the rainbow. With
my left palm extended to shield the lens, I pressed the button.

Mist can also introduce a certain charm, helping to convey
a mood. Very good photographs can be taken early in the
morning, when mist is creeping across the ground, in hollows,
ravines and gorges, over a lake or a river, or enveloping a
monastery. Skiers know how beautiful the mountains are when
far below, beneath your feet, white clouds shroud the valley and
the snowy peaks glint in the sun. Temples look very good when
rising up out of the mist.

The most fruitful time to take photographs is on a stormy
night or evening. The evening is better, of course, because
then the town is lit up. Obviously, if it's pouring with rain, then
you will have to shoot from under an awning, a bridge or an
archway, or from a window. An umbrella is unreliable, because,
as a rule, a storm is accompanied by squally gusts of wind. In
order to take one photograph that will include several flashes
of lightning, set a long shutter speed – half a minute or even a
minute. Subjects photographed in windy weather are especially
striking .

Of course, this does not mean that from now on the
photographer who wants to travel must opt for trips to
faraway countries in the typhoon or hurricane season. But if
bad weather strikes you along the way, know how to make
maximum use of it.

Shooting in waltz time

The ghosts of the Hapsburgs still hover over Vienna to this day, and the very air seems tinged with nostalgia for the golden days of the Imperial age. From Christmas to Lent, the impetuous patriotism of the Viennese finds expression in three hundred balls – a situation which is unique in the social life of modern Europe. At the ball organised by the Viennese Philharmonic Orchestra, the inspired and tireless waltzers included the country's president, the Prime Minister, and also many ex-servicemen with decorations and medal ribbons on their chests - including some I would have guessed were veterans of the Napoleonic wars! After a few hours of taking difficult photos in the cramped closeness of the hall, I became so dazzled by the hundreds of waltzing couples that the room was literally 'swimming' in front of my eyes.

It used to be the case that photographers had to draw all their inspiration from within, but now they can create some very interesting photos thanks to the technical potential of their equipment. One breakthrough was the appearance of photo flash units with a 'rear curtain' function. Rear curtain sync involves the movement of two shutters, not one central shutter, to achieve exposure. Usually, the flash operates immediately after the first shutter opens, but in rear curtain sync it fires at the moment before the second curtain starts to close. At a fast shutter speed – 1/250 of a second, say – the moment at which the flash fires has no practical significance. At a shutter speed of, for example, 1 second, it's another matter entirely. Obviously, here we are talking about shooting indoors or when it is dark outside. So, in that time, a runner carrying a torch will cover 5 metres, a car's tail lights will travel 20 metres, a Spanish flamenco dancer or a Balinese cult trance dancer will manage a full-spin turn, and veterans of the Viennese ball will take just a few steps.

In the past, the photographer shooting this kind of subject had three possibilities: set the camera and flash to automatic and snatch a static shot with 'frozen' movement from the darkness; or, having measured the real lighting conditions, shoot without flash, in order to get a deliberately smudged picture; or finally, at the same slow shutter speed, set off the

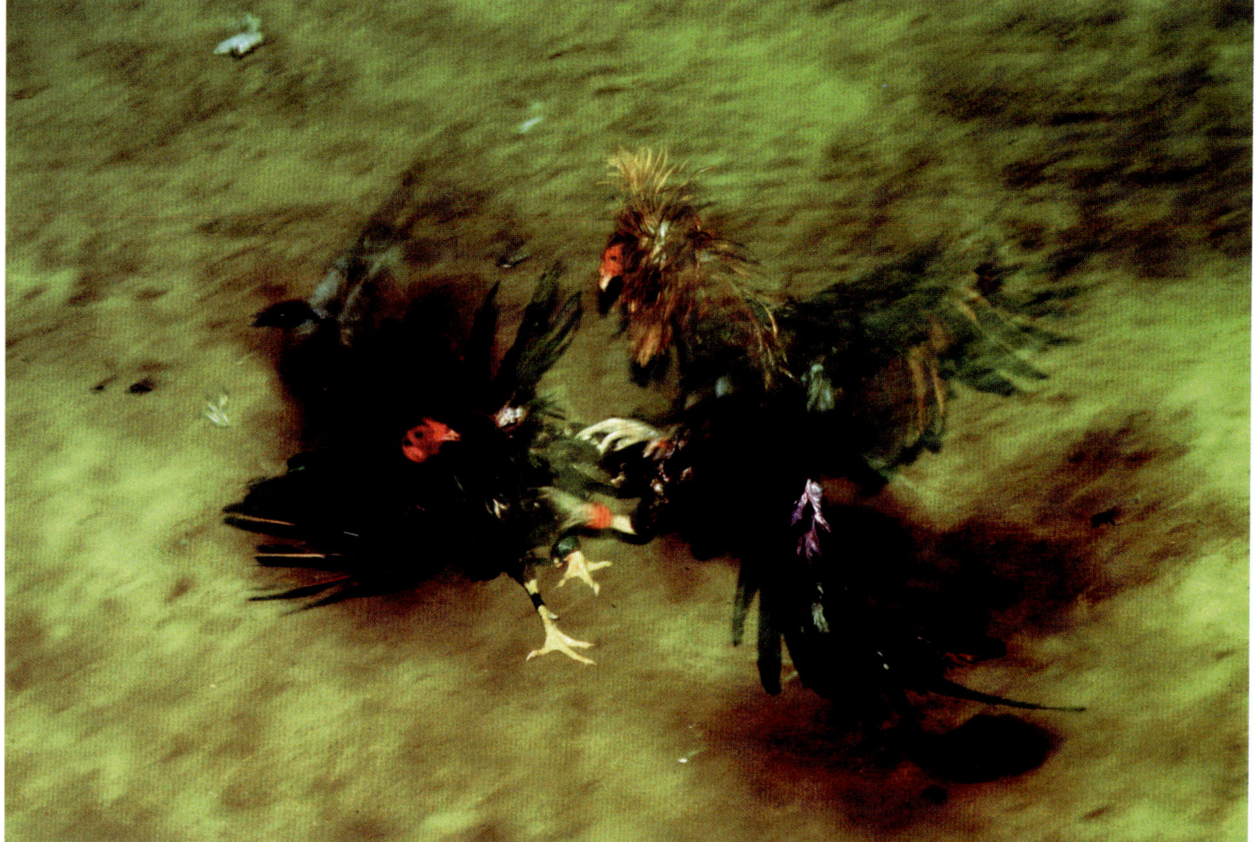

Cockfighting: traditionally the favourite entertainment in the Philippines, very exciting for local people – and very cruel, as the cocks have little steel blades attached to their legs. To convey the whirlwind nature of this single combat, the photograph was taken in the darkened arena using the 'rear curtain' flash technique.

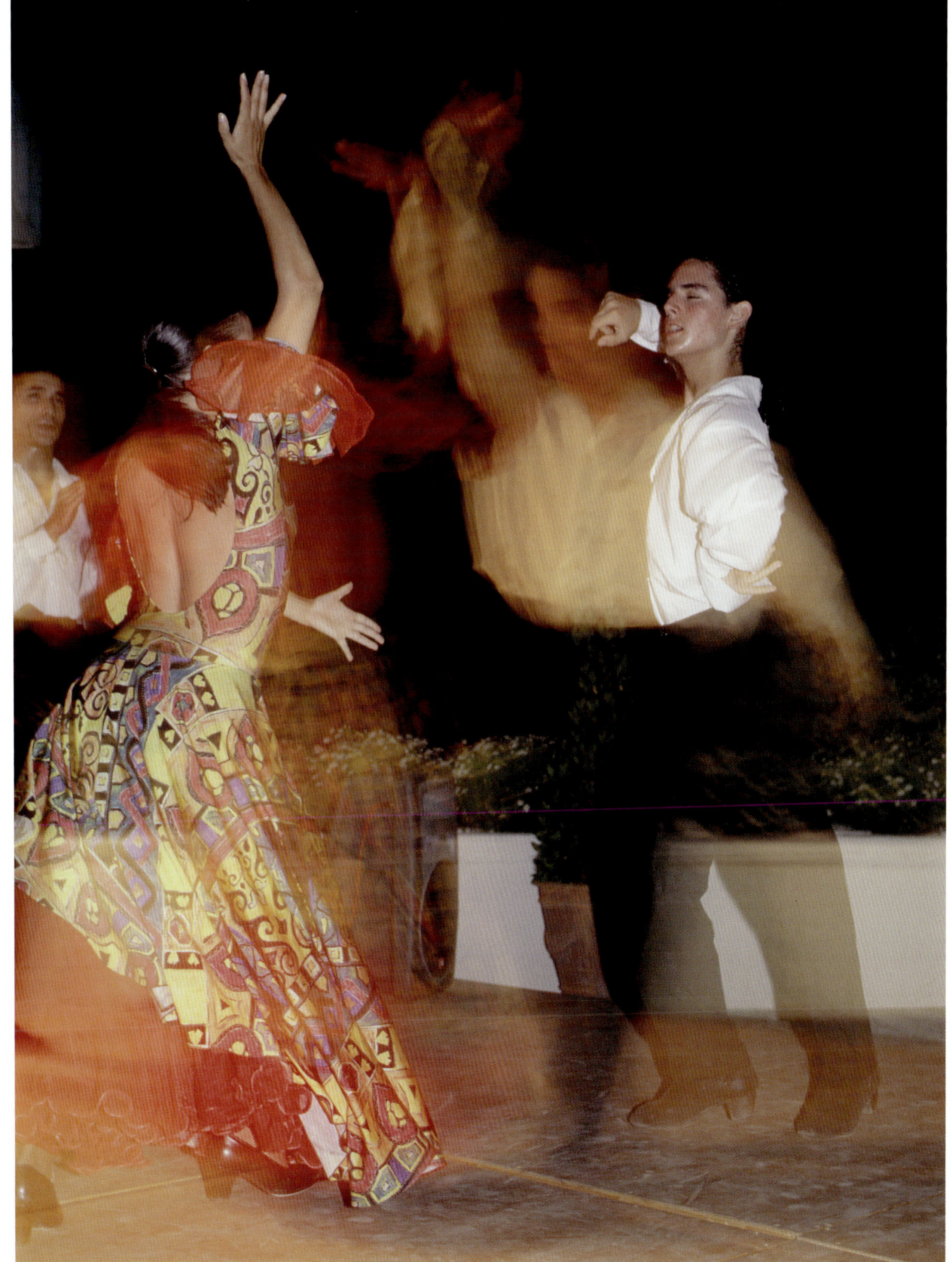

Flamenco, the fiery dance of Andalusia, cannot be represented through the static, 'frozen' movement that results from the use of flash. In this case, the photo is rescued by the use of 'rear curtain', allowing the unrestrained surging momentum of the dancers to be shown as if it is developing within the picture.

A fiery mythological princess, in flesh-and-blood form, spinning in the whirlwind of the ritual *kecak* dance. The photographer is the only one who has the power to convey – in the girl's surging dance, elusive to the eye, snatched out of the darkness – the inexorable movement of continents and the birth of this magical island out of magma and ash, the perfection of the lines of rice terraces and the carmine sunset, the Pandavas and the Kauravas waging war on the astral plane and the melodious strings of the gamelan. Here is the whole chain that links a moment of earthly existence to the eternity of the cosmos, to its primal strength and harmony.

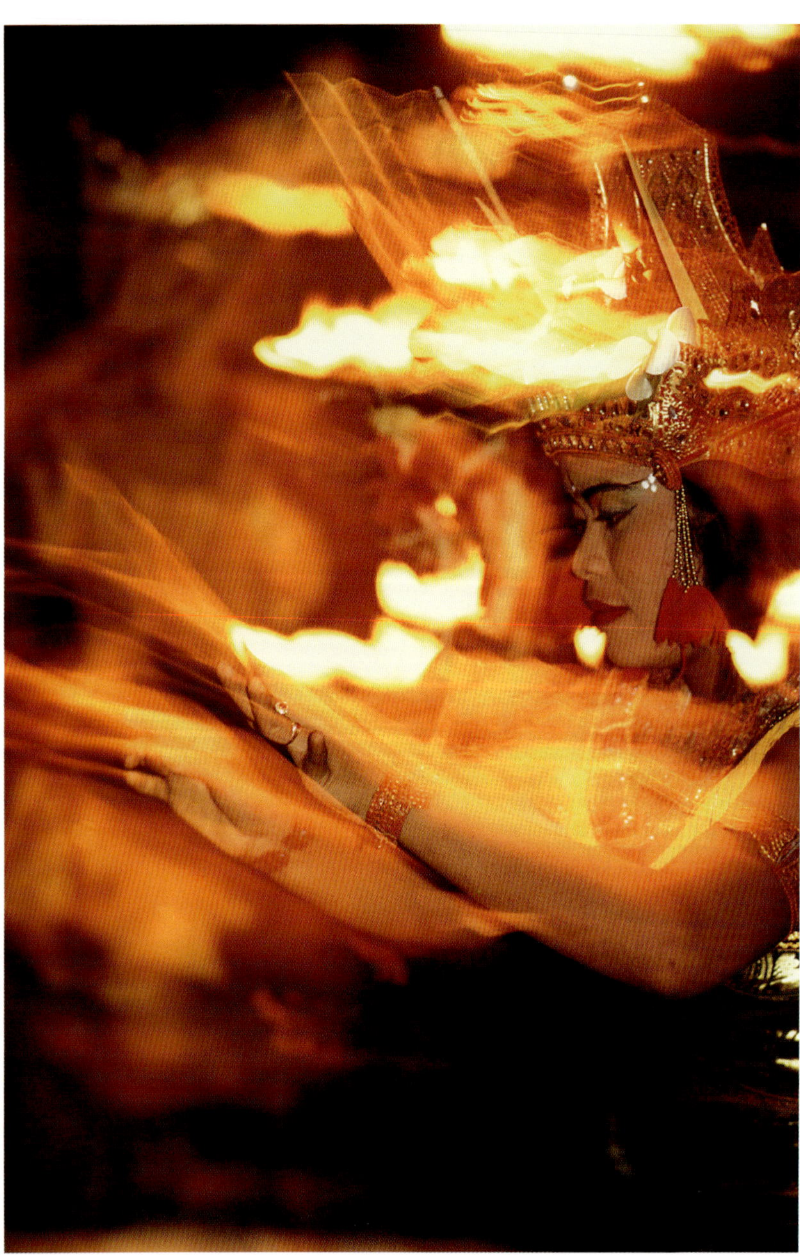

flash , in order to get a blurred picture in which one of the runner's hands, holding the torch, is racing along some 5 metres in front of him.

Using rear curtain sync, the flash lights up the runner at the last instant, leaving the trajectory of the racing torch like a beautiful fiery trail in his wake. The flamenco dancer appears in a magical aureole, conveying a sense of the whirlwind mystery of the dance – but, like the runner's, her face is well defined. And in the Viennese ballroom, the blurred movement of a mass of people will convey the uncontained surge of the waltz, with recognisable faces among the dancers captured by the flash.

Taking photographs in this way inevitably raises some objective difficulties. Your autofocus must be set on the runner at the start of the five-metre distance to be covered, because you must calculate mentally where he will be one second later, and set the focus accordingly. With the flamenco dancer, things are even trickier: she might turn her back on you or even move out of the frame altogether, since the viewfinder will be blocked by the mirror. However, you should take consolation in the fact that these are not ruined shots, but are simply the cost of creating your art. A few good photographs will more than compensate you for the losses. Actually, while there used to be losses with film, now you can simply delete the ones you don't want.

This is the only type of photograph where the amateur has practically the same chances as the professional. So what differentiates one of these photographers from the other? The amateur takes a photograph and waits to see how it comes out. The professional evaluates the potential of the shot and knows what should come out; therefore he or she can make immediate use of all available technical methods and resources. But in this situation the outcome is equally unpredictable for them both.

What does a whirling dancer from Bali have in common with a Thai boxing ring in Bangkok, where masters of this martial art may do battle using both hands and feet? Only the photographic technique used for these photos – which in both cases is rear curtain sync.

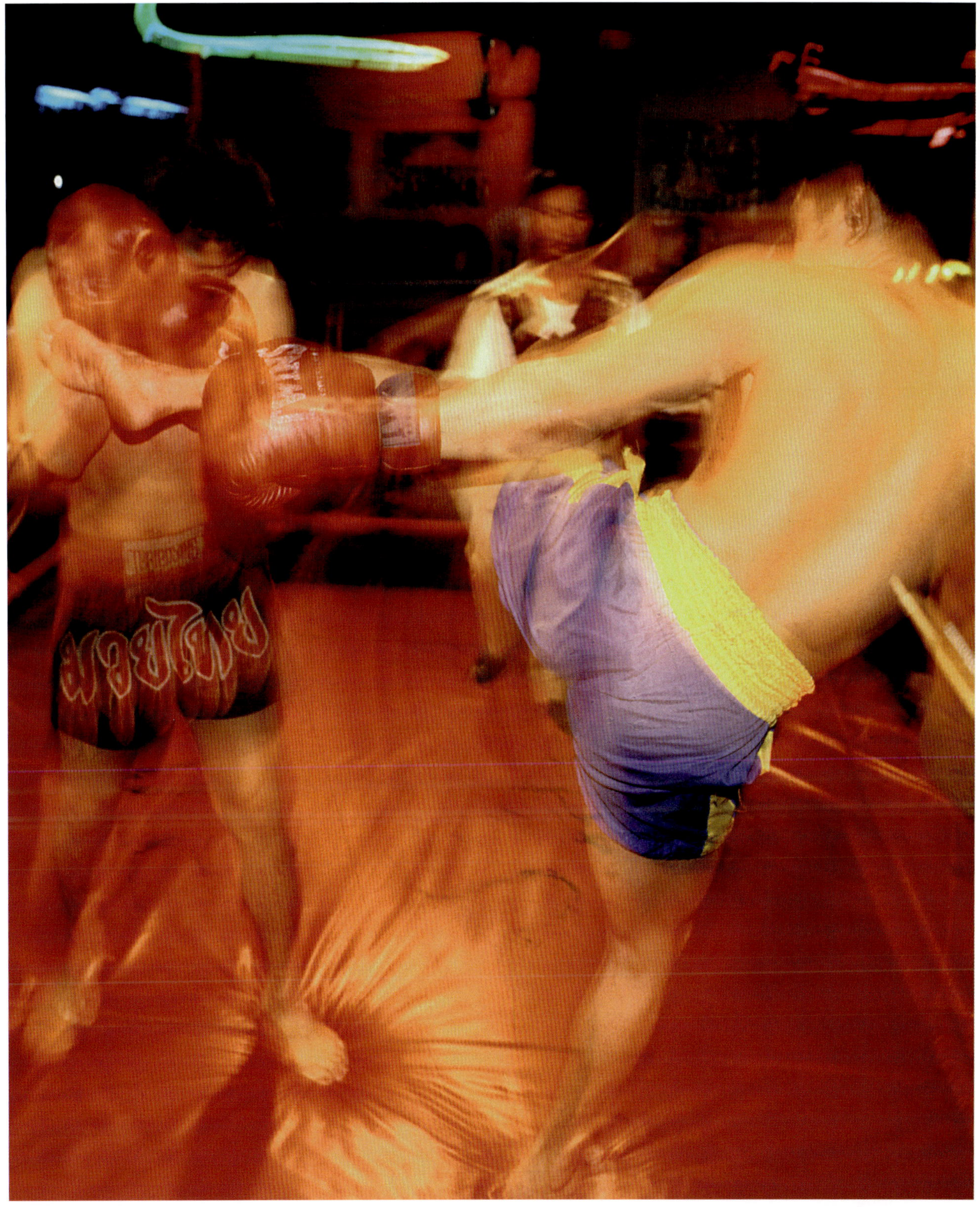

Viennese waltz. Taken with a hand-held camera, on film with a sensitivity of 100 ASA, using the 'rear curtain' flash technique.

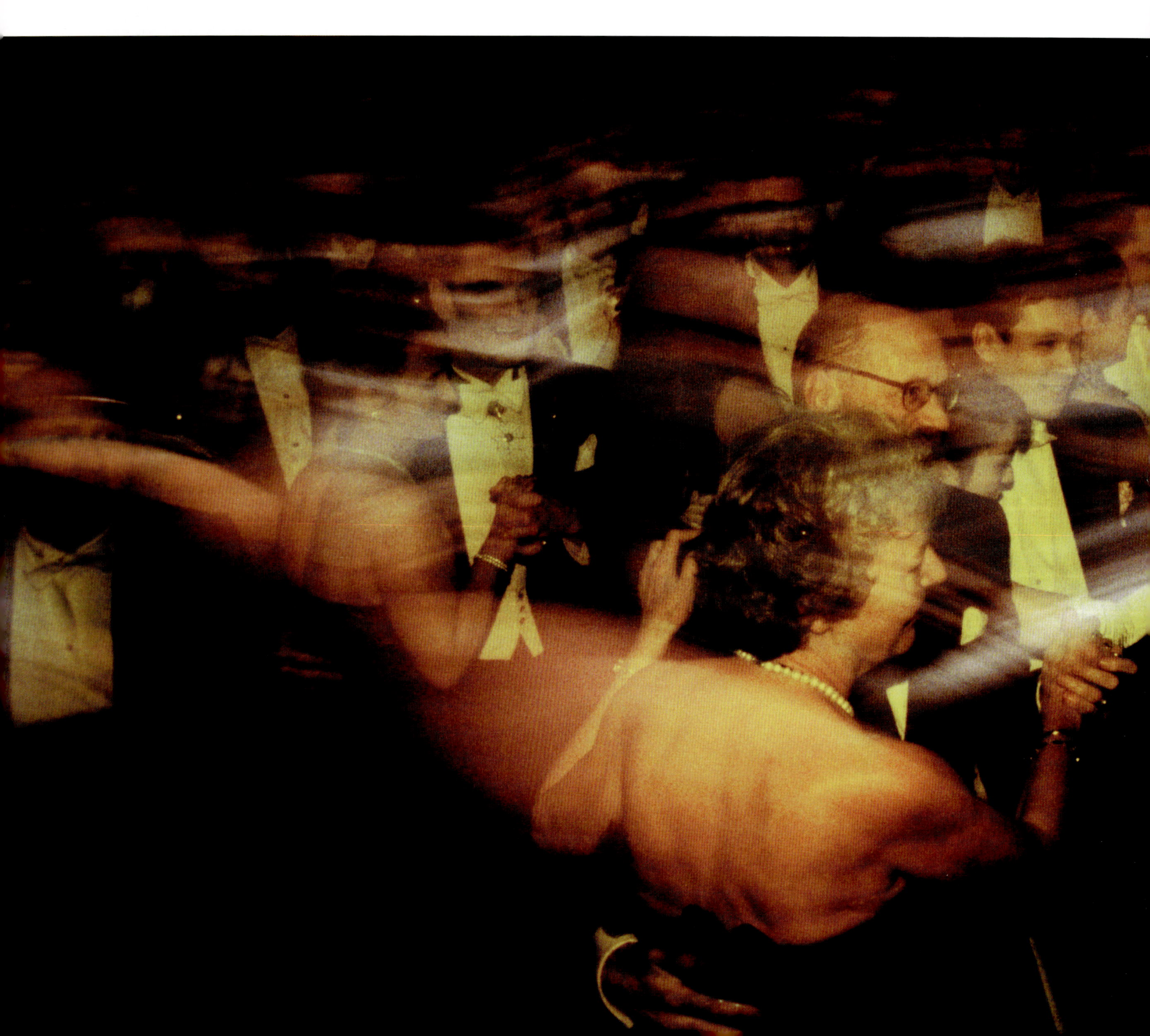

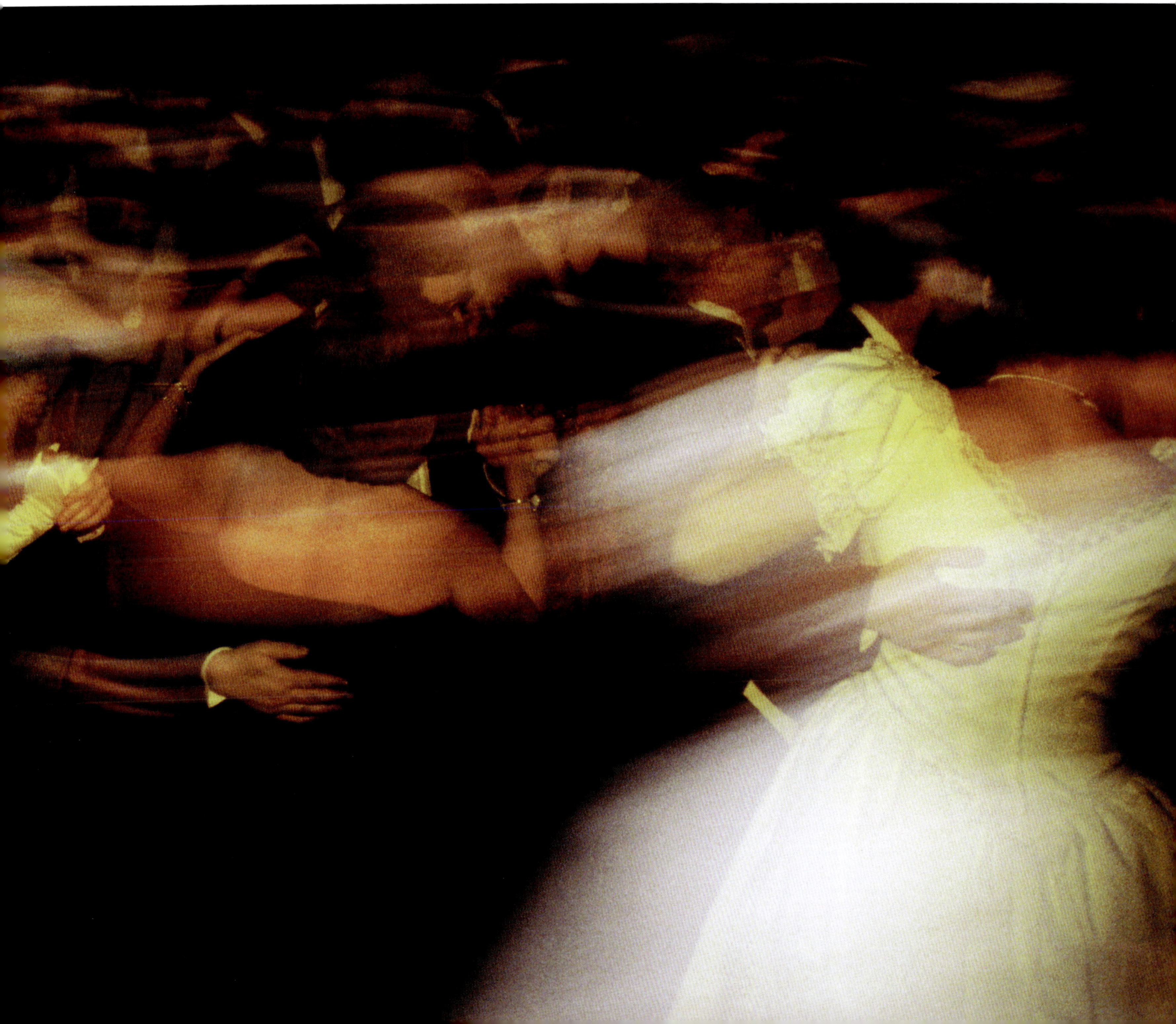

The still silence of black-and-white

In the summer, everyone prefers to dress in white; even the colours of your hire car look somehow brighter. In many warm countries the houses are painted white and even the earth, touched by the sun's rays, is scorched completely white. One can imagine how tricky it is to photograph snow-white peaks. The fact is that cameras, even the most professional ones, are still less perfect than our eyes, which can discriminate the most subtle nuances of light and colour. The Chukchi people,

The highly refined and yet simple forms of the architecture on the coral archipelago of Los Roques in the Caribbean. Venezuela. In this case, the window, a black hole gaping in a white wall, has not betrayed the photographer's eye: it has been photographed without correcting the exposure, just as it is.

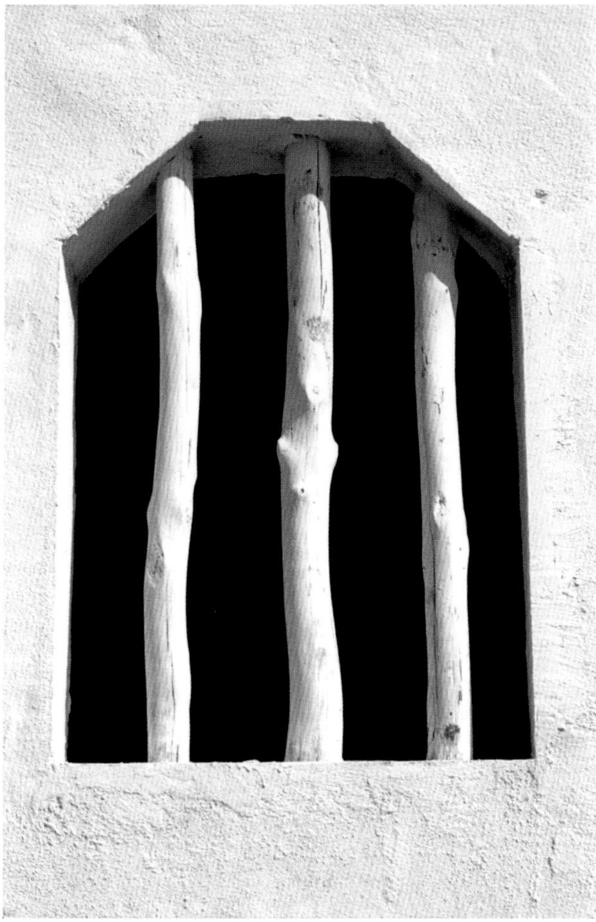

for example, have 18 names for different shades of snow! Yet a light meter cannot recognise colour: like many animals, it sees everything in black and white – its light measurement system is regulated according to the 'grey scale' and any strong deviations of the spectrum towards white or black will mislead it.

The originators of one super-modern camera have assured us that their legendary (and indeed wonderful) camera can differentiate a thousand colours. But in practice, in critical 'black-and-white' situations, its exposure metering is very little different from the similar indicators provided by the least complicated budget cameras.

So what is the threat to the photographer in practice? In the presence of bright white (light-coloured buildings, a beach, snow), the light meter raises the de facto lighting conditions of the lens too high, and as a result you get a shot that is strongly underexposed, by 1.5 to 2 f-numbers – which means a darker shot. On the other hand, if you photograph a sleek black car without any corrections, you will get a surprise when the picture shows a faded grey, unremarkable vehicle. When you print a picture from a film negative, the density can be compensated for, but with reversible (slide) film – which is the only one used by serious travel photographers – there is little room for manoeuvre. The same is true nowadays when taking photographs in RAW or JPG format. With the first of these, an error of 1.5 to 2 f-numbers can easily be corrected using converter programs with practically no loss of quality, but JPG format is not so forgiving of mistakes. In addition, there is the inviolable rule of the true photographer: you must do everything you can to obtain the highest quality source material. This is like the foundation of a building – and being able to rescue the situation by using a computer is not some magical substitute for poor source material.

If your camera has an exposure correction function, remember that, in order to shoot a white building, you must either open the aperture by a factor of 1.5 – that is, say, instead of 16, use a setting between 8 and 11 – or, without changing the aperture, you must reduce the shutter speed, for example, from 1/500 of a second to 1/250. 'Exposure bracketing' can also be very helpful in difficult situations like this, with adjustment of the values on both sides of the 'correct' one. Then you are guaranteed to get a perfectly exposed shot. With a black object, you should take exactly the opposite approach.

Photographers have other well-tried methods of avoiding crude fatal errors. You can point the lens at a blue sky and then use the same settings to shoot your white object. With an automatic point-and-shoot camera, preventing correction of the light meter reading is more difficult, but here too you can find a way out: make sure that your white cathedral occupies no more than half of the frame, while using the other half to balance out the lighting conditions with tree foliage or the deep blue of the sky at noon.

Almost all houses on the island of Minorca are white, but in the little town of Binibeca, even the roof tiles and chimney pots are painted white. Offering the deep blue of the sky to counterbalance the whiteness for the light meter, the photograph was taken without correction. Clearly the whiteness they have in this part of Spain is special because it has managed to slightly brighten the overall shot.

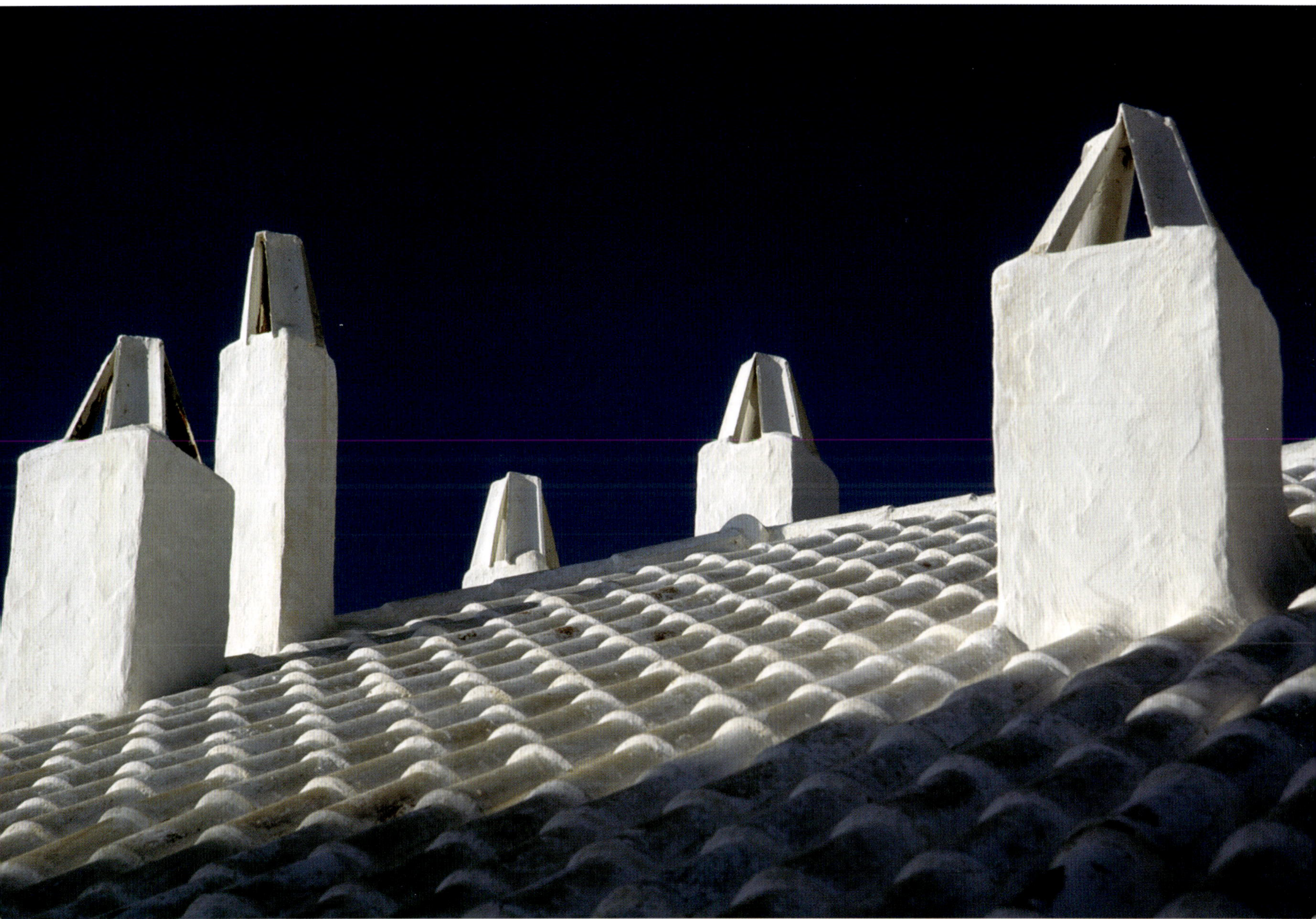

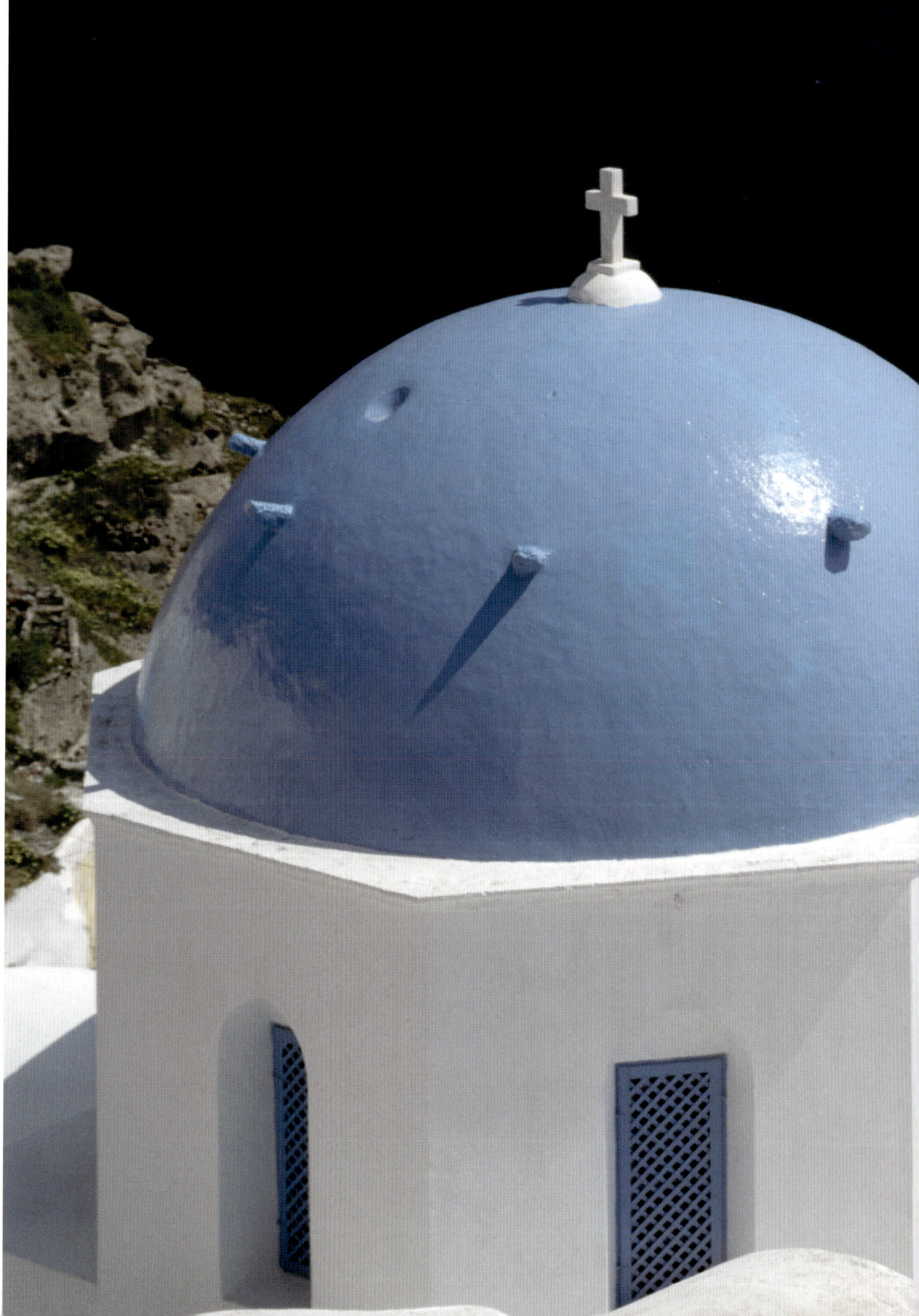

Church on the island of Thera, Greece. The combination of the white church with the brilliant blue dome and the dark surface of the sea is fairly complex for accurate exposure metering. So it is preferable to photograph such subjects by 'bracketing' across two frames, decreasing and increasing the values the camera has given you automatically.

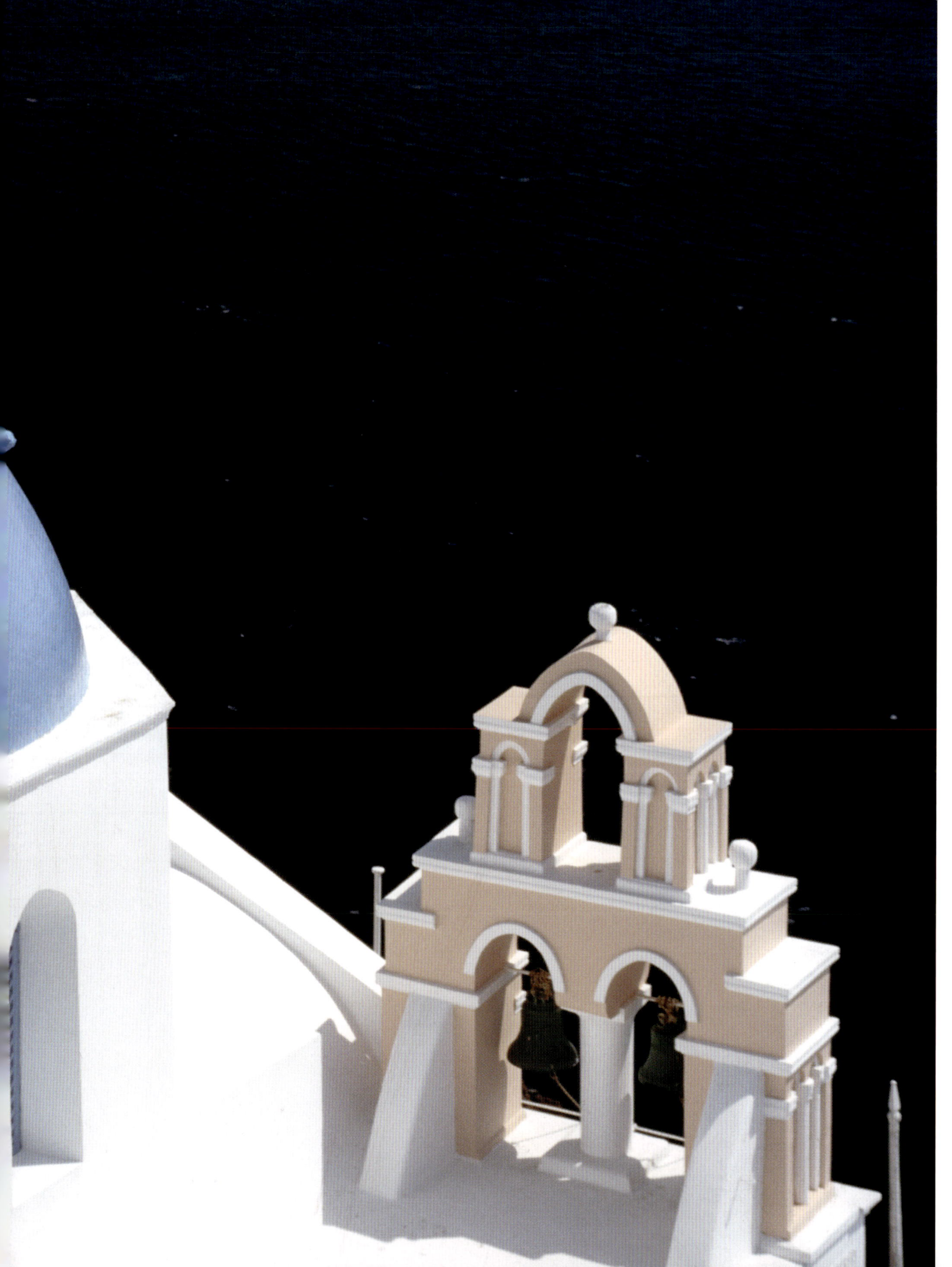

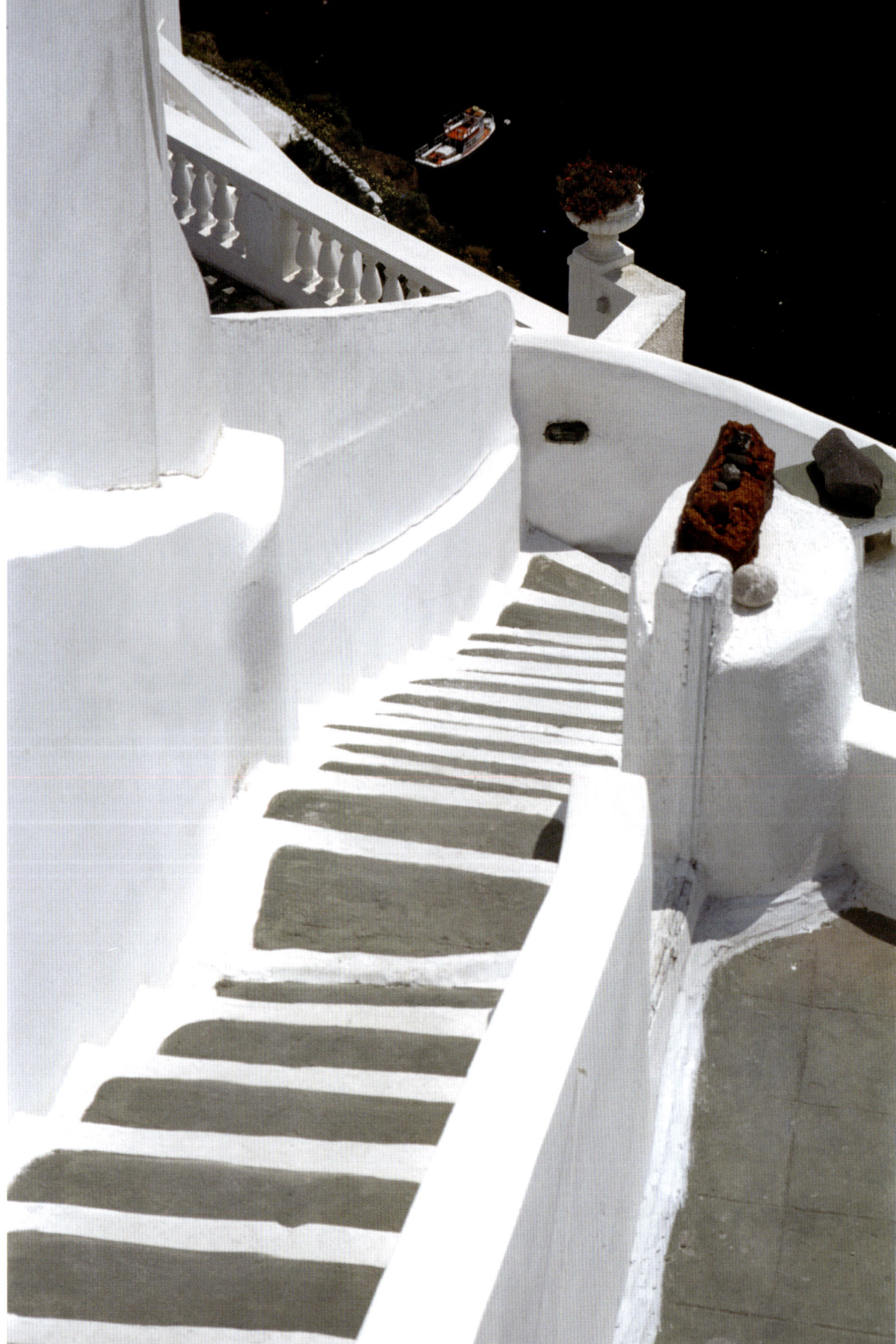

A flight of steps on the island of Thera, Greece. The same approach is also required when photographing these white steps, lit by the dazzling Mediterranean sun.

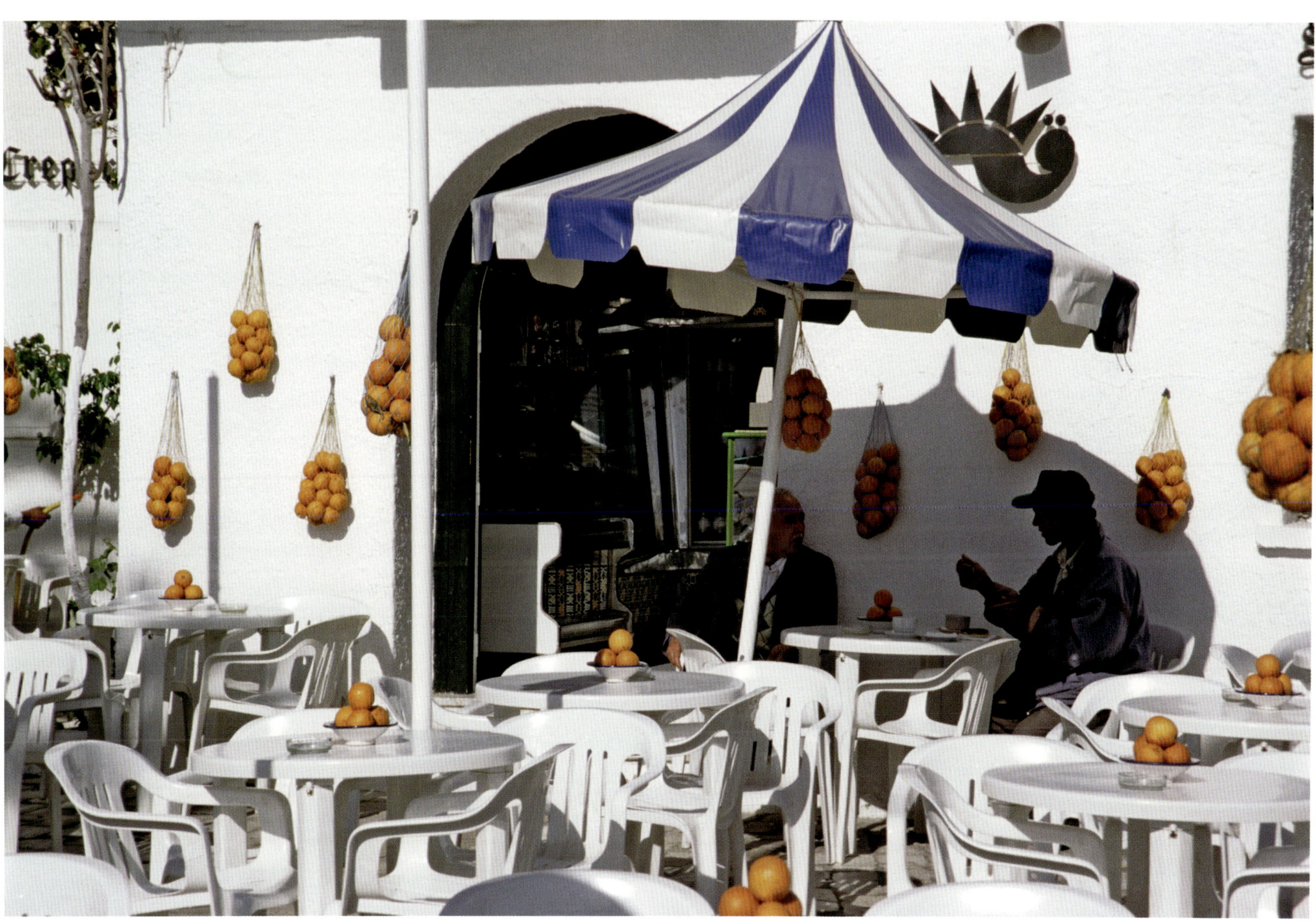

A cafe in Port El Cantaoui (Tunis).
The predominant colour here is white,
and a corresponding adjustment
has to be made, but in the centre of
the shot is a dark gap, so you have
to make a precise judgment as to
whether a correcting measurement
or a central measurement is to
be selected.

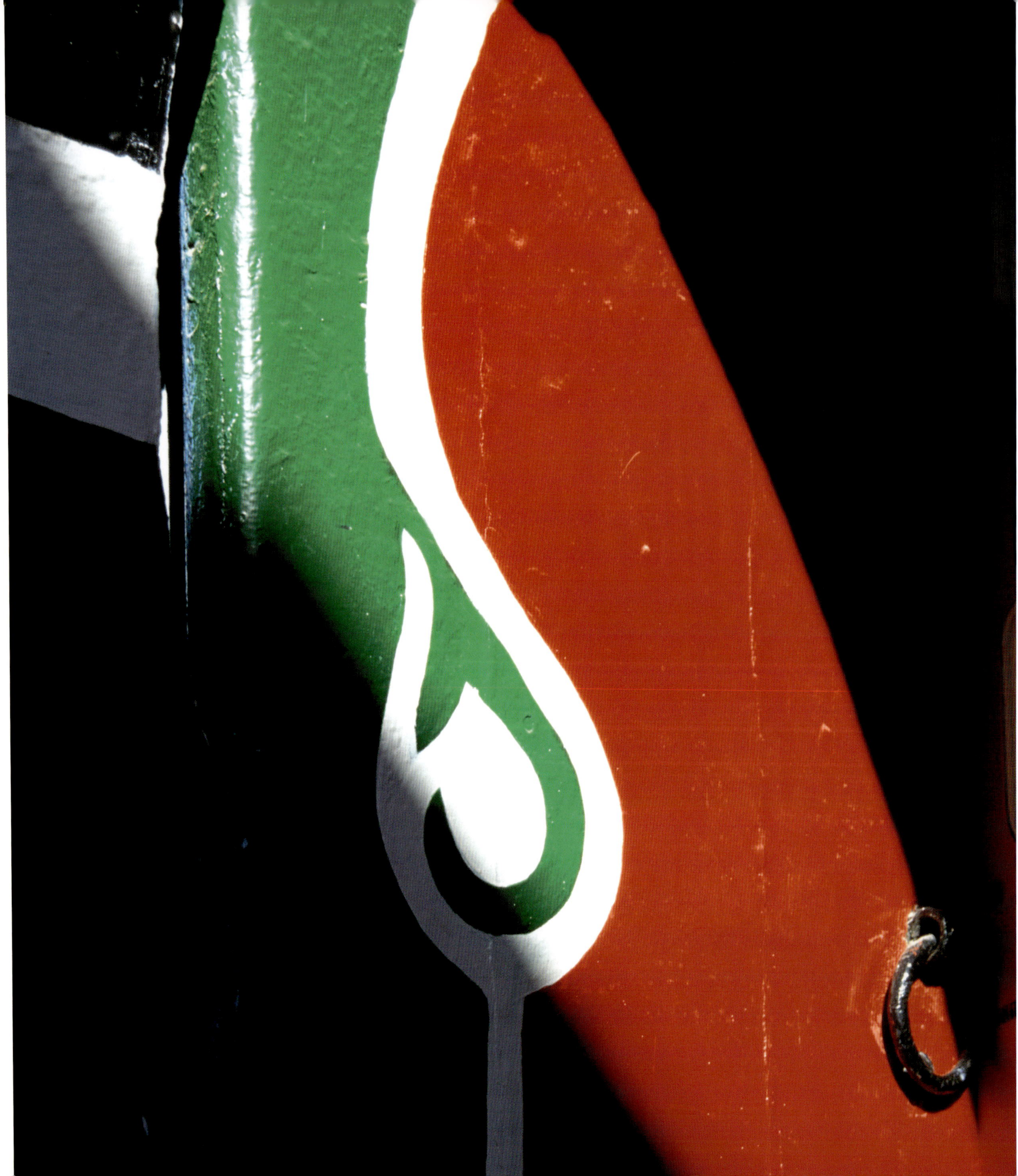

The last rays of the sun have penetrated a narrow little street in the city of Tunis to light up this decoratively painted door. The deep, practically black, shadows covering the greater part of the door's surface 'trick' the light meter, and in order not to bleach the shot, the exposure has to be reduced by one f-number.

The snow of the Chukotka tundra takes up most of the space on this shot so, whatever measurement system you're using, it's a good idea to add 1½ to the aperture setting.

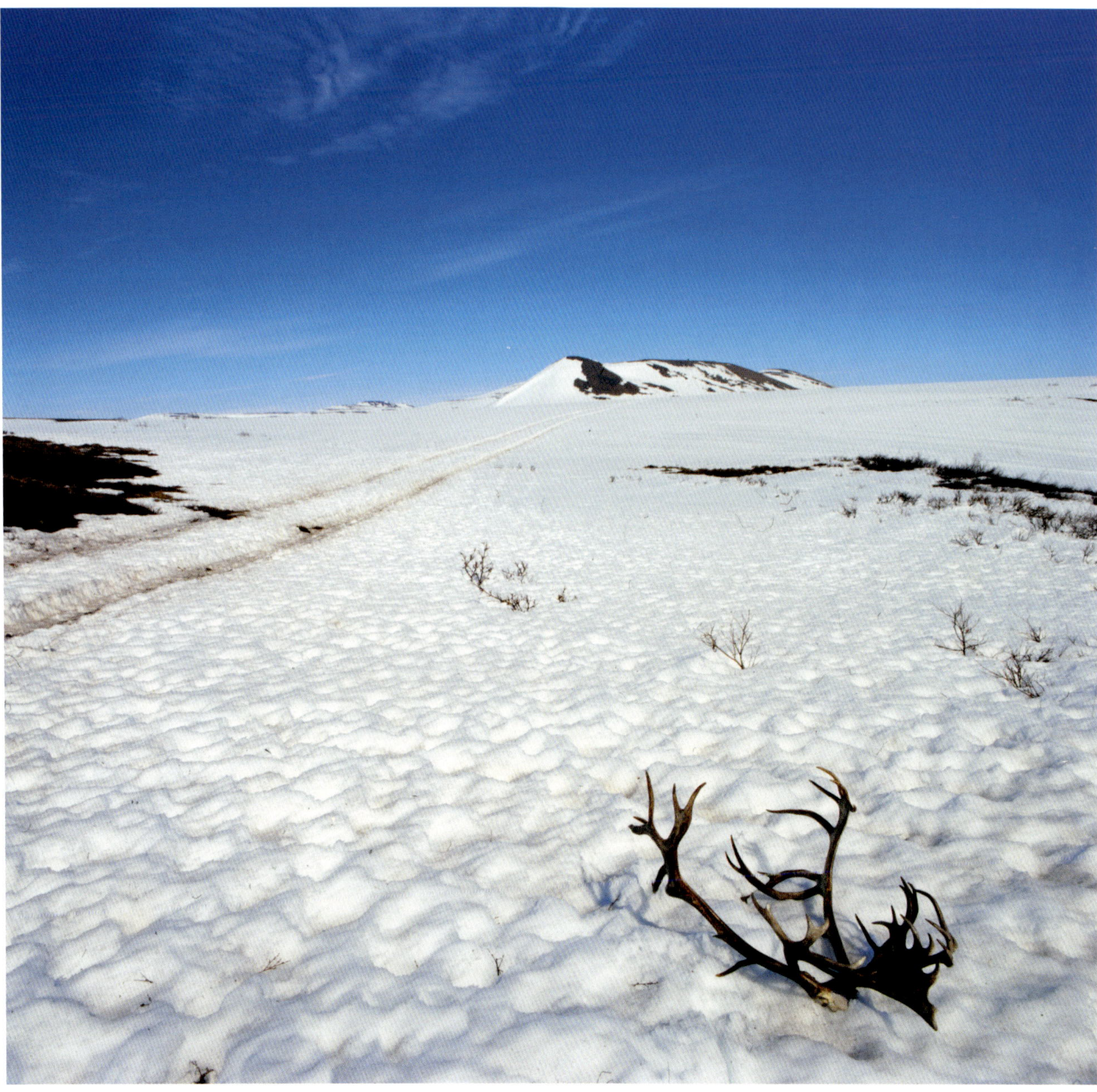

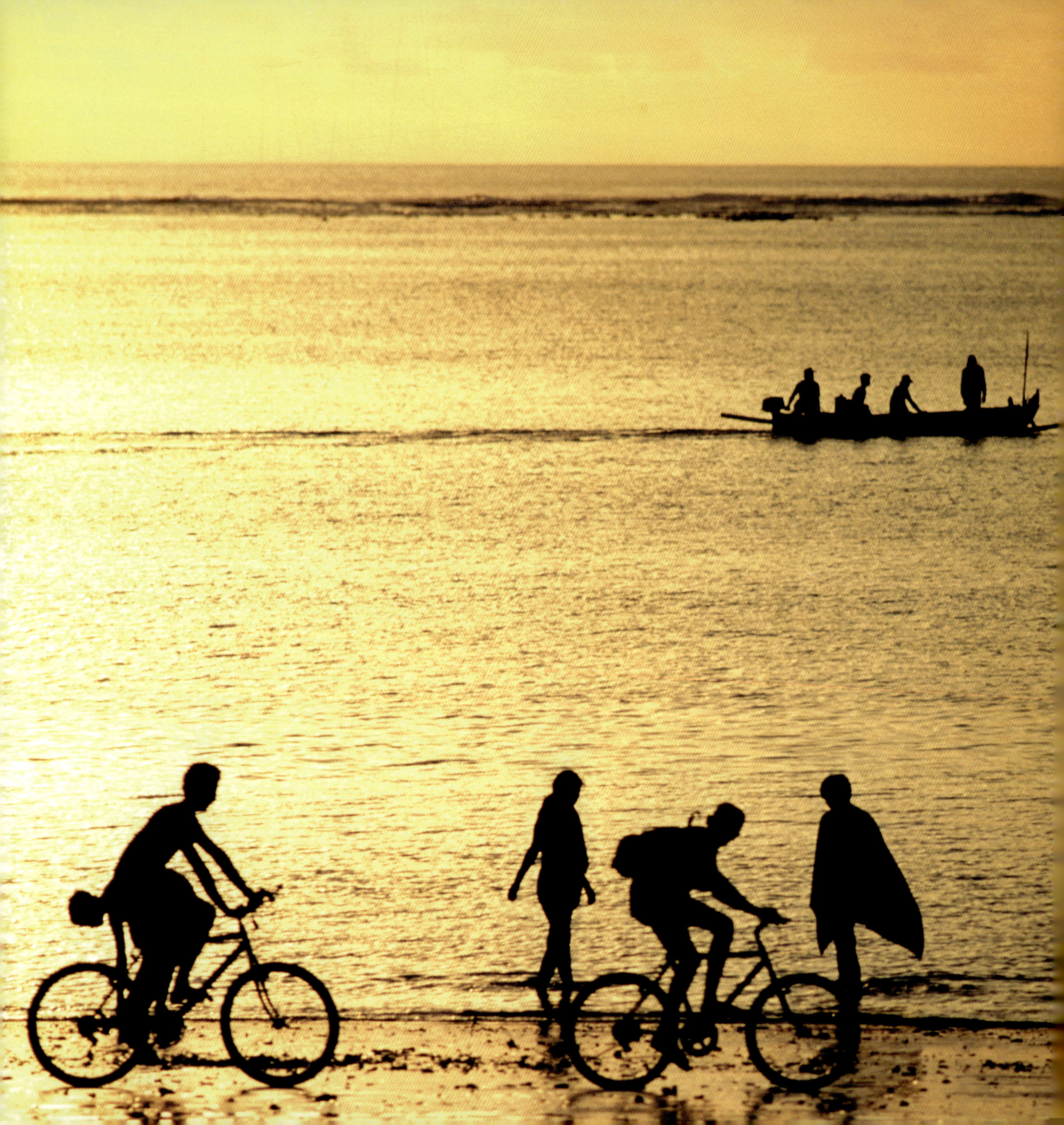

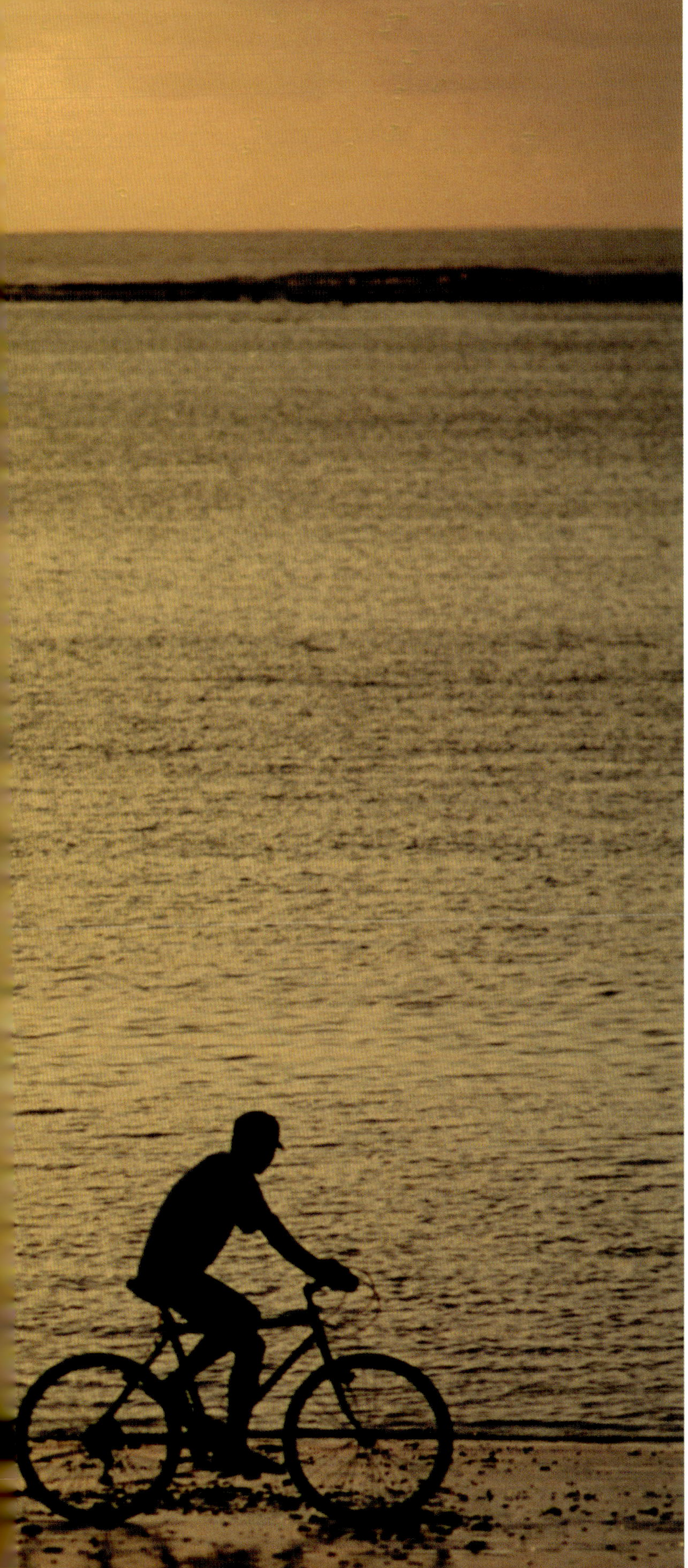

A point in space

Almost everything we have been talking about up to now has related to cameras, lighting conditions or the essential skills of photography. Now we can shift into a higher gear and come to grips with what needs to be learned in order to create not just technically literate but good, interesting photos. The very idea of 'artistic photography' presupposes not only that its technical elements are flawless, but also that the photographer has found an unconventional camera angle, an unexpected play of light and shade or some other way of making a shot stand out from the normal run of photographs.

The key parameter of any photograph is composition – that is, the relationship of its individual parts, which form a coherent whole. Just as a successful poetic phrase achieves the magic of art only by placing a single assortment of words in a specific sequence, the same is true in photography. All the details of the picture must be very precisely matched and adjusted in order for the picture to be perceived as art. In this sense, a photograph is similar to a painting. Clearly, by definition, there can be no precise recipes for true creativity – there are only general guidelines and recommendations.

The first recommendation is that it is preferable for a frame to be balanced – that is, the elements of meaning, light and colour should not be concentrated somewhere in a corner, leaving empty spaces across the rest of the frame. Of course, this aim (just like any other) need not be elevated to an absolute and carried mechanically into any picture – 'straightforward' framing with the chief subject exactly in the centre can simply appear primitive, while a perfectly 'correct' landscape shot with all the space 'filled in' may be completely impersonal and amorphous. This is especially true if it does not focus on some important detail or foreground such as a person, a car or a boat – that is, it has no three-dimensional character.

Let us say that a mown field and a level wooded area behind it appear very beautiful to the naked eye; however, they will make a dull photograph, in no way conveying a landscape. But if this sleepy forest is suddenly ablaze with ochre-red maples, the stubble of the rye field begins to sparkle with hoar-

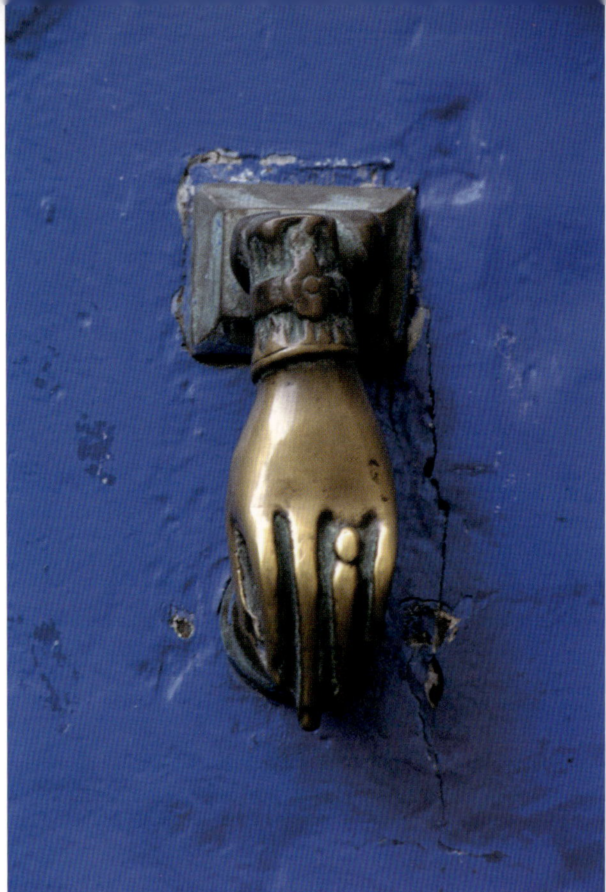

In this photo the light bouncing off the metal of the hand-shaped door knocker combined with the rich blue background of the door itself creates a frame that is perfectly balanced in light, meaning and colour.

In accordance with this rule of one-third, a horizon, especially a marine horizon, should not cut a shot in half, but should be on one of the conventional horizontal lines. A photo will always be a winner if it has an impressive close up which lends bulk to the whole image.

Every frame has its own depth of focus, depending on the aperture you used to shoot it: the more open it is the smaller the area of focus will be. It is very important that the key area of the frame should be as sharply focused as possible. Otherwise, the attention will be attracted by something else. If you're shooting a portrait, then the eyes, or even a single eye, should be the most important feature, and if it's a grandmother knitting a wooly hat, then the focus should be on the needles and the threads, because they're the key area of the shot.

There are some other very simple rules which help to avoid common errors in an amateur photo. The frame should be 'clean', without any superfluous details which interfere with the image as a whole – i.e., the brunette's hairdo should not be streaked by the black coat of someone passing behind her, the beautiful building should not be shot against the background of a construction site littered with lifting cranes.

Photography is frequently associated with poetry. A well-known collection of poetry by Joseph Brodsky is entitled 'A Part of Speech'. A part of speech can sometimes say a lot more than an entire dictum. In travel photography, too, a habit is quickly made into a reflex – the first thing to do is assess the subject as a whole. And yet, again, it must be emphasised that sometimes the detail says more than the whole. The bend of the neck speaks of the body, the headlight tells of the car, the toe reveals the height of a person – or a 40-metre statue of the Buddha.

Another 'canon' of composition: it is preferable to place any moving object in the part of the frame where it is moving *from,* as if giving it room to continue the movement. In exactly the same way, a person should be turned with face towards the frame, but not at the edge of the shot.

Of course, we should not forget that 'the canon' is not an absolute; everything depends on the aim and idea of the picture and on your ability to give it figurative character.

frost and, better still, furrows lightly powdered with snow lead your gaze at a slight angle across the ploughed field towards the maples – then it is quite another matter. And if a family of hares leaps into the frame or a bushy-tailed red fox chases its prey across the field – you can safely send off your 'dull' forest scene to a competition in a photographic magazine!

Of course, 'seeing a shot' comes with experience, but there are a few general rules. Above all, every frame must be there for a reason. For example, in a cityscape – a dominant high point in the shape of a Gothic church, a dense background of terracotta roofs in a European city interspersed by the clear white outlines of churches, the amazing shapes of the architectural fantasies of Gaudi in Barcelona. Make your own mind up about what the main point of attraction is – what do you want to stress? A white church? Great! Here's a tip for you from the conventional 'sacred rules'. The rule of proportion is one-third or two–thirds. Imagine two horizontal lines and two vertical lines on the screen, or in the viewfinder, as if you were creating an image field with 9 equal rectangles, and structure the frame in such a way that the emphasis falls, not in the centre of the frame, but on one of these lines or close to it. Focus the camera on this point and press the button.

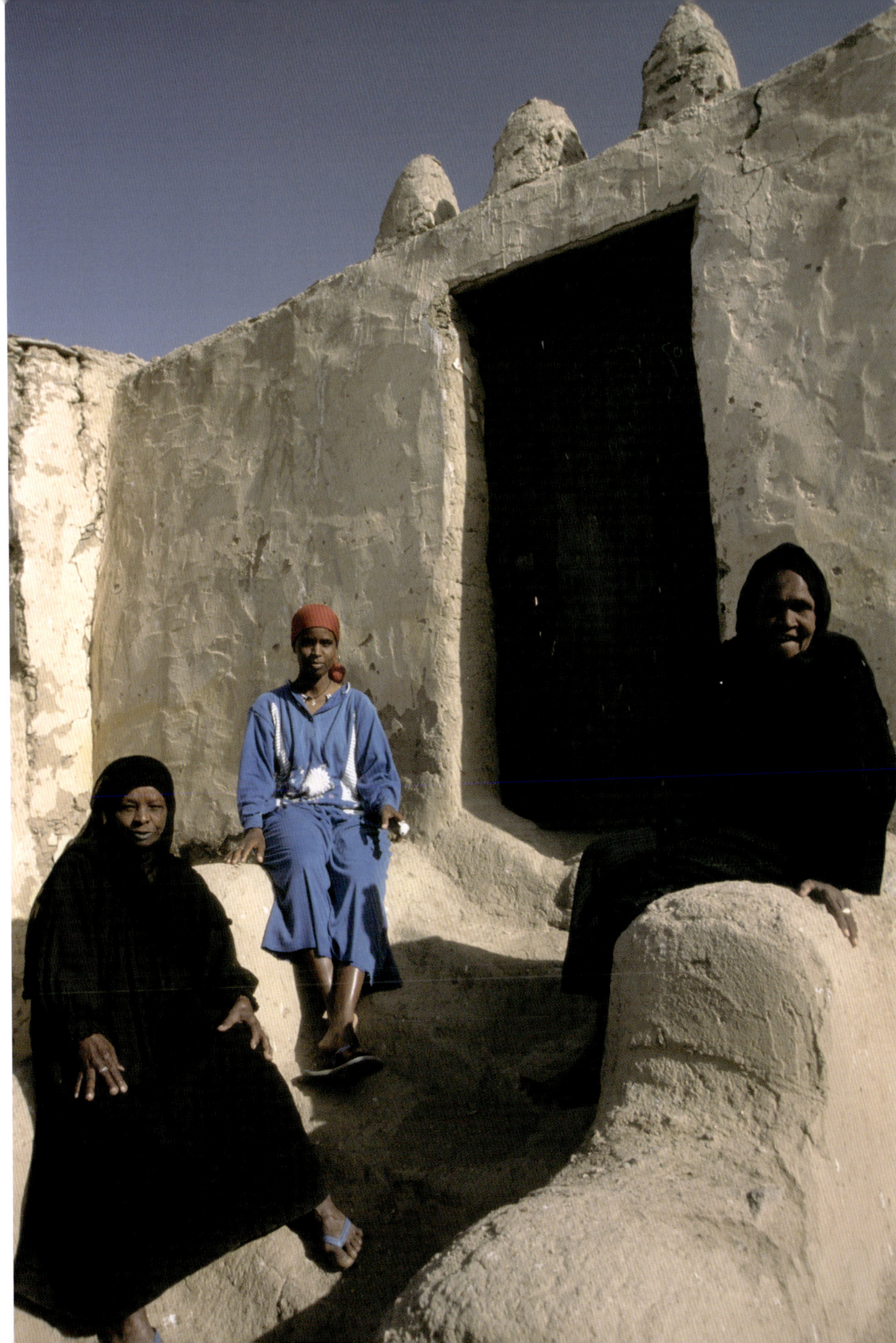

A Nubian village near Aswan, Egypt. This settlement is well off the tourist track, and life here has changed very little in the last thousand years. The obvious focus of this picture – the girl in the red headscarf – has been successfully positioned in a perfect triangle with the other characters; your gaze rests on each of them and then is halted by the darkness of the door, as if drawn to the secret of a legendary people.

This decorated house in Zurich, with primitive figures across the whole wall, presents an amusing contrast with the real inhabitants of this international financial centre. Switzerland. The crudely depicted, Socialist Realist-style peasants and the refined white-collar workers walking below break the classical rules of photography, as they sail out of the frame, although the girl sitting atop the window and the bankers' shadow preserve an ideal compositional balance.

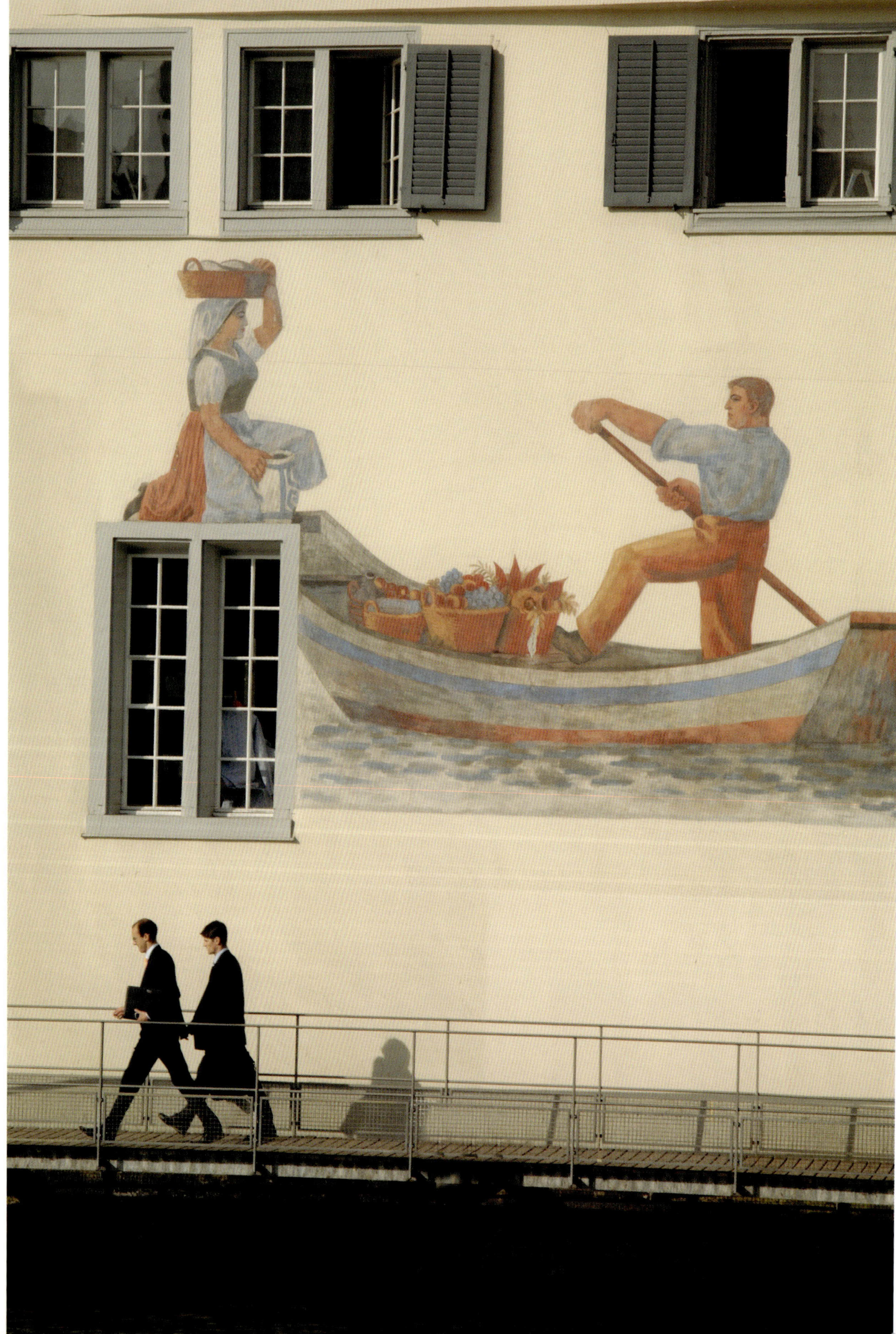

Boats moored along the Nile, Egypt.
Almost everything in this frame has
been set up in breach of the rules,
but the result has really surpassed
all expectations.

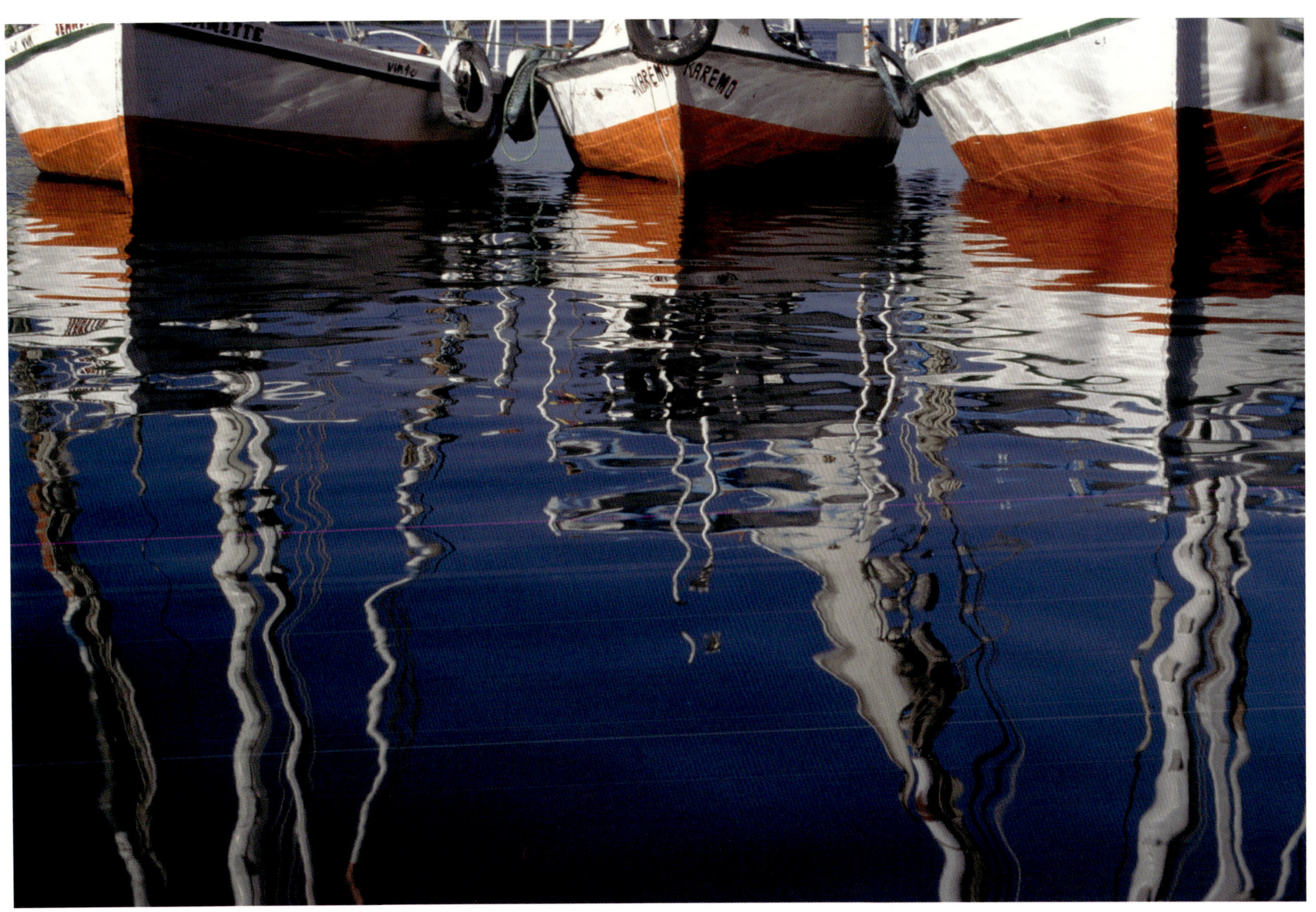

The legendary Truvoroy settlement
at the walls of Izborska. An epic
landscape from the days of Ancient
Rus. The most significant features are
the stone at the crossroads and the
little white church , which balance
each other out at the sides of the
shot. From the huge granite boulder,
the eye is directed along the rut up to
the 17th –century Nikolskaya church
and, further off, to the summit of the
Zheravya Hill.

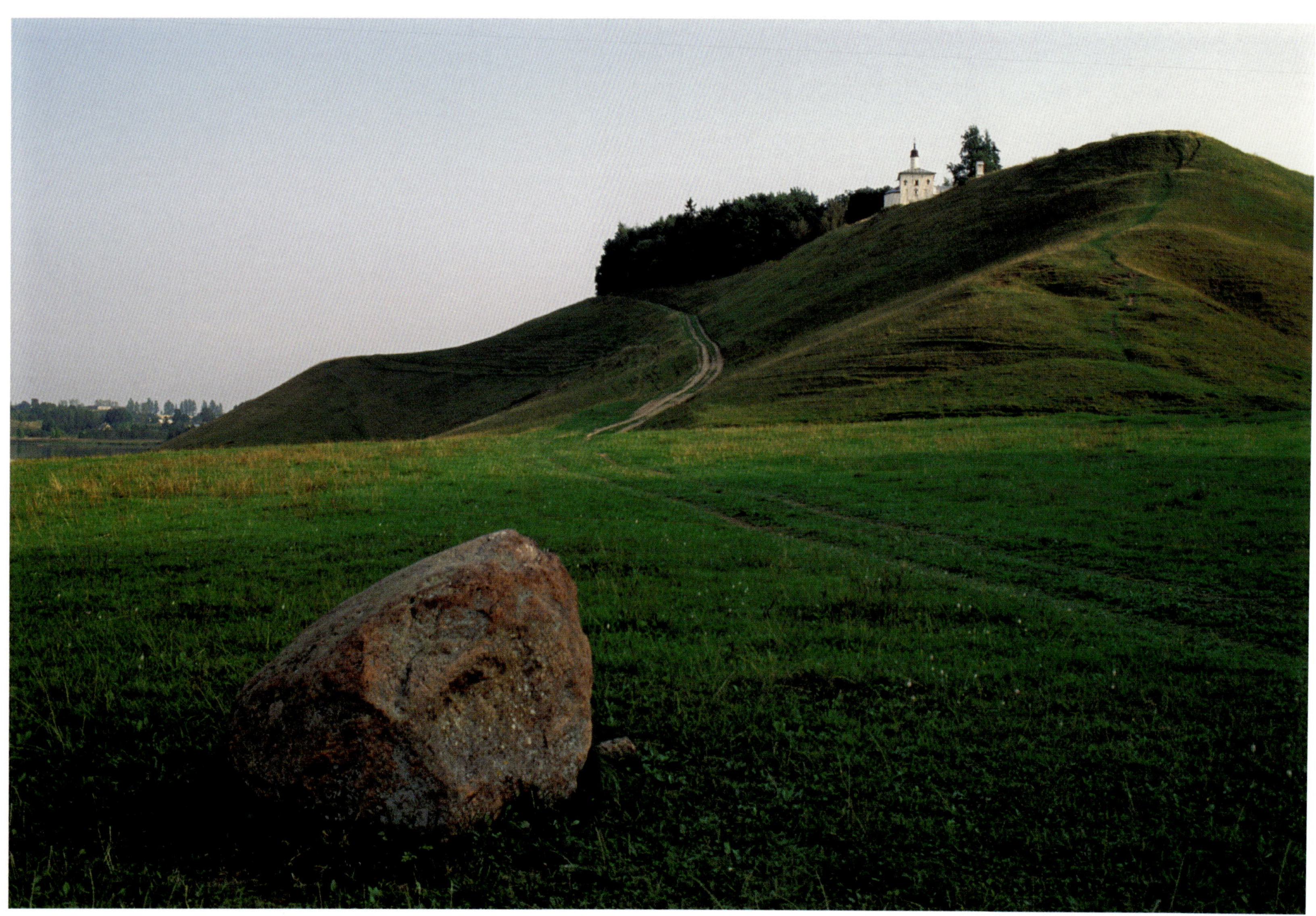

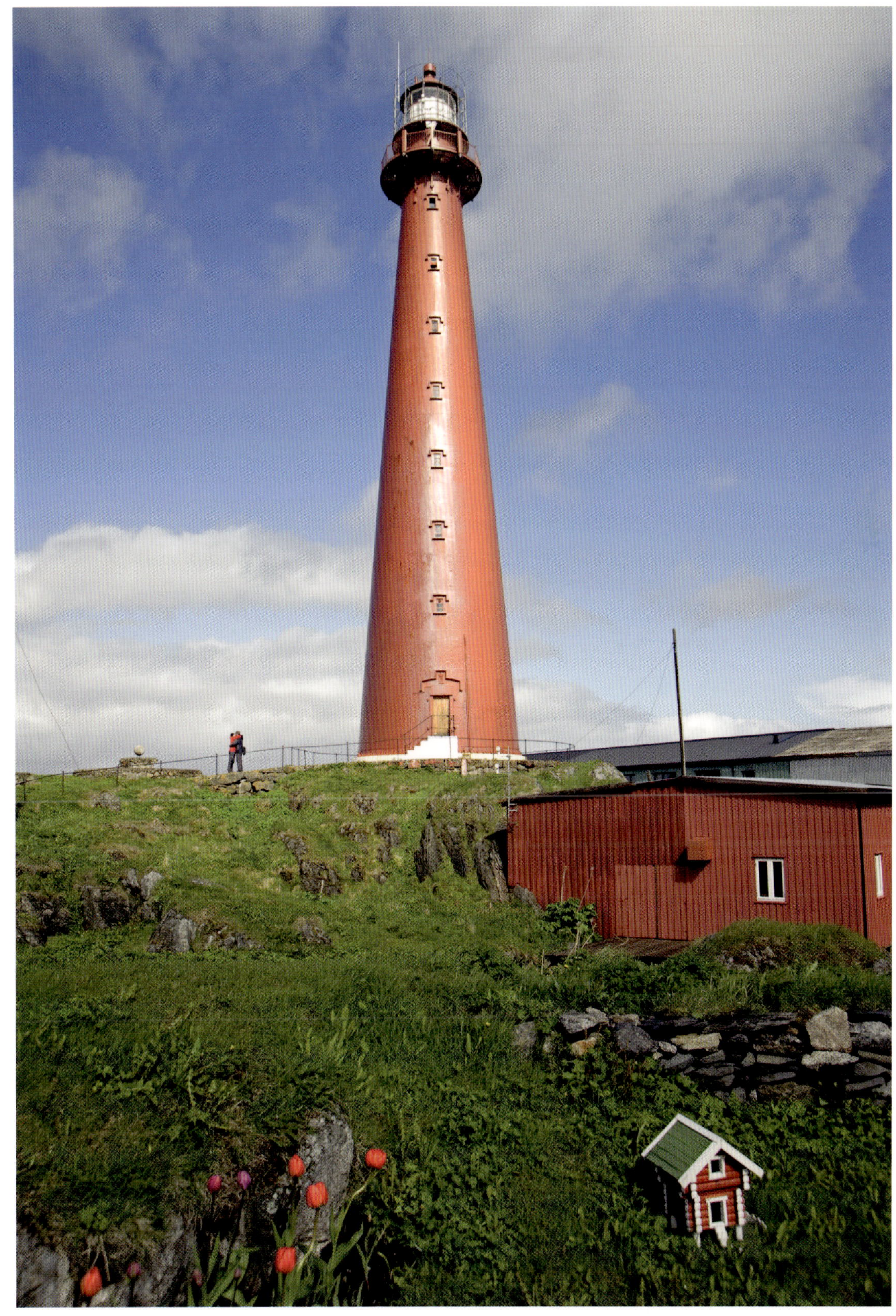

Next to the Whale Museum in Ande-
ness (Norway) stands a 40-metre
high red lighthouse, which has been
there since 1856. But the tiny dolls'
houses with the dimensions of a bird's
nesting-box are built here for trolls.
The picture is completed by the kissing couple who unexpectedly moved
into shot for a few seconds.

Vivid impressions

The desire to bring colour to the travel photograph was so great that the first colour image appeared in a magazine as early as 1910, in the form of a black-and white photograph hand-painted with a brush. The first colour film was produced by Kodak in 1936.

Nowadays, when we talk about travel photography, we mean only the colour image – we leave the black-and-white image to the aesthetic of advertising photographs and a few art photographers. Moreover, colour has become such a weighty consideration in the photograph that sometimes it is a sufficient end in itself, so that other important elements – meaning, information, association – are scorned. A number of magazines that deal specifically with the artistic aspects of photography have printed pages and even full-page spreads of my shots depicting small barrels of powdered dyes, taken by me in the central bazaar in Marrakech. Two barrels piled with spices in two colours – ochre and terracotta. Neither the picturesque vendor nor the buyers, who would make an excellent genre scene, were around. As I saw it, I realized the picture already has everything it needs!

Such vivid brushstrokes are to be found not only in Morocco and Egypt, among the Roma or in India, you can come across them suddenly in a country with a very muted palette. In the Arctic Lapland region of Finland, a post box painted in all the colours of the rainbow – glowing with such artless joy, revealing such a bright attitude – literally begged to be photographed. The same was true of the carmine-red children's water cannon against the rich turquoise background of the hotel pool.

It can happen that a coloured blob about the size of a reflected ray of sun light unexpectedly occupies a huge area stretching to the horizon. That's what happened while I was flying over the Alps, when a crimson ray of light from the setting sun suddenly flared up on the stabiliser of the Airbus roof, which really 'made' the whole picture. In short, there is always colour, everywhere – seek and ye shall find!

A group of snowboarders with their own flash style attracted my attention in the cable-car at the Austrian resort of Ishgl. The bright red wig one of them was wearing, lit by the golden rays of the setting Sun, and the play of the flashes of light on their spectacles form the basis of this shot.

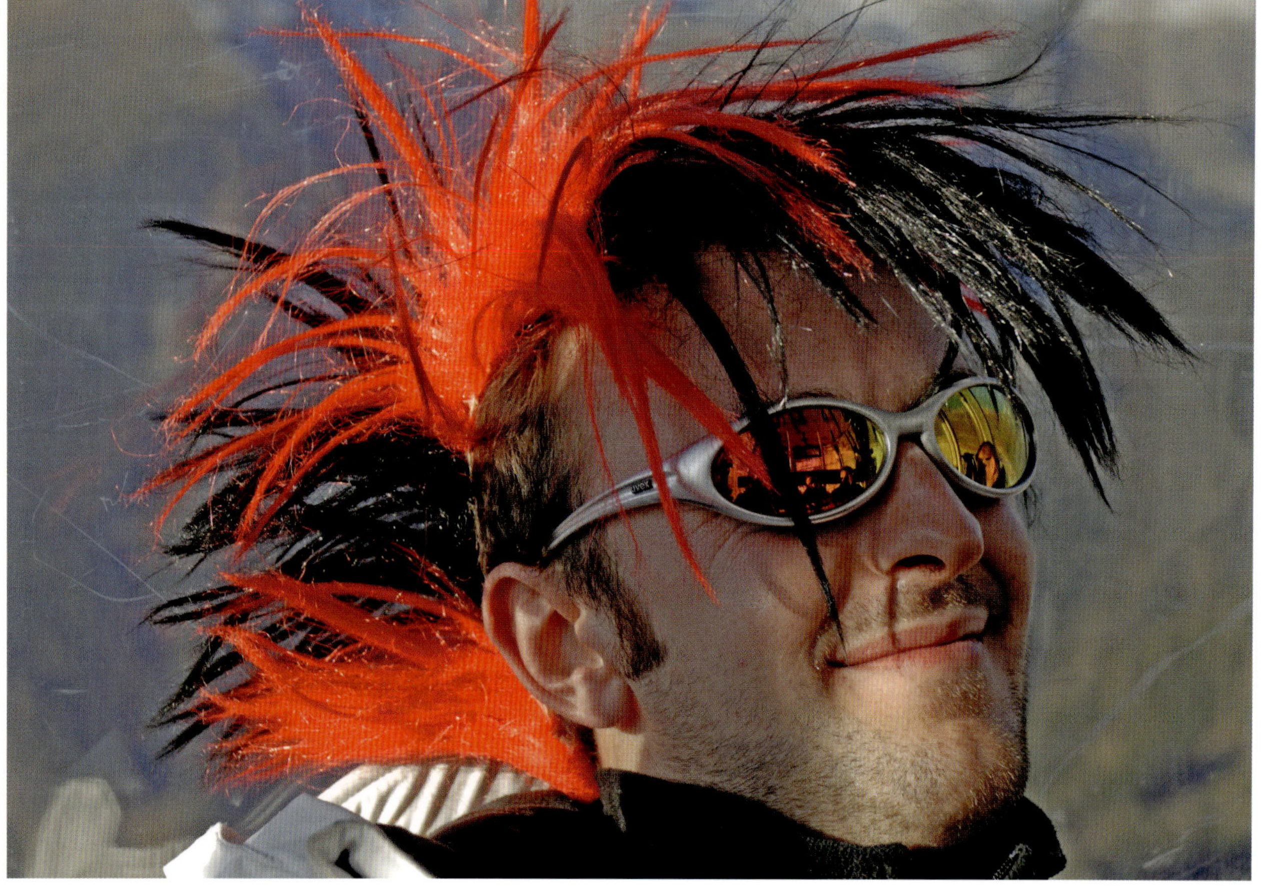

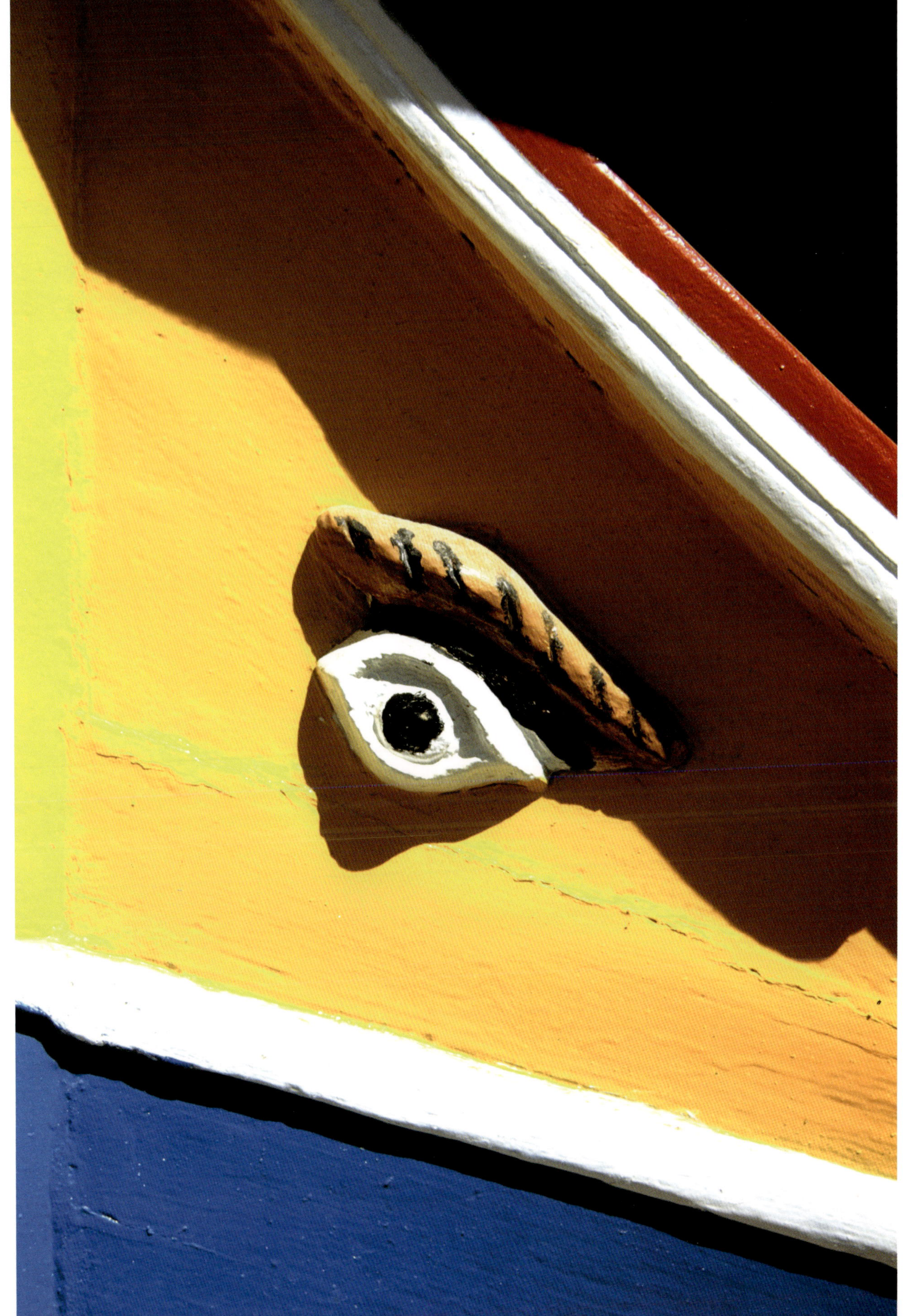

To this very day, the people of Malta feel that they are direct descendants of the Phoenicians – the best navigators in the Ancient World. Maltese fishermen's boats replicate both the shape and the colour scheme of ancient Phoenician vessels, and a famous eye flashes on both sides of the prow – the Eye of Osiris. Need it be said that these brightly patterned vessels are a subject of special interest to photographers on this Mediterranean island?

Marrakech in Morocco is a city whose own special aesthetic consistently attracts artists, photographers, people with a subtle sense of style, beauty and colour harmony. Any genre photograph or still life taken in Marrakech will bring a wall of your home to life. A lot of people have already been seriously 'bitten by the bug' of Marrakech style, as they were in the past by Chinese style.

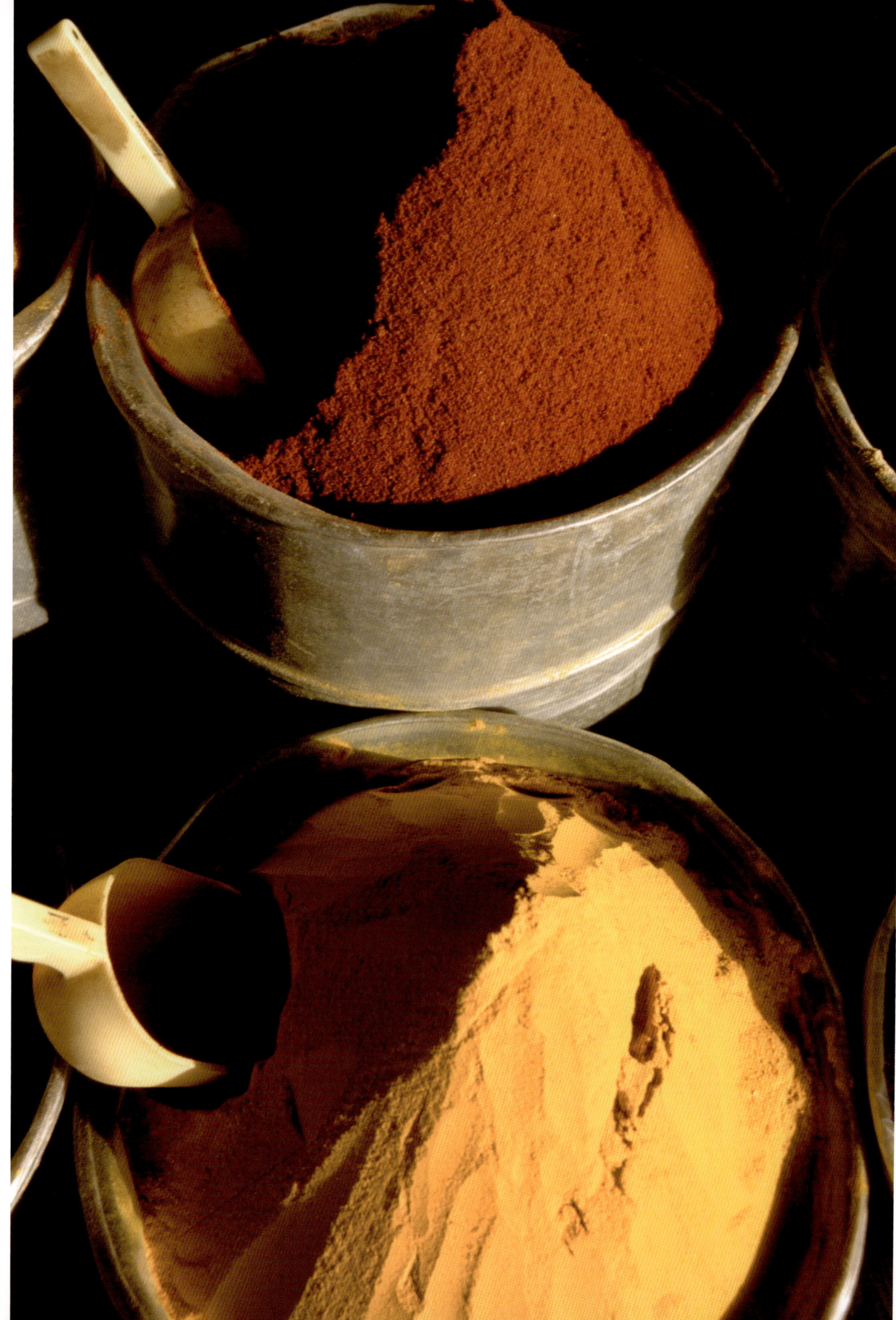

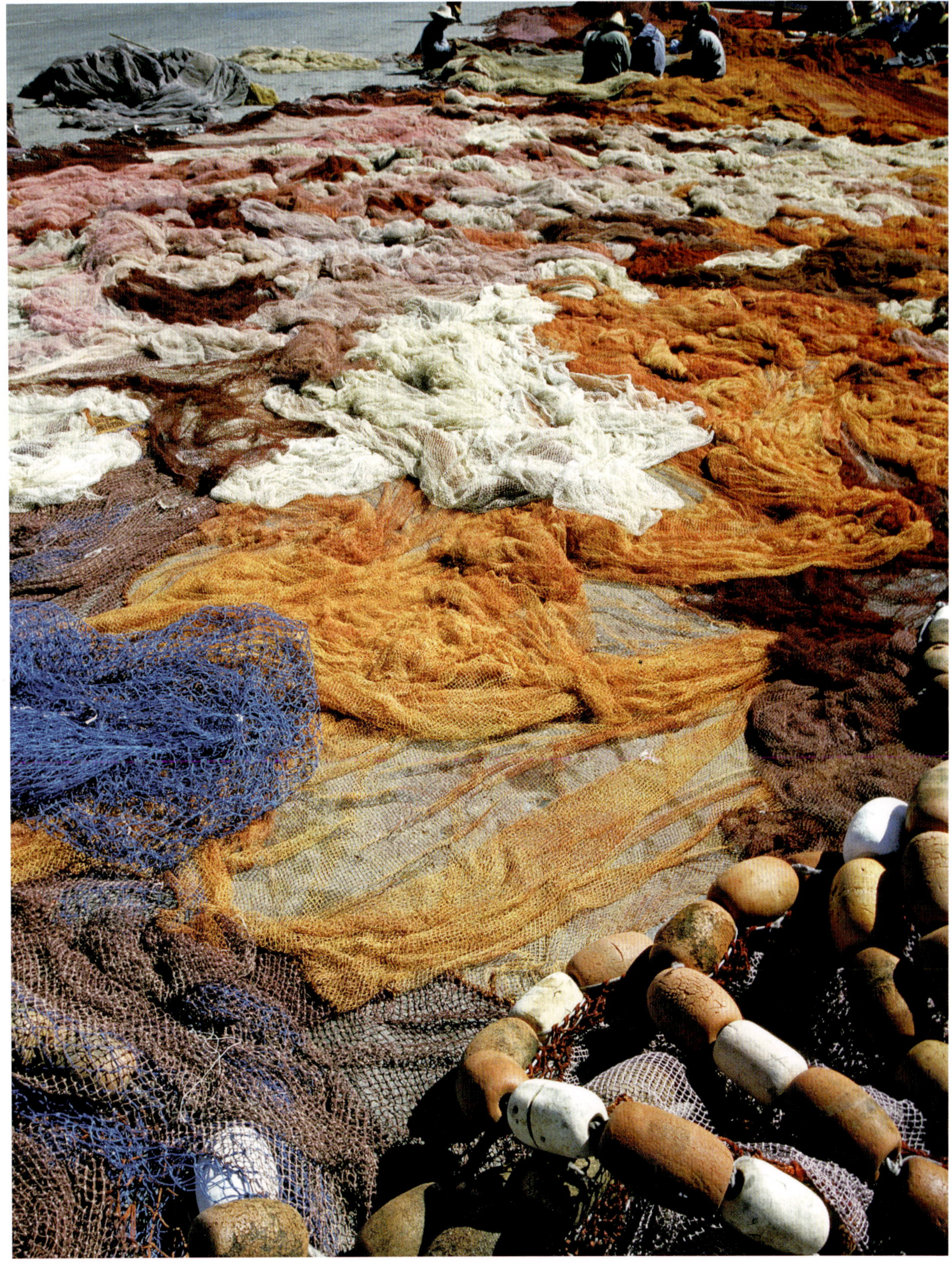

Port of Agadir, Morocco. Nets spread out by fishermen to dry display a wide variety of different pastel tones from a soft straw colour and a pale rust to a cornflower blue and all shades of deep red. They are strewn across the area next to the moorings in artistic disorder, like bundles of coloured wool ready for making a tufted carpet.

Children's water cannon, Turkey.
Logically, one is more likely to imagine
a genre picture with children playing
and jets of water shooting out of
the barrel of the cannon. But the
photographer has been attracted just
by the precise combination of colours
of the toy itself and the water in
the pool.

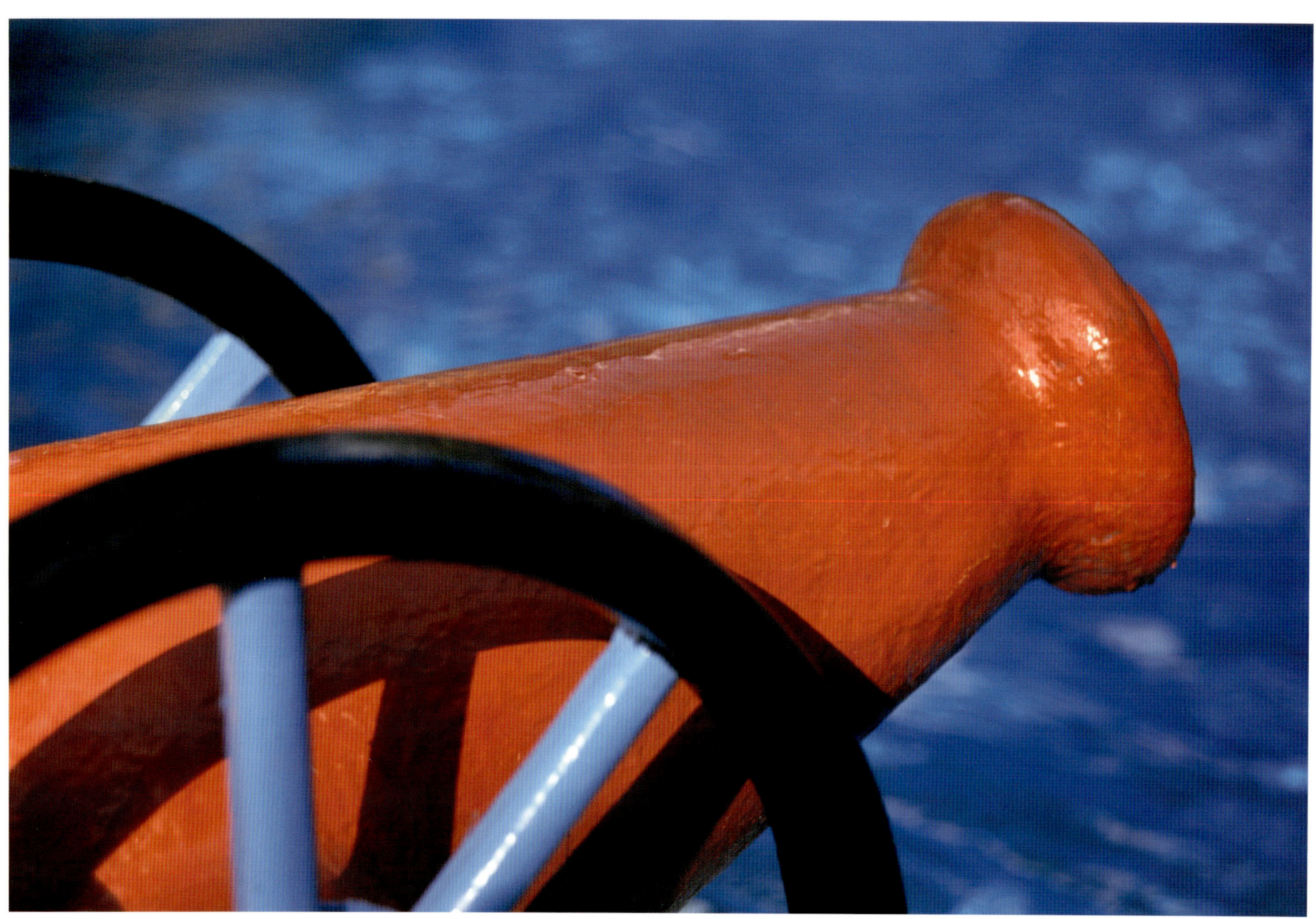

The town of Castellon in Spain. One of
its newest sights is the so-called Sun
House. I don't presume to claim that
the seven-legged sun/octopus feels
at home in the acid-blue sea, but it's
right to a place in this section is clear.

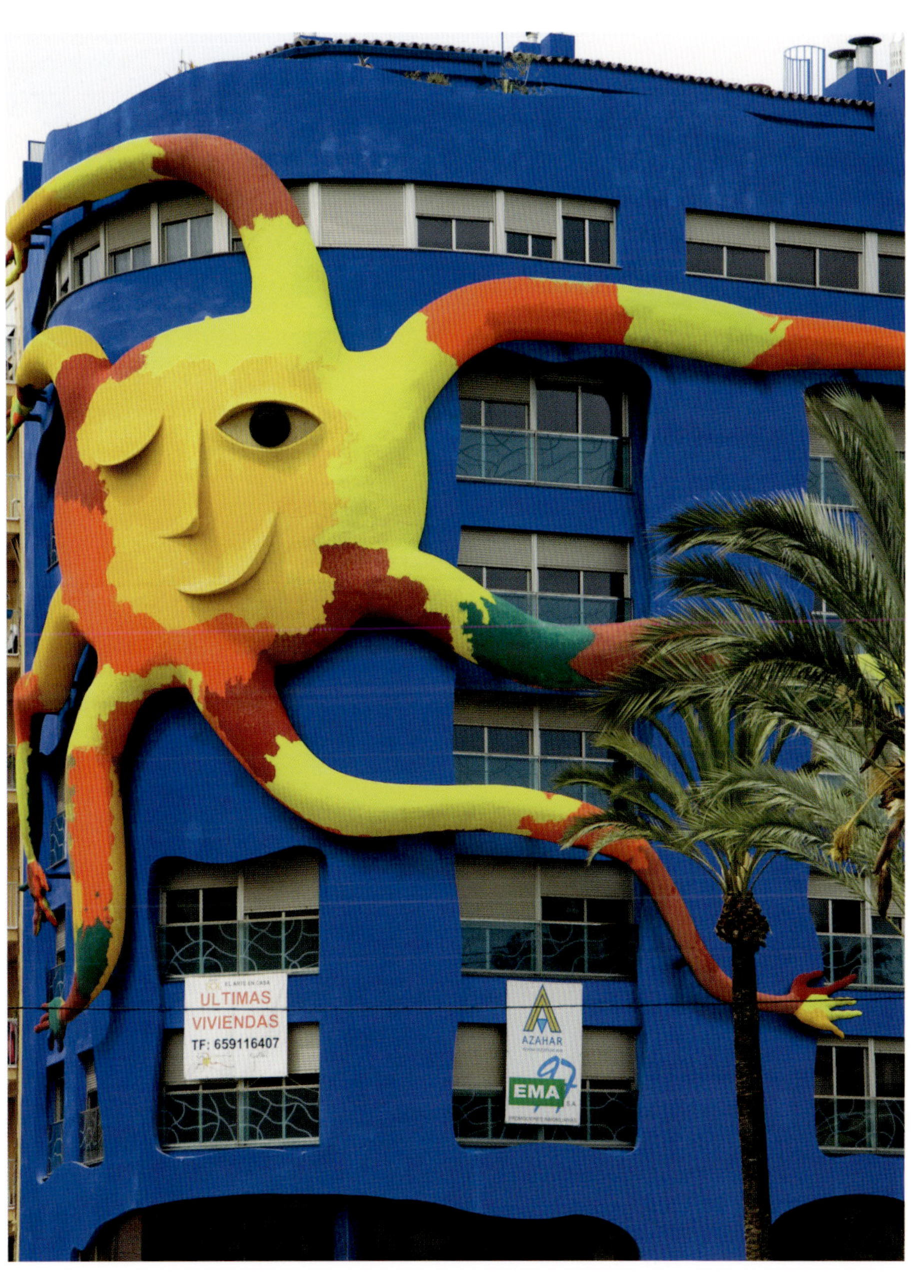

Bergen town centre, Norway. It is
hard to say whether the stylish black
house with red paintwork and its
neighbour – a bright green cafe – are
really compatible, but this eccentric
urban design is just asking to be
photographed and it's likely that it has
been approved by the architectural
authorities: in a UNESCO World
Heritage Centre, you are just not
supposed to paint facades like this.

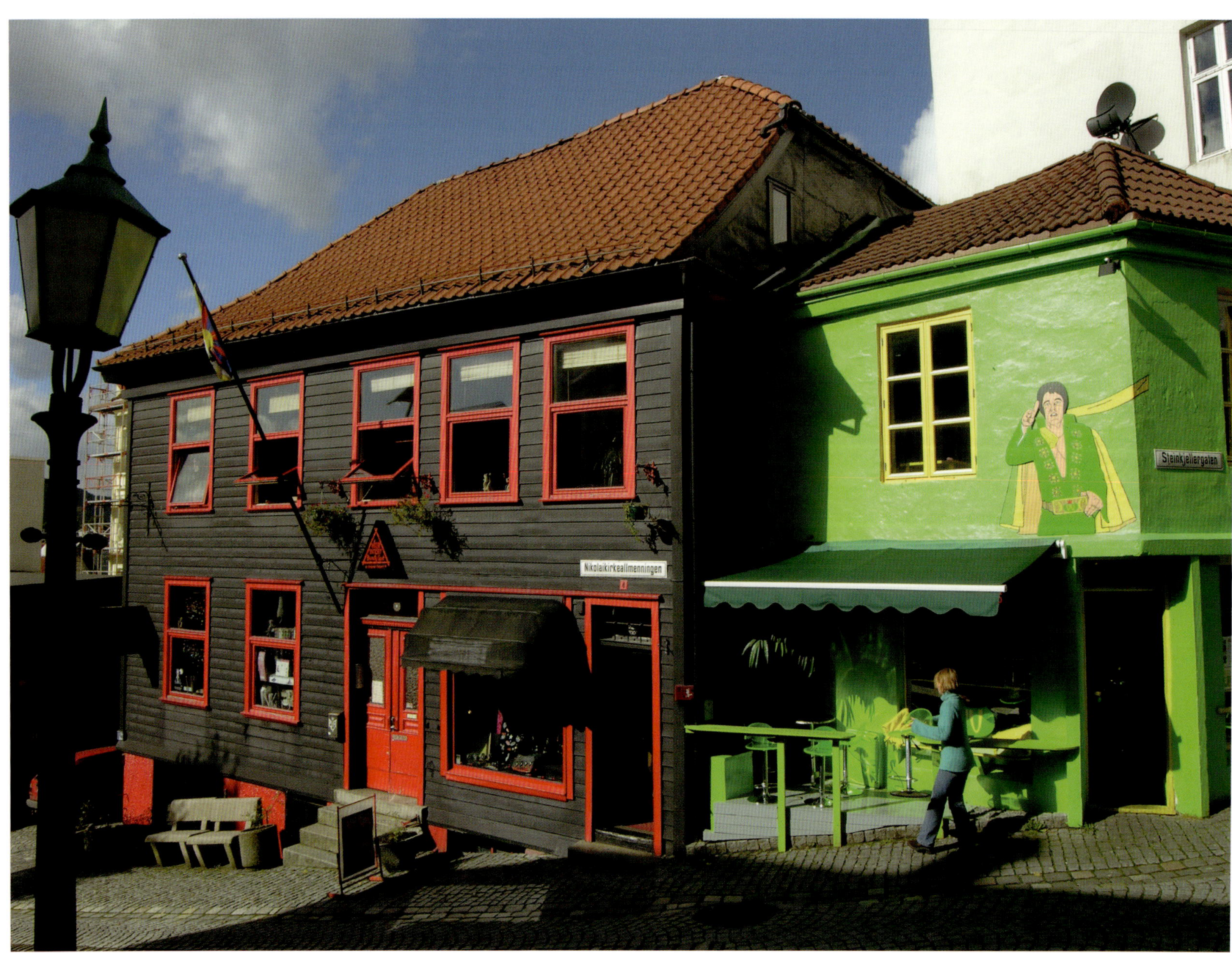

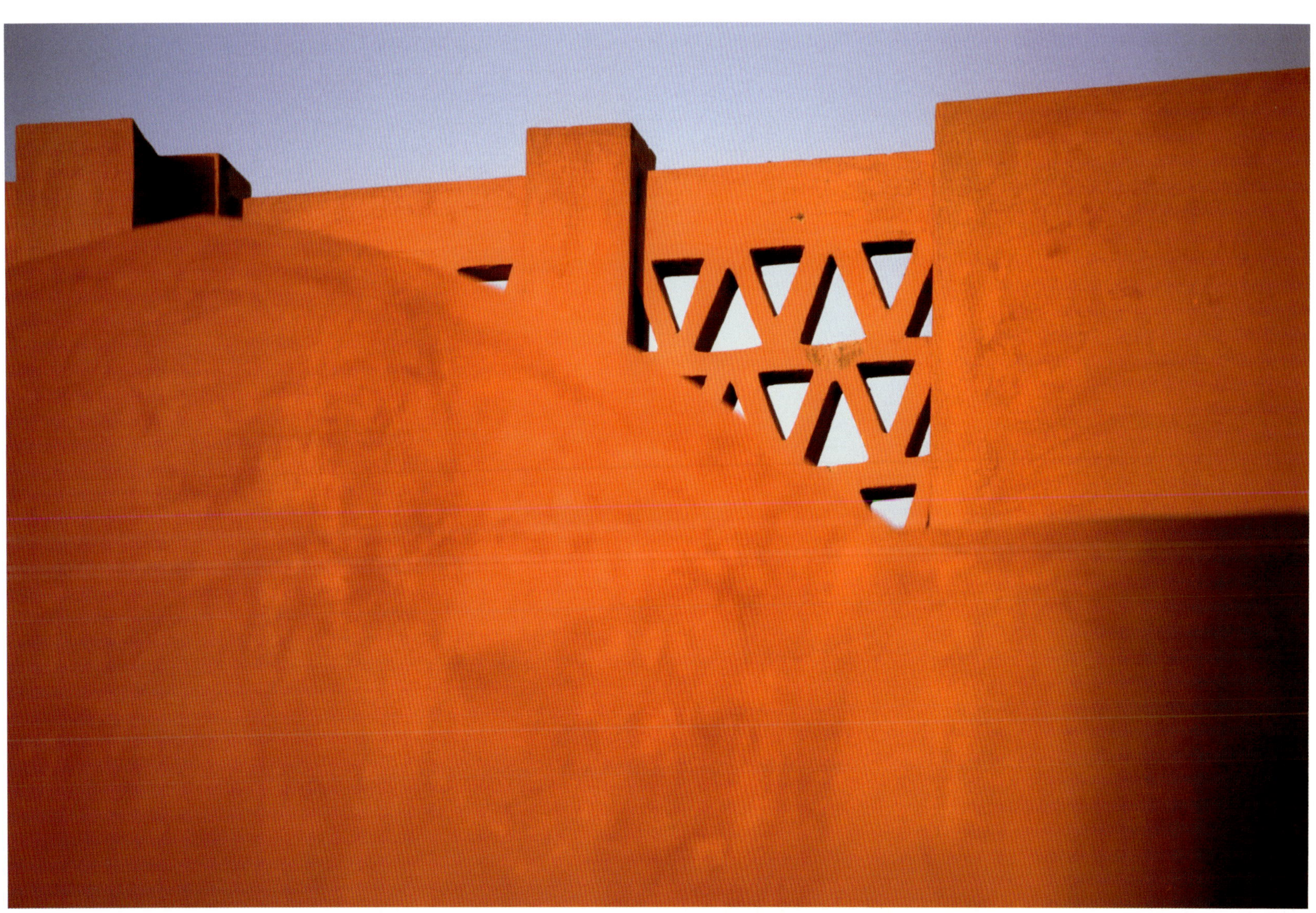

The world in faces, faces in the world

The classic portrait photograph, whether taken in a studio, in an ordinary building or outdoors always involves setting up the shot, the careful choice of angle and lighting conditions and, as a rule, the use of a tripod, umbrella and reflectors. It is a process that involves a large number of takes, taking a lot longer than an hour, and over that time the person may adapt psychologically, tune in to being photographed. In travel photography, everything is precisely the opposite. There is no setting up, because your shots are almost always absolutely impromptu; moreover, it is highly desirable that your model doesn't even suspect she or he is being photographed. Otherwise the face will be tense, if not stony, while gestures and behaviour will be unnatural. This applies especially to children. In exactly the same way, a static shot is usually not very interesting; a person is much more striking when moving, relating to others or busy with something. So you should usually take a few seconds' break in shooting – hang around a little bit – and the person will dissolve into the crowd or go past, or other people will obscure him.

This way of shooting places greater demands on your photographic equipment: a compact camera is just too slow and will do nothing more than get on your nerves. Your main tool will be a telephoto lens, preferably the fastest possible, with a fully open aperture, so that you can shoot at a fast shutter speed and also be able to blur the background. A 70–200 mm or 70–300 mm zoom is ideal in this situation, but getting one to fit a reflex camera with a 2.8 aperture is enormously expensive, prohibitively large and heavy, and will unintentionally attract the attention of people around you. Therefore you could settle for a lens with an aperture of 4–5.6, which then means increasing the film or sensor speed to 200–400 ASA, in order to avoid blurred shots. It should be borne in mind that using lenses and cameras with stabilisers at slow shutter speeds will not be helpful when shooting moving figures.

A telephoto lens severely reduces the depth of field, and even more so with an open aperture, so focusing requires special care. You will get the best results if the model does not blink, if you choose the most expressive face, and if the

I don't know how someone on a modest little boat taking passengers for cruises on the Nile heard of the cult musician, rastaman and prophet from Jamaica, Bob Marley. Maybe the young Egyptian with the mischievous eyes is 'blown away' by reggae.

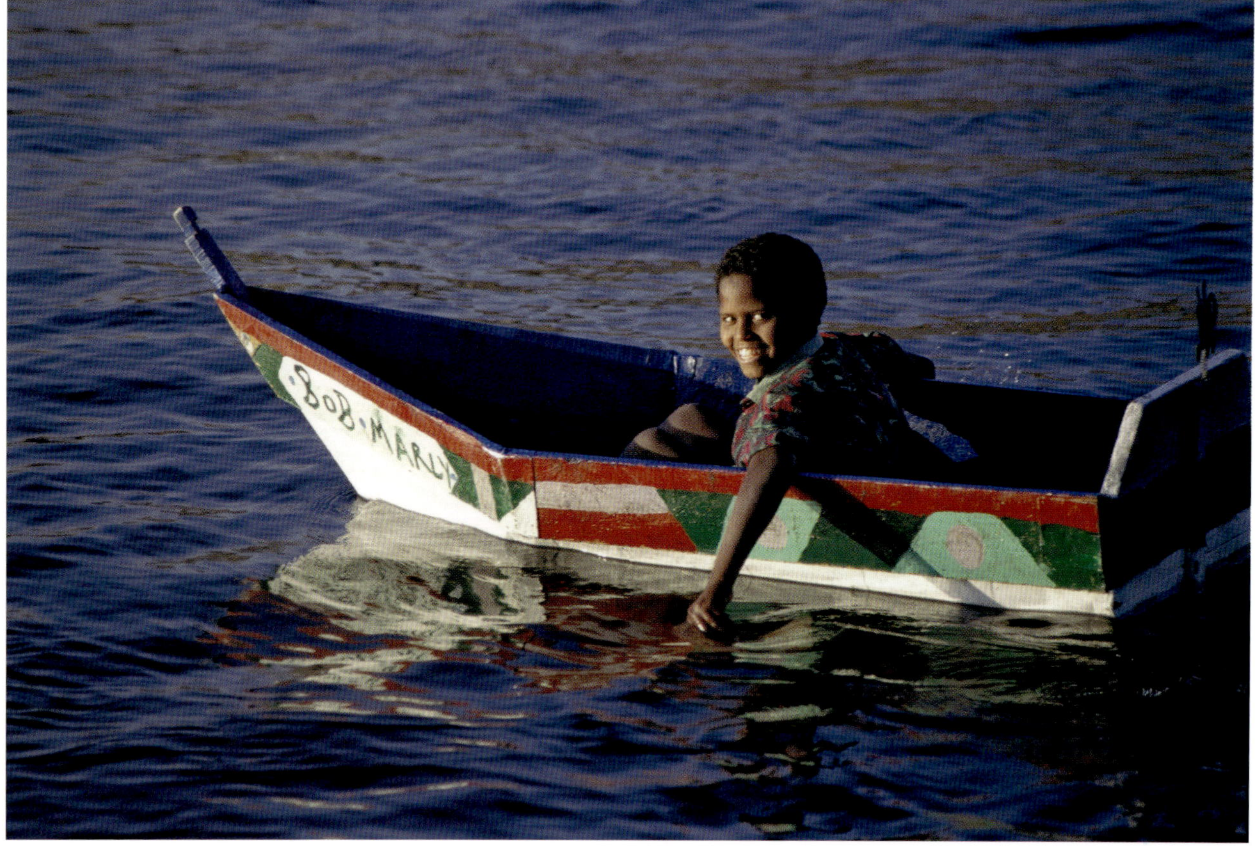

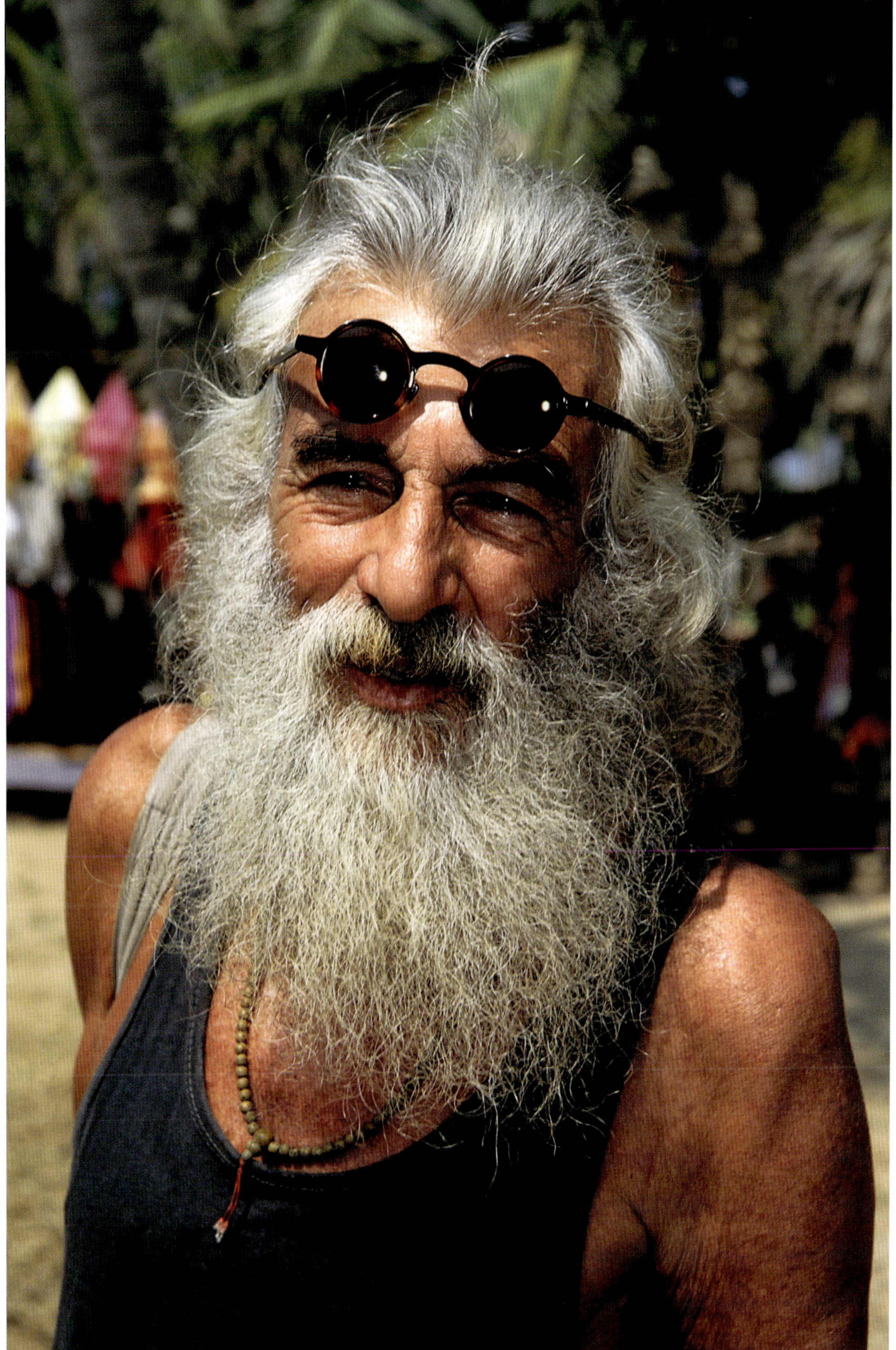

A hippy. India. This ageing hippy spends his carefree, semi-vegetarian life, with friends and without responsibilities, on the warm beaches of the holiday state of Goa. His eyes, covered by deep shade from his brows, have been filled in using flash.

'Mohawk, Potsdam, Germany.' This splendid hairstyle clearly doesn't match this lad's modest, bashful face – he is clearly just a victim of fashion.

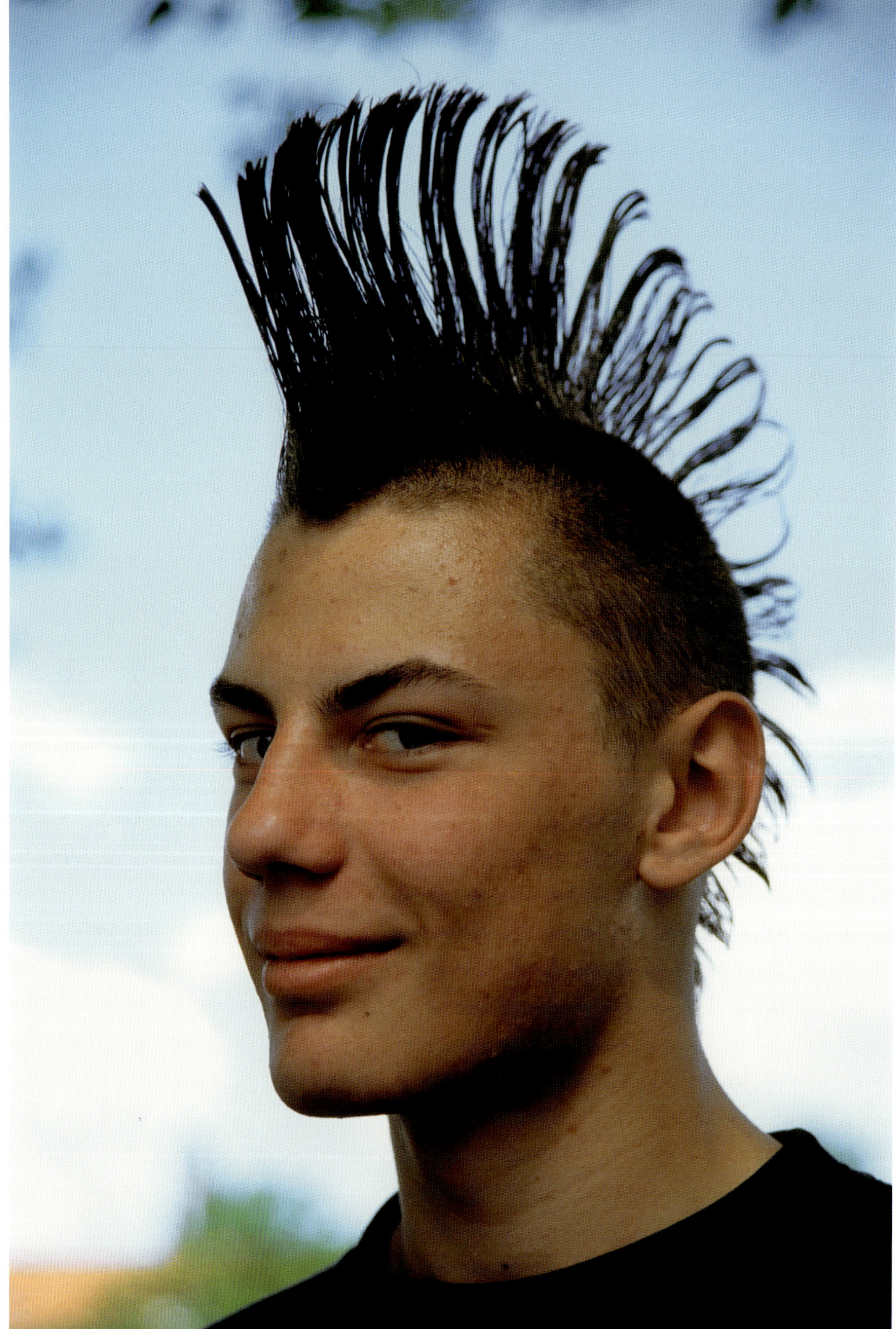

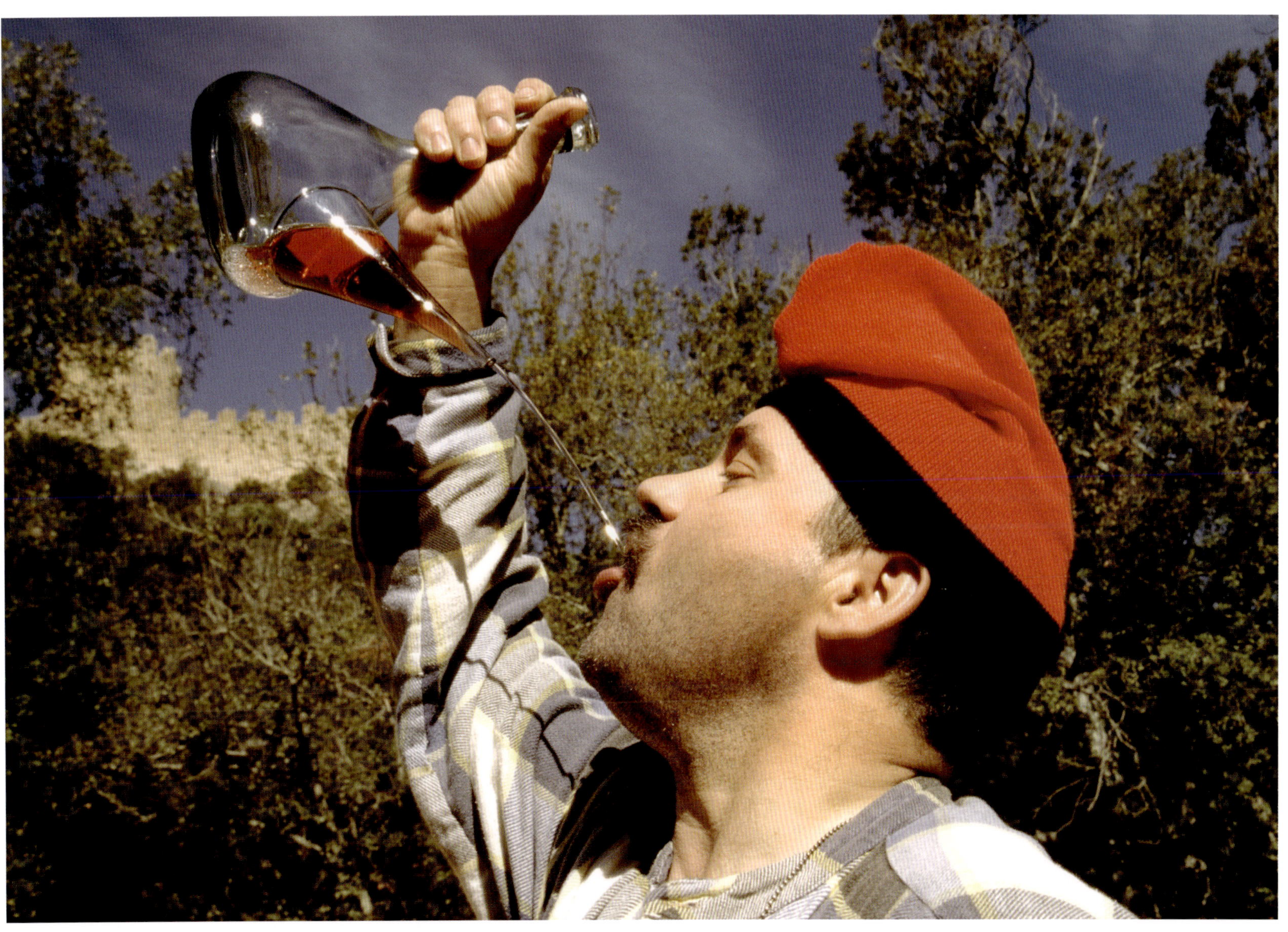

Catalan winemaker, Spain. You mustn't spill a drop of red home-made wine on your shirt when you are learning how to drink from the *poron* – a glass vessel with a narrow spout. But without this skill, you will be an outsider at any Catalan festival!

On the road from Bangkok to Pattaya, the 'Safari World' park is waiting for tourists, with obedient elephants which have been trained by clever people. But there are also some attractions here which are not for the faint-hearted – for example, when an elephant winds its trunk around you and carries you off. You should just see the look on the punter's face!

The Freundorfer Tavern is the most famous in Gasmisch-Kirchen Germany, and its host Joseph Freundorfer is an absolutely typical Bavarian. This portrait was taken using bounce-flash deflected onto the outstretched right hand; slow synchronization was used to bring out the detail of the interior of the tavern.

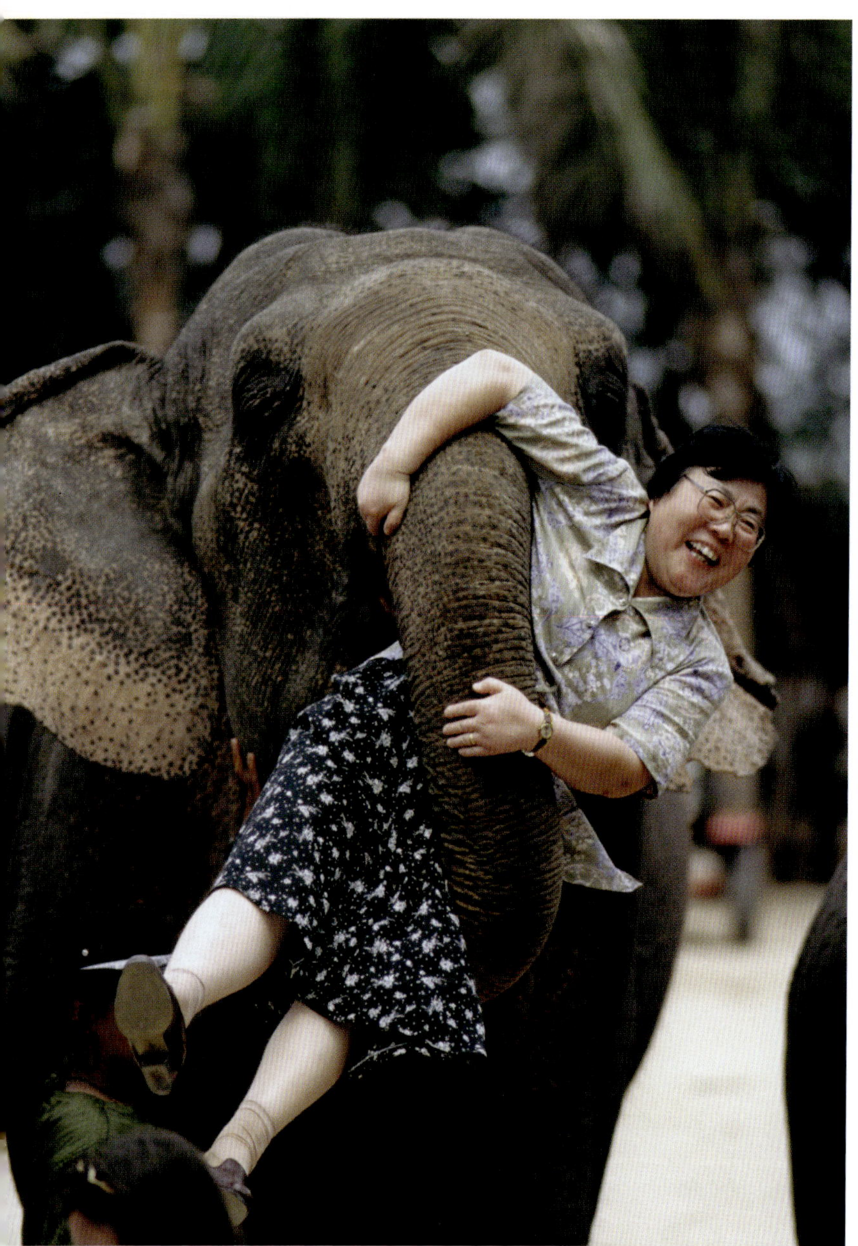

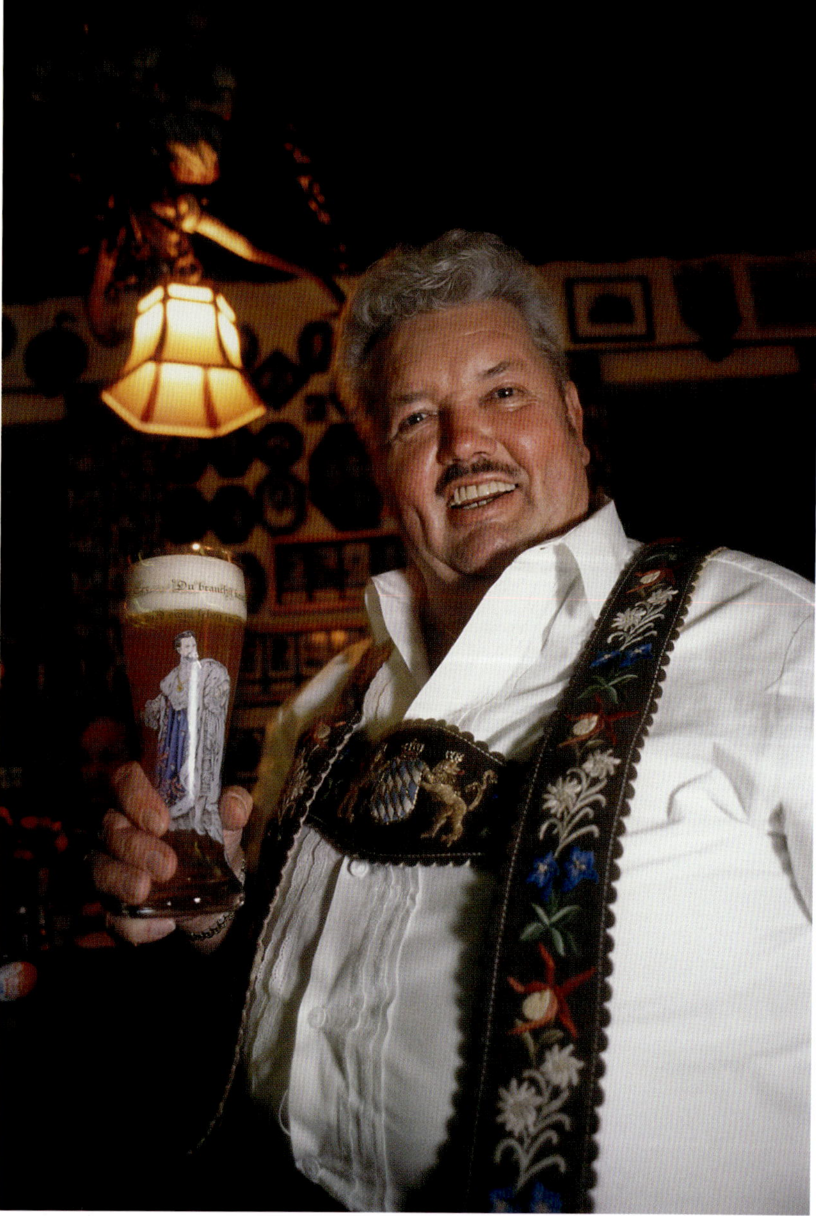

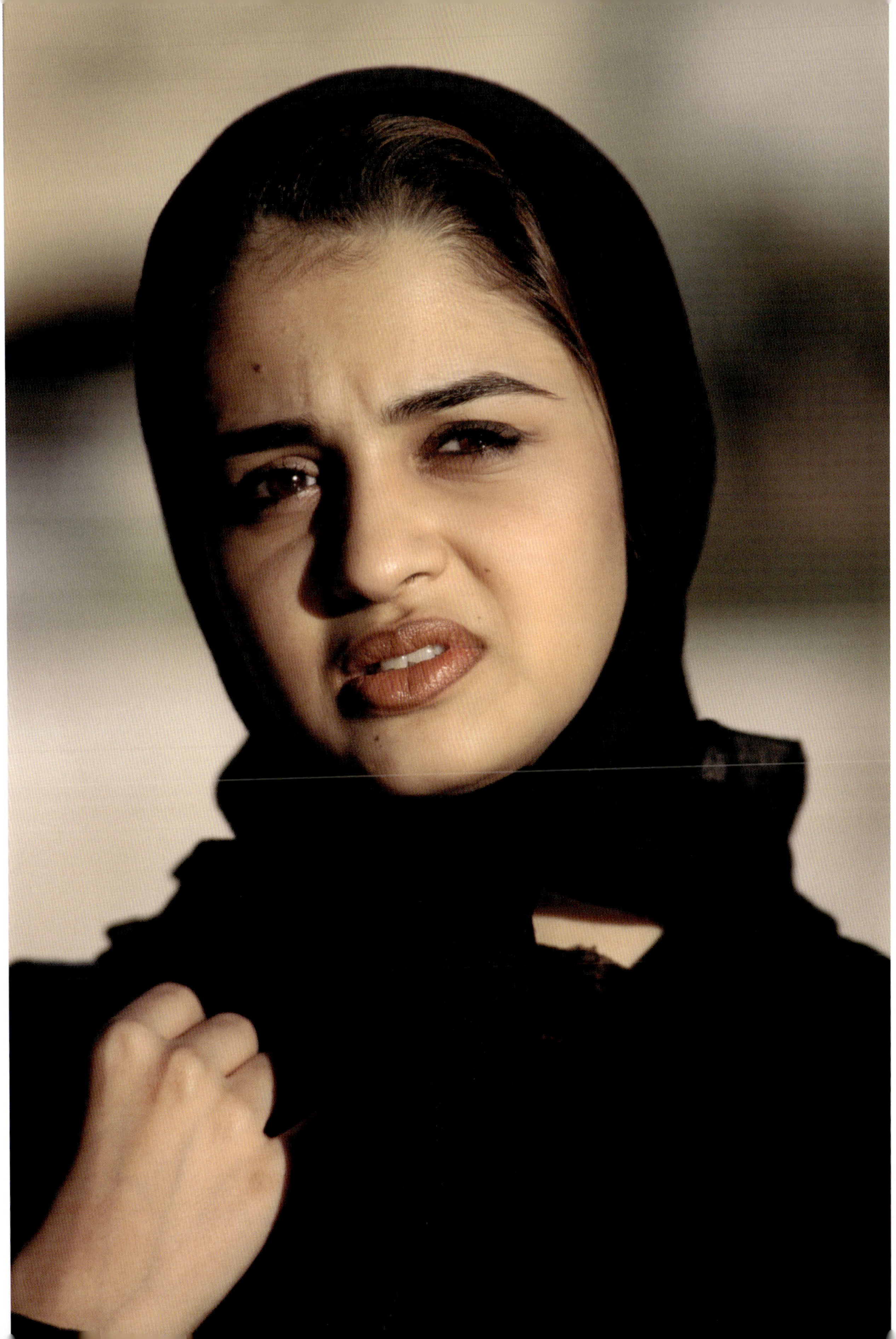

Young Iranian woman, Tehran. The modesty of the hijab that women are required to wear cannot disguise the lively eyes of this young resident of the Iranian capital.

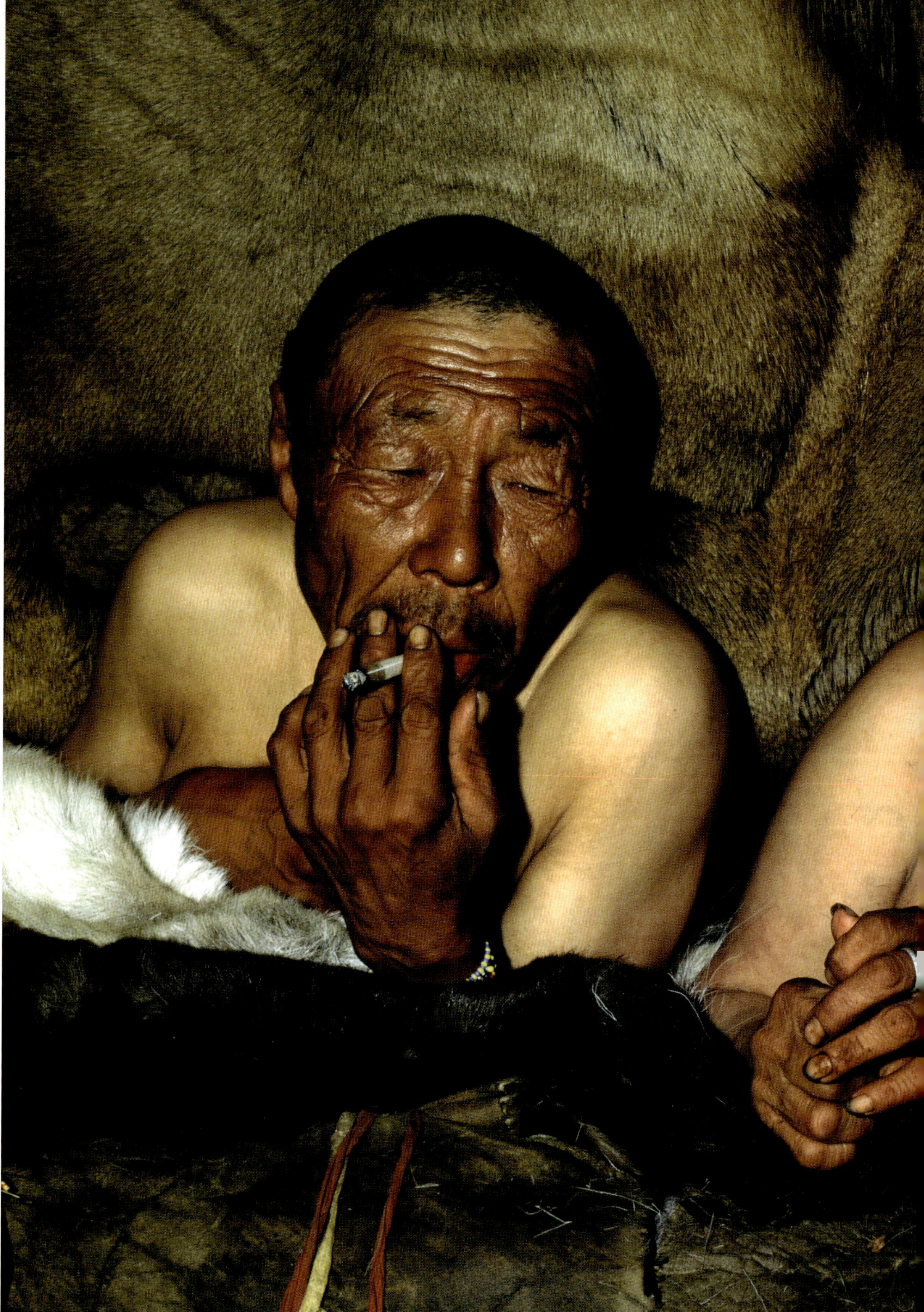

Chukotka. One of the most successful portrait photographs, taken with flash and printed as a full-page spread in many magazines across the world, deliberately used none of the prescribed technical devices. Taken early in the morning, in semi-darkness, this photograph of the primitive setting of the *yaranga*, lost on the snow-covered tundra – the faces with their richly contrasting elements, the ethnographic details, this whole microcosm swathed in deer skins – was definitely enhanced by the direct, harsh light from the head-on use of flash: 'correctly' diffused light would damp all this down and could not convey the significance of the setting and the special emotional atmosphere.

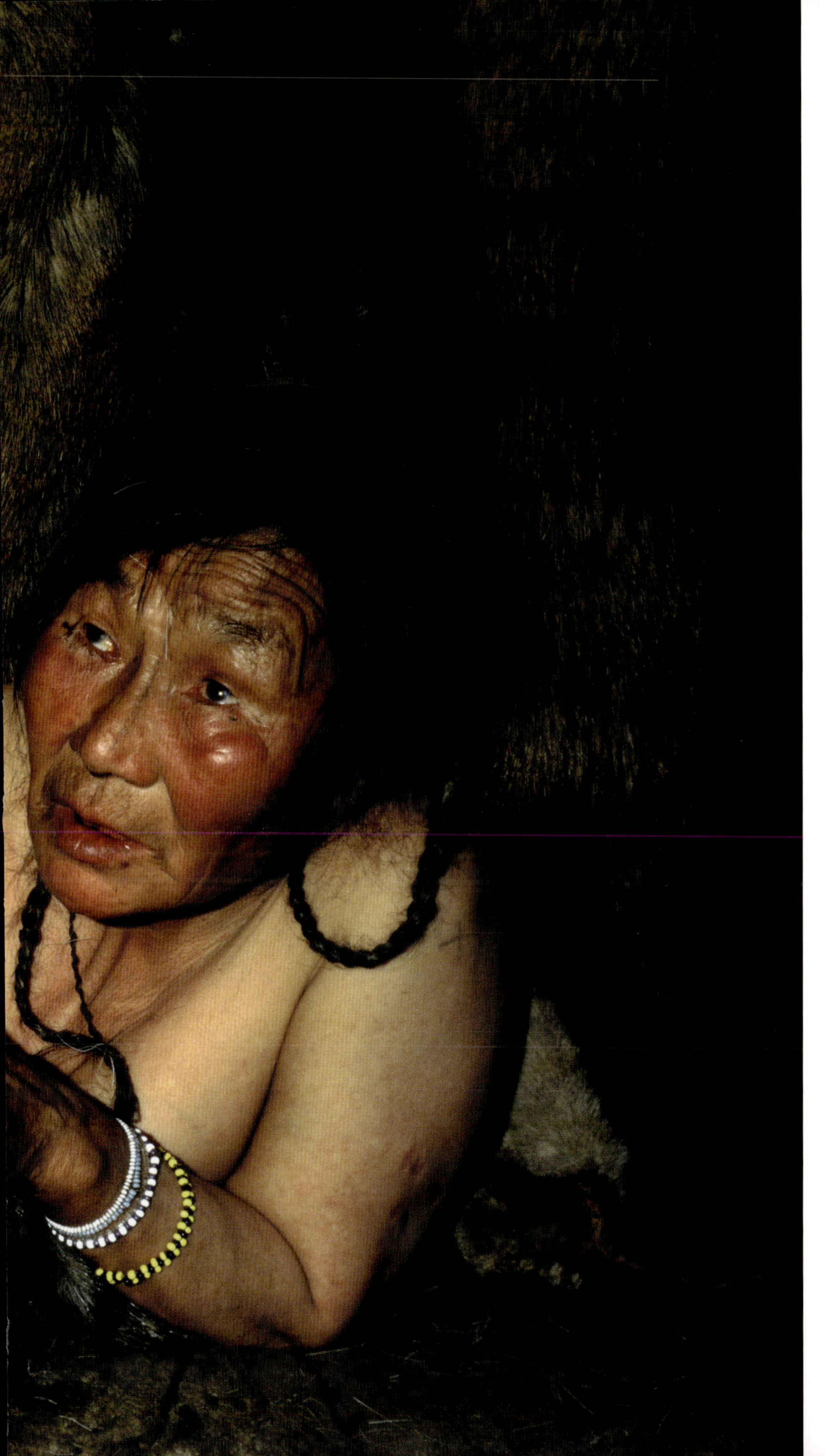

People in Thailand are much more tolerant of photographers than they are in Muslim countries. With rare exceptions, you can even take photos in temples. The only time problems can arise is in the red light districts of Bangkok and Pattaya. But even there things can be sorted out with the help of a few dollars. It's a great place to take genre shots and portraits – the floating market, where the traders sell everything from their boats, from finished products and ready-to-eat food to souvenirs and clothes. No-one pays any attention to you. All you need is a good telezoom.

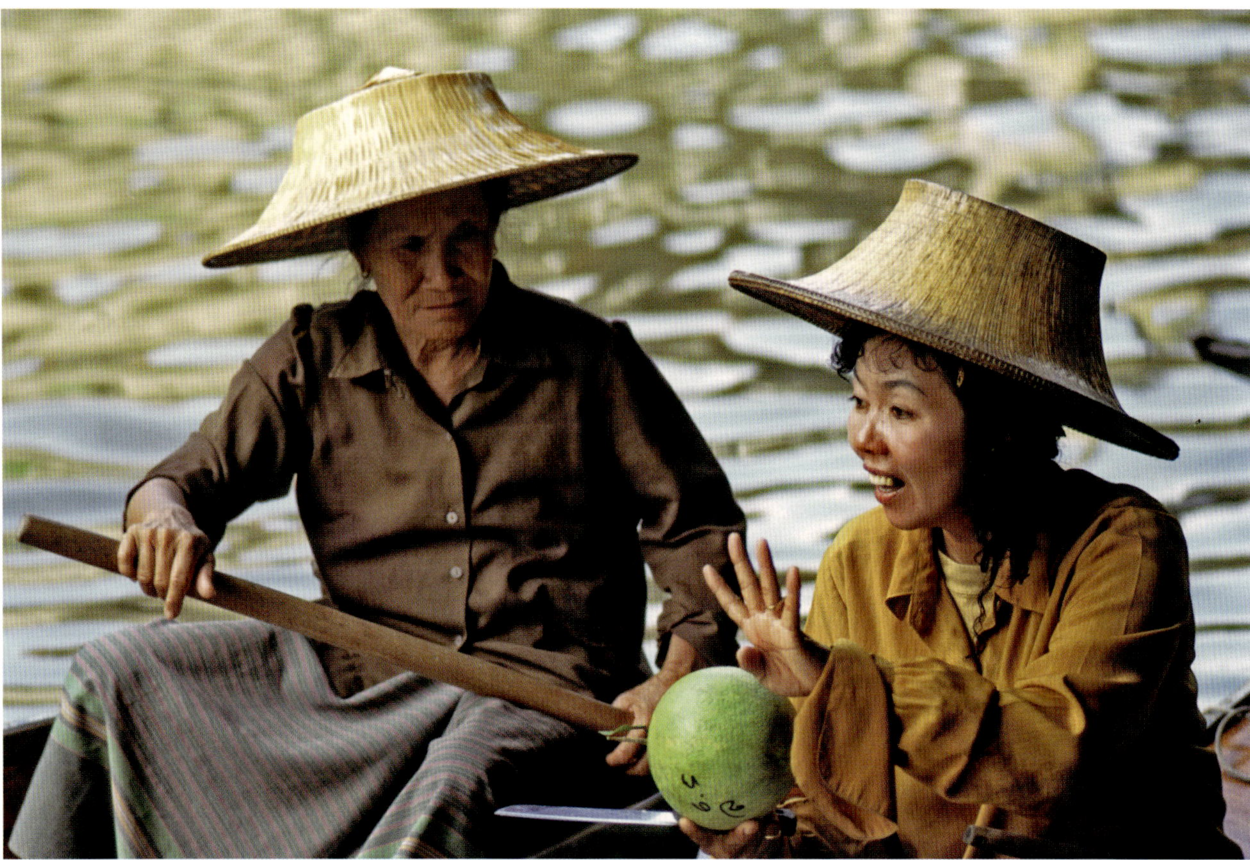

head does not merge with the heads of other passers-by.

The probability of taking a good portrait photograph is significantly increased if you do not simply wander along the street in the hope of meeting a colourful character, but settle yourself in the correct position early; this is especially important in Arab countries, where women either turn their backs or shy away to one side as soon as they catch sight of a foreigner with a camera. Take a stroll through the Medina – the old town centre of a Tunisian or Moroccan city – and note the direction from which the main stream of local residents is coming. Find a sheltered spot, which must be in the shade of a building or the crown of a tree, so that the sun will be behind you and the people moving towards you, and hold your camera at the ready, so you don't miss the moment. If the street is in deep shade, take your photograph when the subject comes out onto a square or crossroads that is flooded with sunlight. Firstly, against the background of the dark street, he or she will be lit to advantage; secondly, the sunlight will make it less likely that he or she will notice the photographer.

Of course, portrait photography is subject to the basic rules of composition; but it also has its own peculiarities which,

strange as it may seem, are often unknown even to the photo editors of illustrated magazines. Posts, poles, ropes, cords, wires, the line of the horizon or of a fence – indeed, anything similar – must never in any circumstances cut across the person's head and neck. So, if you shoot on the beach, make sure the subject's head is against the background of either the water or the sky – but do not divide it between them. A TV antenna or a lighthouse in the distance must not grow out of the crown of the head, and black hair must not merge with a deep shadow on the wall.

Situations can occur in which a secret snap either doesn't allow you to get a good photo or is just impossible in principle. That's what happened in Marrakech, on the huge central square of Djemaa el Fna, when I noticed an Arab sitting on the asphalt with a face of rare distinction, nobility and charm. People were coming up to him one by one, talking to him for a few moments, and then moving on, yielding their place to the next in line. Who was he – a philosopher, a wise man, a fortune-teller, an interpreter of the Koran, a neighbourhood judge in disputes?

I had to get a good close-up portrait of this mysterious person. I tried to photograph him with a telephoto lens, but

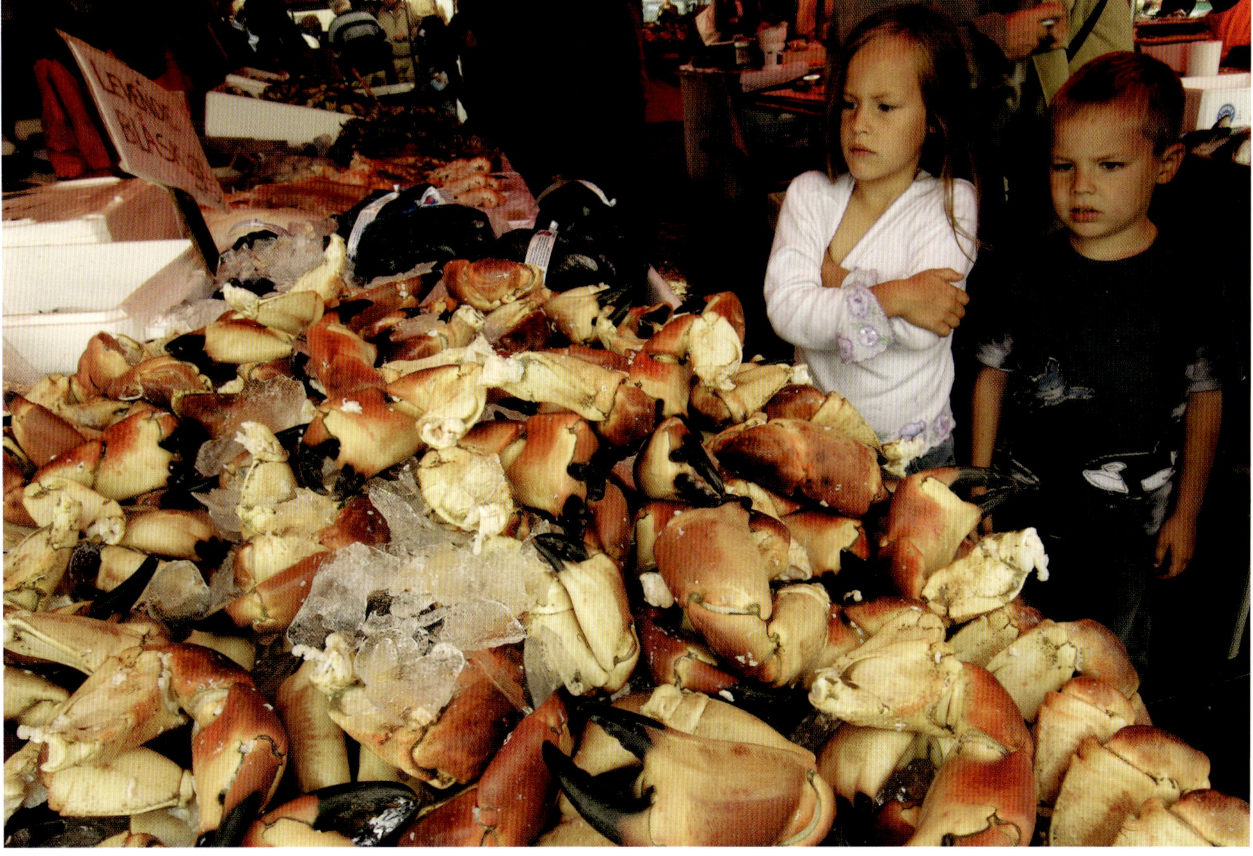

he noticed, and I felt awkward. Usually in such places people will let you take their photos for a little 'baksheesh', and some people even do this professionally. A few hours earlier I'd taken a photo in just this way of a splendid water-carrier on a market square, who was inviting tourists to 'photograph a colourful character', while his colleague collected money for this. But offering such a distinguished-looking man a few dollars, seemed unthinkable, and there was nothing for it but to approach him like the people who were in front of me in the queue and were waiting to talk to him.

We discussed the essence of things and the destiny of mankind on Earth, and I told him the truth about myself. I was from Russia, a journalist, a photographer – I was not a Muslim, but I respected everyone's right to their own faith. Half the world went by, everyone could see us, but you don't often meet such an inspired person, and it would have been an honour to take his photo. A gentle, scarcely perceptible smile appeared on the Arab's face and he nodded his head slightly. Manliness and goodness, aloofness and sympathy – everyone sees something new in this portrait.

The main thing to remember is that, if you are lucky enough to meet a person on your travels who is clearly out of the ordinary, you have the opportunity to create that special shot that meets the goals you have set yourself as a photographer.

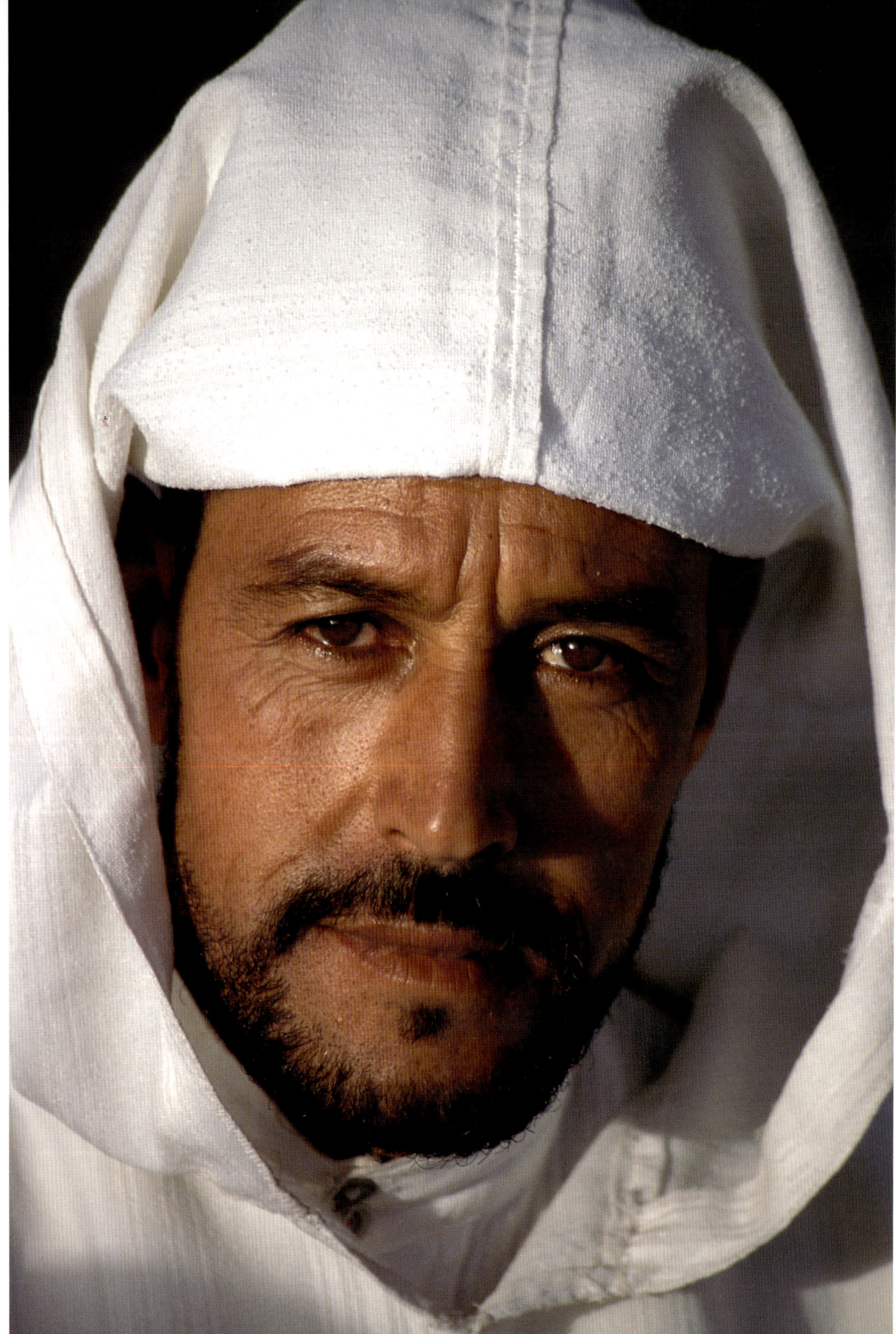

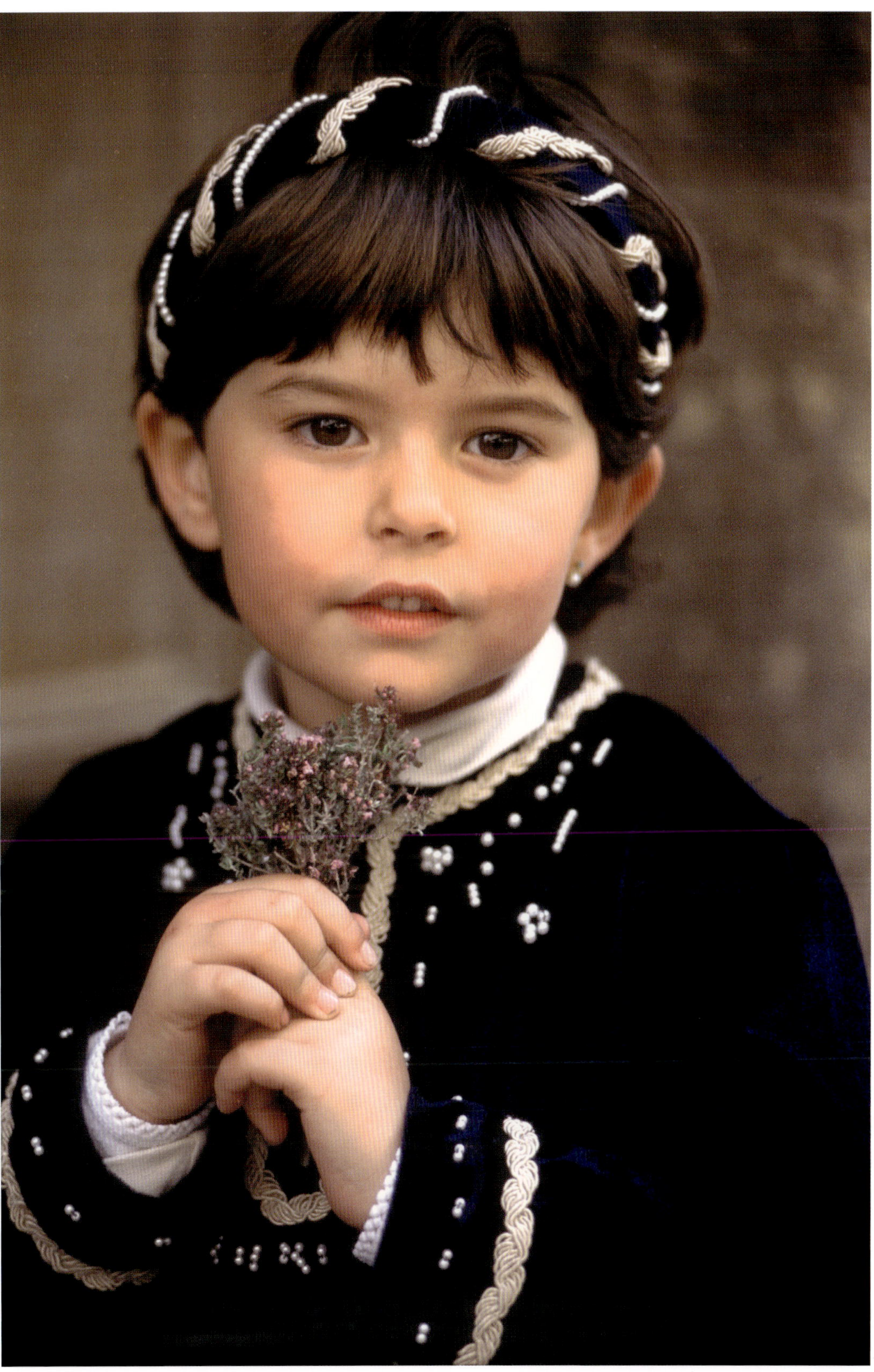

LEFT

Wisdom. This Arab with a noble, spiritual face was sitting in a marketplace in Marrakech, chatting with anyone who approached him. It wasn't possible to create a good portrait from a distance, and so permission had to be asked to take this photograph – and was graciously given.

RIGHT

Medieval Spanish girl. How can you photograph a little girl in an old-fashioned costume? It's very simple: travel to Catalonia, just find out which towns celebrate 'Medieval Fairs' and when, and you will find yourself plunged into the atmosphere of that historical period..

The law is the law

Travelling around the United States by car, I was taken to visit an Indian reservation on the Northeast seaboard; I wanted to get closer to the house of one of the residents and photograph the beautiful carved totem pole standing by the porch.

'Stop! Don't go even a step nearer – shouted my guide from the car – You'll have to photograph it from the pavement: He might shoot at you – and the law would be on his side!'

In most developed countries, both the law and public opinion defend a person's rights and private life: however, this doesn't stop the paparazzi secretly or unceremoniously photographing celebrities, preferably in risqué poses and situations. Indeed, they can get a fee from the tabloids in the tens, if not the hundreds, of thousands of dollars for just one lucky shot, which compensates them a hundredfold for the many days they spend in pursuit of their desired subject. The tragic death of Princess Diana acted as the clearest possible expression of the ethical values of this genre of photography... And the courts in other countries are planning to clamp down on photographic intrusion into private life.

Therefore what we mean by 'shooting with a hidden camera' on your travels is taking tactful photographs of people solely in public places – in the street, on the beach (but not the nudist beach, where it is usually strictly forbidden to take a camera), in a park, at a discotheque, where you can carry on unnoticed by the subject of your 'photo shoot' for the sake of your photograph's artistic expression. To put it simply, you are trying to capture people as they show themselves to be naturally – their situation, emotions, gestures, facial expressions – before they can become strained or frozen, or before they turn away because they have noticed you pointing your lens at them. It's just that your photographer's eye is caught by the characteristics of these people. You are not invading their privacy. After all, if a couple in love kiss under the eyes of everyone in the Luxembourg Gardens or on the banks of the Seine, rather than at home, this is no longer the couple's private life – it is an expression of the social life of Paris. It would be tactless to photograph them obtrusively at close range, but you can shoot them with a telephoto lens, from somewhere behind

At a portside market in Morocco. The only way to photograph female traders in an Arab country is surreptitiously, using a telephoto lens. They make the photograph startling. It's an ordinary scene – two ladies selling beautiful coloured caps in the port town of Essaouira – photographed using a lens with a focal length of 200 mm.

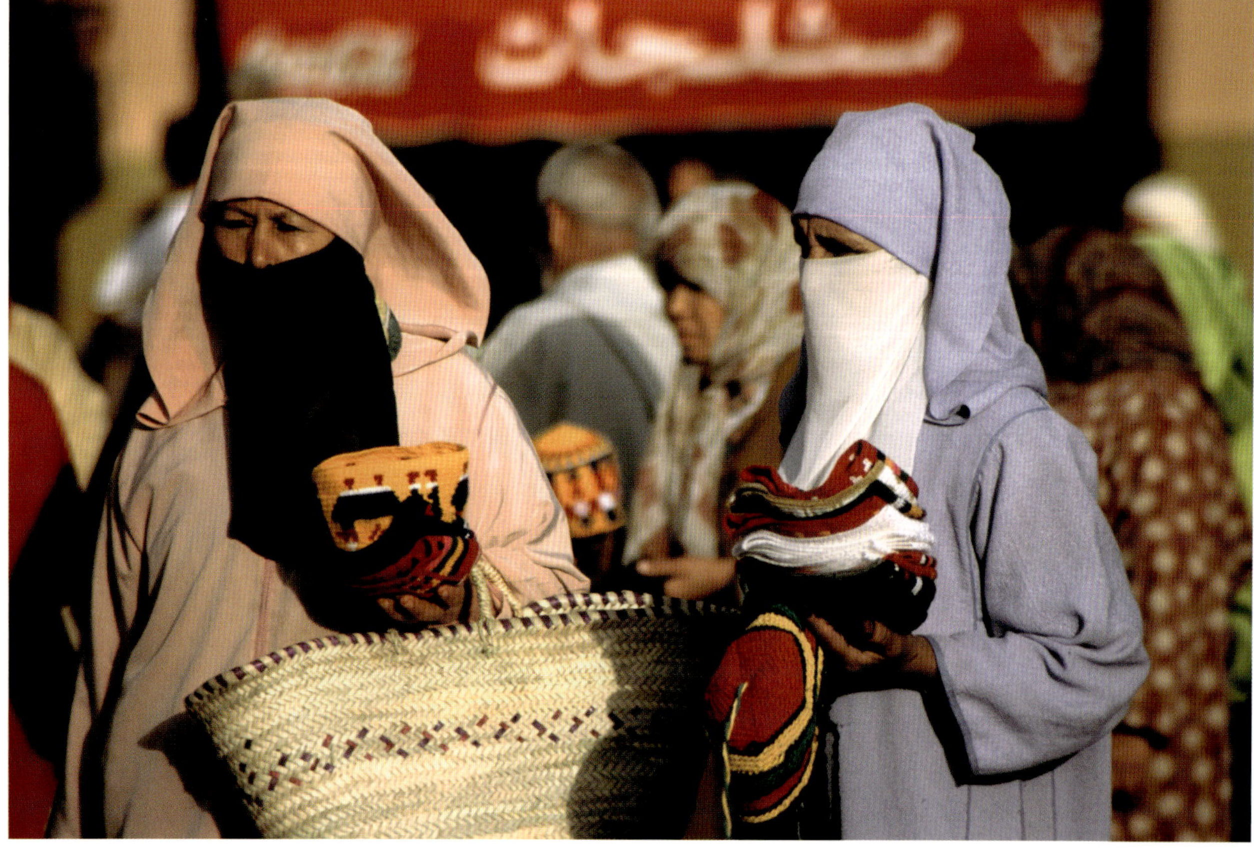

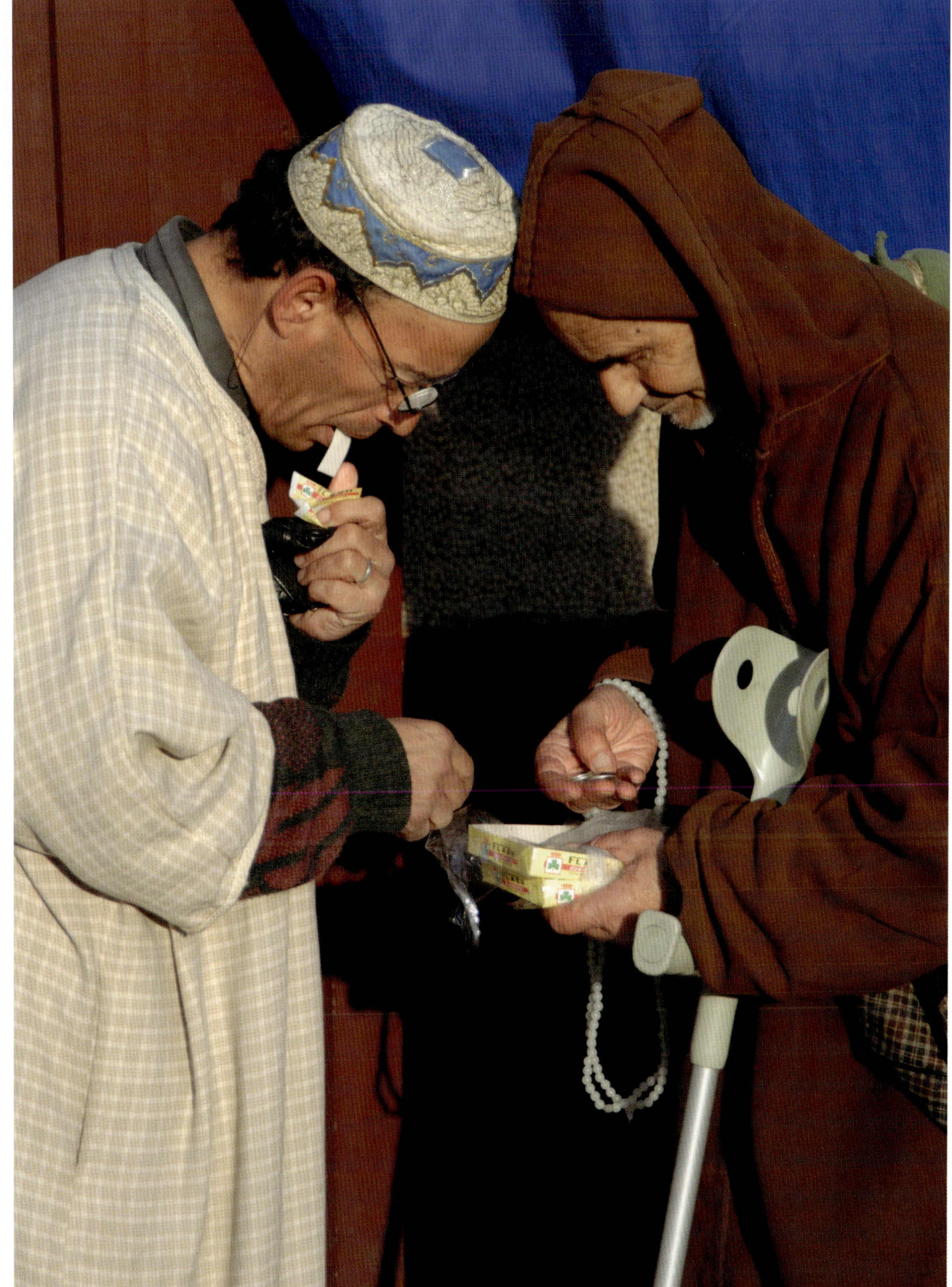

Market in Rabat. Morocco. It is not entirely clear what is being traded here – some kind of vouchers or tickets. Perhaps for some kind of local lottery or sweepstake? In any case, buyer and seller have the look of conspirators.

Love in the North, Norway. Perhaps this is how it was when the conqueror Erik the Red gained the love and favours of girls from among the local peoples he encountered during his sea campaigns. This photograph was taken with a telephoto lens on a Sunday morning beside the Nordfjord.

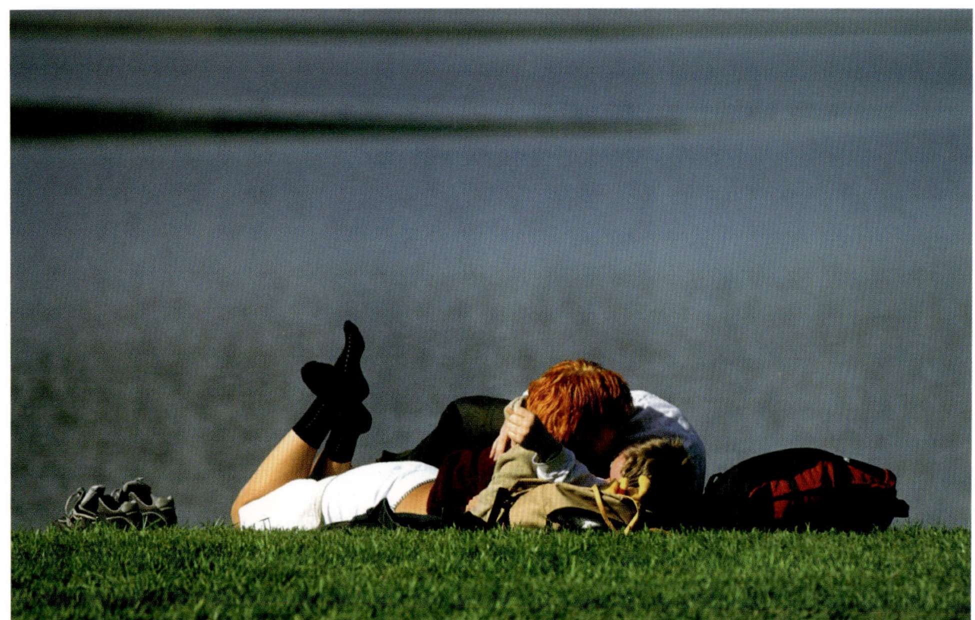

a tree, without being tormented by remorse and without fear of prosecution.

This is also the only way you can take good shots of children at play, because they usually freeze like statues as soon as they notice the photographer. You should use a hidden camera at a bazaar, because the traders really dislike being photographed. It can also be handy here to have an inconspicuous compact telephoto zoom lens. And you can shoot with a telephoto lens at a shutter speed of 1/30 of a second out of the car window, raising the glass to the top to create a vice-like clamp for the lens.

It is important for people who are keen on shooting with a hidden camera to guard against the serious danger to which they are exposing themselves if they start photographing street disturbances, terrorist attacks or crimes, since this makes them accidental witnesses to these events. Similarly, it is categorically ill advised to point your lens at people in military uniform (except, of course, at a military parade or specially rehearsed 'changing of the guard'), military equipment, airfields (including civil ones) or bridges, especially in areas where there are ongoing wars or ethnic conflicts (the Middle East, certain African or Latin American countries), or indeed at people or cars that look in any way typical of the criminal underworld. If this advice is ignored, the photographer may need the services of a lawyer or a good surgeon.

Apart from portraits, genre photographs of people also occupy an important place in travel photography. These may include shots of people haggling in a bazaar, or scenes at discotheque, sports ground or swimming pool. In slightly risqué situations such as a bathhouse or coming out of a steam room to swim in an ice-hole, you can only take photographs with your models' agreement and ensuring that they understand clearly that other people may see the pictures or that they may be published somewhere.

The main thing to remember is that, if you are lucky enough to meet a person on your travels who is clearly out of the ordinary, you have the opportunity to create that special shot that meets the goals you have set yourself as a photographer.

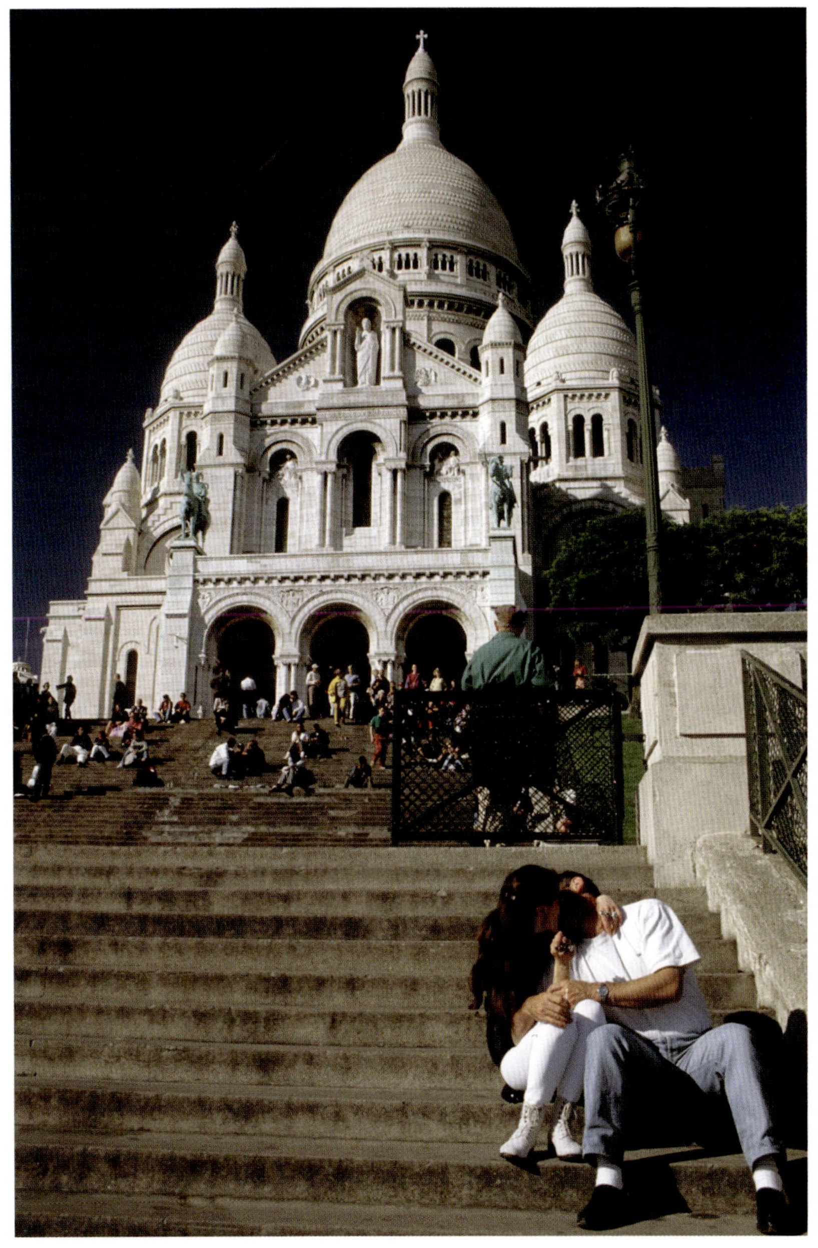

The steps of Montmartre, France. Paris is the capital of allthe world's lovers – so wherever you point your camera, you will find a kissing couple to photograph.

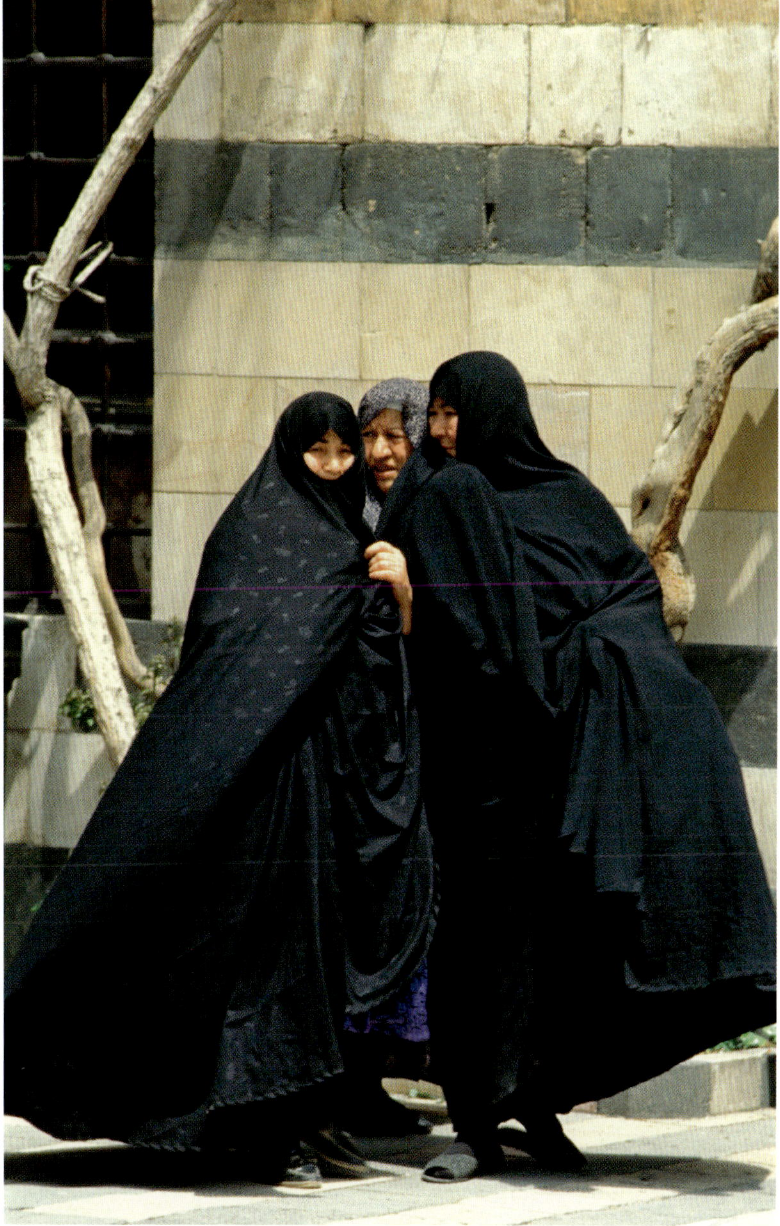

Damascus, the Omeyadov mosque. Surely these three Syrian ladies who'd come here to pray in the mosque hadn't been thrown into confusion by catching sight of me looking into my telephoto lens? I tried to make myself inconspicuous. But can anyone or anything be concealed from the eyes of Eastern women? Sorry, madam.

Religious followers completely detached from the world are to be found even in Nepal. This man has embraced life as a hermit at the Pashupatinath Temple, one of the largest and most respected in the Himalayan kingdom. The photograph came about by chance, when the old man and the photographer came face to face in the ancient stone labyrinth – a surprise for both of them. It only took a split second to shoot, but the reaction did not disappoint.

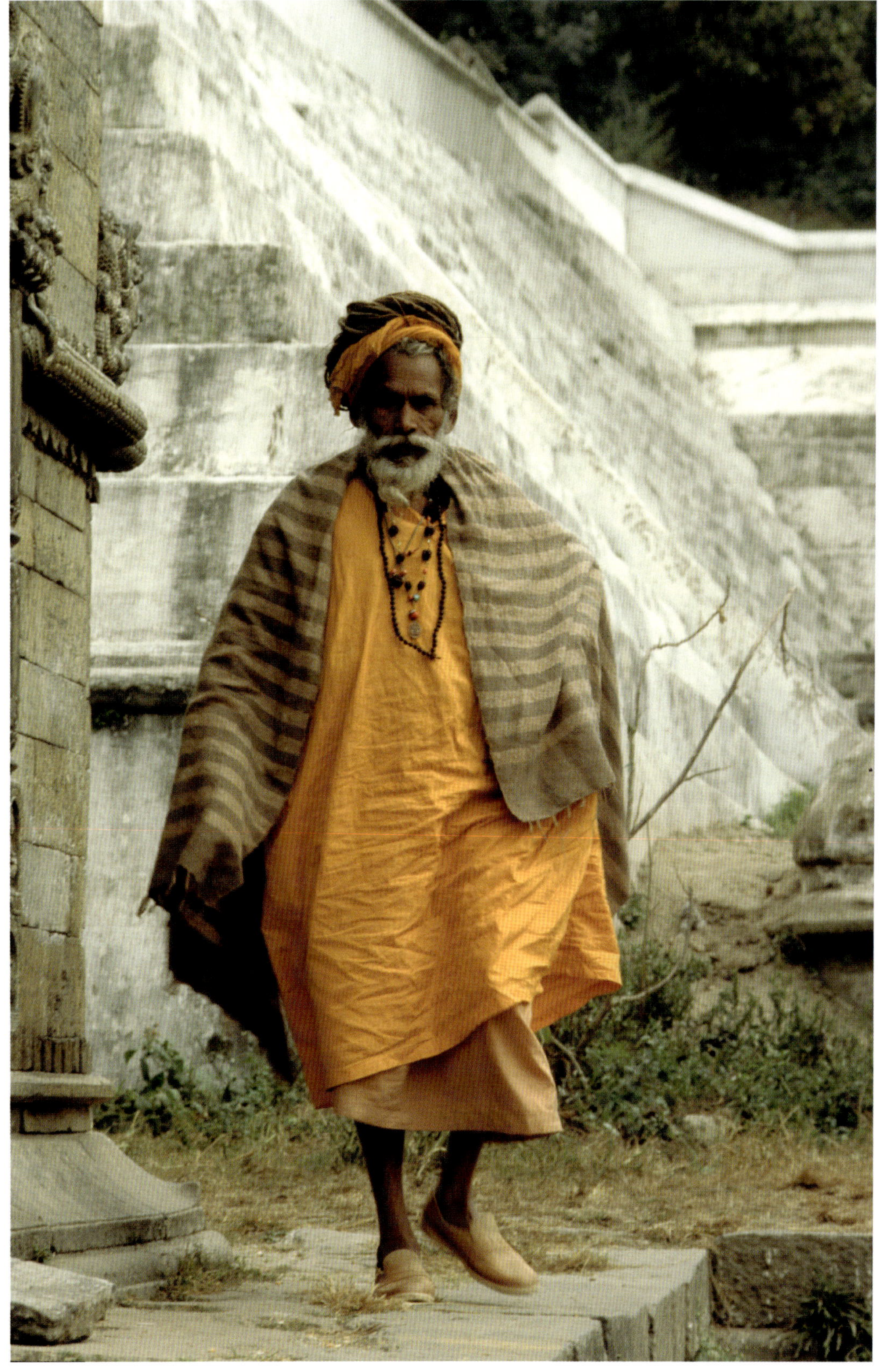

The women of the Tunisian island of
Djerba still wear national dress to this
day – loose white linen tunics with
kerchief mantles and straw hats. I
was able to photograph this group of
women, but only from cover and with
a powerful telephoto lens. As soon as
they noticed someone with a camera,
they whipped round like lightning and
went off in another direction.

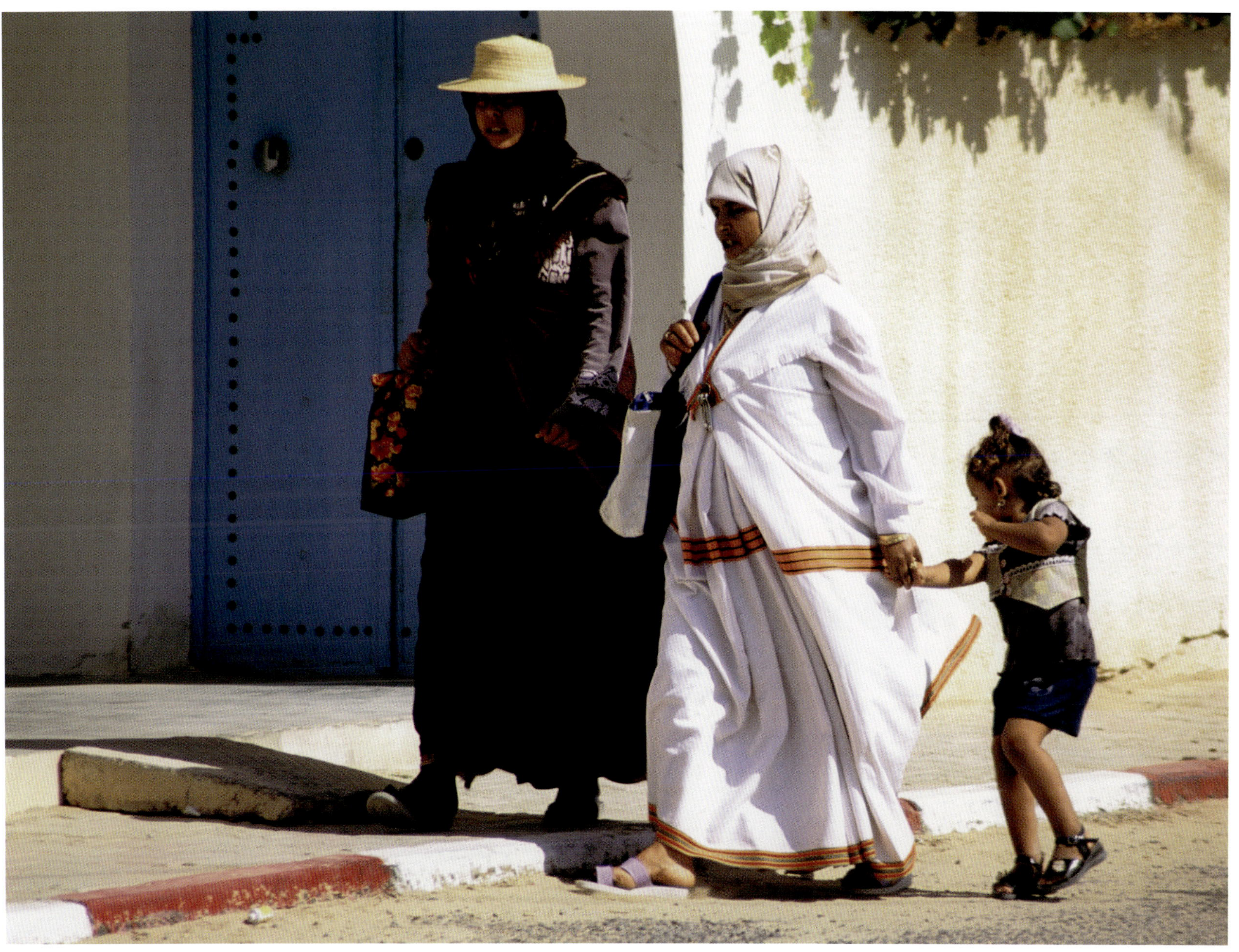

Taking genre to new heights

If giraffes could take photographs, then people would no longer get a look in because when shooting photographs, occupying the heights is the key to success. It is not for nothing that mountains, high buildings and television towers are equipped with viewing areas for tourists – and that you have to pay to use them. The only 30th-floor view of Manhattan's Central Park in all its beauty is to be had from the office of George Soros. But from the top of the Empire State Building you can see the whole of Manhattan. So you can go up to the top of this famous skyscraper, bring something you can stand on, and you can photograph this fascinating view over the heads of the crowds of visitors!

A high-rise hotel offers excellent possibilities. Even if your hotel room doesn't have a balcony and the only part of the window that opens fully is right at the top – or indeed the window doesn't open at all – you can always think of something to get round the problem. In Jakarta, I had to photograph the city's central square from the hotel corridor by standing on tiptoe and struggling to poke my lens through the slats of the Venetian blind, just below ceiling level. Obviously, it is impossible to put one's eye to the viewfinder, and I had to shoot blind. In Bangkok, I am always lucky to stay in high-rise hotels. The beautiful 30th floor view over the river offered me a full-scale panorama of the building boom that has gripped the city, as if I was holding it in the palm of my hand.

There's another first-rate position for a photo which you can use at least twice in any lengthy journey – sitting in a seat next to the window in an airplane. What can you photograph from a height of 11,000 kilometres? Beautiful clouds, together with fragments of the wing, an engine, mountains, islands, a beautiful shoreline – and when you're landing, more precisely when you're approaching your destination, you may chance to fly over a town, which you can photograph from no more than a few hundred metres up. There are no technical complications.

The way that the architects of old competed to build the highest bell tower seems to show that they were especially concerned about the needs of future photographers! The panoramas of cities and the surrounding natural environment which open up from such steeples or from fortress towers, are incomparably better than any vista you can capture at ground

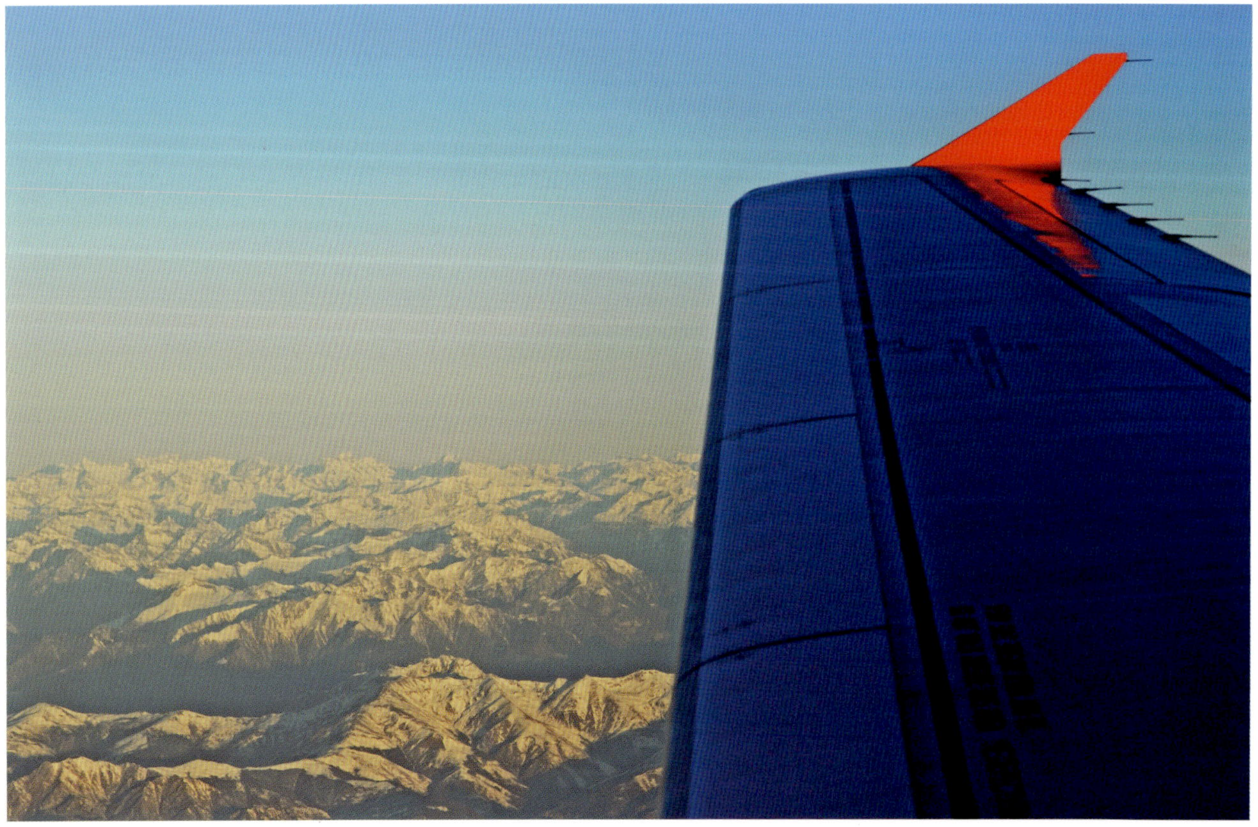

On board an Airbus, at a height of 11,000 metres above the Alps. The low evening Sun brightly lit up the wing's red stabiliser. An example of how one slight emphasis can 'make' a shot.

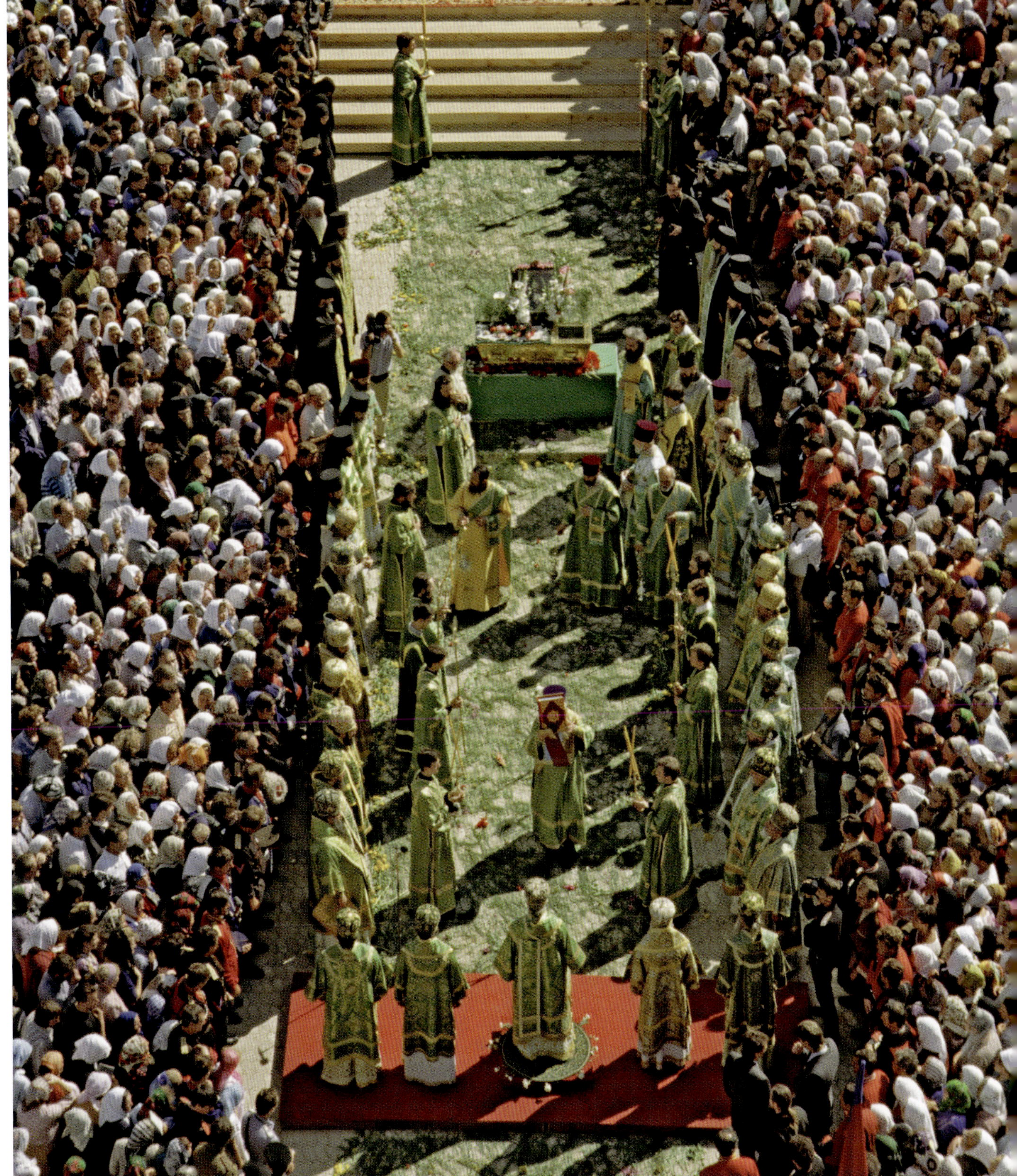

The Patriarch of Moscow and All Russia, Alexei II, in the presence of all the members of the Holy Synod, leads the commemorative service of worship at the Serafimo-Divyeyevski monastery on the occasion of the transfer (re-dedication) of the relics of Saint Serafim of Saratov. Taken from the belfry.

A 'bouquet' of Hong Kong's towers,
photographed from the 66th floor of
a skyscraper located on a high hill –
taken through the thick glass walls of
a rotating restaurant. The picture was
shot using a fisheye lens.

A bird's eye view of farmland can be
very graphic. It may resemble a multi-
coloured blanket patchwork quilt,as
in this shot, taken in Austria. The road
is included in the picture with cars
moving along it to give an idea of the
scale.

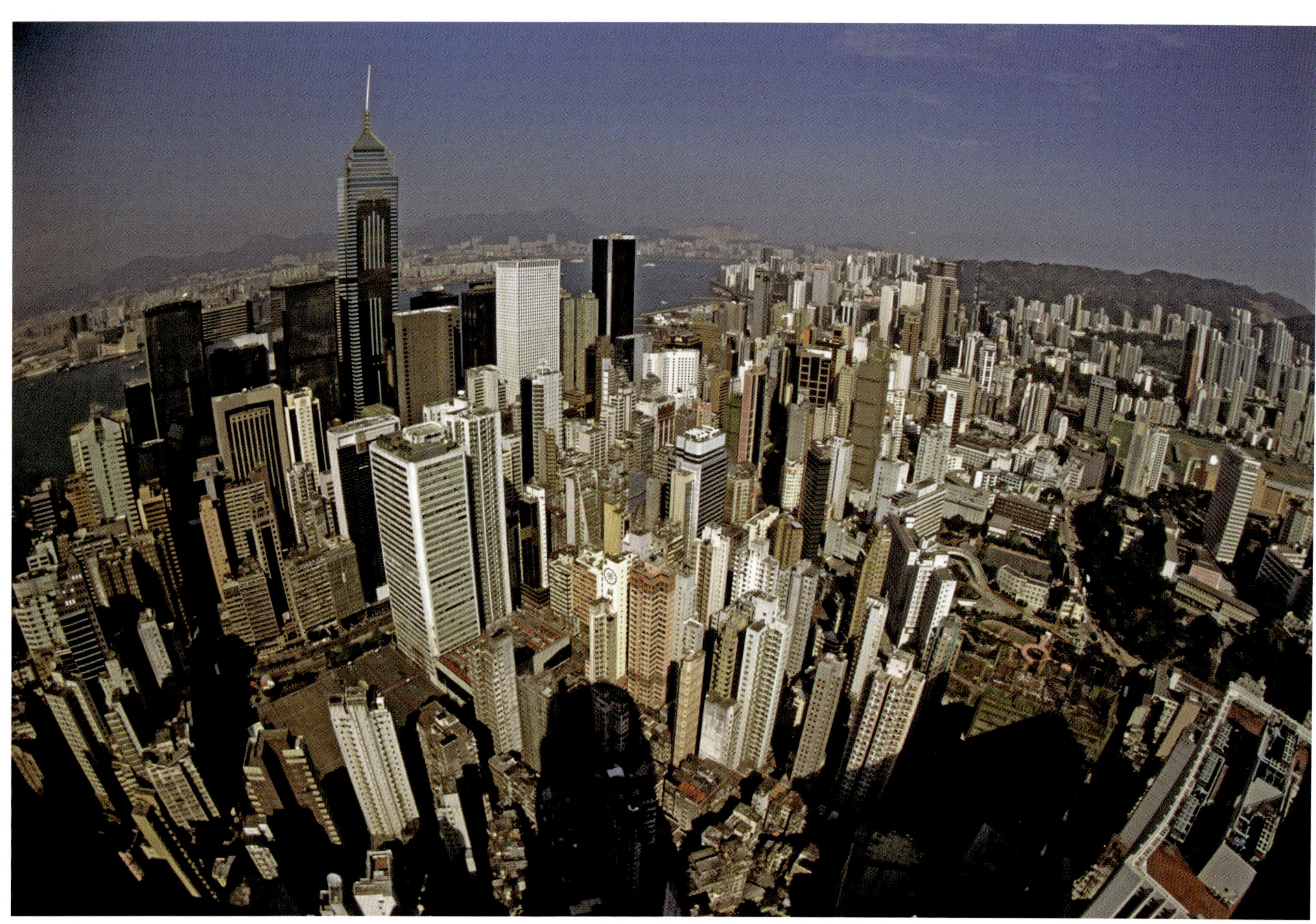

level. Architecture is best photographed from a high vantage point outside the architectural ensemble itself.

But this is all child's play compared to what awaits the photographer on a yacht in heavy seas if he decides to photograph it from the top of the mast. Of course, just as you can shoot a monastery from the ground or through the window of a tourist bus, you can photograph a yacht from her deck or mooring, without risking your neck – but if you are seriously trying to master the skills of the travel photographer, then you need to put yourself on a footing with the professionals. This means that if a specific subject can be photographed better from above than from anywhere else, then it should be photographed in exactly that way and no other. So your task is to come up with whatever you can – a ladder, the roof of a vehicle, a truck with a telescopic ladder, a crane, a tree, a telegraph pole, a roof, a pole with your camera stuck on the end, a hot-air balloon or a flying carpet – it will be a good exercise in ingenuity.

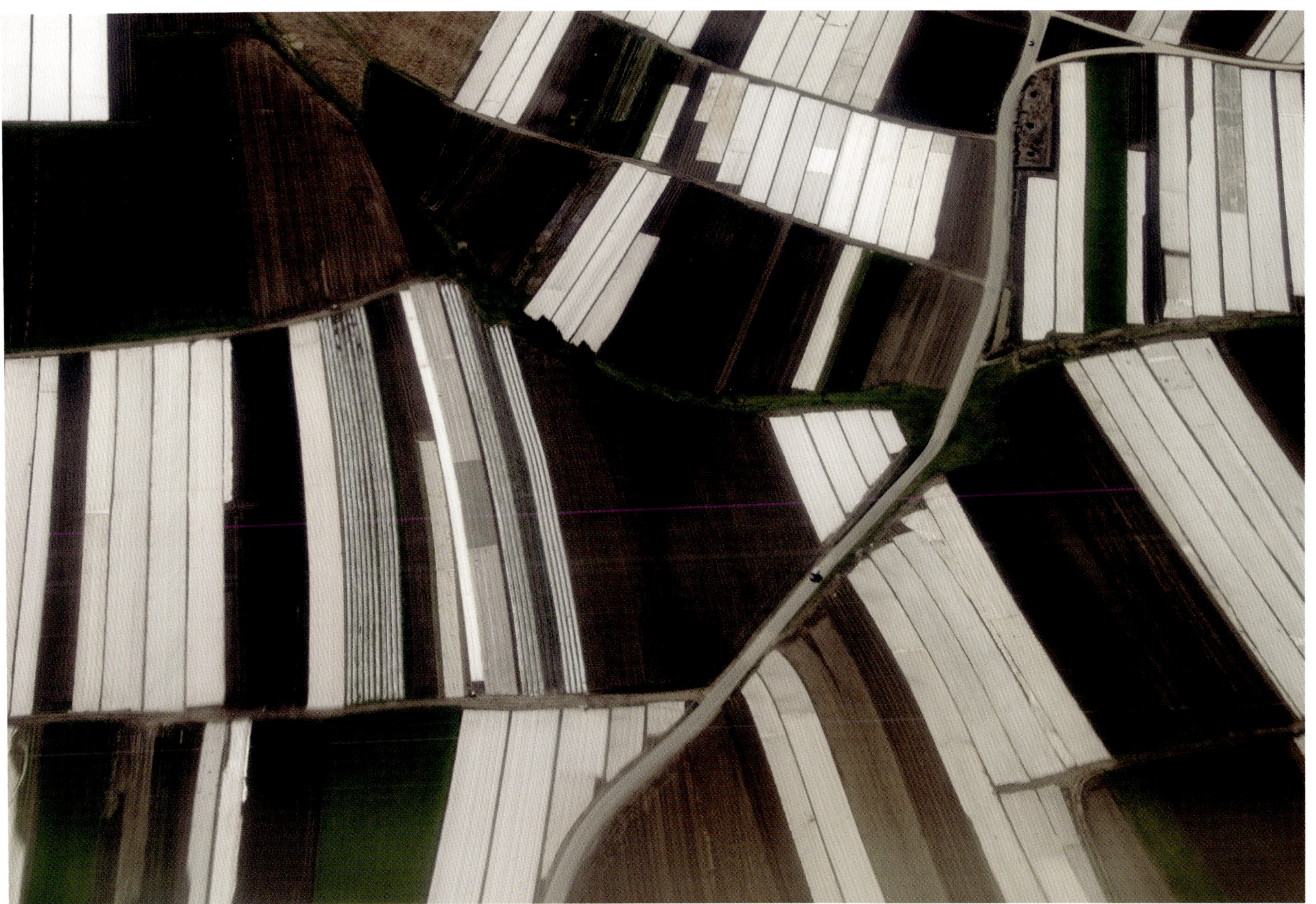

By the way, when it comes to going up in a hot air balloon, helicopter, aeroplane, light aircraft, delta paraglider or even making a parachute jump – no opportunity to take photographs from the air should ever be missed! Always try to command the strategic heights – both literally and metaphorically.

In many countries around the world, resorts and tourist sites have a well-run airborne armada of small pleasure or light aircraft available, as well as hot-air balloons, delta paragliders and parachutes, from which excellent photographs can be taken without any risk to life. The cost of these short excursions by air varies greatly (in Brazil, for example, they are fairly cheap). But even if this turns out to be expensive as a form of entertainment, you shouldn't turn it down if it means you could photograph the most beautiful atolls in the Indian Ocean or the almost inaccessible Angel Falls in Venezuela. So keep your camera at the ready and don't miss your chance. And for the time being, buy a compact camera with an articulating display, so that you can hold it above your head and take photographs over the crowd – or get hold of that little two-step ladder. It will come in handy...

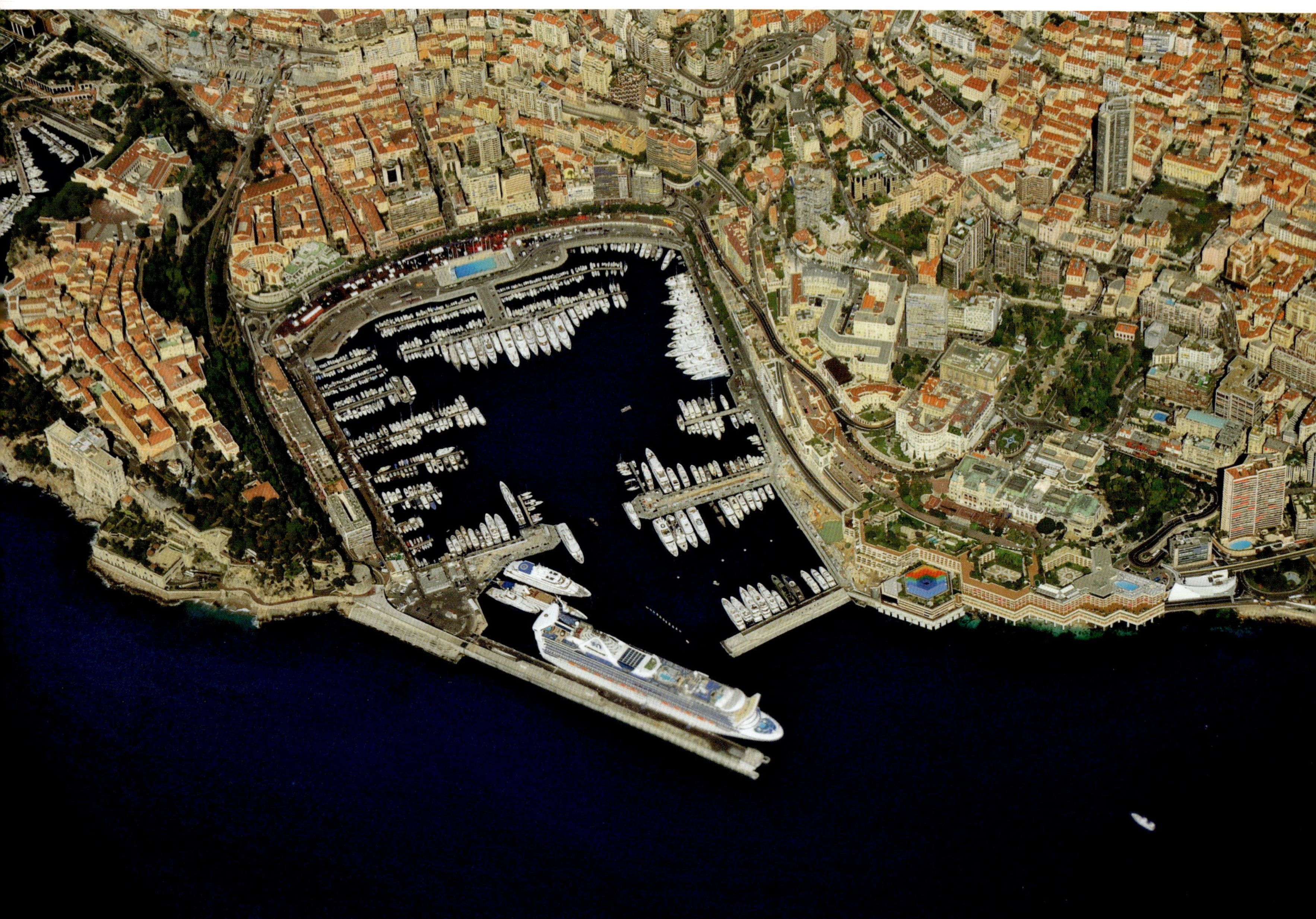

On the approach to its landing at Nice airport, the aircraft flies over Monte Carlo, the capital of Monaco, giving a good view of the playground of the millionaires and the international beau monde, the world-famous casino, the palace of the Grimaldi princes and the harbour with its very expensive yachts.

A ship in a narrow section of the Geirangerfjord. Norway. A shot taken from a height of 300 metres clearly reveals the scale, grandeur and beauty of this natural phenomenon.

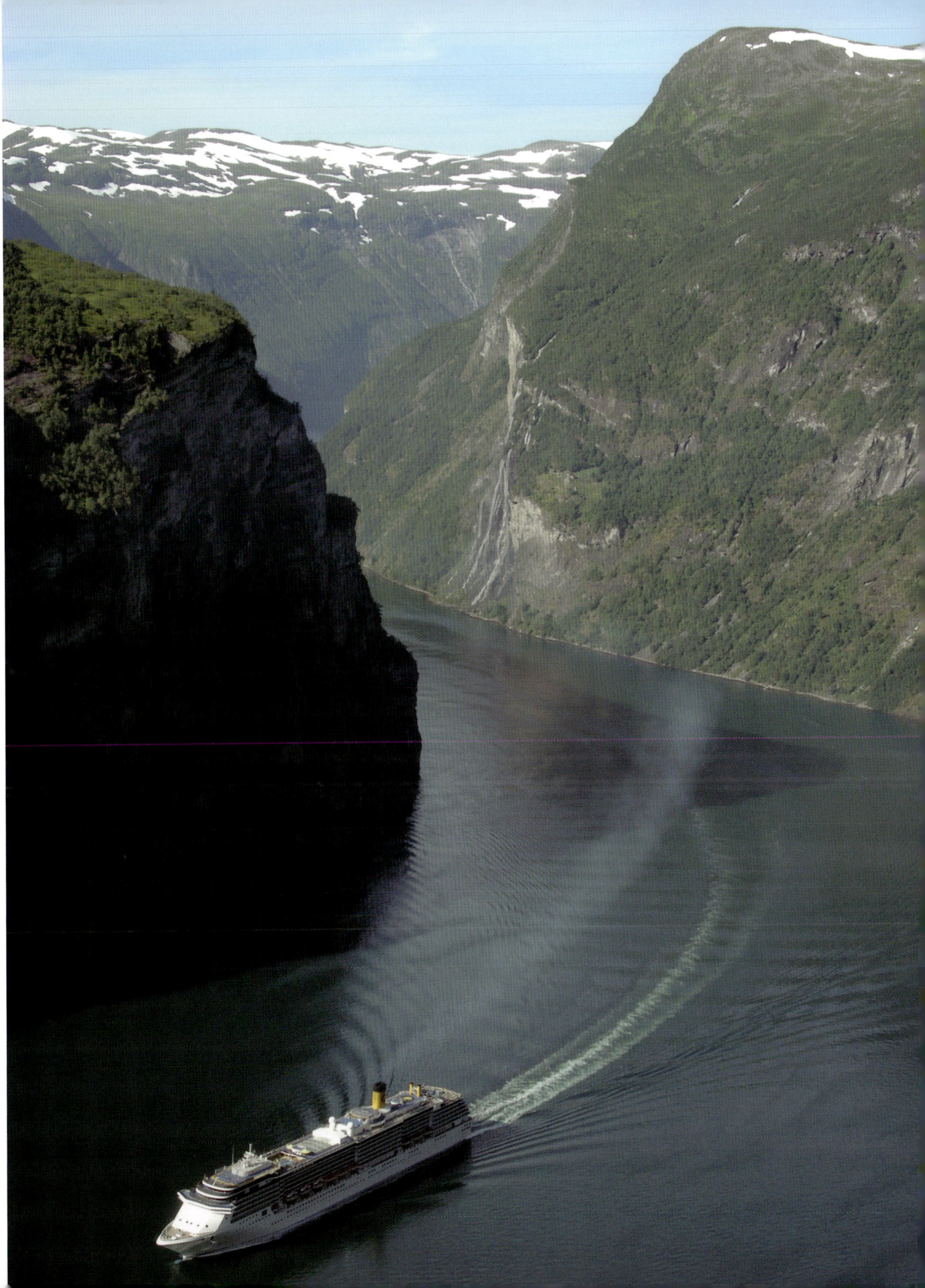

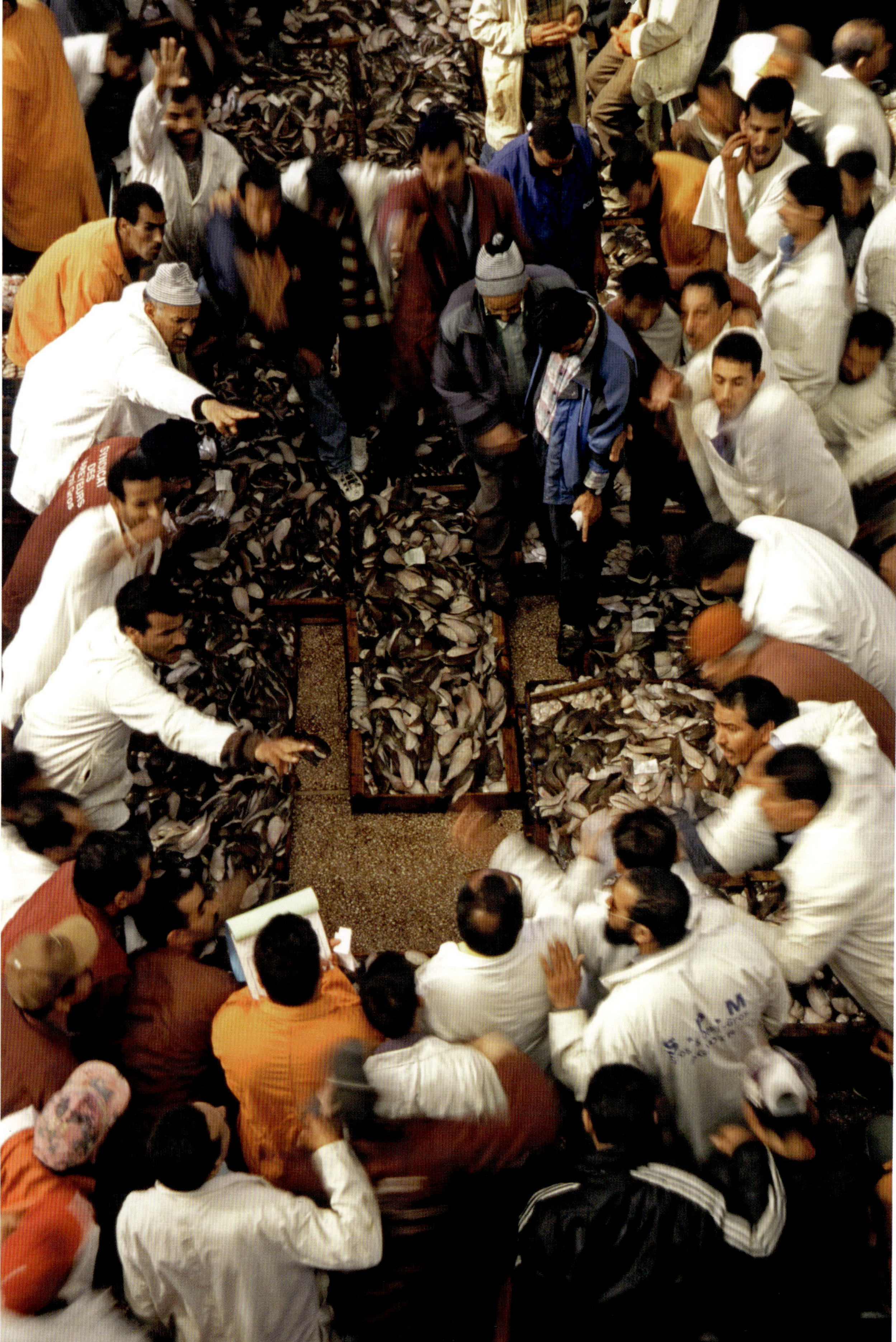

A fishy stock exchange in Agadir (Morocco). The huge shed is overflowing with fresh fish, and also with traders – purchasers in white djellabas and brokers in orange dressing-gowns. Moving from one pile of fish to another, all this noisy crowd is animatedly gesticulating, exclaiming and chatting. The excitement and the hullabaloo all around remind you of the New York Stock Exchange.

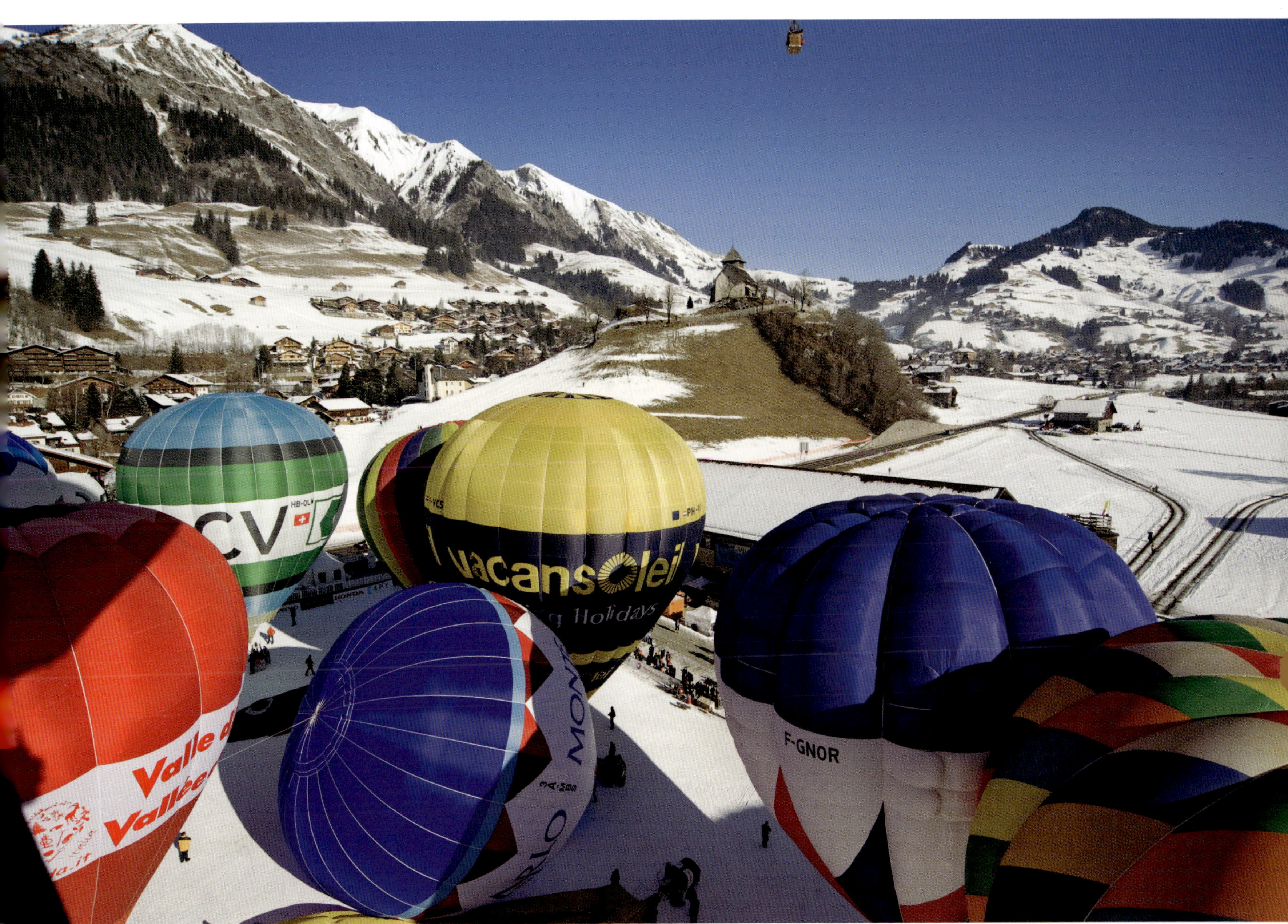

2008. The Swiss resort of Chateau d'Oex. The biggest Winter balloon festival in the world. Taken from the basket of the 'Allied Nippon' balloon, piloted by one of the best Russian balloonists, Sergei Grishini.

Playing with reflections

Among many peoples of the world a mirror is thought to have magical attributes and is a tool of enchantment or clairvoyance in fairytales and myths. A reflected image does indeed harbour a miracle of transformation and a photograph containing a reflection can be both a mirror to the soul and a soul for the mirror.

When you are travelling, reflections are to be found everywhere, so it is important to learn how to observe them as attractive subjects for photographs. An architectural ensemble, whether it is a Chinese palace or an Italian *palazzo*, is always reflected to advantage in a still, smooth surface of water. Sometimes an effective shot can be achieved with an undulating reflection on the surface of a lake or river, while the subject itself remains outside the frame. Classic examples of reflections – sunrises and sunsets over the sea, a path of moonlight – are fairly banal in themselves so they need something in the foreground of the frame to liven up the whole picture (for example boats). Or else you need some additional effects. Snow-covered rocks or mountains that look as if they have tumbled into a mountain lake can be very good. You might even copy in a red canoe reflected in the water.

If there is no sea or lake, it's not a calamity, because the less water there is, the more interesting the result can be. A staggeringly beautiful and expressive photograph of this type appeared many years ago in an illustrated magazine: an oil worker, his face smeared with oil, cupping a handful of black liquid in which a derrick is reflected. A pool, or even just the damp asphalt, immediately after rain can be an excellent mirror. Find the focus of the shot where your cathedral, or some part of it, is reflected in a puddle and take your photograph using a wide angle lens, kneeling down and leaning towards the puddle.

Even if the barometer needle has been pointing to 'Very Dry' for ages, look carefully around you and you will see just how many potentially reflective surfaces there are. The plate-glass windows of modern buildings, in which reflections of surrounding older houses are repeated many times; shop windows, vehicle windscreens and wing mirrors, motorcyclists' or skiers' protective goggles and helmets, the dark glasses of sunbathers on the beach – with some imagination, the photographer can make use of all these. And of course, don't forget ordinary indoor mirrors – for example, in a boutique where a lady is trying on a hat. You can also take an effective self-portrait in a mirror in some kind of exotic surrounding.

There are not usually any technical difficulties taking photographs of reflective surfaces: a modern light metering system corrects the shot effortlessly – as long as the surfaces concerned are not too bright or too dark. Here the usual rule of exposure compensation comes into force: light – increase the exposure, dark – decrease it. But photographs of sunsets showing a path of sunlight on water allow a significant range of values – for example, a third-stop setting in the aperture diameter on either side of the optimal one. In short, you must find a 'theory of reflection' in your own photographic practice!

The reflection of the Nikitski monastery in Pereslavl-Zalesski in a car's rear view mirror.

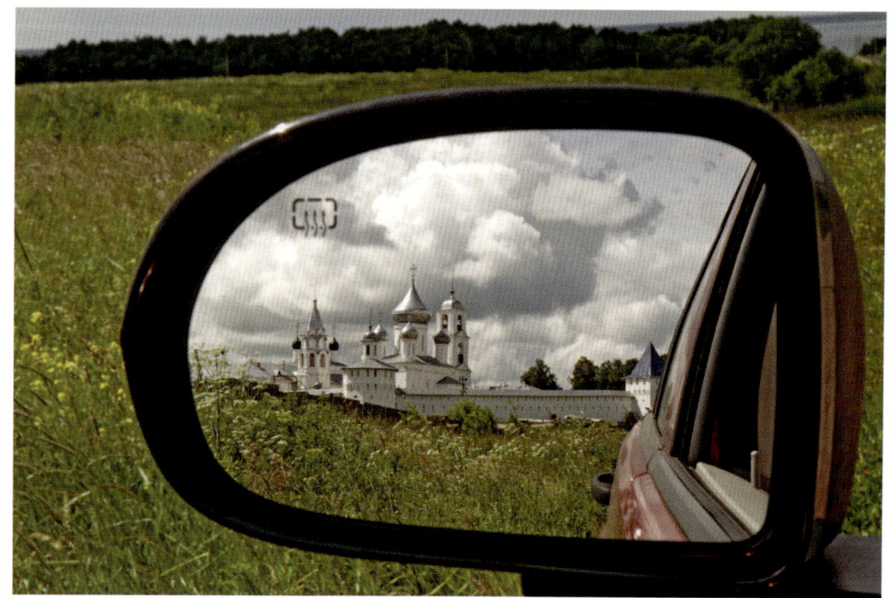

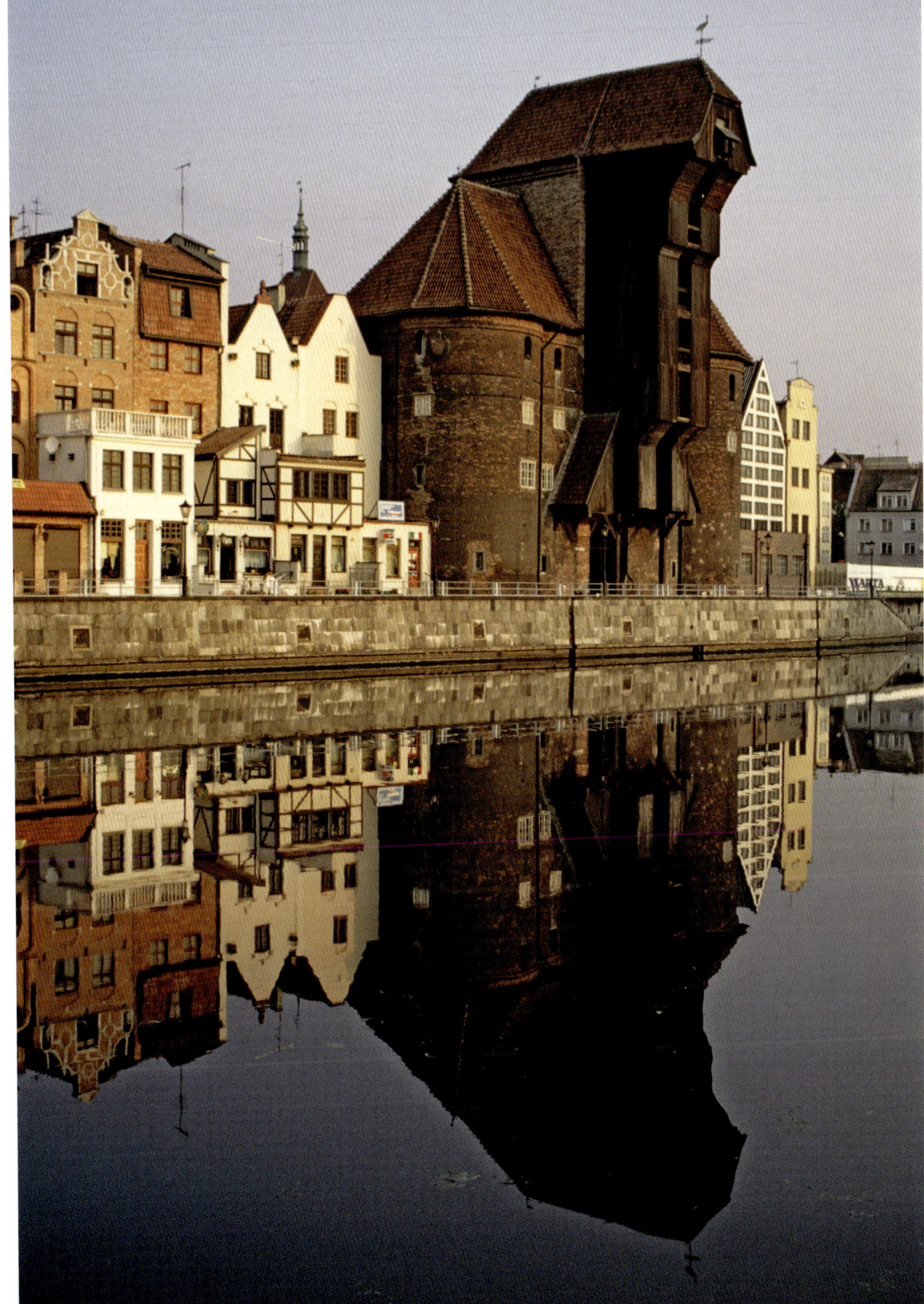

The medieval wooden 'stork' at Gdansk, in Poland, erected in the midfifteenth century after a fire. It was used to load cargoes onto ships, and also to instal masts. Nowadays, it's the Gdansk Maritime Museum.

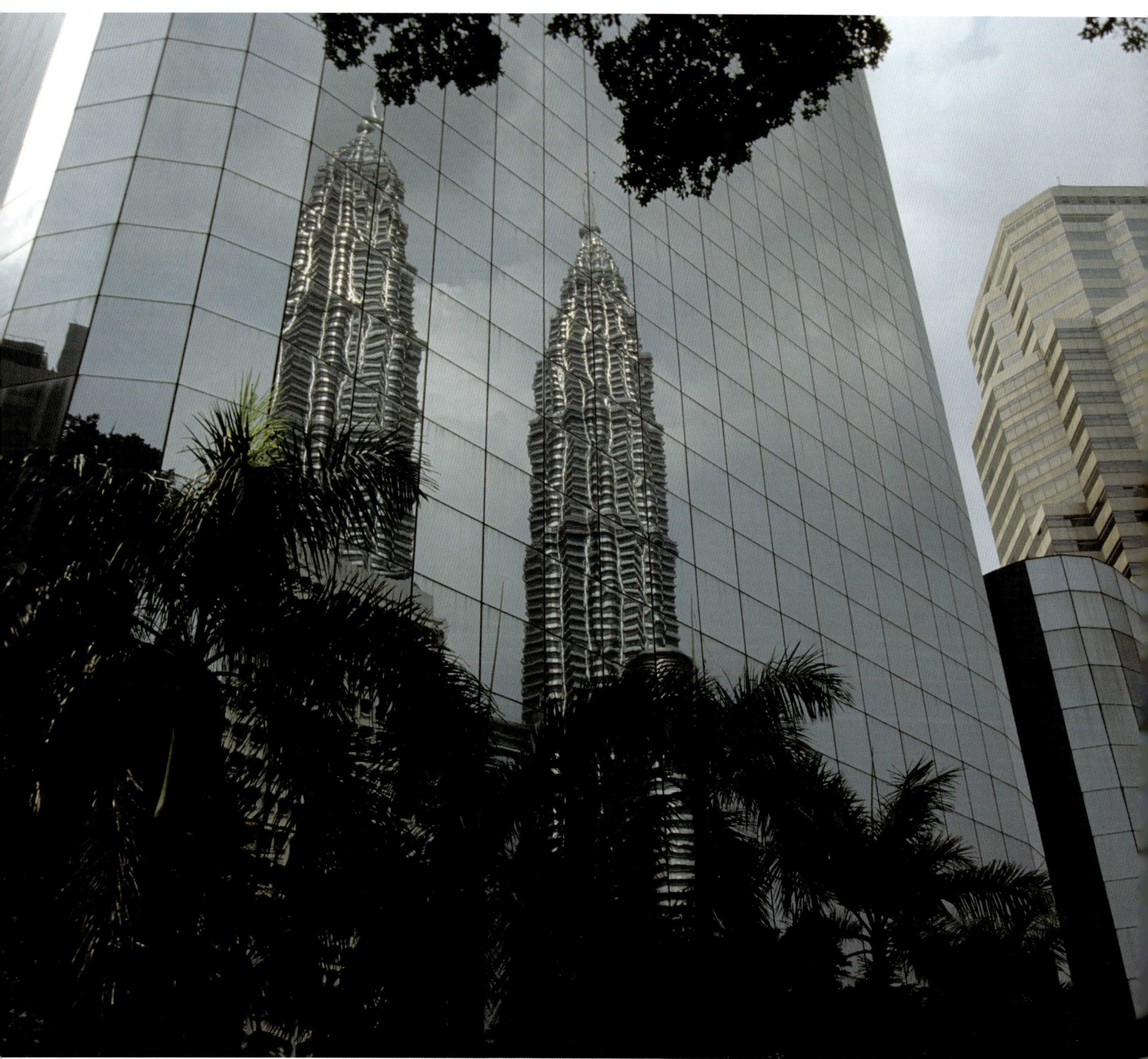

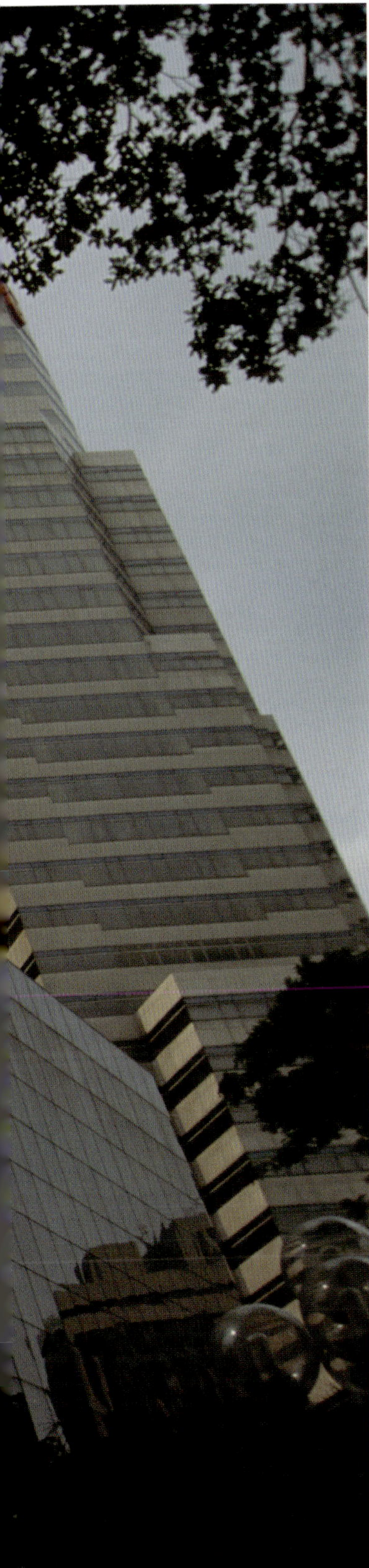

Kuala Lumpur, capital of Malaysia. A reflection of the 110-storey Petronas Twin Towers – until recently, the tallest buildings in the world (452 m).

The centre of Venice. In the mirror-like facades of the modern Haas Haus building are reflected the architectural details of the surrounding structures put up in the olden days. Taken from a distance using a telephoto lens, so as not to 'muck up' the vertical lines.

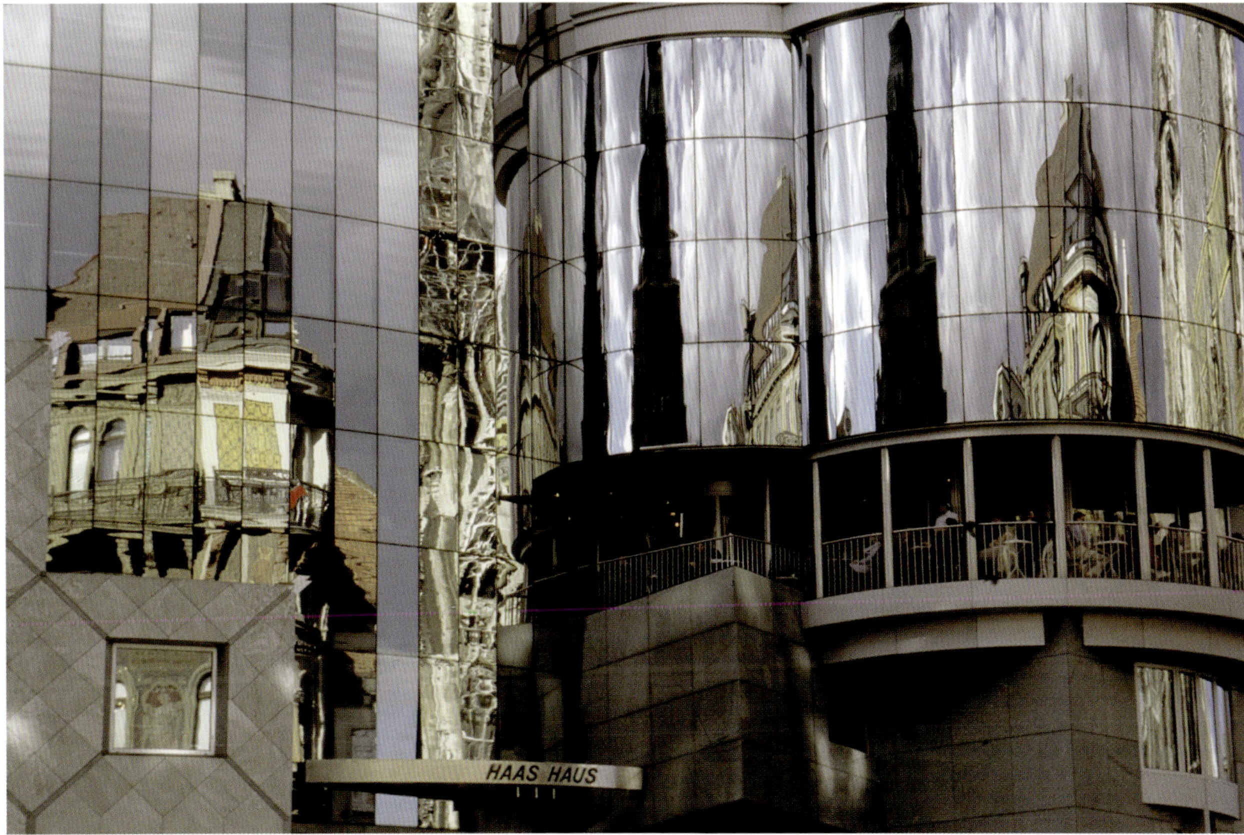

A reflection in water may appear to float in the air like a phantom, with no sign of the material which originally carried the image, as with this shot of old-fashioned wooden houses on log piles in the Norwegian town of Trondheim.

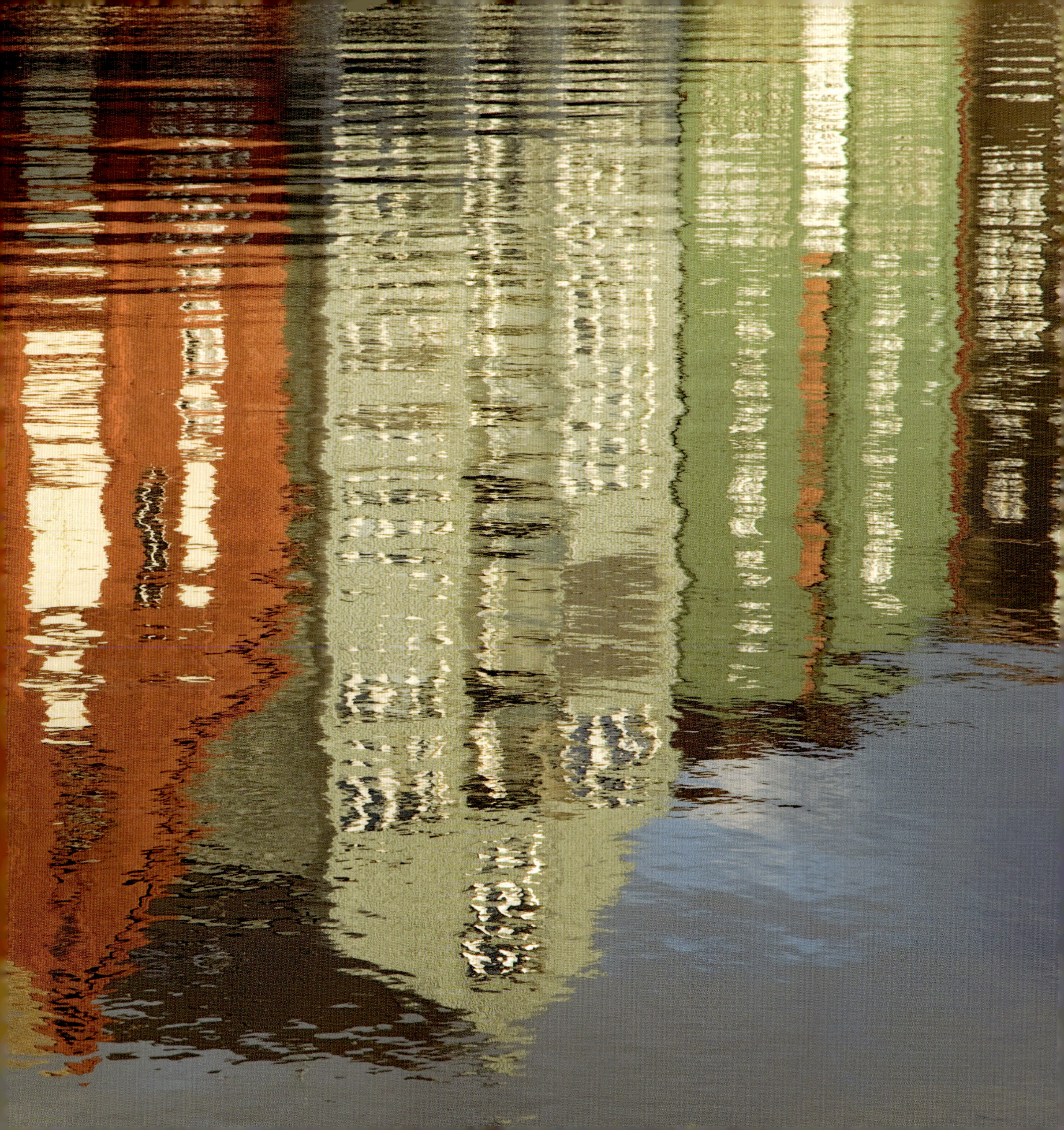

Down shady avenues...

In its essence, its physical nature and its magic, the shadow –
the doppelganger – is similar to the reflected image. It existed
in an incorporeal state until the light touch of the storyteller
Hans Christian Andersen gave it flesh and blood as an immortal
character in his story 'The Shadow'. This phenomenon is also
well known in travel photography: on our stage, a shadow is
capable of taking not just a minor role but one that is equal to
the leading characters – and even, strange as it may seem, of
leaving them in the shade!

One memorable picture, which turned the graphic
possibilities of shadow to masterly advantage, was taken from
an aircraft flying over a camel caravan – the dotted line of the
caravan, barely legible in the perpendicular projection, and the
huge shadows cast by the low rays of the setting sun were
like long-legged animals lying on the sand among the dunes...
It was mesmerising.

We have already mentioned, when talking about composition, the importance of balancing the frame, its solidity and
its spatial qualities, when the distance to the main subjects
is evident from just a few details. So a good shadow with
recognisable contours is an excellent tool for all this. In some
senses, it is even better than reflected surfaces, which are
always arranged strictly along the vertical of the frame,
whereas the direction and angle of a shadow depend on the
angle of the shot and are under the photographer's control.
You can position an effective shadow right across the shot
from one corner to the other! Obviously, when the sun is at
its highest point in the sky, there is not much you can do with
shadow; but the lower the sun, the more opportunities there
are to give your imagination free rein. Shadow can also be
serious hindrance. Shooting with the sun directly behind you
during the hour before sunset, you will cast a characteristic
shadow, several metres in length, onto the subject of the
photograph – and this, as a rule, spoils the shot. If you have
nowhere to hide, then the only thing that can rescue you is
the Photoshop brush.

Shadow can work well in travel photography if you use
the 'shadow puppet theatre' effect, with your subject in deep
shade but silhouetted sharply against a light background.
This technique works very well in places where national
dress, head-dresses or hairstyles, facial profiles or musical
instruments have distinct silhouettes with an unmistakably
ethnographic flavour. Like, for example, inhabitants of the
Peruvian cordilleras or lamas in Tibet and the Himalayas.
Oh – and you will simply never confuse the shape of a yak
with that of a cow. You can introduce an interesting play of
light and shade into your picture if the light is passing through
a latticework awning, a wicker hurdle or other light 'sieve'.

Morning in the Alpine resort of
Avoriaz (France). A backlit picture
– the solid-looking shadows and the
clearly outlined relief of the snow
make for a graphic photo.

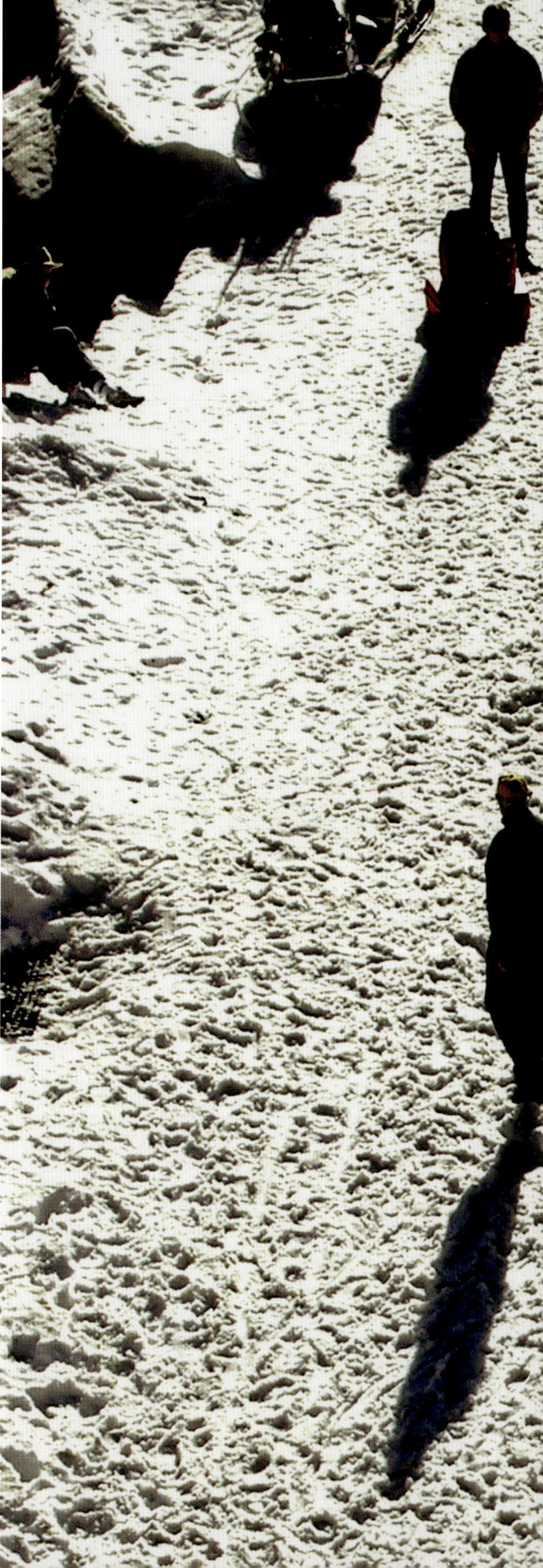

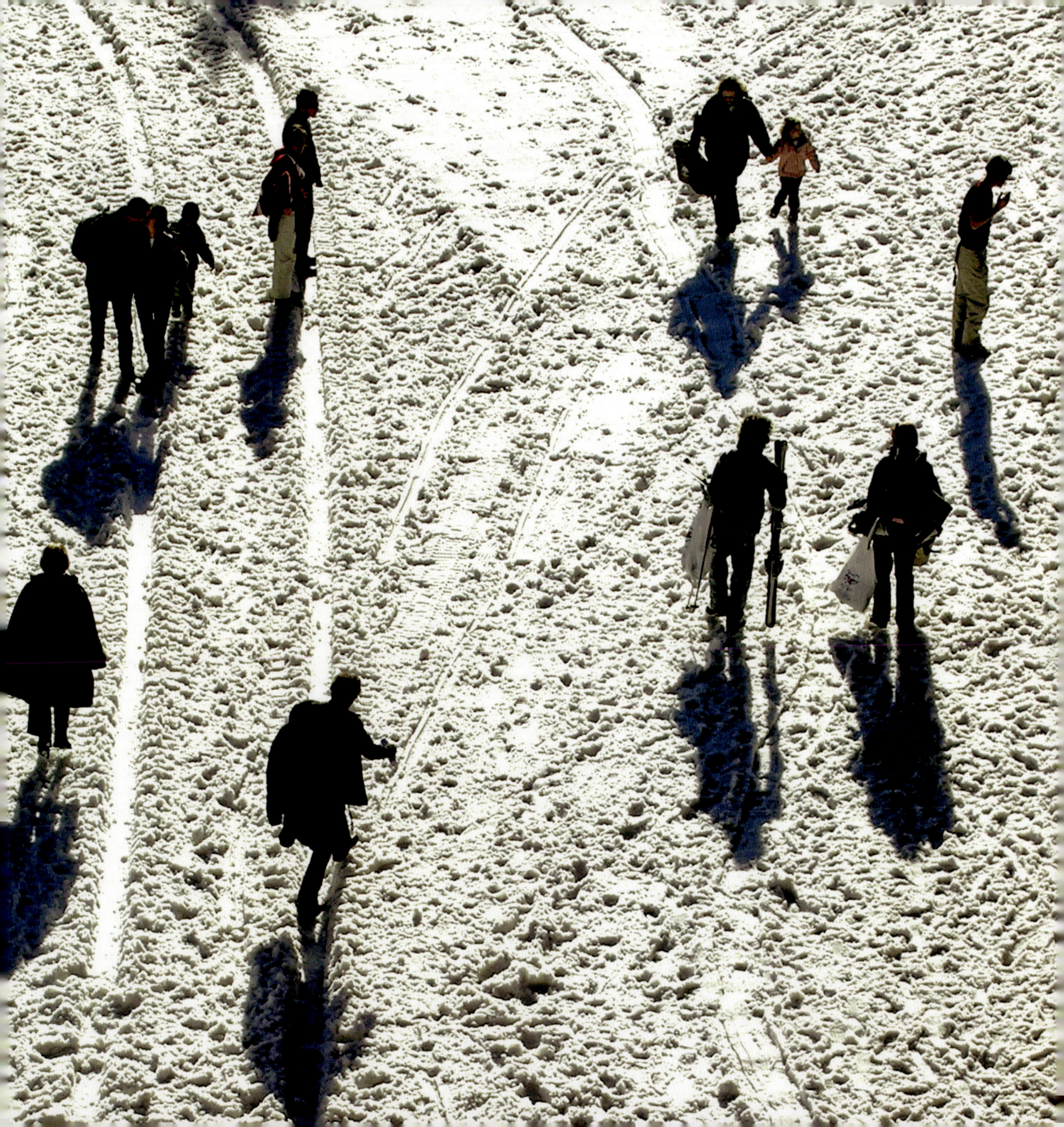

Journey across the Sinai Desert. Of all the imaginable types of transport that a travel photographer has to use, the camel is the most uncomfortable and unpredictable. But just look at the shadows it casts!

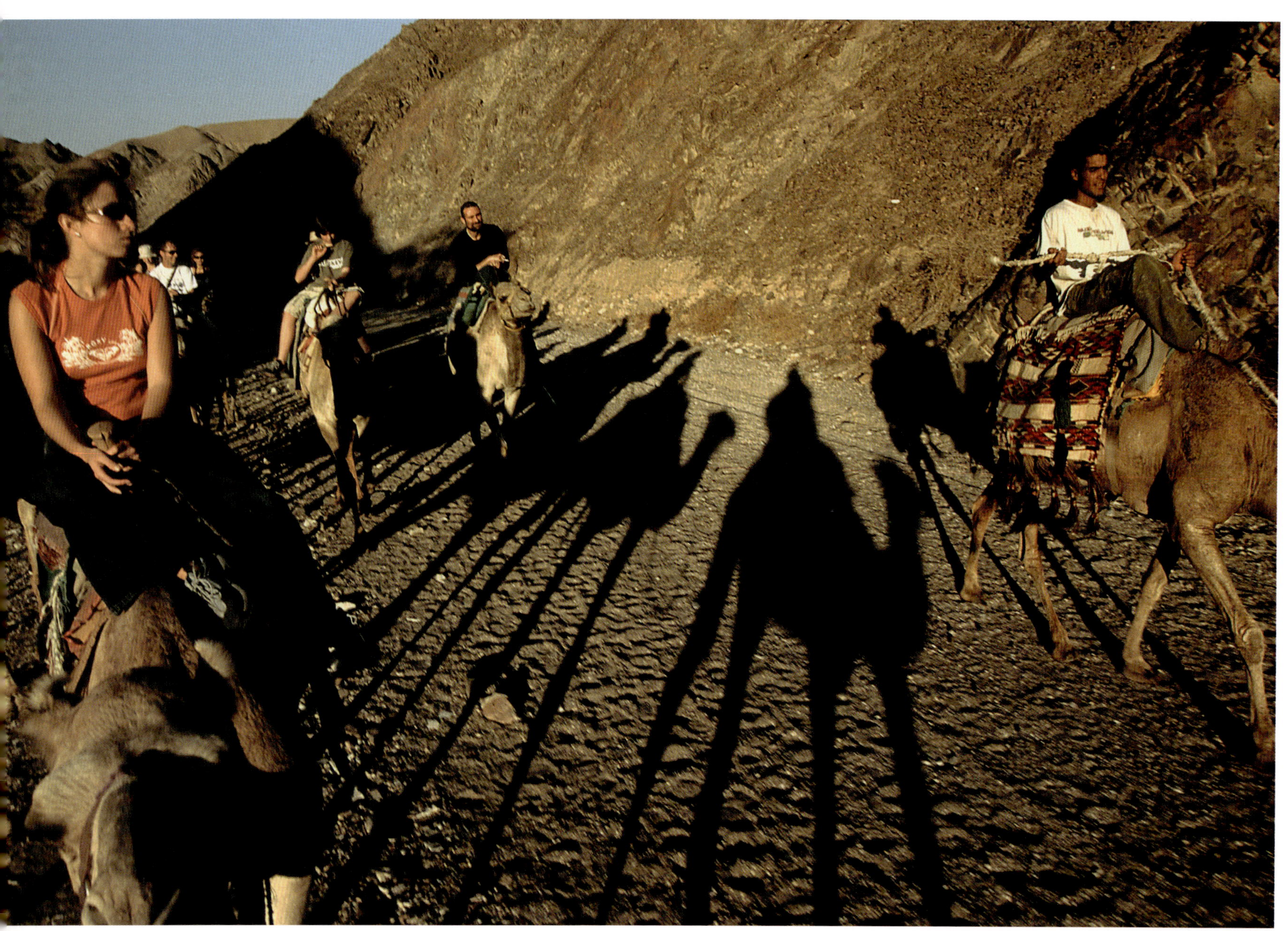

The most beautiful and famous of
the palaces in the Moroccan town of
Ouarzazate. These mediaeval citadel
palaces, which in Morocco are built
of clay, are called kasbah. The play
of shadows simply highlights their
distinctive architecture.

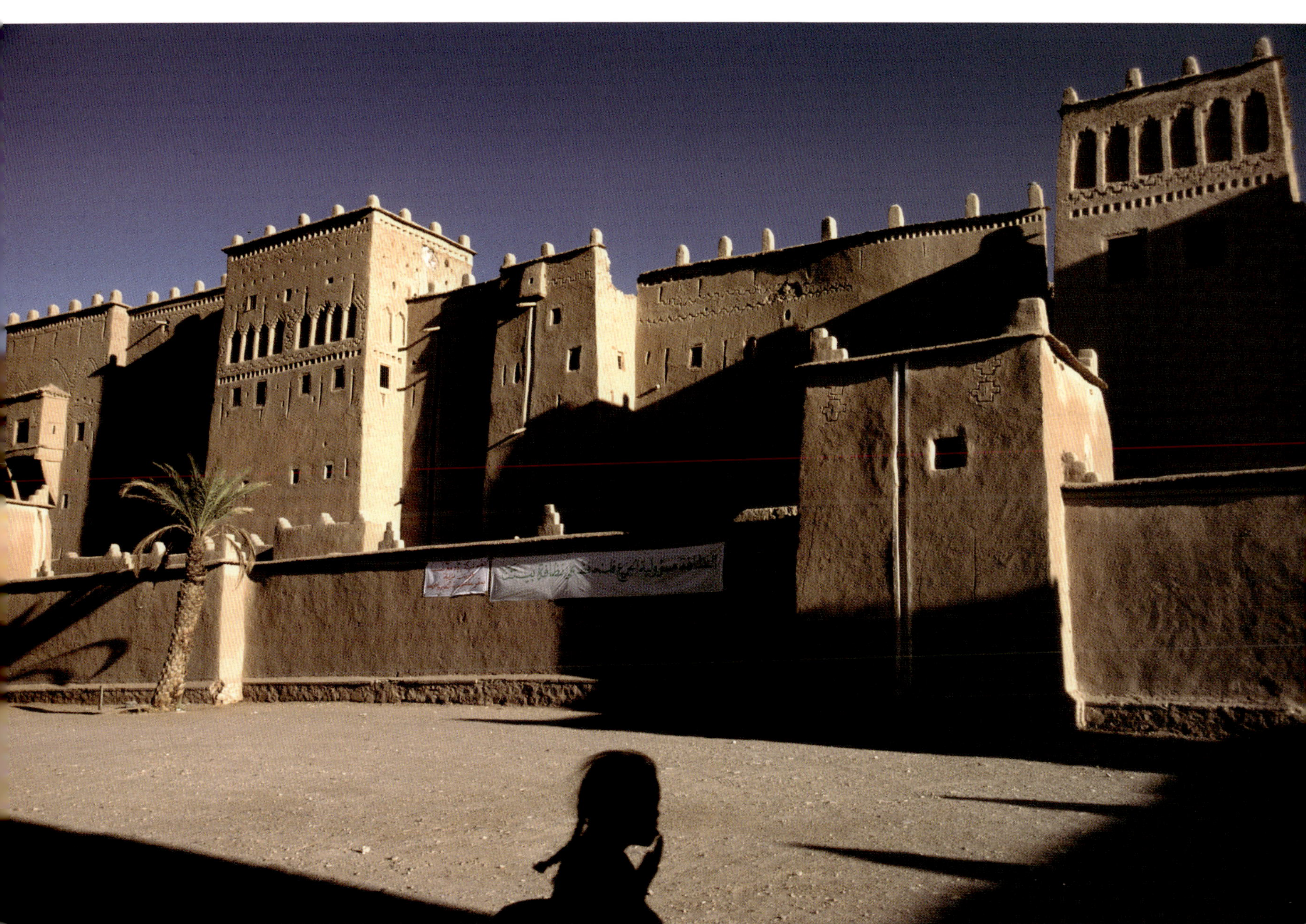

Are you still a prisoner?

Yet again we must revisit composition, but now alongside the topic of shade. Happy and liberated, you have arrived at last, after years of waiting and hard work, on the beautiful island of your dreams. You bask on the sand or the warm shingle, while not far from the shore snowy white yachts bob out in the bay, just ready to sail. Is there anything that wouldn't make a great subject for your photograph? You even remember all the advice: stand a little way in front of the prow of the vessel rather than at the stern, for example. If you take a beautiful picture from the coastline you will get a banal, boring shot – for which you didn't need to fly to the Balearic Islands or Mauritius, but could simply have made a trip to your nearest reservoir.

It is essential – or, to be more precise, desirable – that the basic motivation for taking the photograph should be to reveal the main characteristics of the subject. To photograph the same yacht that you have seen with sails drooping at half-mast, you need some kind of special circumstances: usually, she should be flying across the waves – better still, taking part in a regatta, heeling over hard. After all, that's what she's designed for. Or, if you are looking at a tourist excursion boat, your attention as a photographer should focus on what it would be like to take a trip on her. Of course, a yacht is a special world with its own language of signs and consequently can provide you with a lot of different 'motivations'. There is a whole cult associated with the well-known process of polishing the decks and shining up the sparkling brass or bronze. Even the anchor chain housing or the deckhouse bell, engraved with an anchor and the name of the vessel, could provide a legitimate individual subject.

But what kind of special circumstances might allow you to photograph a yacht without sails? Go up onto one of the high cliffs that frame the bay. A photograph taken from there will reveal an intimate, exclusive space, showing a sweet little bay with blue water and golden sand, with the crew of the yacht relaxing on the beach. The other approach would be to stroll

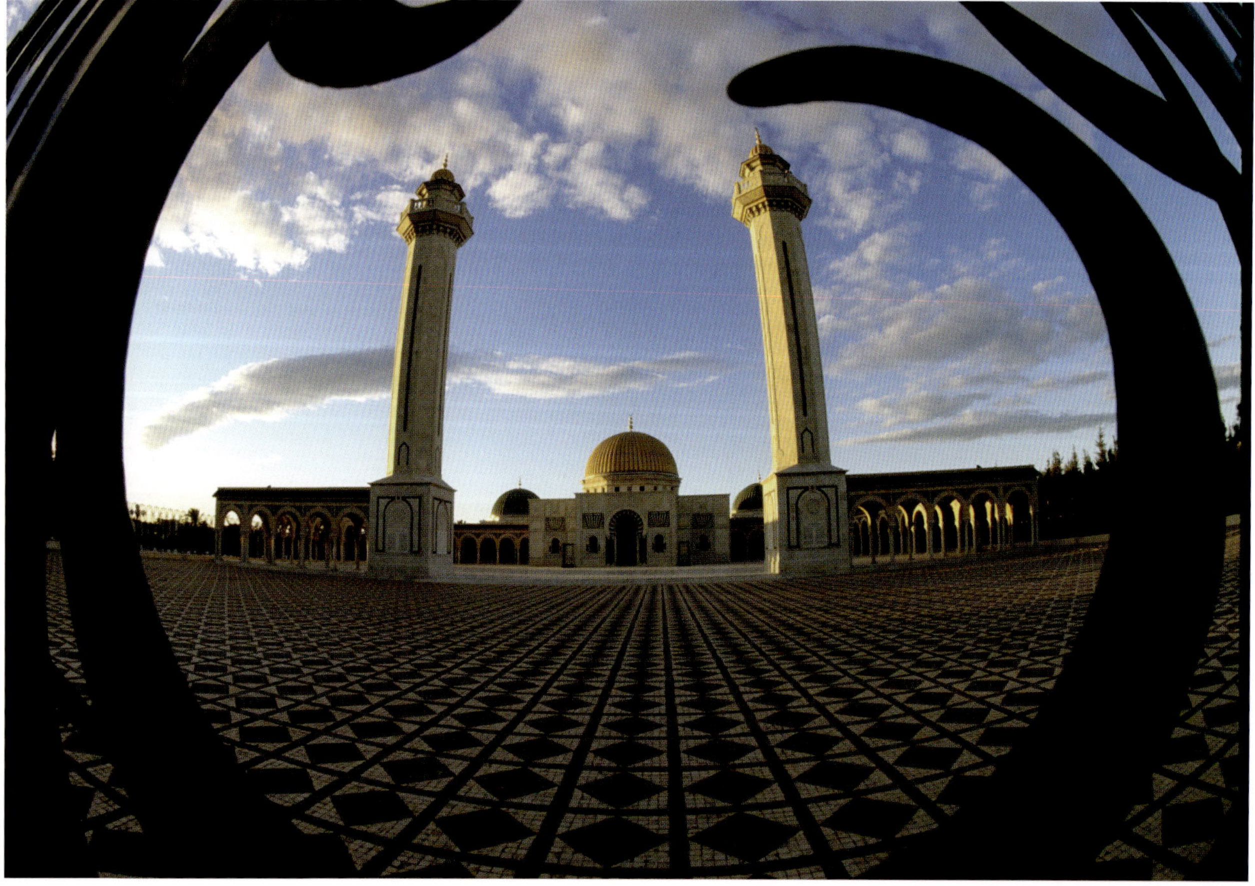

Tunis. Monastir. The mausoleum of the Bourgiba family, where the first president of the country, Habib Bourguiba, was laid to rest. Taken with a fisheye lens, framed by the pattern of a wrought metalwork fence.

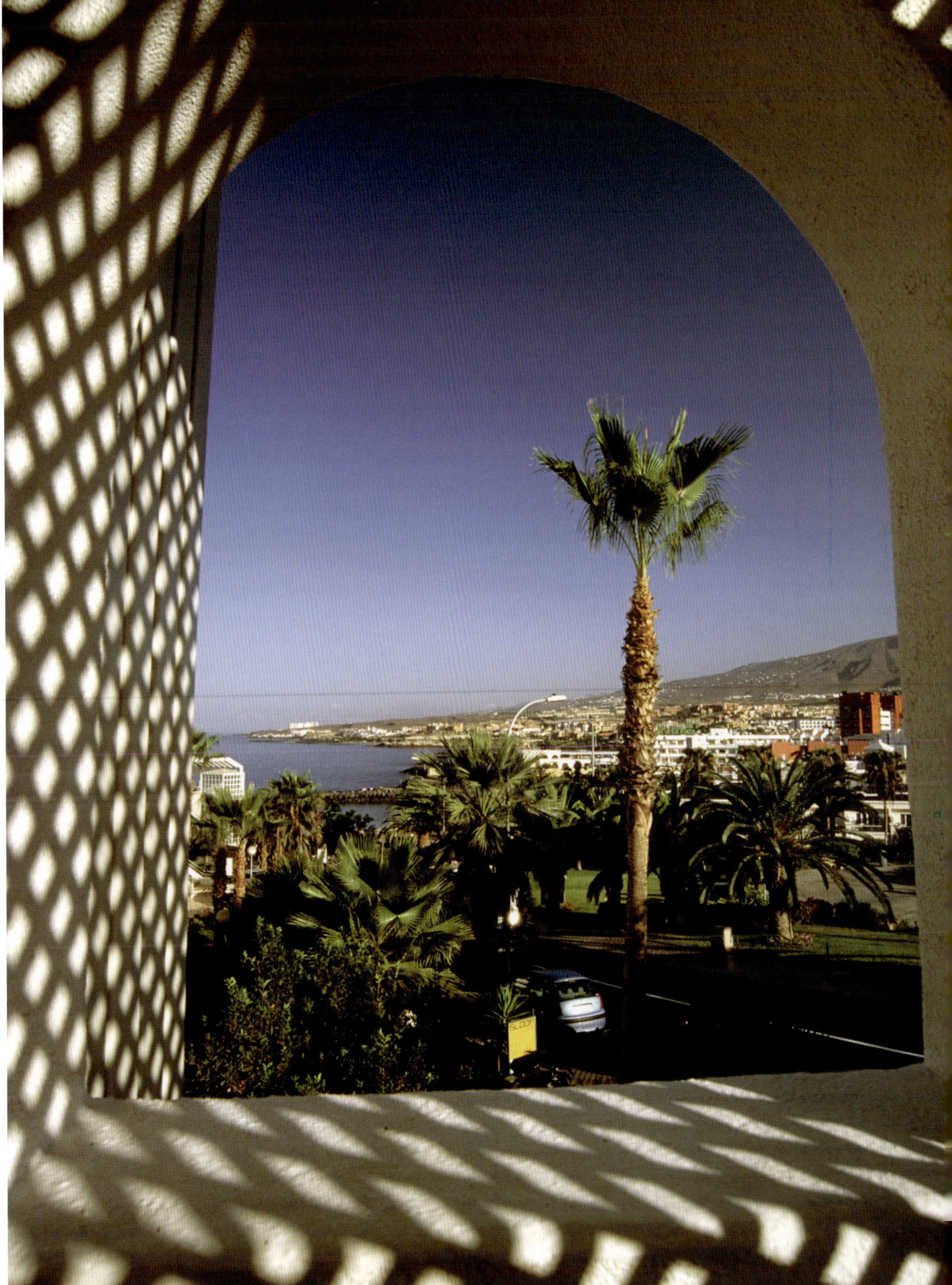

The holiday island of Tenerife, Canary Islands, Spain. Naturally, this arched embrasure framing the resort of Los Americas was not chosen at random. What 'makes' this picture is essentially not the simple plaster arch, but the play of light on it – the beautiful mosaic of light and shade.

A highly unusual effect has been
achieved in this photograph taken in
a temple in Firozabad City, located
an hour's drive from Agra with its
famous Taj Mahal, India. Although
the legendary mausoleum is primarily
magnificent as an example of
architecture, this Firozabad temple
is a masterpiece of decoration in
particular. From outside, it looks like
a precious carved ivory casket, while
from within, through its delicate
walls, the yard and the people walking
about can be seen as if through a lace
curtain. So that is how these pictures
were achieved – through a marble
'filter'.

round the tiny bay with its many yachts, which the island of
Majorca has in profusion, find a cave, opening or crack in the
rocks, through which just one boat can be seen, along with
that crew sunbathing on the beach, and frame your shot. By
giving your shot this dark uneven framing, you add a little
bit of mystery to the intimacy of the bay in the first version.

'Mounting' a photograph like this frequently rescues
it, and you can use it in the simplest situations – such as
photographing an architectural ensemble from underneath
an ordinary arch or even through a window. A 'frame' is
especially useful when you want to half cover an unremarkable
sky. Examples of the photographer having recourse to this
simple device can often be found in illustrated books on old
architecture. And not just for decorative purposes. It often
adds more information to the shot, giving a bigger picture
of the subject of the photograph. Thus, that masterpiece of
Hispano-Islamic architecture, the Alhambra Palace in Granada,
is much more interesting seen through a narrow embrasure in a
two-metre-thick stone wall. It immediately becomes clear that
in fact this delicate, refined carved palace is also a
mighty fortress.

I took a photo with a quite unusual effect in a Hindu
temple in the city of Firozabad, which is within an hour's
journey of Agra and its famous Taj Mahal. But if the
legendary mausoleum is outstanding, above all, because of its
architectural state, then the Firozabad temple is a particularly
decorative masterpiece. From the outside, it resembles a
precious carved casket made from ivory. Once you go inside,
however, you suddenly realise that, through open-work walls,
you're looking at a courtyard with people going by, as if seen
through lace. That's how I photographed them – through a
marble 'filter'.

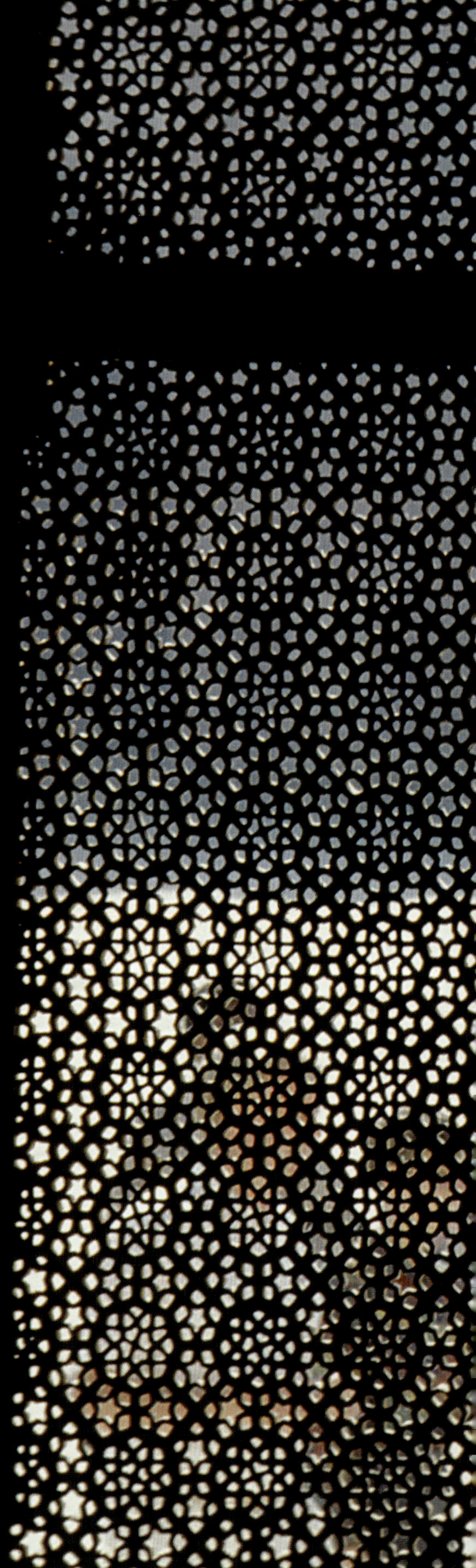

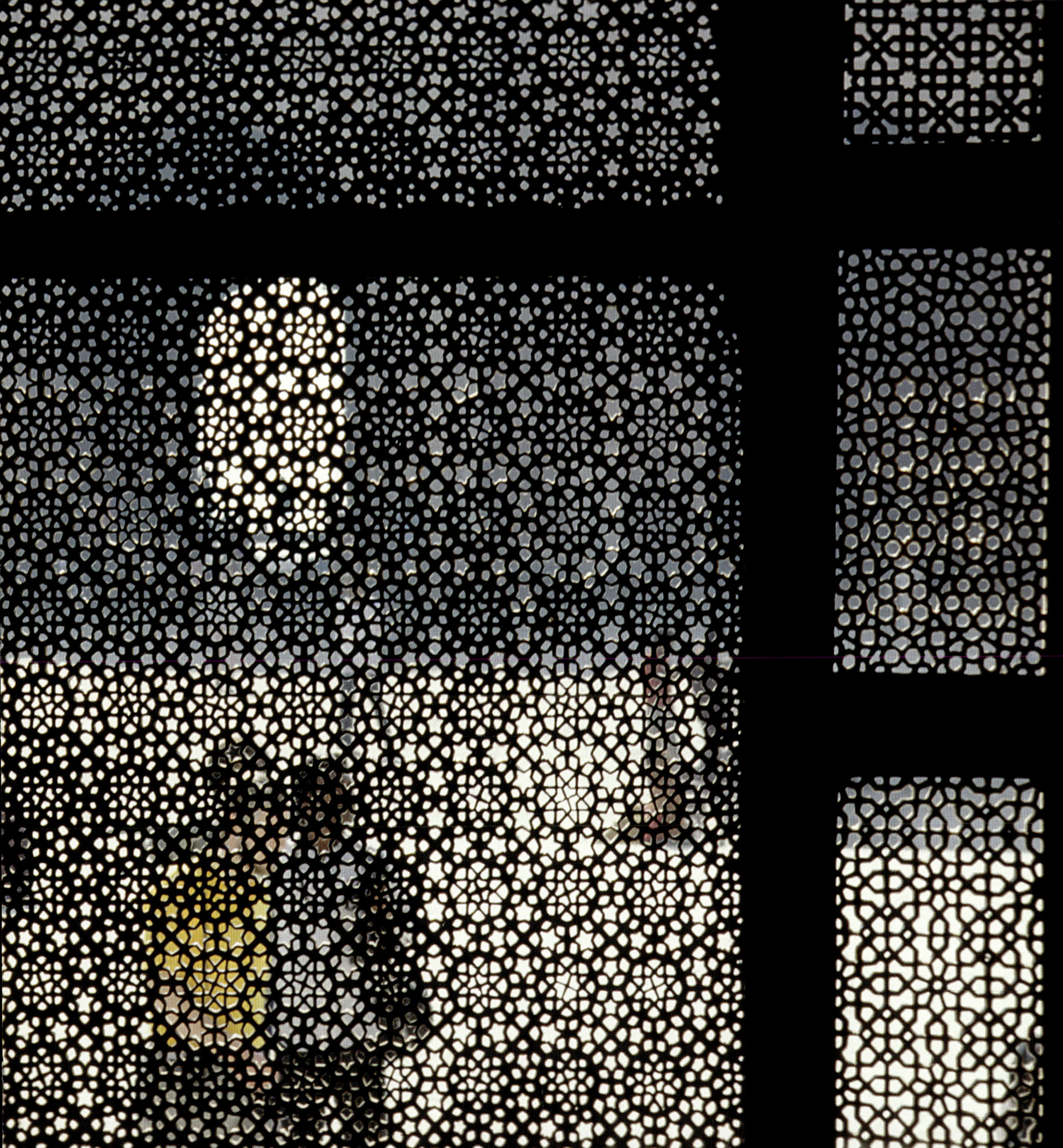

In the ancient city of Petra, the only
path leads through a narrow gorge –
or rather, a crack in the mighty rocks.
Jordan. Without the camels and the
human figure in the foreground, the
picture would have lost a great deal.

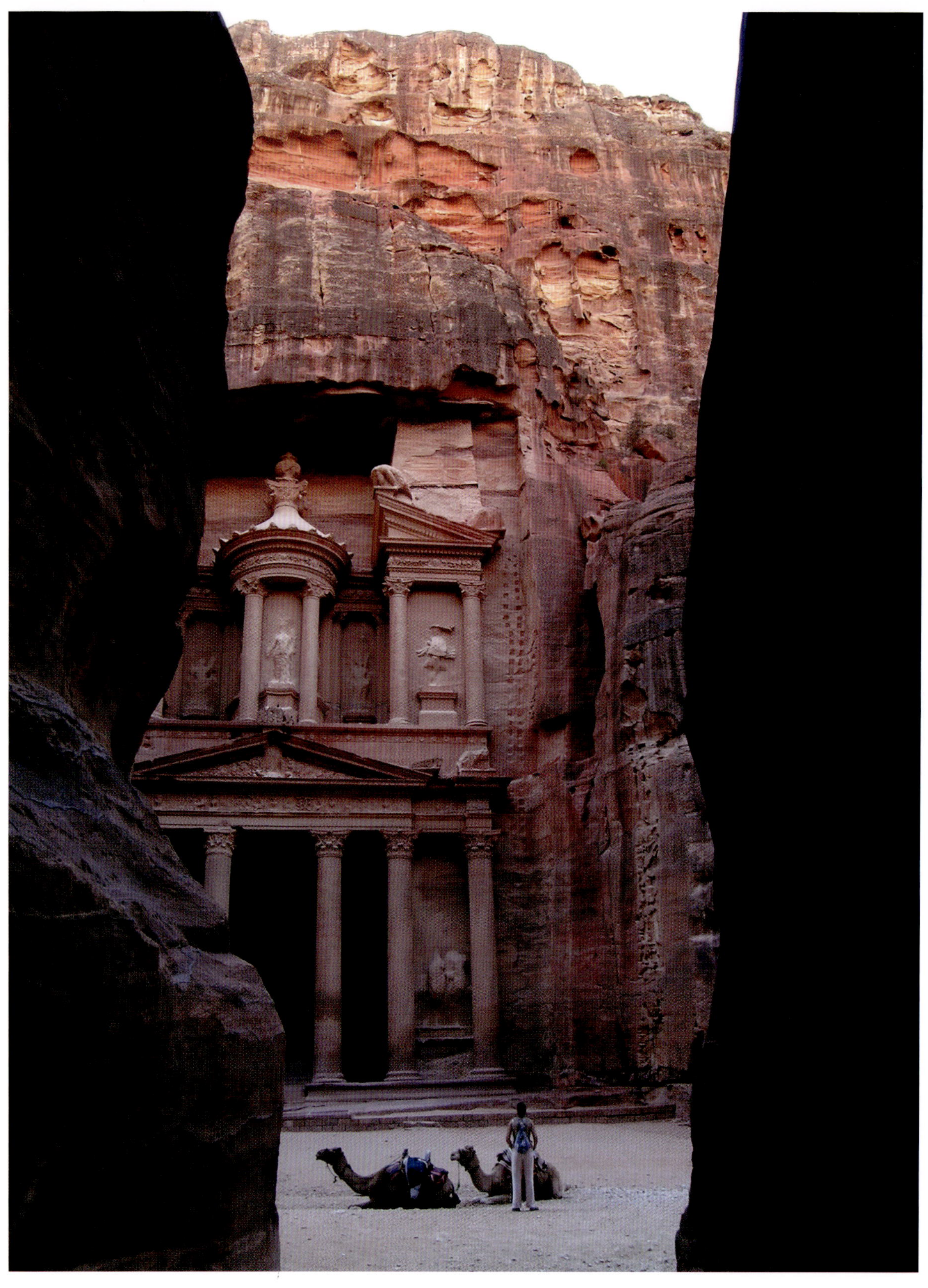

Spain. The palatial fortress of the Alhambra. The deep shadows in the niche can scarcely be made lighter by Photoshop. When taking a photo through an arch, be careful not to outline its shape or to bring out the acute angle of the archway at the bottom, lit by the sunlight.

Jordan. The biggest of the crusader castles, Kerak, built on a high cliff – a labyrinth of towers, galleries and secret passages. Taken from a deep niche, using flash at the 'fill in' setting.

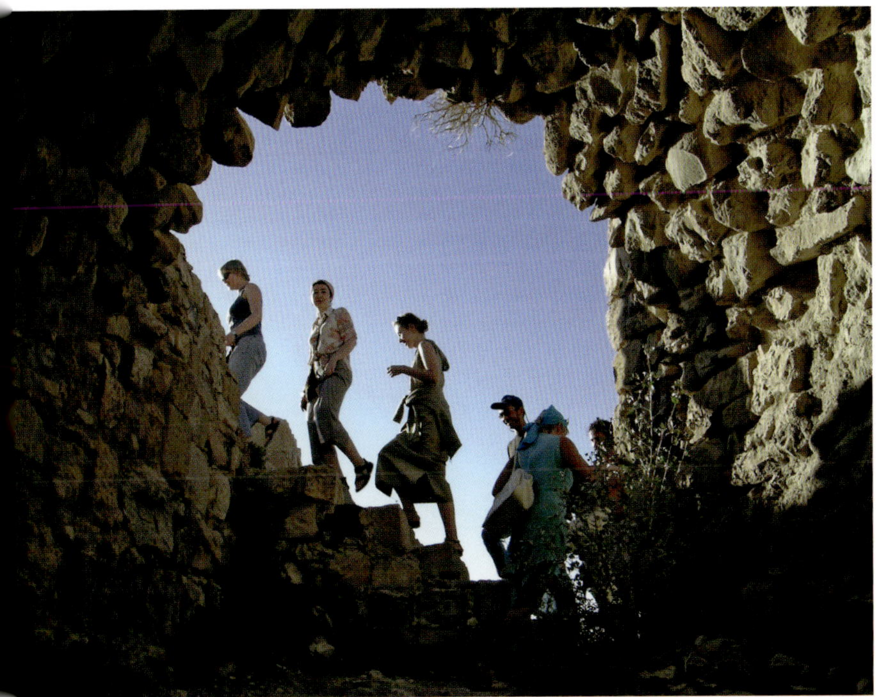

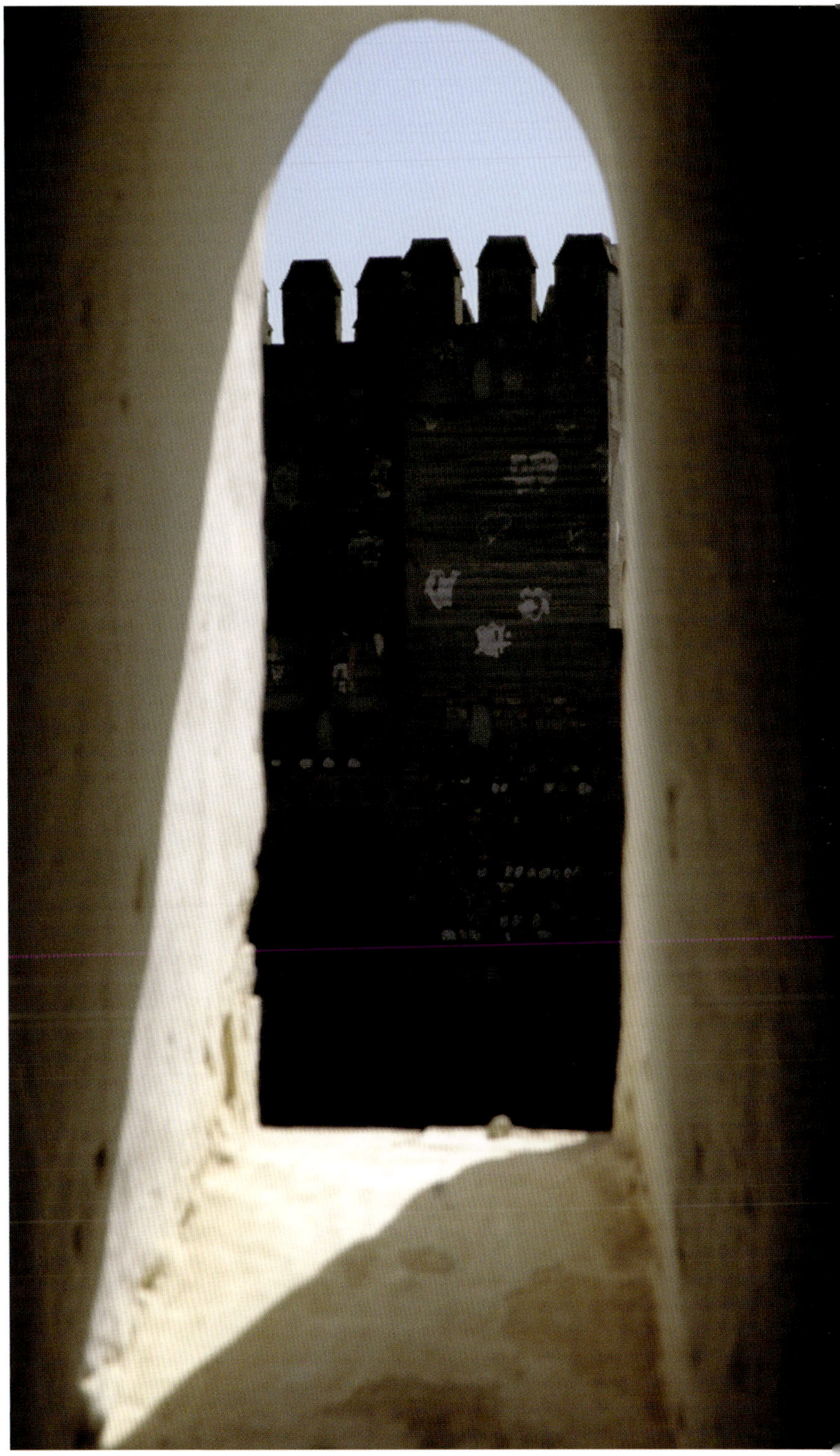

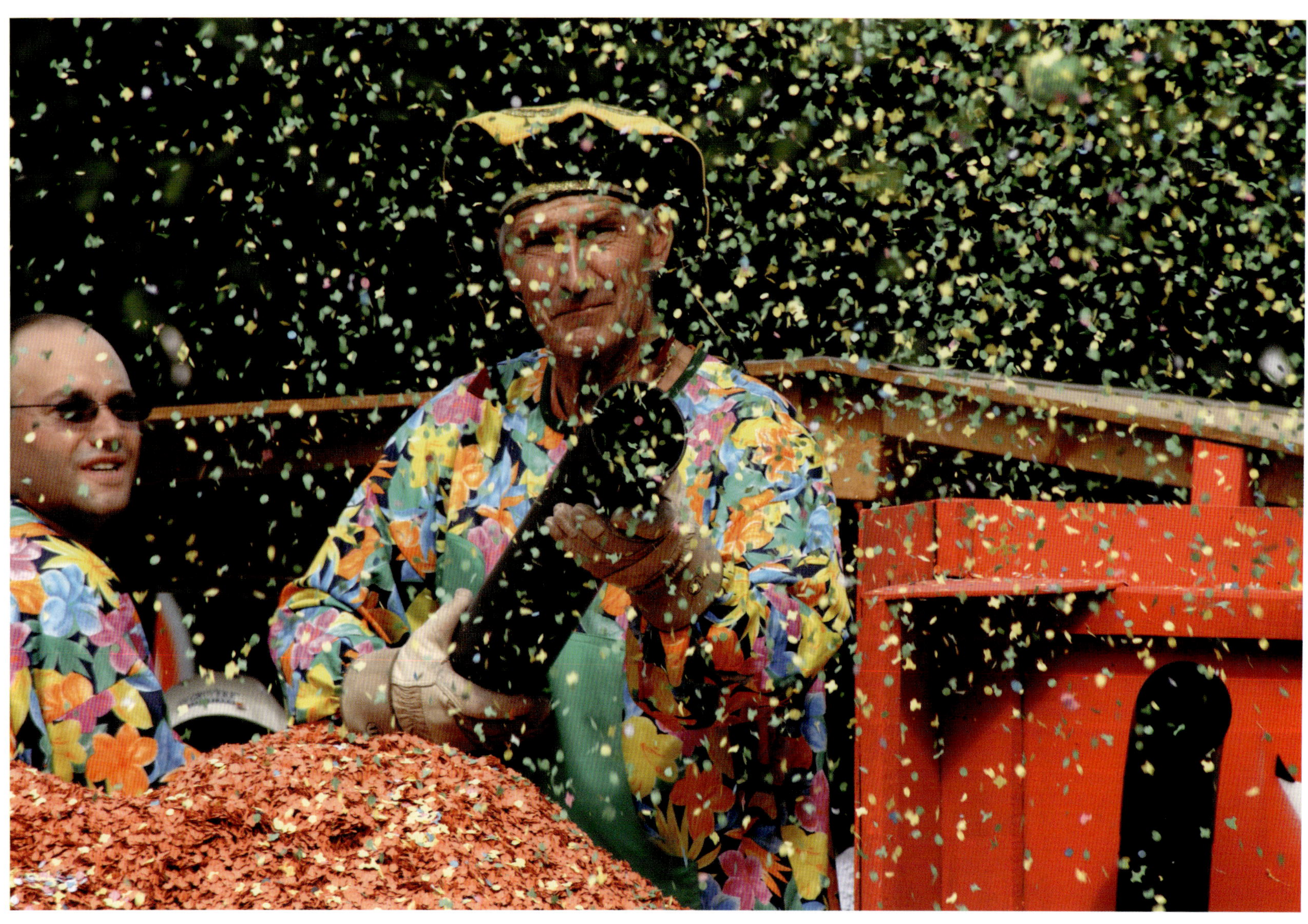

Wine Festival in Neuchâtel. Switzerland. The ideal 'sieve' can also unexpectedly materialise in the form of a volley of confetti, which this brave warrior is shooting at his fellow citizens from his 'bazooka'. The essential point is that the artificial barrier between the lens and the subject has added expression to the chosen shot.

One of the secluded coves on the island of Majorca, Spain. The enigmatic framing of this picture, with the yachts at anchor, creates a certain intrigue and, involves the viewer's imagination. In addition, this simple device makes it possible to shoot at midday, in the most unfavourable lighting conditions.

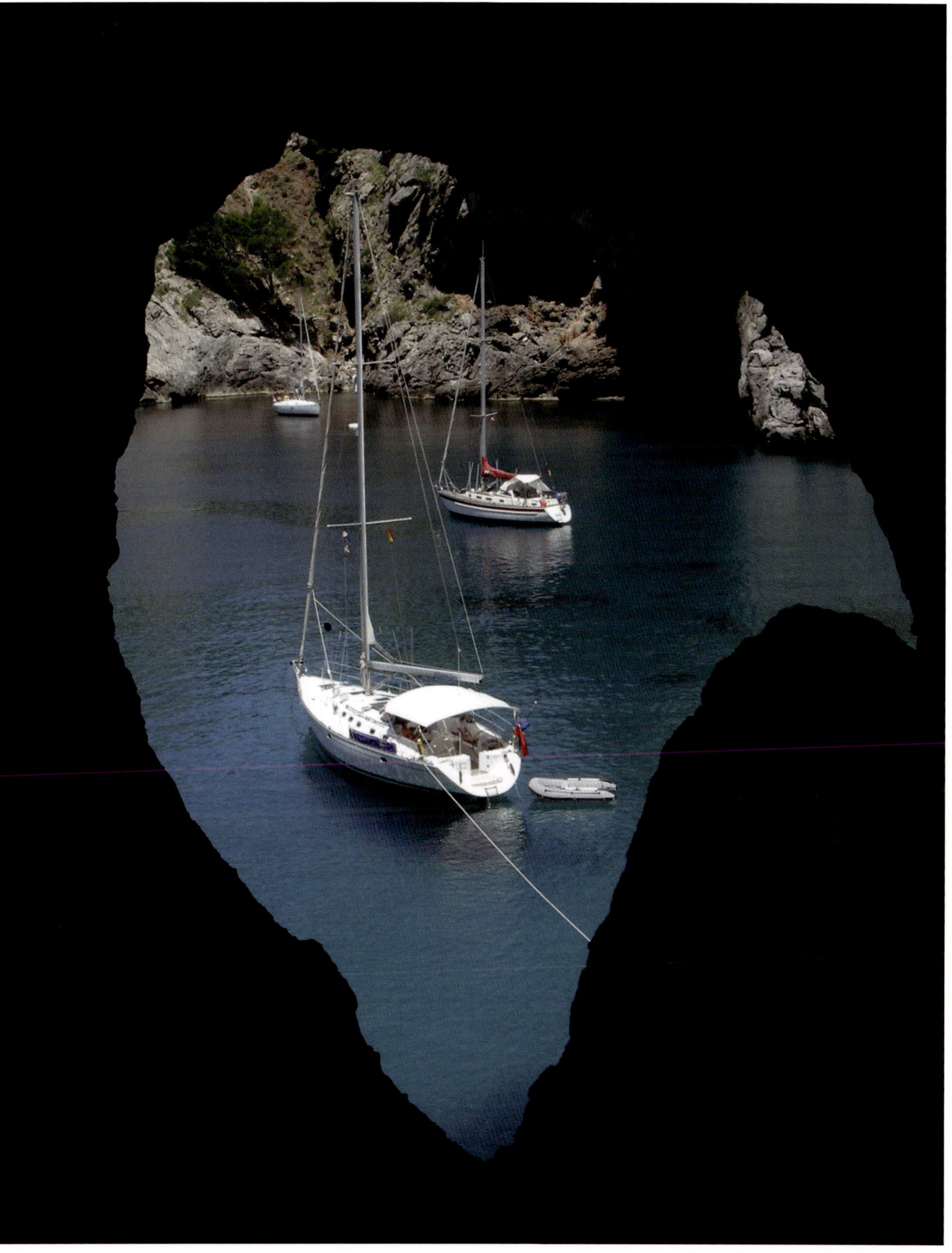

Sparring with Euclid

Do parallel lines intersect? One motorcycle racer told me that, at speeds of 300 km an hour, even the widest road converges into a single point right in front of the motorcycle, so they have to travel blind, completely by instinct. Photographing the Summer Palace in Beijing, I found myself between the lines of two high terracotta walls stretching into the distance, and I felt like that motorcycle racer. The Chinese architects have created a graphic illustration of the law of perspective. Because theories of light and the laws of space do not fit neatly into 'correct' geometry, when we photograph a right-angled building the shape we get is a trapezium or a truncated cone.

Symmetry is tempting – and yet at the same time perfidious. An absolutely symmetrical face has an idiotic look.

Symmetry that results from accidental regularity of line is a 'motivation' for a photograph: a dozen identical Fiats parked on a narrow little street in a small Italian town, a line of coloured gables atop the houses in an Eskimo settlement in Greenland, a dotted line of 200-litre fuel-oil barrels marking out a pathway through the snow to a polar station, rows of finials on the Red Fort in Delhi or of stupas in a Himalayan valley – all these draw the photographer's eye. However, the great Gaudi would turn in his grave at the word 'symmetry', and in the architectural masterpieces of ancient Novgorod you will never see parallel lines, and no two windows are carved in the same way! So work out your own photo-correspondence to this asymmetry of genius!

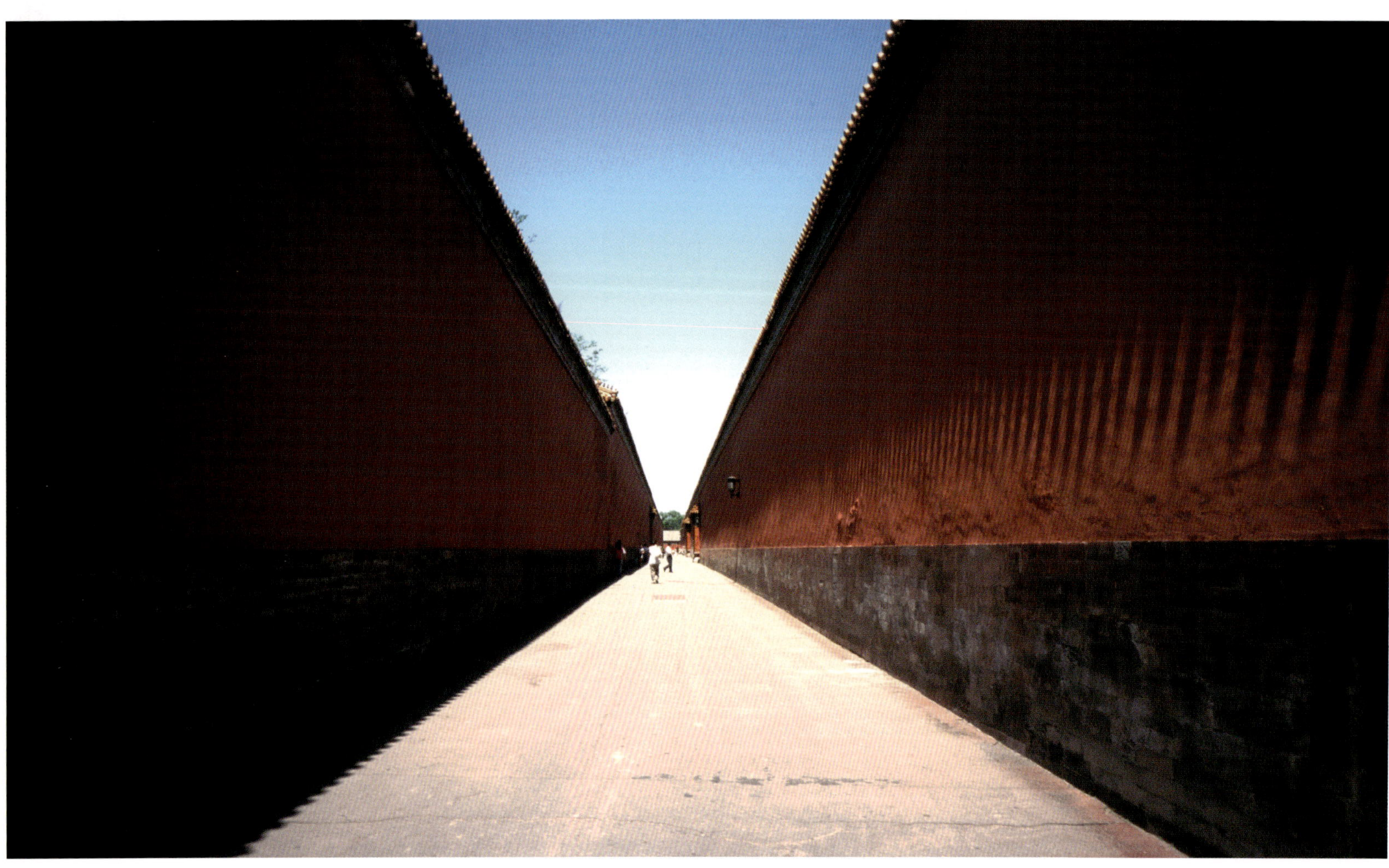

LEFT
Royal Palace. Beijing, China. This
photograph is iconic – and yet we do
not know what is waiting for us where
the walls meet, at that magical point
through the looking-glass.

RIGHT
The City of Arts and Sciences,
Valencia: the impressive 'symmetry'
of this huge complex of buildings
bears the stamp of the best Spanish
architect of our times, Santiago
Calatrava. Contemporary large-
scale, extravagant urban design
projects in Valencia, Berlin, London
and other European cities offer
the photographer inexhaustible
possibilities for creative imagination.

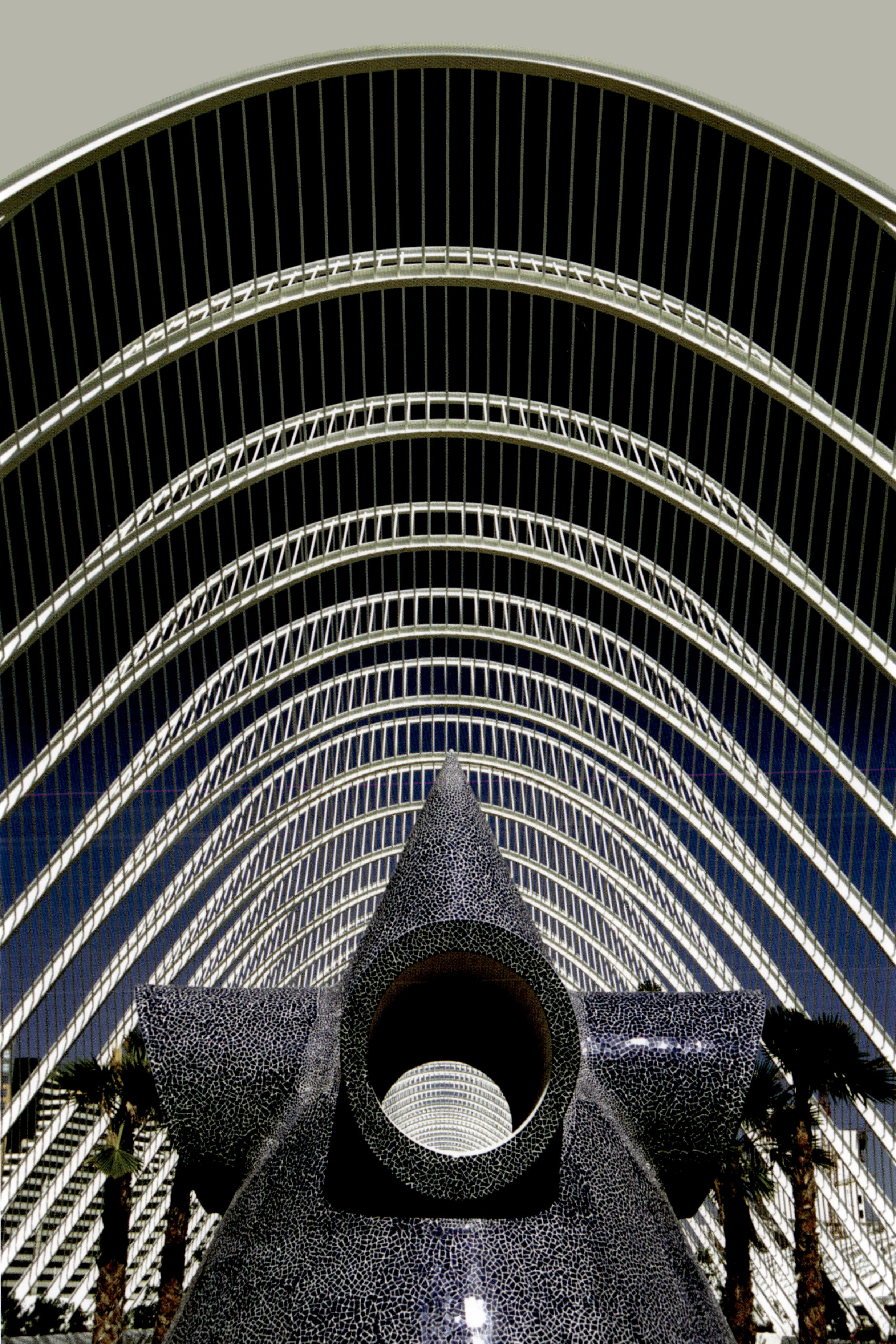

A regular formation of glasses of aquavit – the highly alcoholic national beverage of Norway – taken in the galley of a boat during a sea fishing trip.

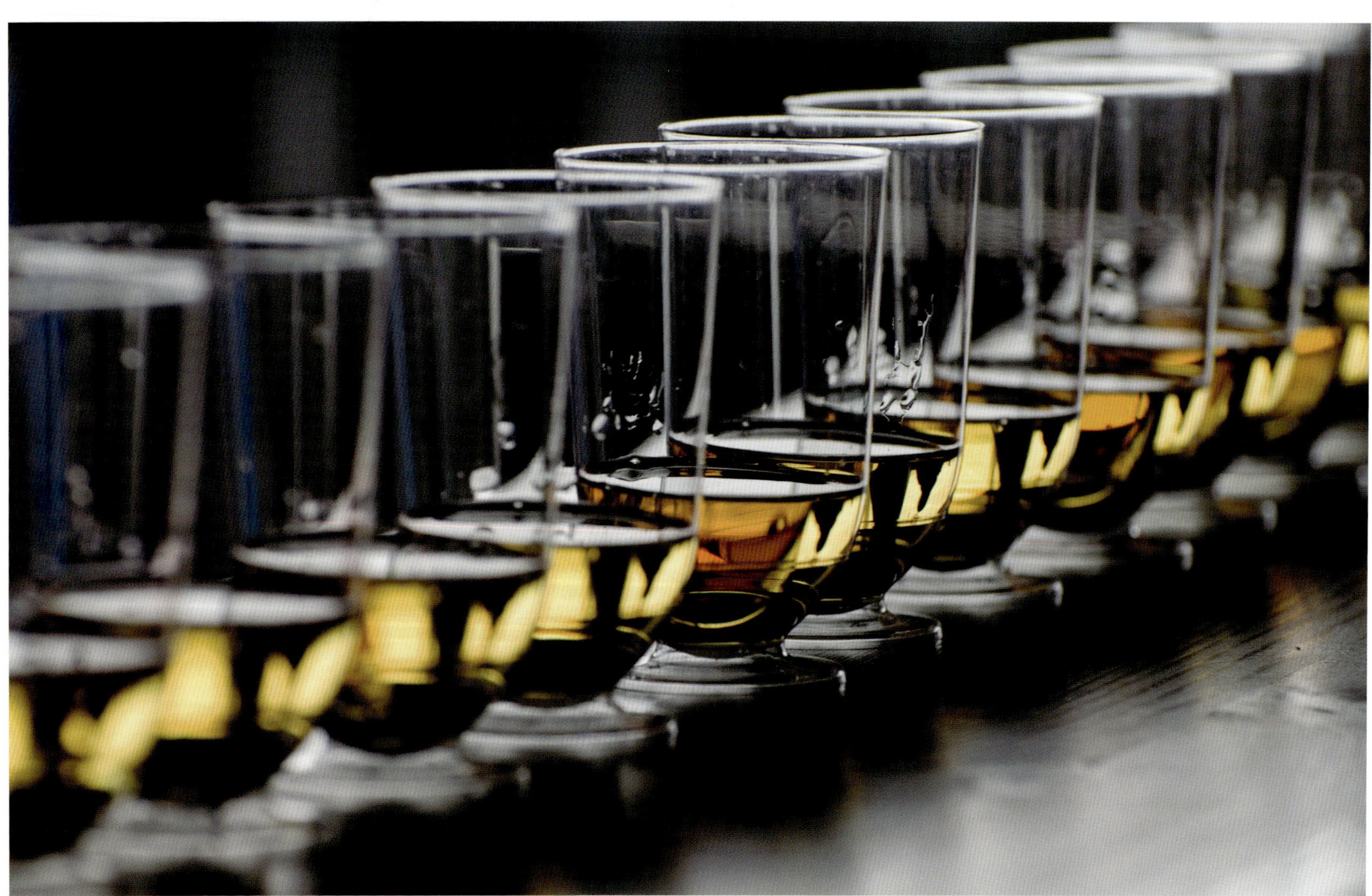

The heavy, cloudy sky has
artistically poured out its 'mercurial'
reflection onto the wavy surface of
the Norwegian fjord. Taken from
the deck of a ship.

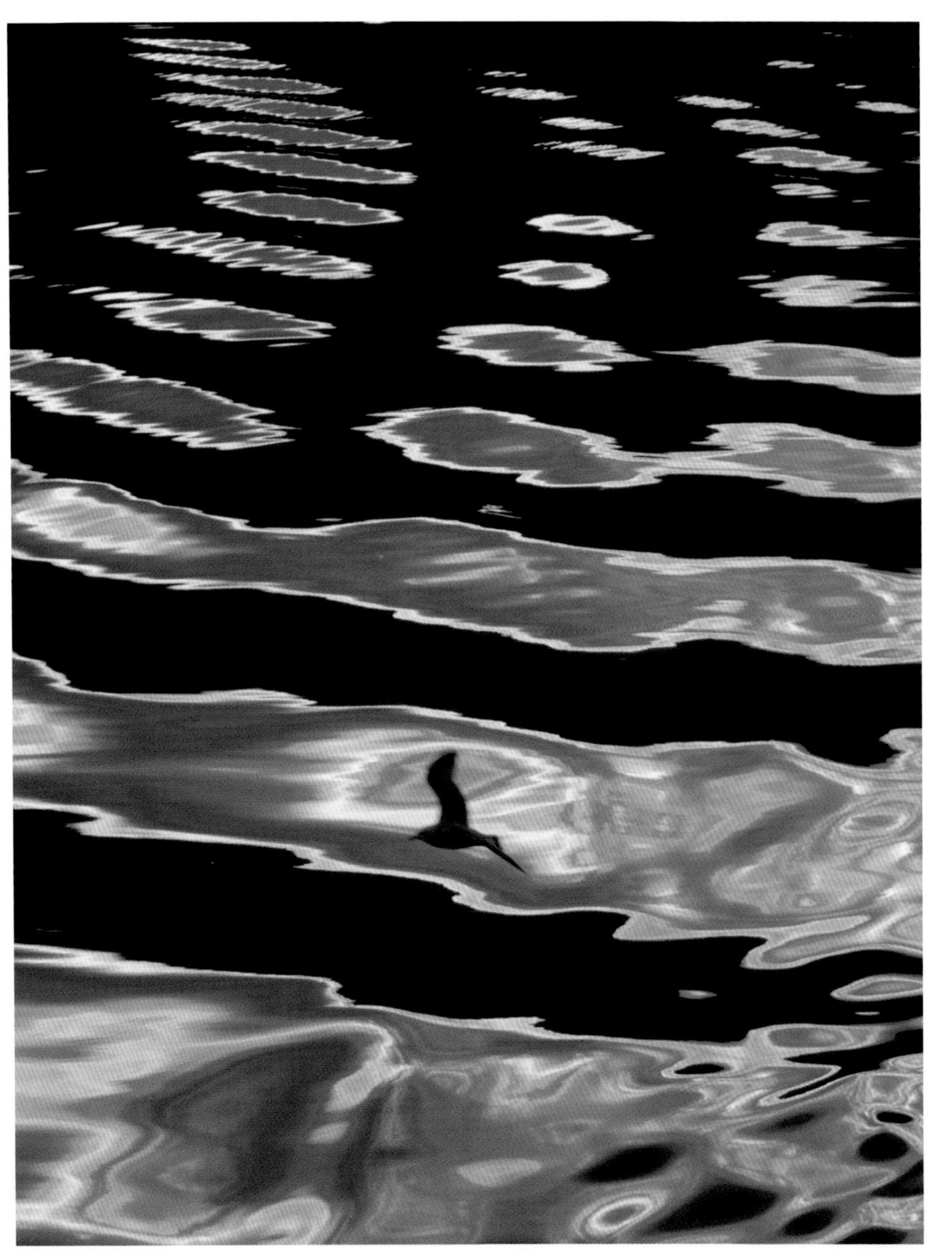

Big things are seen best from a distance

I have a favourite photographer's model in Switzerland, a chaste young goddess - the Jungfrau, in the Bernese Alps. I've been photographing this beauty for many years, from every possible angle – from the Alpine ski resort of Klein Scheidegg, from the saddle between its two snowy peaks, from the window of a train on a mountain railway, on its curving slopes, and through the thickness of a glacier, from the 3,000-metre high Schildhorn next to it. But until recently I'd never taken an outstanding photo of the legendary mountain.

And now, having once again spent a whole day on the road taking photos whenever I felt inspired to do so, I felt tired. As dusk was falling, I returned to my hotel at Interlaken, opened the curtain on the wooden window of my hundred-year-old chalet, and noticed that my best-beloved was sparkling in the

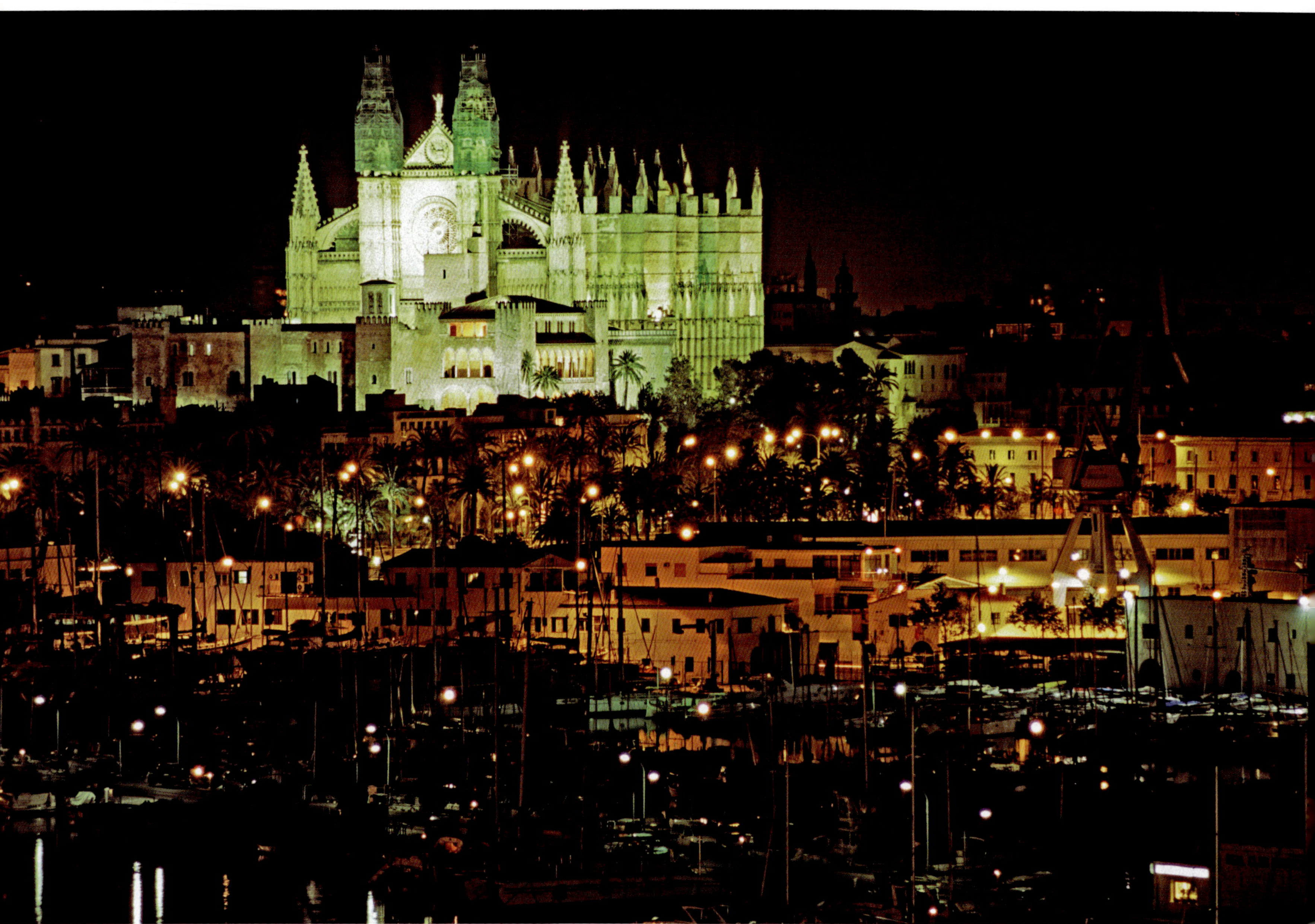

warm golden rays of the sun, right in front of me, in the ideal frame for a photo, like an Alpine stage set! The mountain must have been forty kilometres away in a straight line, but in the extremely pure and transparent Alpine air each of its crevices was visible. As everyone knows, big things are seen best from a distance!

I've had many chances to discover how true this statement is. Just as with the Jungfrau, I was going through torments trying to photograph one of the biggest churches in the world – the cathedral in Palma de Majorca. I walked around it more than once. I tried to shoot it from the coastline and from the harbour area. While I was able to get a shot of the carved façade, the massive edifice of the cathedral was still on too great a scale. And once again it was a hotel located at the other end of town which came to my rescue as I came home in the evening! I can't even remember what floor I was on. I think it was the eighth, or even higher, because the harbour was all laid out below. But with a Nikkorom 180/2 stand, I photographed the cathedral, floating above the nocturnal town like a huge ship.

Here's my advice on photographing large architectural structures and groups of buildings. When you take the tourist bus to a monastery or a church, take note of good perspectives as you approach it. If the driver stops right under the monastery walls, you'll never be able to get a good shot from there. You'll need 20 minutes to get half a kilometre away, in order to be in the right place to take your photo. That's why buses are the worst form of transport for a travel photographer, who needs complete independence and autonomy. In Europe, bus drivers can't just stop on most roads, even if they're willing to help you with the photo. The regulations are strict on that point – no stopping except at special purpose-built points.

I once travelled from Casablanca to the Moroccan capital, Rabat, on an excursion bus. I caught sight of a splendid perspective – the surrounding fortress walls of the city, ideally lit by sunlight, with a big black cloud extending over half the sky which was just on the point of covering it. And even better, there was a good foreground, with boats on the sea. I shouted wildly to the guide and the driver: 'Stop!' The bus had scarcely stopped at the side of the road before they were opening the doors for me, and I was stepping off the bus. While literally in motion, I managed to press the button a couple of times. If you're seriously interested in being a travel photographer, then the very best way to take photos is on your own. Even the most loving and patient spouse will not always understand why you have to spend hours waiting for the right light, instead of going to a café.

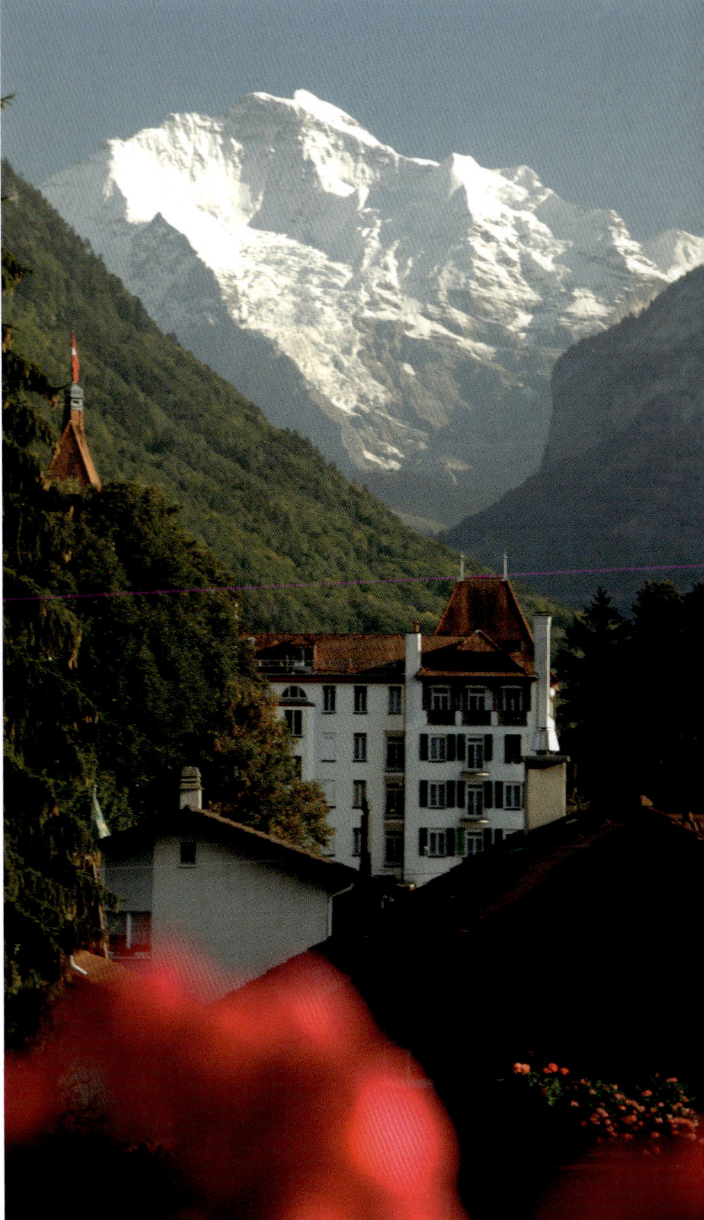

Getting down to the nuts and bolts

It is important for travel photographers to learn how to perceive the world around them not just at the scale of the Eiffel Tower or the Pyramid of Giza – a tower made up of thousands of metal section with hundreds of thousands of nuts and bolts, and a pyramid built out of millions of stones – they should always remember that a detail is frequently capable of conveying an image better than the whole. It's impossible to stop looking at London's Tower Bridge – one of the most beautiful bridges in the world: the graceful lines of its load-bearing sections cut out on the template of a great artist; its openwork cast-iron mouldings; its nuts and bolts; its rows of rivets, neatly painted in red, white and blue. The virtuosity of this beauty's technical resolution is equal to that of her architectural merit. Having taken in the magnificent sight, you should focus on its industrial and design aesthetic.

Artefacts from the golden age of machinery, lovingly preserved by enthusiasts, open up a real space for creativity: locomotives in museums or sometimes even still in service, carriages from Orient Express trains, old ships, American classic cars on the streets of Havana, early-20th-century mining hoists in the Alps. The same is true for absolutely up-to-date products and processes that still use old technology. This could be brewing beer, making wine or blowing glass. You might also come across extravagant objects – for example, a house in Finland made of empty bottles.

The photographer can find material with texture in old doors, gates, windows, locks, latches or bolts, weather-vanes – or the tools of the sea, ranging from a rusted portside bollard and coils of rope to the hulls of ships smashed against the rocks. Very good antique machinery and appliances are also to be found in mining museums, at salt mines in Bavaria, Austria and Poland and in European flea markets. Designs in the high-tech style can also look very good. I photographed the brand-new bridge in Trondheim, Norway, rather than snapping the model for the delectation of journalists – and yet I couldn't decide from which viewpoint and with what perspective it gave the most profitable picture.

It is important not to overstep the mark and not to stoop to the 'aesthetics of garbage'; always and everywhere, remember that human dignity overrides everything else – and treat the heroes of your photographs with tact and sympathy. It's a different thing if you want your picture to draw the attention of the authorities or the public to people's poor living conditions or to a gross invasion of the natural world – but that is no longer travel photography.

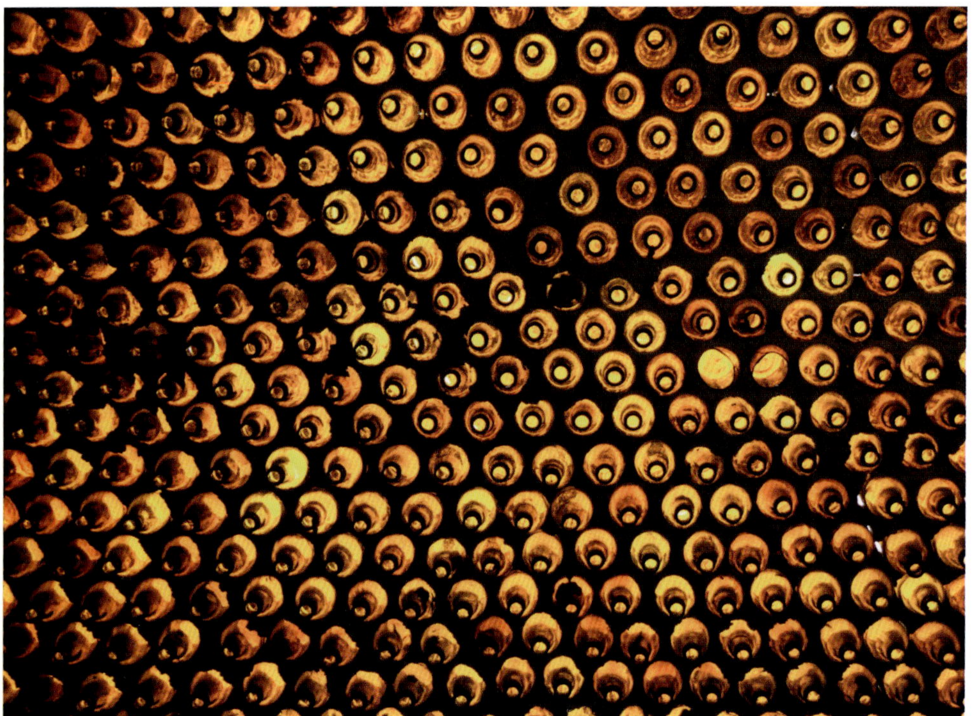

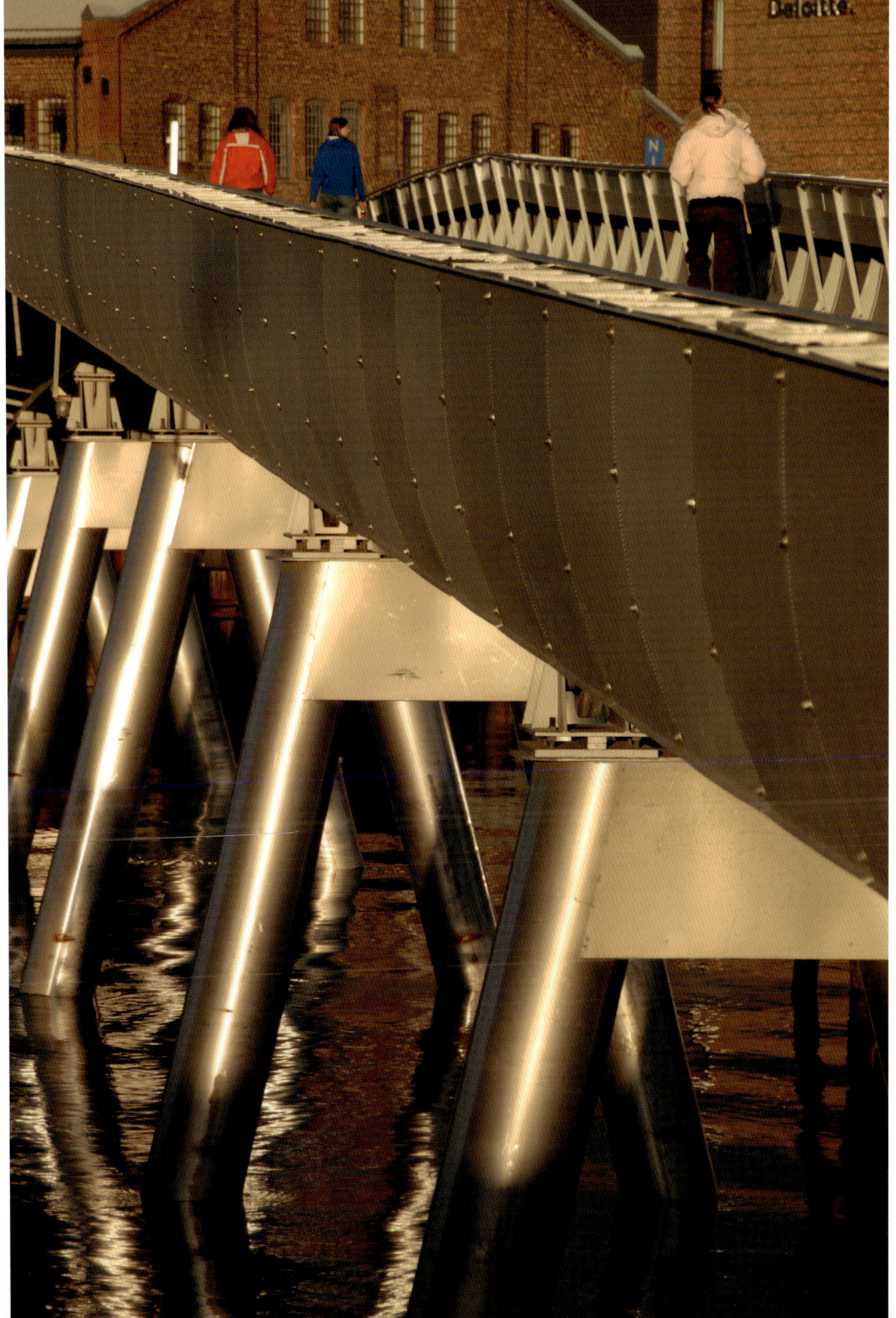

A century of architectural
development lies between Tower
Bridge in London and the new bridge
in Trondheim, but the older beauty
has not aged at all. Tower Bridge is
painted in the colours of the British
flag, making it a wonderful visiting
card for 'Foggy London'.

Wind farm in the Øresund Strait,
Denmark. Up-to-date technology has
brought its own aesthetic into our
present-day world.

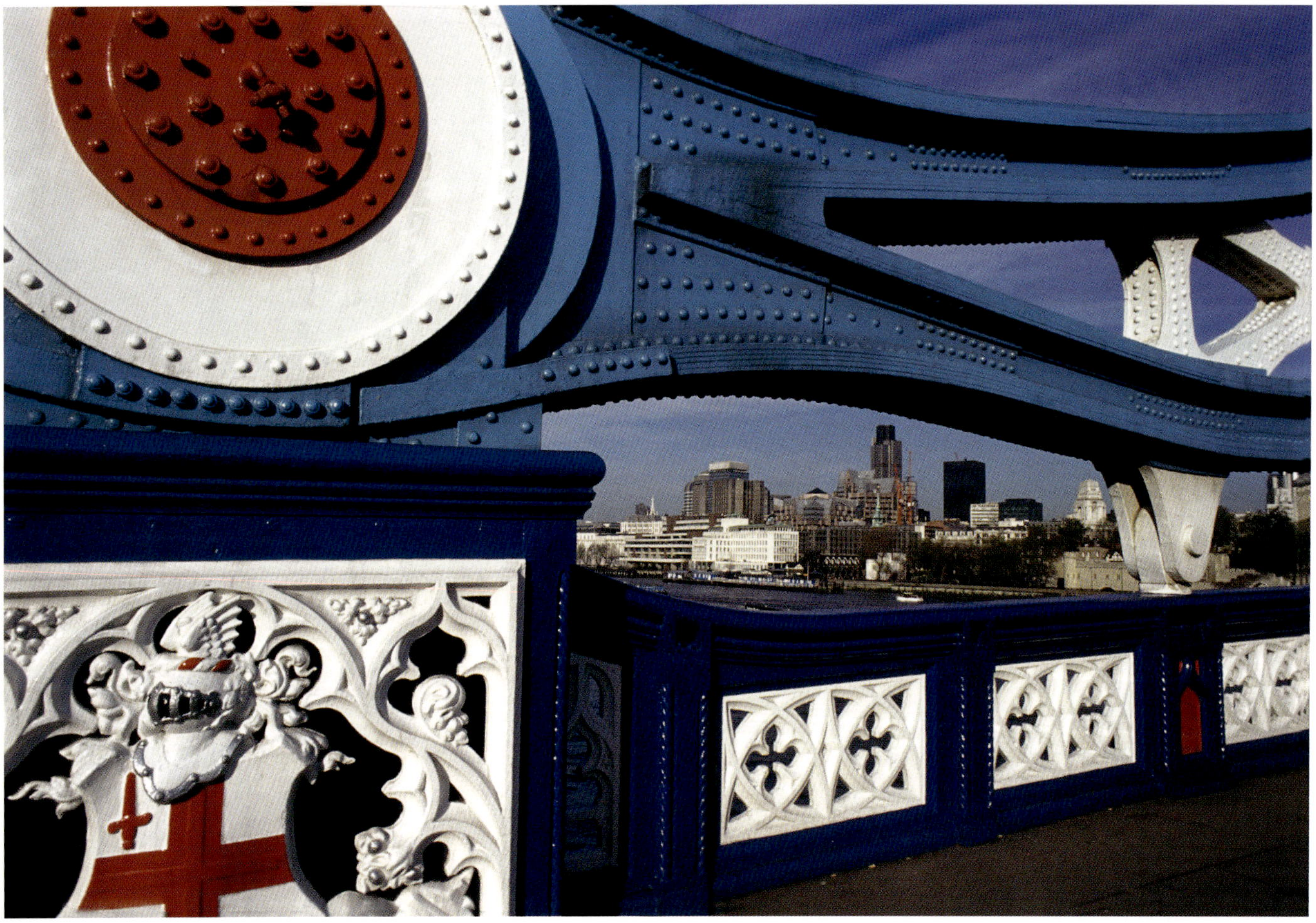

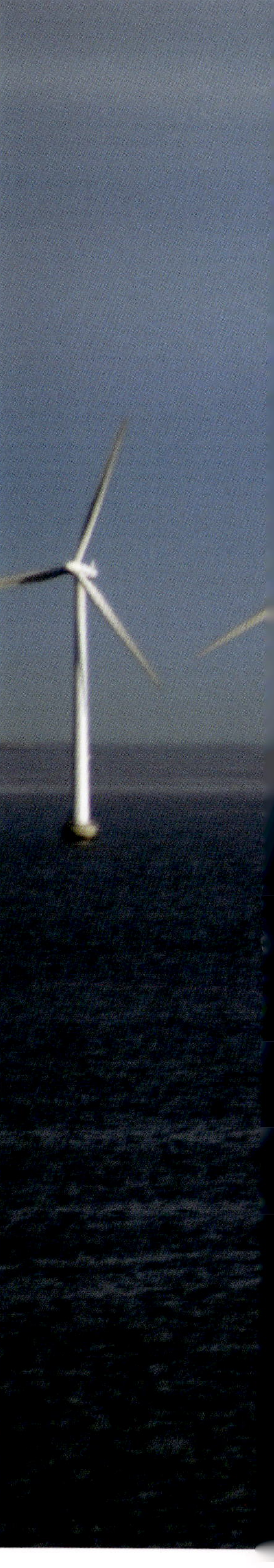

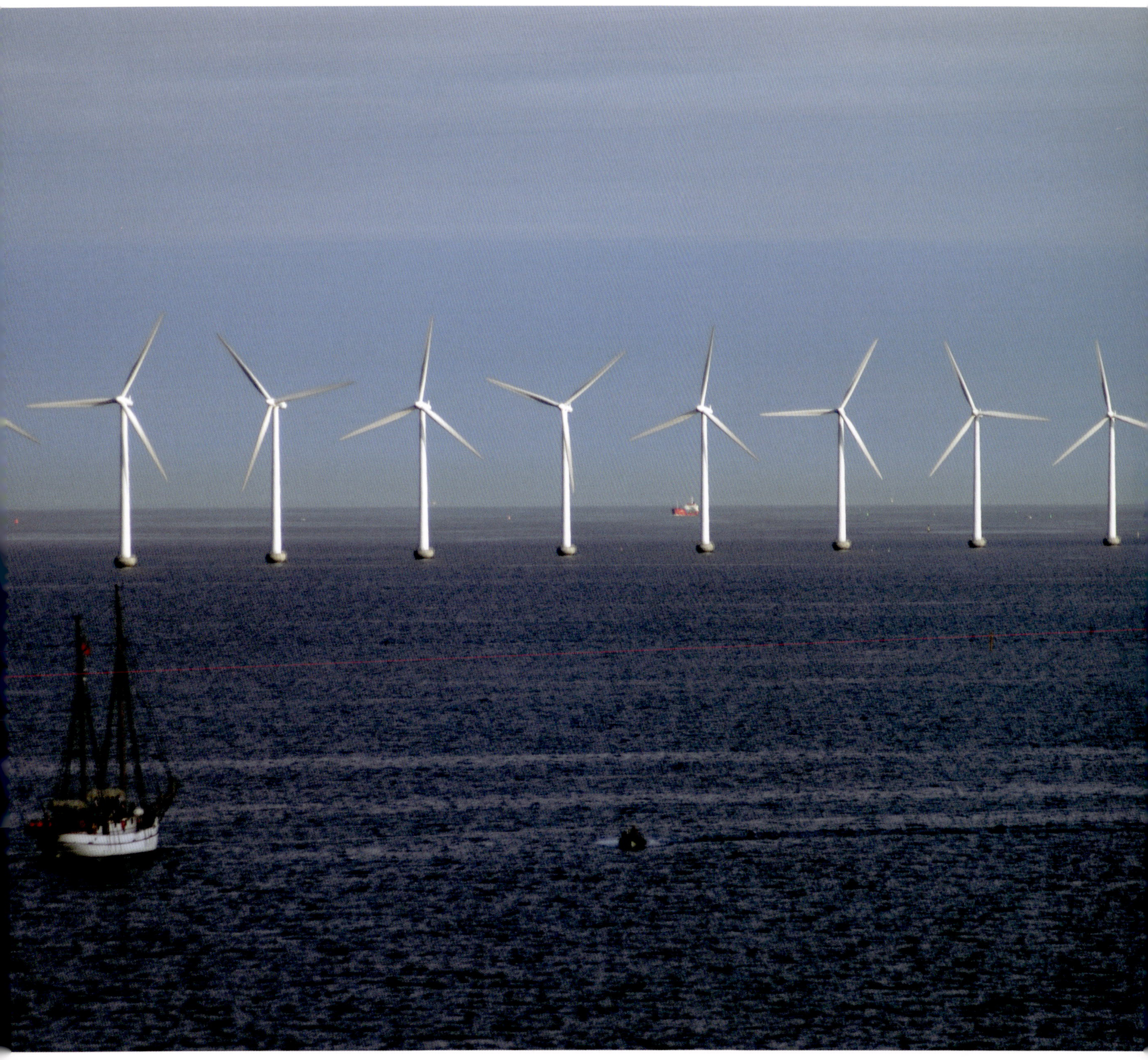

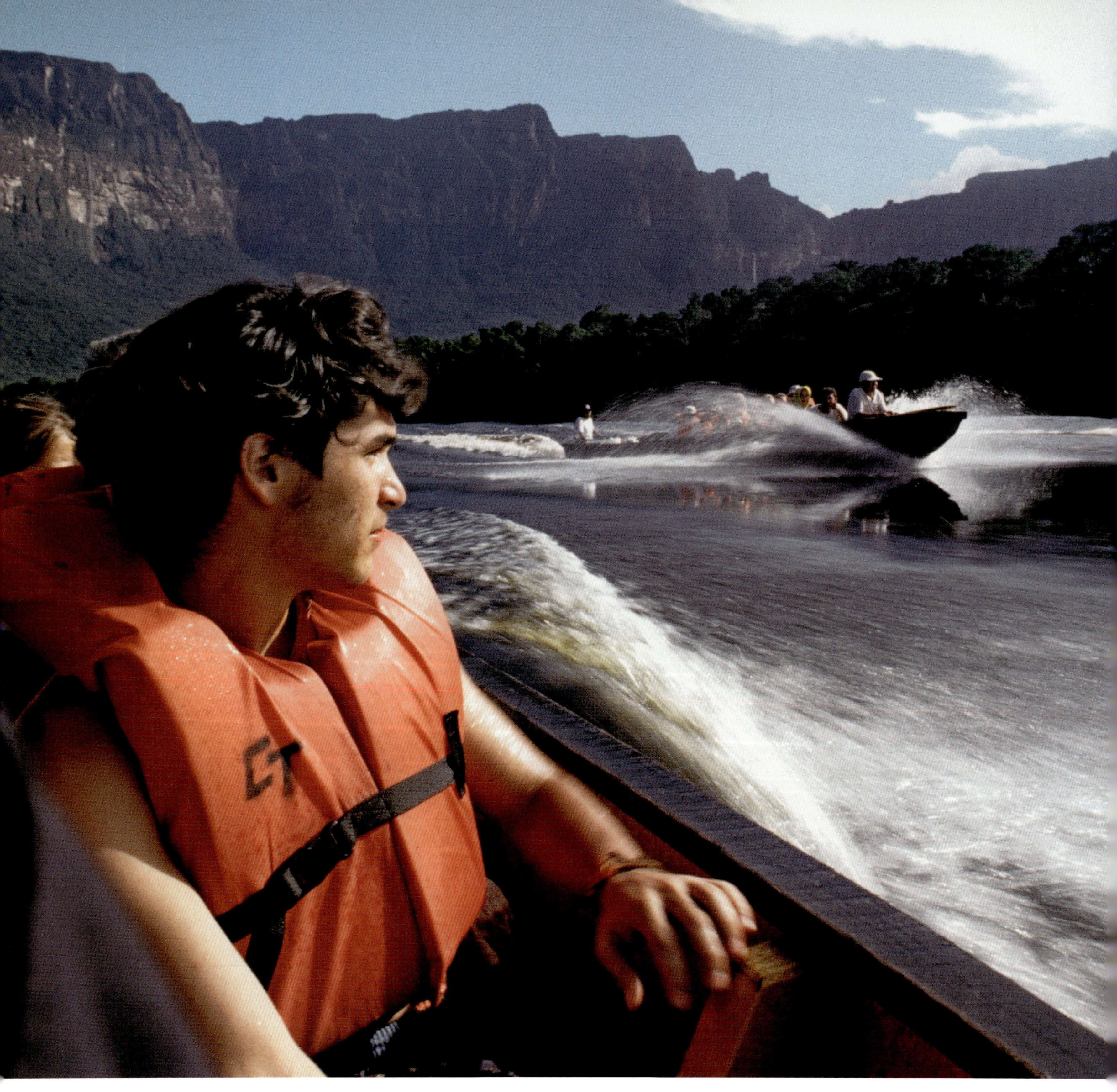

Guardian angel

The desire to take rare photographs can sometimes be seriously risky. Many years ago, having arrived on the almost inaccessible island of Paramushir, in the North Kuril Islands, I naturally succombed to the temptation to visit its famous sulphuric volcano, Ebeko. In order to take photographs of the steaming yellow fumaroles in a mist of toxic vapours, I had to walk along a thin crust of scorching, bubbling and spurting mud, with the risk of toppling into a smoking, sulphurous Hell.

Mountain climbing, mountain tourism, rafting on the mountain rivers, hang-gliding and parascending – all of these offer a photographer clear, dynamic photos, but at the same time there's a risk that he may lose his equipment – not to mention his life! And we all have to make our own choice here. I'm obliged to counsel my readers to think through everything as completely as possible, and to avoid any ill-considered adventures. And even if everything does go pear-shaped – don't miss the shot!

When I'm asked to list the most beautiful places on Earth, I choose Bali, the Norwegian fjords and the Lofoten Islands, Monument Valley in North America...and I always add Canaima, in the jungles of Venezuela. But right now, as I think about this tiny dot on the map, I'm remembering just how extreme my trip to cover this area was fated to be.

The hotel – or, more precisely, the comfortable tourist campus and the Indian village, made up of neat little houses – stands on the gently sloping, sandy beach of an amazing lagoon formed by the Carrao River, into which seven mighty waterfalls plummet from a height of 50 metres. Their quivering panorama unfolds before your eyes from the restaurant terrace. Steaming jungles go right up to the edge of the pure water, in which it's perfectly safe to swim, and there are three picturesque palm trees growing in the lagoon itself. Walking along the beach, you can be wonderstruck by each of the waterfalls in turn. One of the most beautiful and impressive natural tableaux I've ever seen. I came back with hundreds of pictures.

The normality of the air flight from Caracas, and the landing strip of the local aerodrome, five hundred metres from the hotel, combine to create the illusion of a location which is civilised and completely safe. Neither the skin of a 7-metre anaconda, casually hanging above the registration desk, nor the 1-metre long iguanas prowling through the grass put you on your guard. But you gradually come to realise that you've landed on a tiny island of civilisation in the midst of wild jungle country with crocodiles, freshwater boa constrictors and leopards. Giant grasshoppers with orange abdomens fly over the hotel's grounds. Over-ripe mangos fall onto the paths with a heavy thud. You don't need to go far to find the exotic.

The tourist schedule includes a canoe trip to the lagoon and the waterfalls. As the boat draws nearer, the cataracts of Canaima, so picturesque and attractive from a distance, start to look less and less friendly.

Over there in the distance are the gigantic peaks of the famous high plateaux so often described, which the Indians call 'tepui', which translates as 'The Abode of the Gods'. These geological marvels, which have been about two thousand million years in the making, witnessed the division of the extremely ancient continent of Gondwana into Africa and South America. Where Venezuela borders the jungles of Brazil and Guyana, there are about a hundred such 'tepui', most of them untrodden by the feet of any human being. The Guyanese plateau is one of the most inaccessible areas of the planet, but concealed in the depths of the 'lost world' is the highest waterfall on the planet – Angel Falls. It was named after the American aviator Jimmy Angel, who first spotted it in 1933.

To begin with, I photographed the tepui using a telephoto lens, not suspecting that a day later I'd be given the very rare opportunity of entering the 'lost world'. But first I duplicated Angel's flight. Admittedly, I was a passenger in a little tourist plane paying 80 dollars for the round trip. The plane flew around the gloomy plateaux, and then the moment of ecstasy when, through a gap in the grey clouds and the green jungles, a ray of sunlight tore apart the stream of water gushing down from the sky, those clear impressions will remain in my memory for ever.

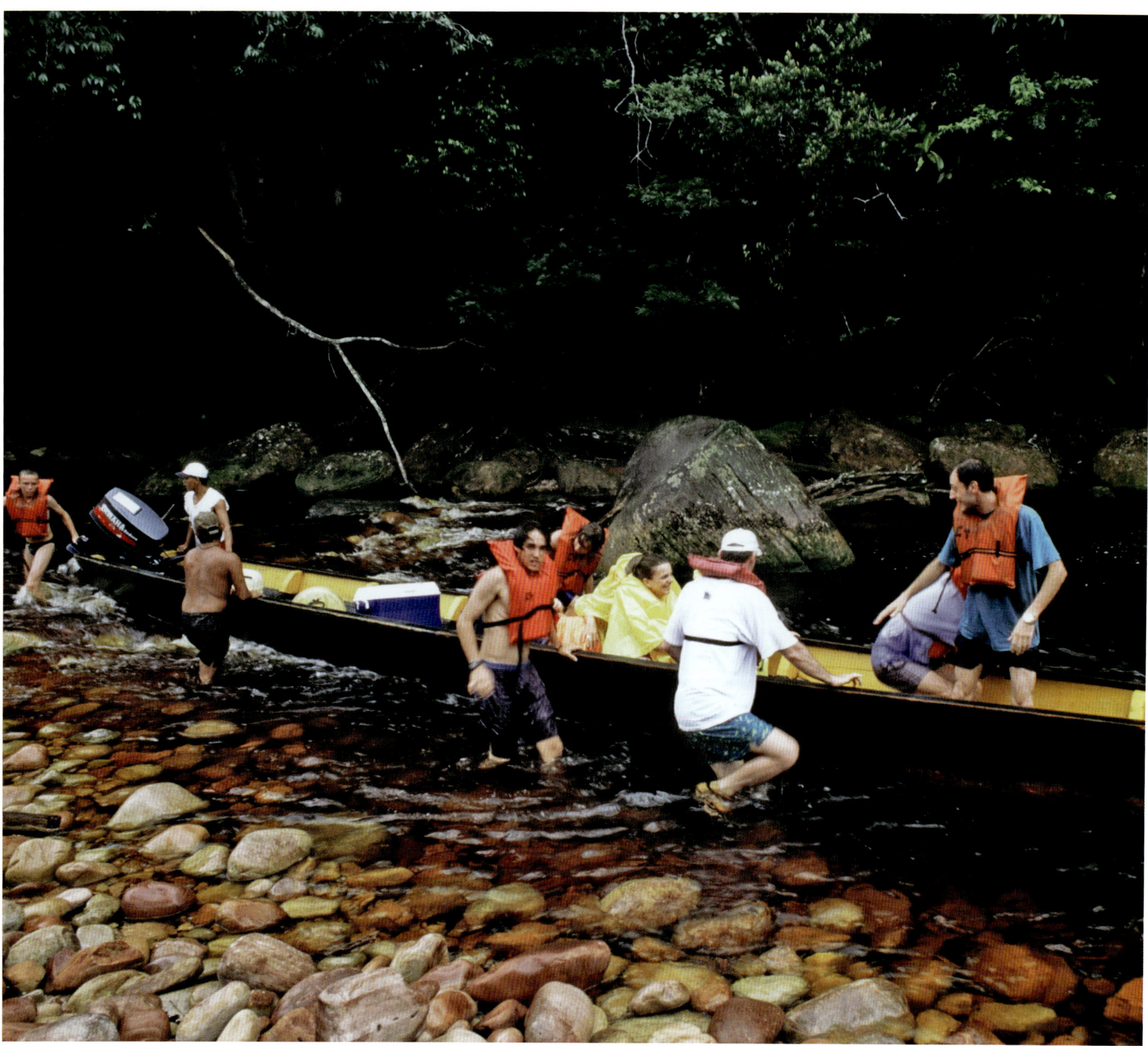

At the height of the rainy season, in July and August, when the water level in the rivers rises, another way to rendezvous with the Angel Falls is possible – an 80-kilometre canoe trip up-stream against the current of the Carrao, which is pitted with the boiling currents of swirling, extremely dangerous rapids all the way. When I asked what the chances were of capsizing and submerging my photographic apparatus, my guide politely replied that it was all in the lap of the gods. Only later when the adventure was over did my guide pull up his 'cowboy' sleeves to show his palm, with a deep scar from the jaws of an anaconda, admitting that anything could happen. Boats did capsize in the rapids and people did drown. I was lucky that year.

I got my first taste of the rapids at dawn, after an hour's murky travel along the nocturnal river. That was when we – seven Spanish adventurers and I – were on our way to rendezvous with the Angel. The water ahead of the boat suddenly boiled over the whole width of the river, and our helmsman guided us through the only gap between the rocks, where the river was agitated by violent jets a metre high. I'd scarcely managed to get my Nikons stowed into their box when the boat's prow rode up. I was drenched with water from head to toe. The hull trembled, driven onto the rocks by the engine. Then the engine suddenly went silent. The helmsman damped down the auxiliary engine to stop the propeller from churning against the rocks. At first, the boat spun round menacingly, but the Yamaha spluttered back into life and got up to full revs, and we won through into calm water. How I regretted that I hadn't brought my all-weather camera with me. I couldn't photograph the most interesting thing – our passage through the rapids – without soaking my kit with water!

With fast-beating hearts, we succeeded in making it through almost all the rapids before our luck changed, in the Devil's Canyon. As we went over a long shoal, the boat became wedged fast between the rocks. Luis, the Indian seated at the prow, tried to push us off with a short oar. The boat tilted over

menacingly. Without wasting any time, he jumped over me into the boiling waters and began to drag the canoe off the rocks. The boat was shipping a lot of water on the starboard side, it was up to my waist. The powerful current whipped the sand away from under the little Indian's feet, and he was dragged under the keel, at risk of being crushed against the boulders. Abandoning my Nikons, I plunged in to help him, and found myself up to my chest in the icy, red-brown melt water. Leaning my shoulder and my arms against the boat, I managed to hold it back for a moment. Luis pushed against the slippery bottom with his feet and, with superhuman effort, we pushed the boat off the rocks. The engine came to life, and the Devil's Canyon admitted defeat.

However, we hadn't won yet – not by a long way. The water level in the channel was too low, and our guide into the 'lost world' had to take a difficult decision. Everyone had to get out of the boat and drag it for hundreds of metres up a side-channel against the fast current.

Turning into the River Churun, the right-hand tributary of the Carrao, we overcame the final barriers towards noon, and now – heart-stopping rapture. The heavenly cataract of the Angel beat down from an unimaginable height! On foot, throw-ing off my thoroughly soaked outer clothing and hastily pulling out my photographic kit, I hurried into the jungle, thrusting through the lianas, so that I could photograph the waterfall before it rained. 'On autopilot', I photographed some bright, wild-looking flowers. There were huge butterflies too, but I had no time to spare for them. And then there I was in a glade, facing the cataract itself. At the base of a tepui, you feel like a Lilliputian. In this projection, at an acute angle, it appears that the miracle of nature is pouring down straight from the sky. A huge bird soared above me, like the ghost of a pterodactyl from the dreaded 'lost world'. I managed to press the button twice before a tropical downpour spread over the jungle, concealing the waterfall from me.

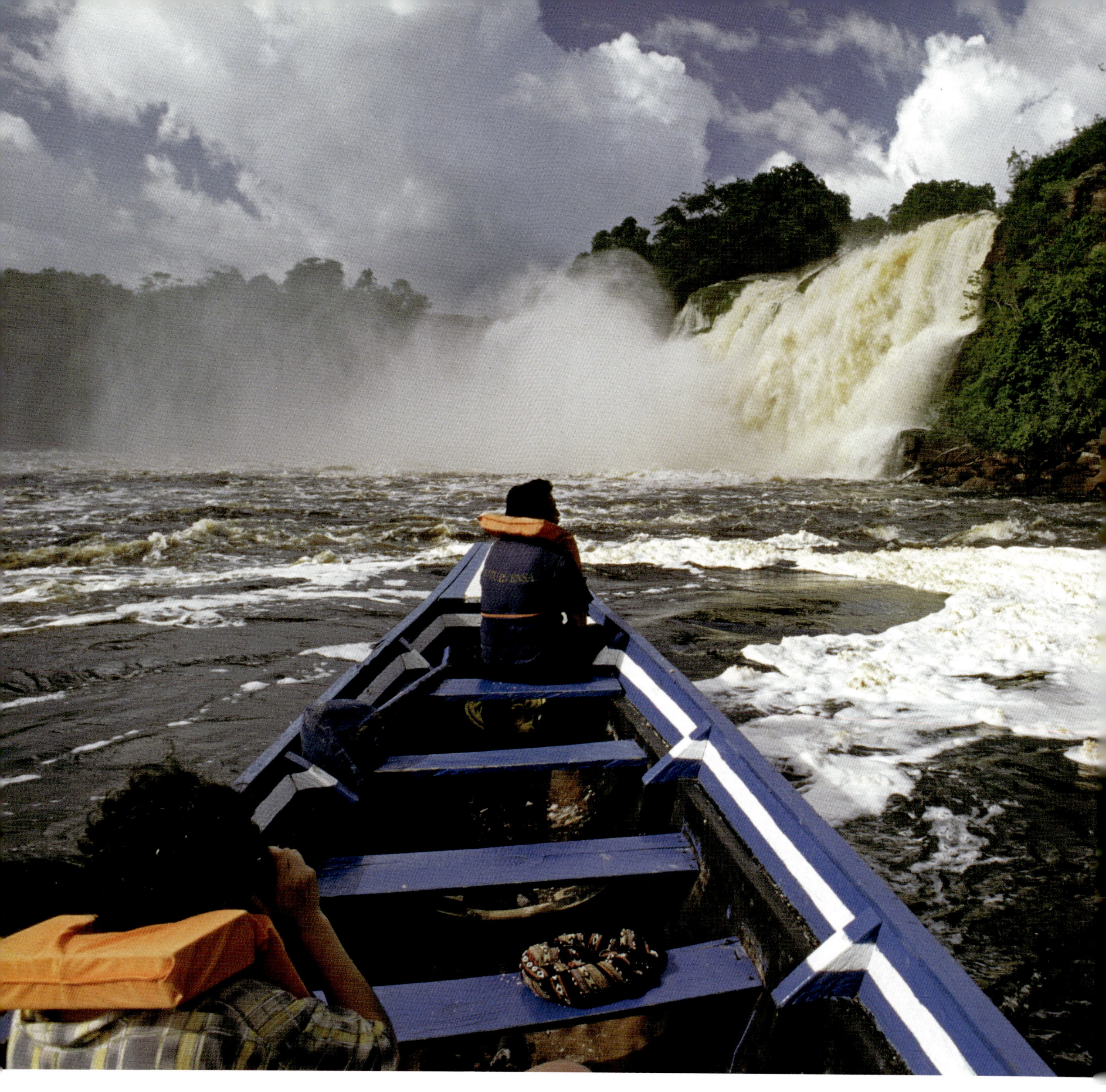

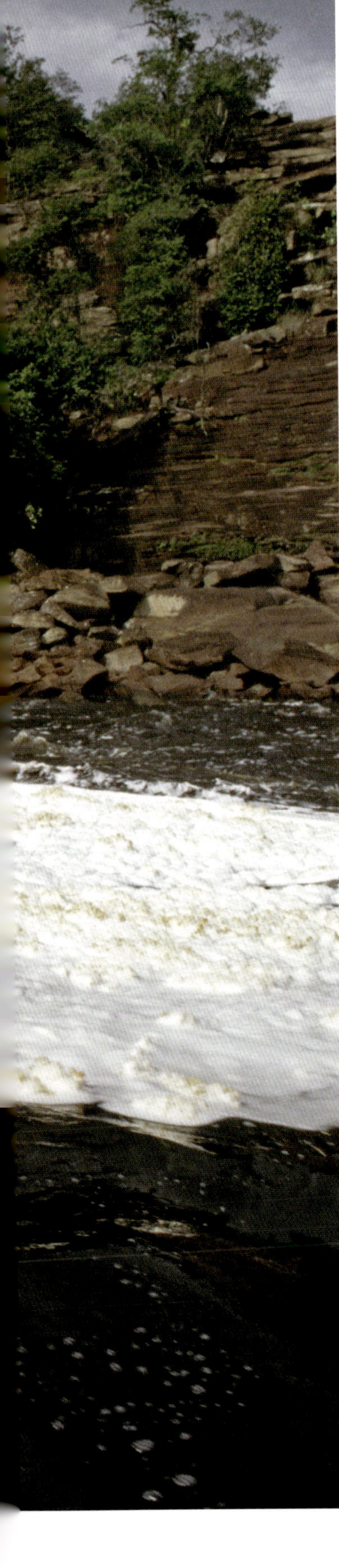

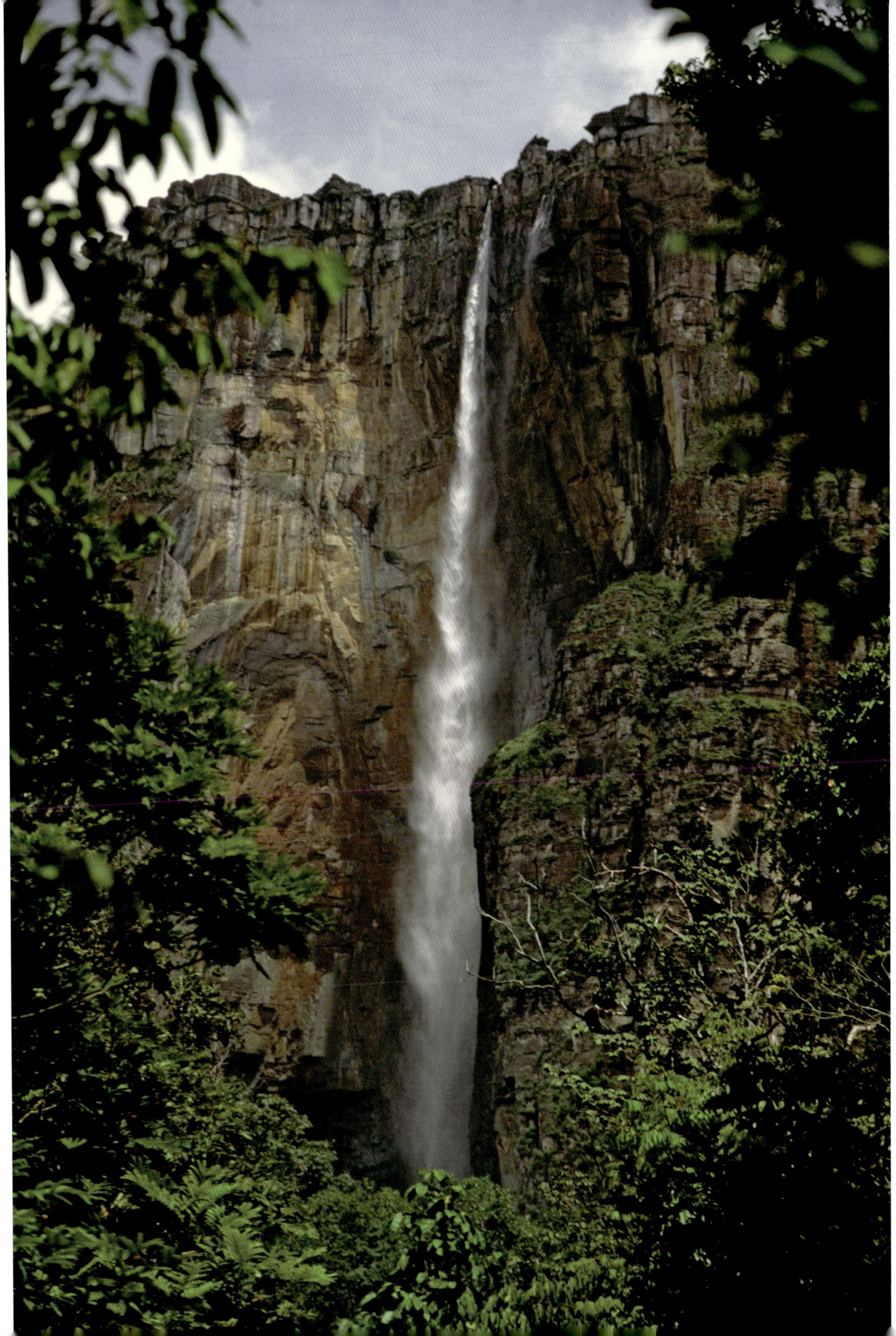

Whale fat for dessert

I wanted to photograph the highly colourful and exotic life of an Eskimo settlement of maritime hunters on the Chukotka coast of the Bering Straits. It has a name which sounds charming in Russian – Sireniki ('the little sirens'), which appears to have nothing in common with the cold hills of the Chukotka tundra, and even less with the pungent smell of blubber, and the freshly-removed walrus skins, the bloody fragments of dead whales and walruses scattered all along the shore and the uncollected rotting remains which attract hordes of flies and flocks of seagulls.

The existence of the Eskimos – the most Northerly people in the world and one of the most ancient peoples living on Russian territory – has depended, from time immemorial, entirely on whatever they could get from the creatures of the sea.

Externally, whale flesh reminded me of an old outer tyre from a car, and I cut the thin outer layer away. The fat was easy enough to chew, but the flesh actually still remained rubbery, although its tubular structure at the point where I had cut it open resembled the spores of an old brown mushroom. It's hard to convey the taste - perhaps something like the taste of unsalted pork fat.

On the map of the Arctic, both now and in the past, Eskimo settlements extend in a chain stretching thousands of kilometres, from Chukotka to Greenland. The daring seafarers navigated among the ice sheets in stable, manoeuvrable little boats.

In the Soviet era, at a time of massive population movement for the Eskimos, only Sireniki, by some miracle, managed to stay in its ancestral location – on the open shore, exposed to all the winds that blow, where the sea doesn't freeze even in the winter. It's only due to the absence of a sheltered bay at Sireniki that a traditional Eskimo vessel has managed to survive right down to our own times – a light boat, covered with walrus skins and known as a *baidar*. So that now the seven vessels of this type to be found there make up the entire whaling fleet of Chukotka.

From the beginning of July to the end of September, the walruses leave their breeding-ground on the Rudder promontory; migrate from South to North, travelling through the Sireniki area along the shoreline itself.

The weather was finally propitious for hunting, and I joined the team of the experienced hunter Andrei Ankalin. The powerful motor lifted the prow of the light *baidar*, and ice fragments flew at me from over the sides and from the motor shaft. Behind me, at the wheel, was Andrei Ankalin. In front, with his back to me, his brother-in-law, Vladimir Alexeyev, was handling the motor. Behind him was the steersman's brother, Nikolai Galgaugie. And in the prow was his nephew, Sergei S'haugie, in charge of the harpoon – a family crew, as in days of old. Andrei also had a carbine. It was lying on the deck under his arm. On the port side, Sergei and Nikolai had metal harpoons already prepared on their long shafts. Their strong, coiled lines connected them to big bright plastic floating buoys and 'flares'. The Eskimos' most ancient invention – the rotating harpoon – has an anchor which opens under an animal's skin. Skilfully thrown, it is a guarantee of a successful hunt.

The *baidar* boats swiftly moved out in a fan shape from the shoreline. Everyone was watching the sea, in the direction from which the walruses might appear. But then one of the boats turned. At that very moment, a shot rang out, and then another, and then our neighbours let fly with both barrels.

It was the Tiypiyhkakov family's boat that caught the first walrus, after it had dived five or six times. It had scarcely appeared above the water when the hunters were beating on the water with rubber paddles, imitating the sounds of a killer whale, the terror of the seas. The walrus poked its moustached head out of the water. The boat swooped on the badly wounded animal, and in a trice the harpoon had been flung into it. The shaft detonated, and the line swiftly paid out under the water, dragging two floats behind it. It was clear that this was an old bull, since the red float, which had a volume of not less than 100 litres, went on moving in the water for a long time. But now the walrus couldn't get away.

We managed to turn the boat round and fired twice. We chased after the walrus, and the young harpooner got ready to throw. 'Don't stand up!' Andrei managed to shout, seeing that I was rising with my camera. Then everything happened at lightning speed. Not having heard Ankalin, I stood up, and, leaning towards the side away from the backs of the hunters, I managed to photograph the heavy harpoon going into the walrus's chest. The boat was dragged forward by inertia. The thick line, with its steel spring, darted after the harpoon, scraping some skin from my neck, and the red float flew past, like a huge cannonball, a few centimetres from my head.

The walrus opened wide its suffering eyes in its death agony. It was a sight that really made me feel awful inside, and I knew that my first walrus hunt would be my last.

At the final moment of the hunt, I needed to get the baidar into a photo taken from as high a point as possible with the red floats, the hunter in the act of throwing the harpoon and, of course, the harpooned walrus, and so I waited for 'our' walrus with an AF Nikkor 24/2.8 wide-angled lens.

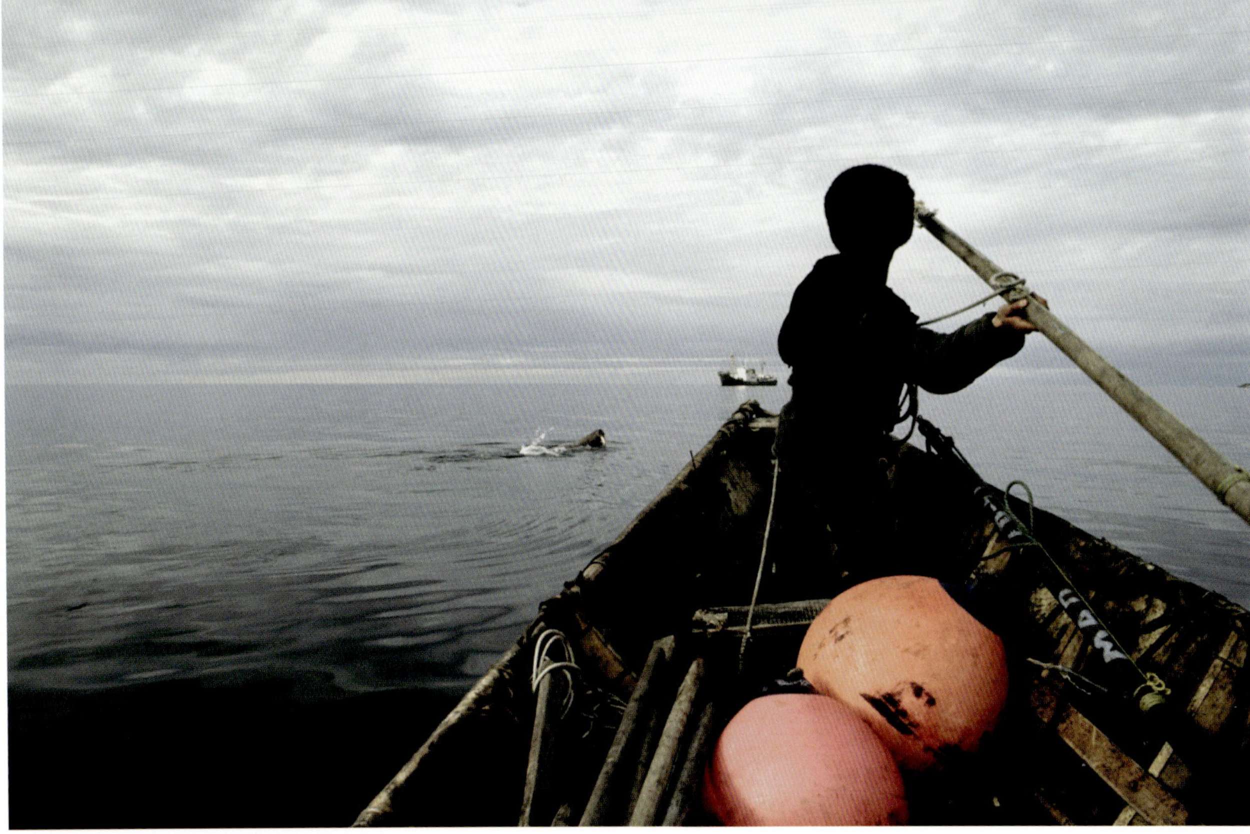

The Eskimo village of the walrus hunters – Sireniki, Chukotka. The whale festival takes place every time one is killed. The entire population comes out onto the shore of the ocean. Drums are beaten, and songs ring out. The Eskimos' favourite delicacy is the pink fat blubber under the whale's skin, with a strip of glossy black skin. When a whaling ship divides a grey whale's carcass up with long flensing knives, the whole village gorges on taro – scraps, pouches, polyethylene bags full of blubber.

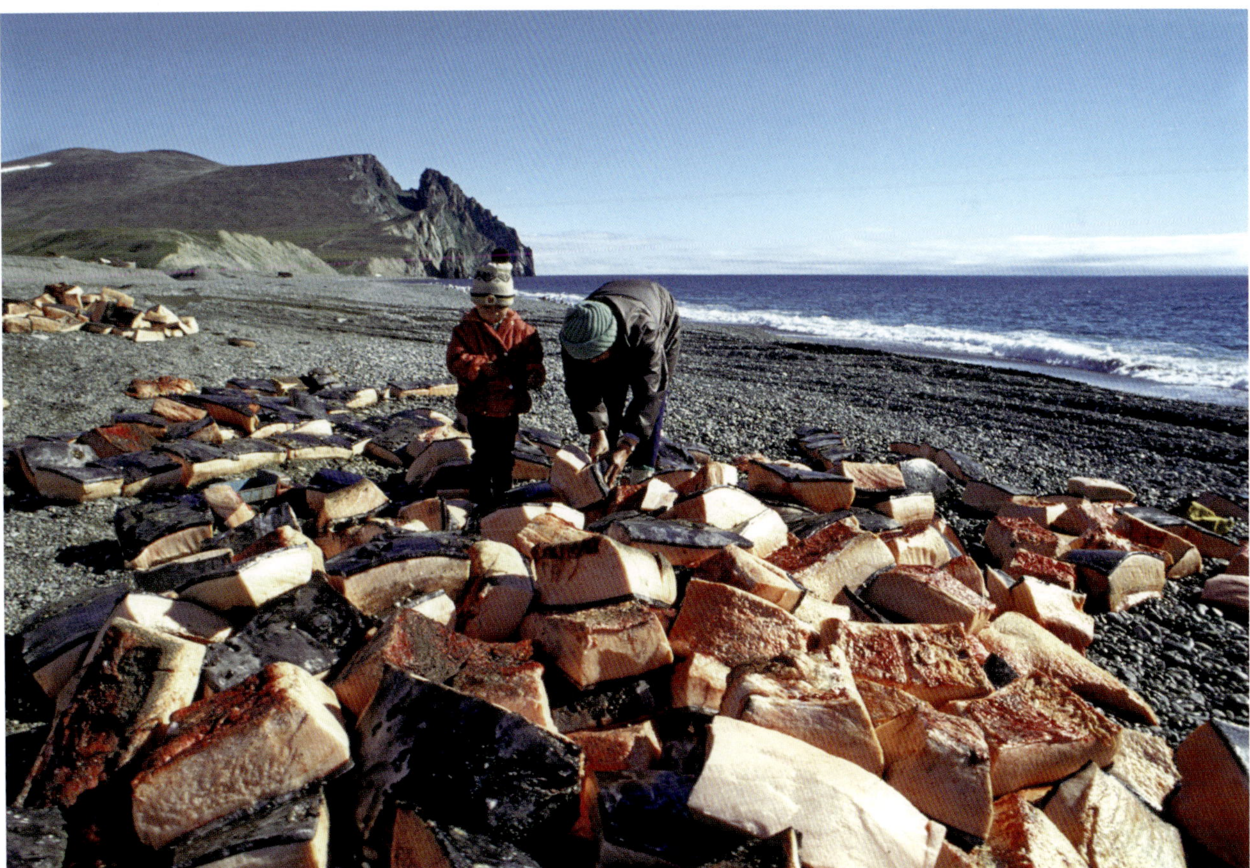

The life of the Eskimos – the most
Northerly people in the world, one
of the most ancient nations living in
Russian territory, has been entirely
dependent, since time immemorial,
on what they can obtain from the
sea by hunting. On the Chukotka
peninsula, and in the Behring Straits
region, there are about one and a half
thousand Eskimos. Their ancestors
arrived there a few thousand years
ago. When I arrived in Sireniki I was
amazed to find, near the dining-room,
the jaw-bones of a Greenland whale,
eroded and turned grey with time, on
which children's clothes were spread
out to dry. When I asked with interest
whether they had been embedded
there long, I received the completely
serious reply: 'Probably about two
thousand years'.

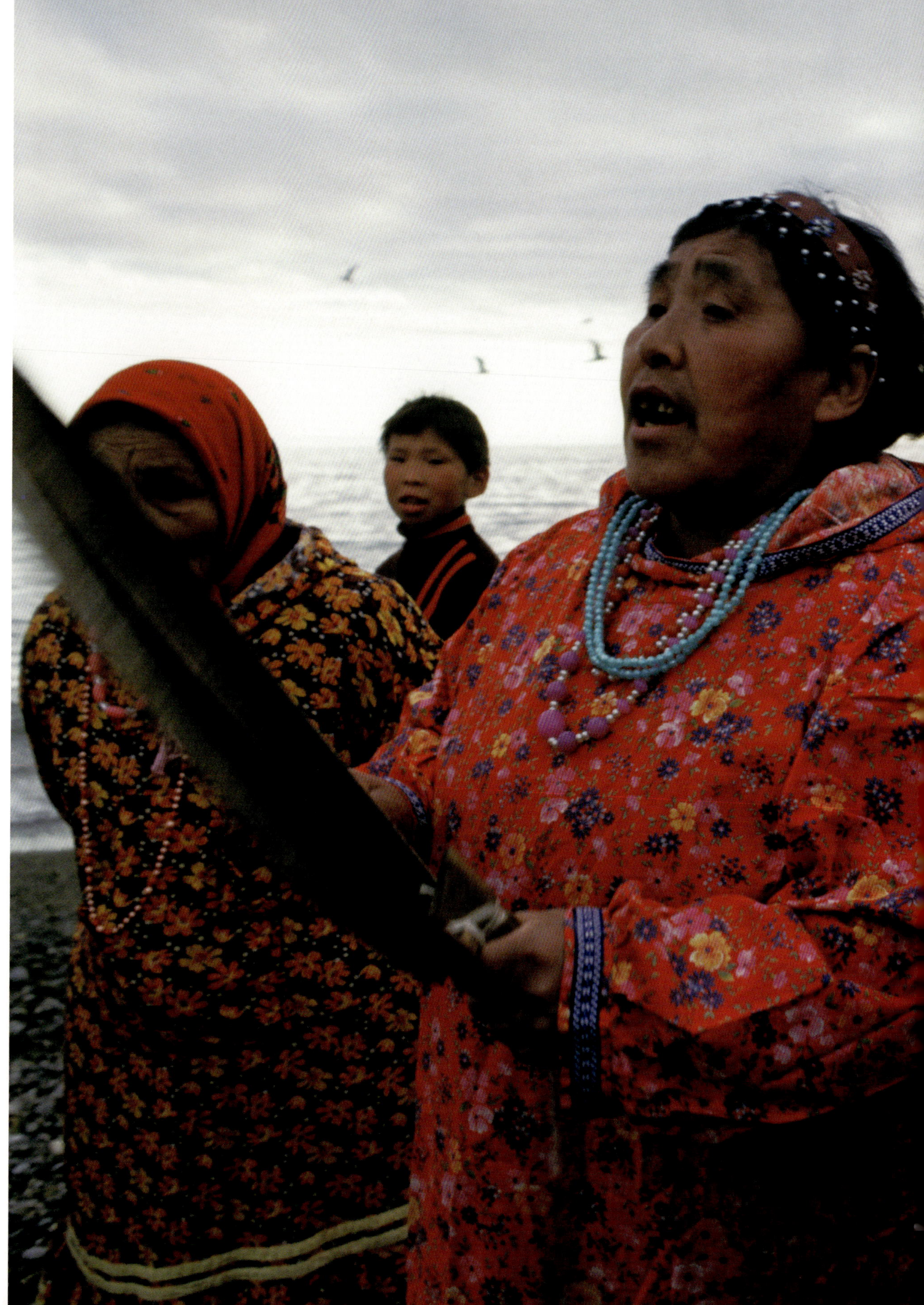

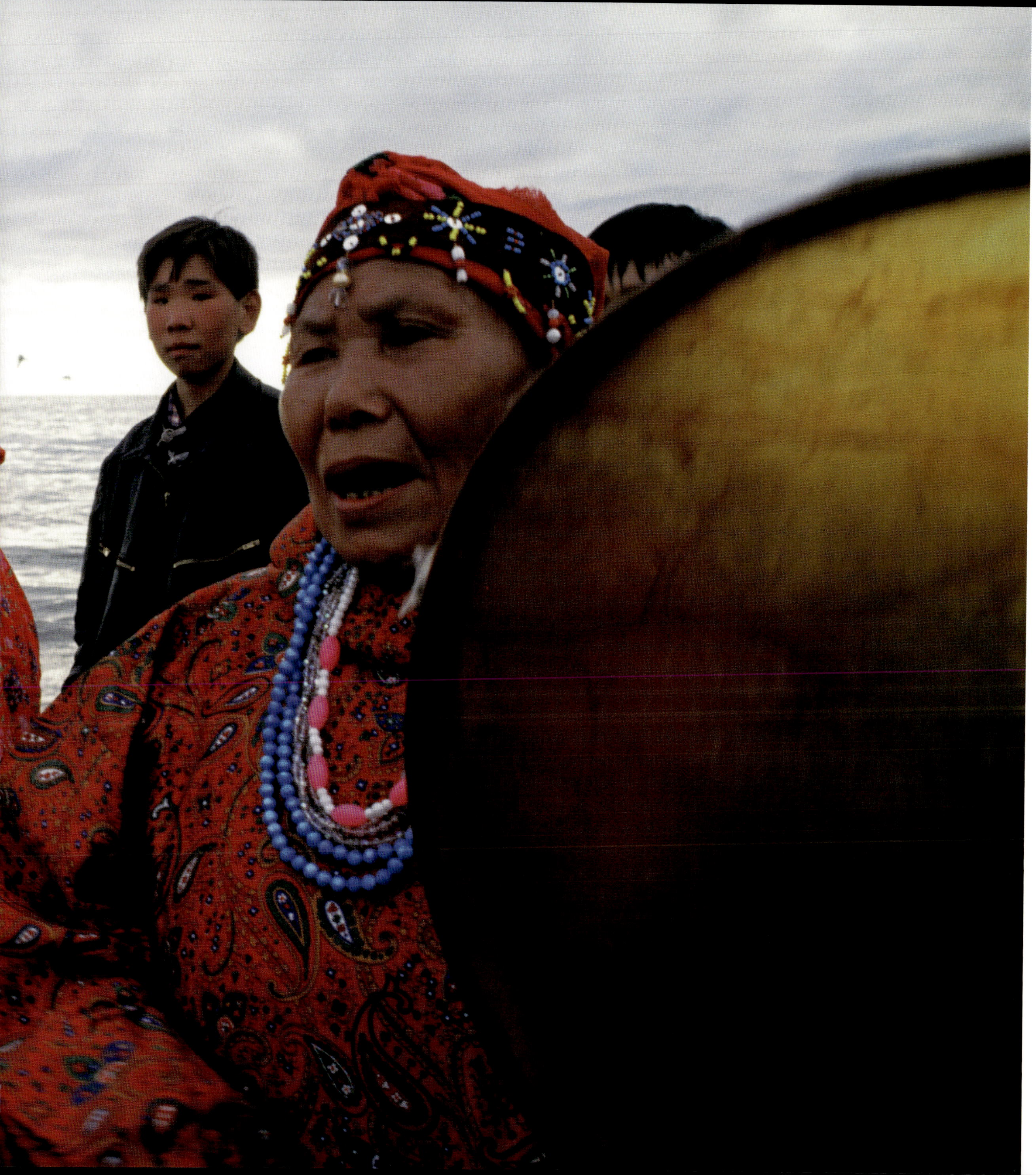

The best hills are still only hills!

I know better than anyone that a downhill skier with a camera – or, vice versa, a photographer fascinated by downhill skiing – will have a difficult time. A casual observer might see something like this: an extremely clumsy person trying to keep his balance on a steep, slippery slope and holding a camera in his frozen fingers. He is at risk of being swept away by a passing gang of frost-bitten snowboarders. On the very brightest screen on a sunny winter's day, you can hardly see anything, because you have to have a camera with a viewfinder. On the other hand, any shot will include some hills with sparkling snow, and off-piste skiers executing graceful turns on the steep slope, desperate leaps, rotating 'saltos' in 'high pipes' and on trampolines, plus the bright cabins of the cable-cars!

After years of fascination with skiing, I've taken photos at half a hundred resorts in all the important downhill skiing countries in Europe, and I've worked out a series of rules for myself. The most important is that I must have spare accumulators and manage with one universal zoom. Just imagine taking a photo from a chairlift seat – the best position for taking photos in the mountains. The abyss is before you – a very beautiful ravine with constantly changing décor. Every few seconds, a chair comes up to meet you with brightly dressed skiers. On a cliff, you notice a mountain goat, and a long way ahead the legendary Matterhorn rises up with its standout profile. I would love to see how you take a lens out of your camera bag or your rucksack and fit it with your unresponsive numb fingers. But the most important question is – what can you actually photograph?

The ski resort of Hemsedal (Norway). Apparently, the suspended ski-lift is able to weave a magic spell to bring together the grid-like support and the structures, the red 'saucers' of the seats and the skiers' bright clothing.

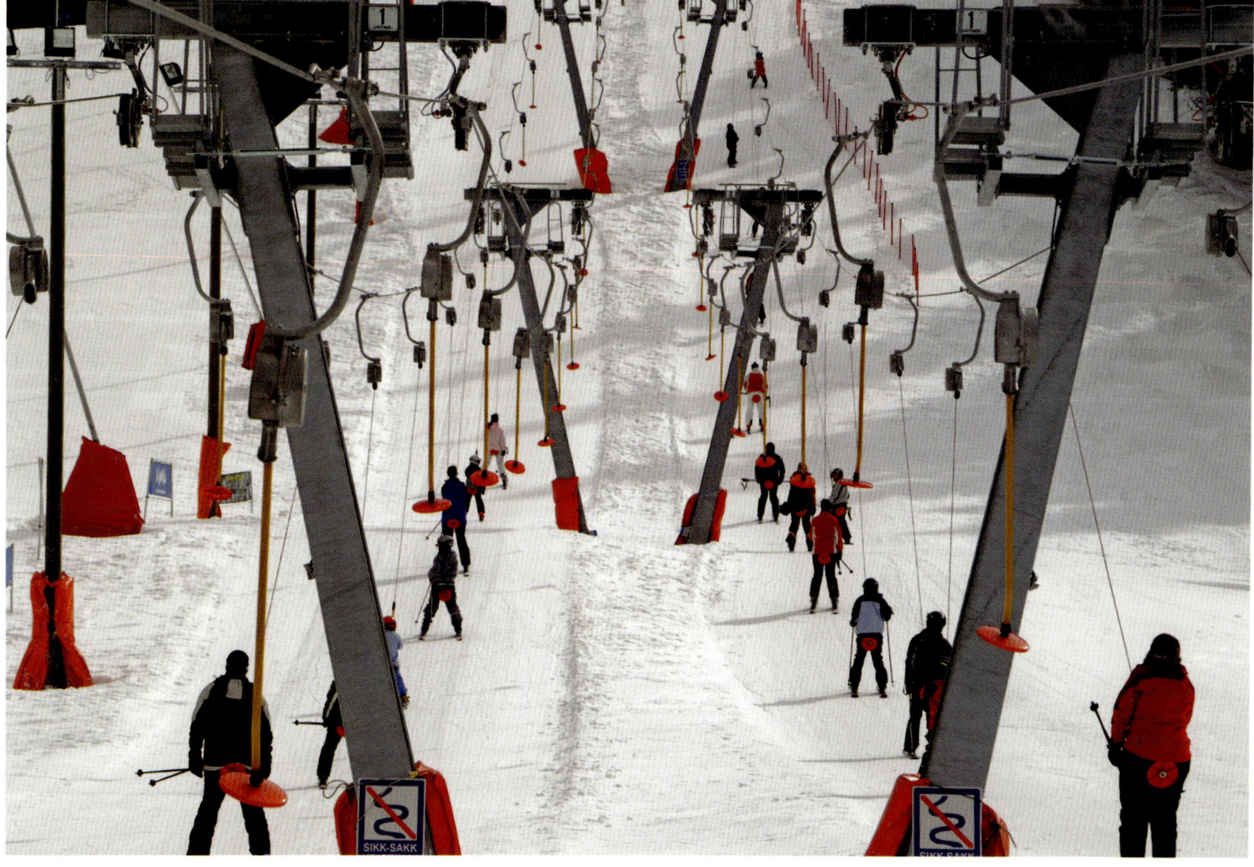

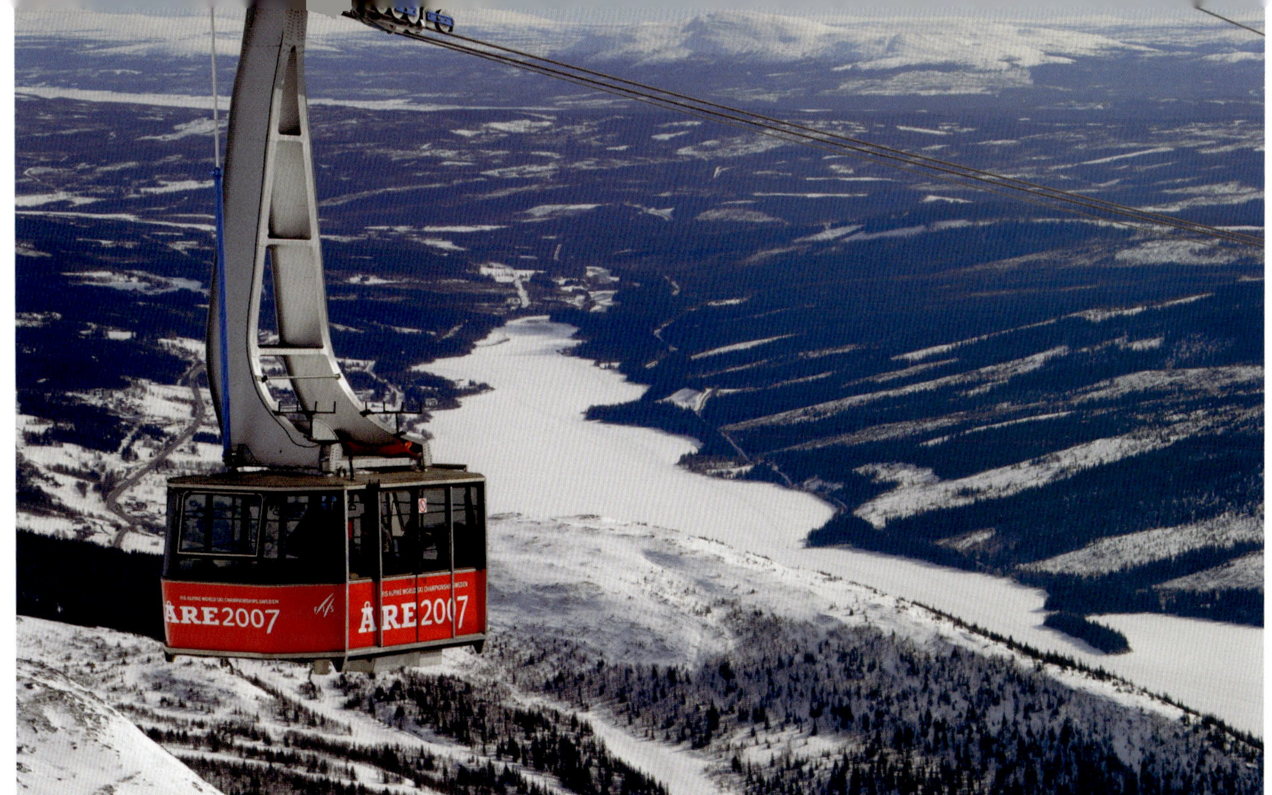

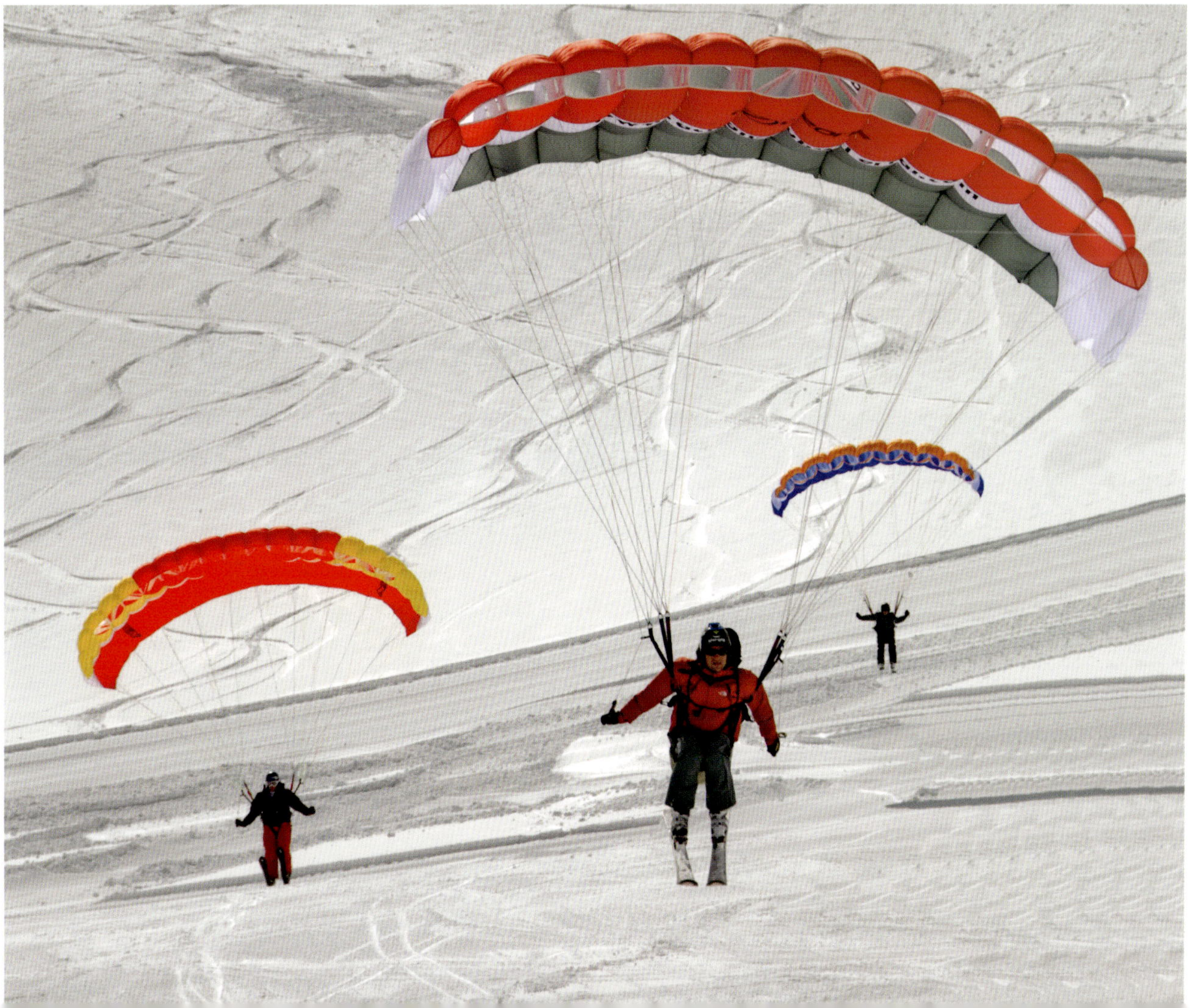

The ski resort of Are (Sweden). The Scandinavian tundra is not the Alps and although it's beautiful in its own way, it's better to photograph it with a rich foreground – here with something like a carmine or crimson car in a 'pendulum' system, for example. Only these tramways in the sky move quickly, although rarely – the entire fleet actually consists of two, as opposed to the tens of 'gondolas'. The paragliders at the Austrian resort of Zelden stopped me in my tracks. I photographed some of them with a telezoom lens and then, turning round, I saw some more heavenly riders coming straight for me. I had seconds to spare in which to rotate the lens into the minimum focal setting and succeed in pressing the button without 'cutting off' the skis or the parachute.

Higher than the Spassky Tower!

In mid-June after coming home from one of my photography trips, I visited St. Basil's Church, and I couldn't help noticing an unusually large police presence and a cordon around Red Square. Apparently the basketball match of the century was about to begin at any moment, pitting the previous champions, the USSR, winners of the Seoul Olympic Games in 1988, against a representative NBA team – the stars of American basketball. I composed a picture in my mind – the legendary Sabonis was leaping higher than the Spassky Tower and flinging the ball into the net. The game was absolutely unique. Up until now, Red Square had been used as a sporting venue only once in its many centuries of history – in 1936. As a special favour to Stalin, an exhibition football match had been staged between Dynamo and Spartak.

I had a few shots left in my Nikon, but there was a cordon of police blocking my path. 'Comrade Colonel' I said, rushing up to the senior officer and matching steps with him 'You did promise that journalists would be allowed in without any excessive bureaucracy!'. The colonel hesitated for a moment. Then he decisively took me by the arm, waving away his subordinates, and escorted me to the basketball court.

The sky and the warm early evening light were ideal for photography. The Spassky Tower was golden in the rays of sunlight, but alas, Sabonis did not sign up for my plan. The ring of American team members, at whom he fired off apparently unbeatable shots one after the other, were actually positioned on the Spassky Tower side, and I had to take my photos on the mausoleum side – and indeed, against the light, right into the sun. I quickly ran across to the ring of our team members, wriggled through their legs like an eel and, knowing perfectly well that I wouldn't be given long to crawl around the pitch, got the hoop in my viewfinder with the star on the tower, scarcely managing to compose the picture in the space available. My cheek was pressed against the ground, and I just waited for some dramatic moment in the game. I photographed an attack in a horizontal snap – to be turned round later – and at that very moment I felt, rather than saw, that the gigantic chequered sole of a boot was flying over my temple. Evading a hundred kilograms of muscle (with some difficulty), I followed the continuation of the attack. The ball had been seized by a powerful two-metre high black man, who was preparing to shoot, while Sabonis vainly attempted to block him. I managed to press the button as my legs were seized and I was dragged off the field of play. There were about forty people sitting on the Press benches, but anything you could see from there was against the background of a high brick wall. To get the shots I needed, I just had to be right under the hoop.

The most interesting thing about travel photography is to shoot events: holidays, festivals, tournaments, etc.. In Rio de Janeiro, Venice and Valencia, that means carnival. In Tibet, it's the Buddhist festivals. In Borodino, it's the historical reconstruction of the legendary battle. In the Alps it's wine and cheese festivals, in London it's trooping the colour. Of course, it's better to know about such happenings in advance, but you sometimes stumble on them by chance, and the fact that you haven't got a seat or you've got no official papers is no excuse for failing to take photos from the best viewpoint – better photos than anyone else!

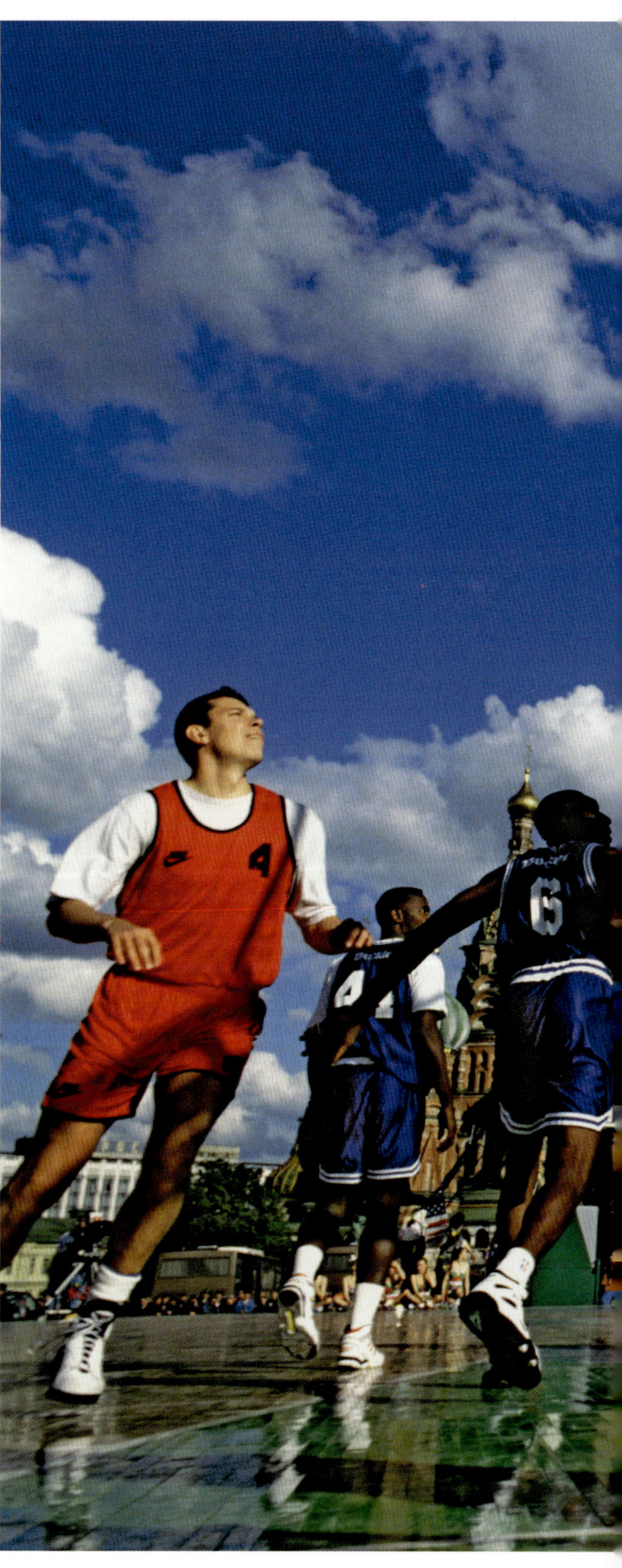

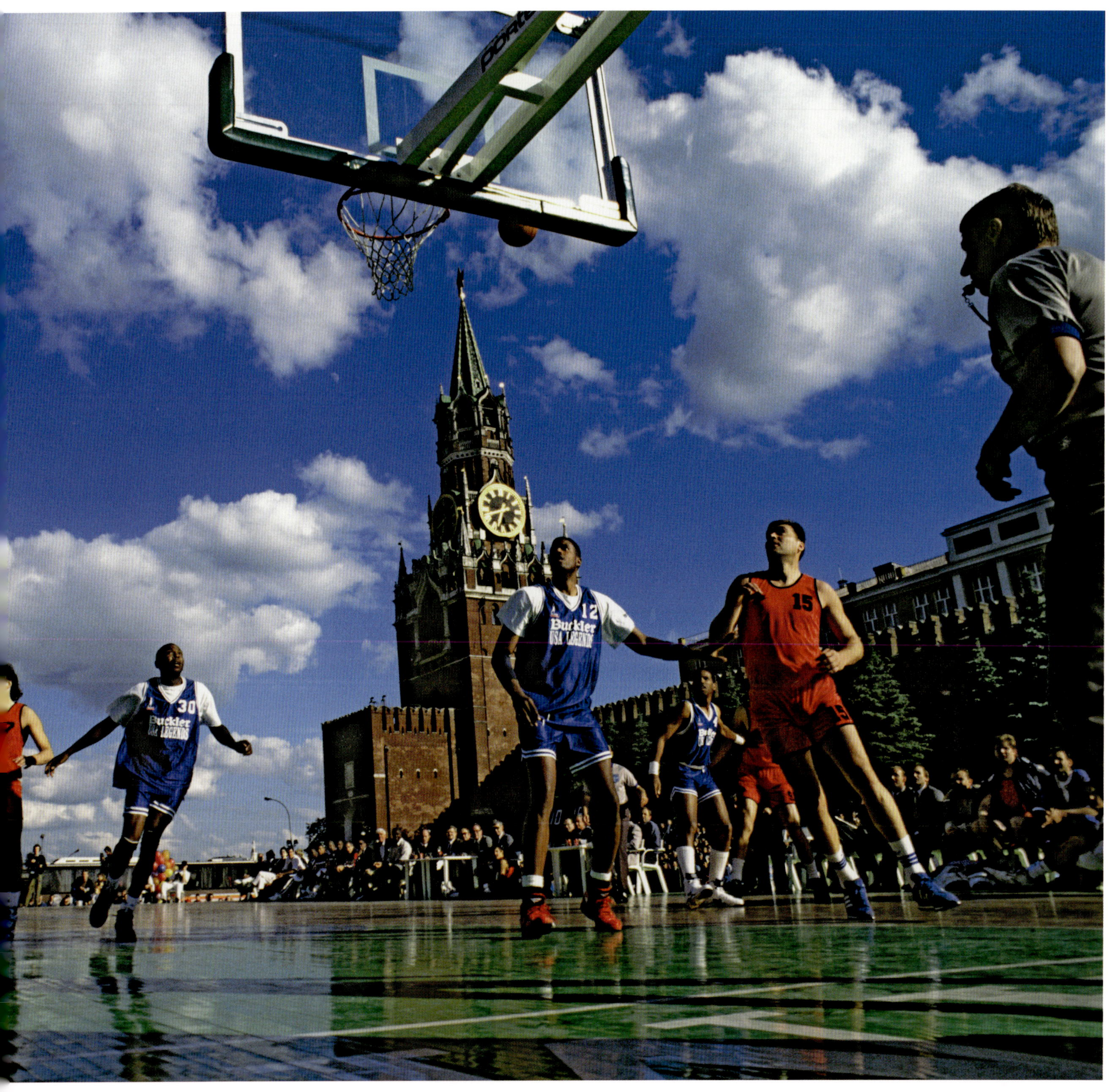

Buckler
USA LEGENDS
12
Buckler
USA LEGENDS
30
15

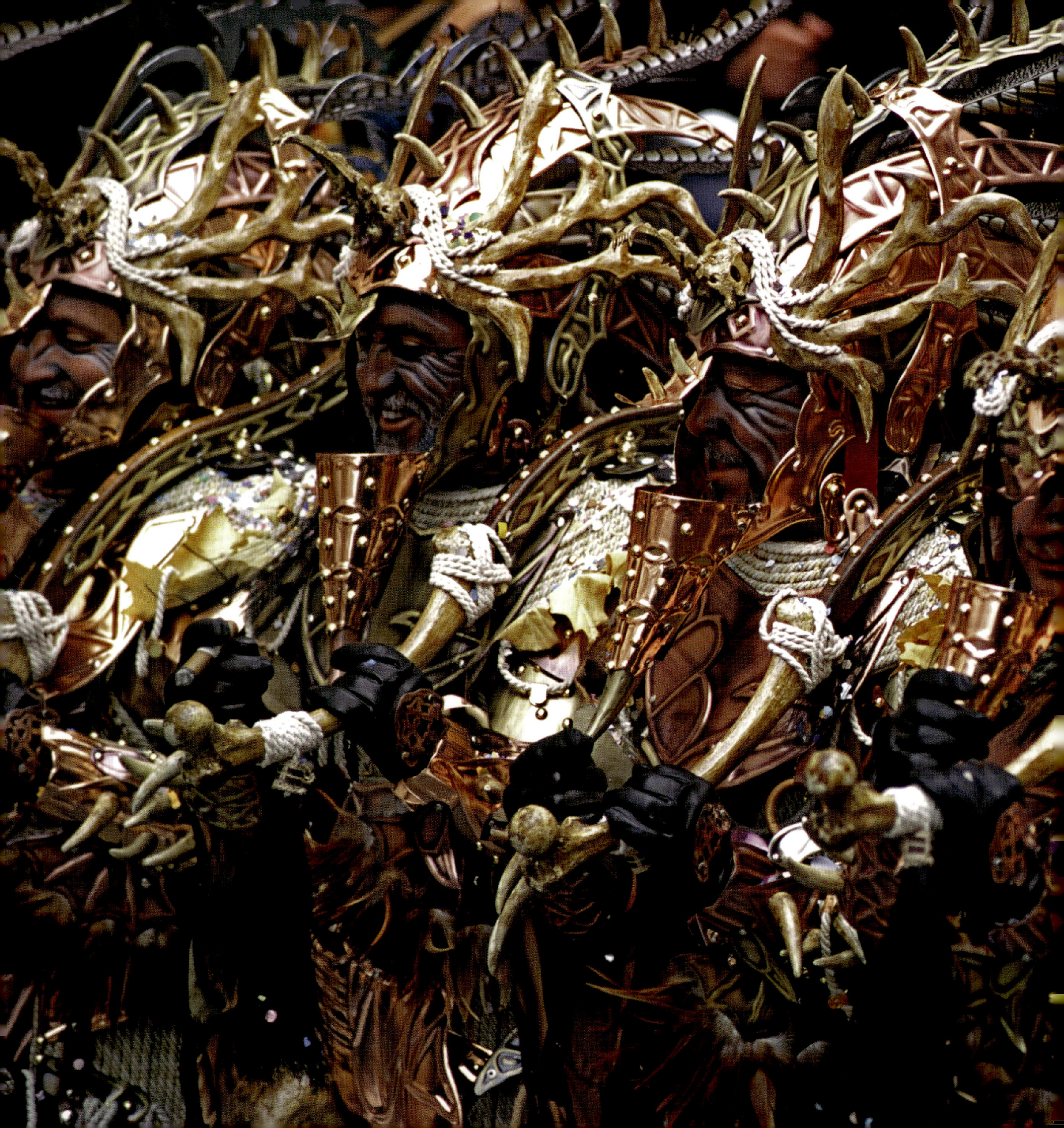

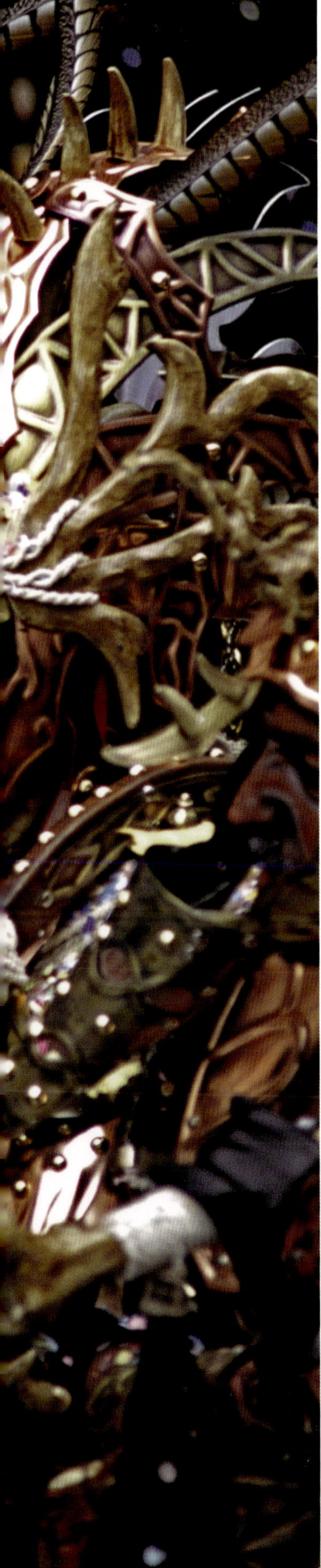

Captured by the Moors

Spain is famous for its great number and variety of festivals. The Spanish love to have a lot of fun and make a lot of noise – and they find any excuse to do so. In one Valencian community alone, there are more than 600 bright, ethnographically colourful events a year – almost two a day. The most famous and the grandest spectacle of all is the 'Festival of Moors and Christians'. Its main events unfold in the town of Alcoy, north of Alicante, from 22 to 25 April. It then rolls out in a great wave to hundreds of other small towns and villages throughout the remainder of the year. So whatever time of year you come here on holiday, you will almost certainly be able to take part in this national fiesta. Just go to the local tourist office and ask for the 'Moors and Christians' schedule. In Alicante the festival begins on 15 August, while in coastal Calpe, it runs from 21 to 25 October. However, the most famous festival is in Alcoy. Residents re-enact real historical battles that took place in the 13th century, during the reign of King James I of Aragon, known as the Conqueror. In 1276, Alcoy was captured by a detachment of Moors under the leadership of Al-Azraq. Townspeople and Christian knights fought the enemy bravely, but the odds were on the Moors' side. And then, as legend has it, St George appeared on a white horse, Al-Azraq was defeated and victory went to the Christians. As a mark of gratitude, the defenders of Alcoy then vowed to build a temple in honour of St George and to hold a feast day once a year on the 23rd of April, the anniversary of victory over the Moors, in honour of their celestial patron.

At first, residents just performed a few individual scenes on the feast day, but over the last 200 years the festival has gradually become the whole town's raison d'etre. For three days, thousands and thousands of fully armed soldiers in luxurious garments parade along in an endless stream, led by captains on horseback, and endless columns of swarthy, dark-skinned warriors of Allah roll by in their colourful strings of carts, with silk-clad 'Arab beauties' reclining in seductive poses. The presence of the Berber and Arab conquerors in the territories now occupied by modern Spain and Portugal endured for eight centuries, and it has left an indelible mark on the history, culture, architecture, language and customs of Europe as a whole – but first and foremost, of course, of Spain itself.

Even though the Moors were a constant presence in southern Andalusia for centuries, they made only a few separate incursions into Valencia and Aragon. Perhaps that is why the 'Festival of Moors and Christians' which is enacted in Valencia and has come to symbolise the liberation of Spain from the Moors, is very peaceful and cheerful in nature–even though it involves both the battle and the siege of the fortress and tons of gunpowder being exploded! Over the years it has developed more and more imagination and scope, and now virtually the entire town turns into a grand three-day carnival involving thousands of people. For many of them, taking part has become not so much a hobby as a way of life – if not the meaning of life itself.

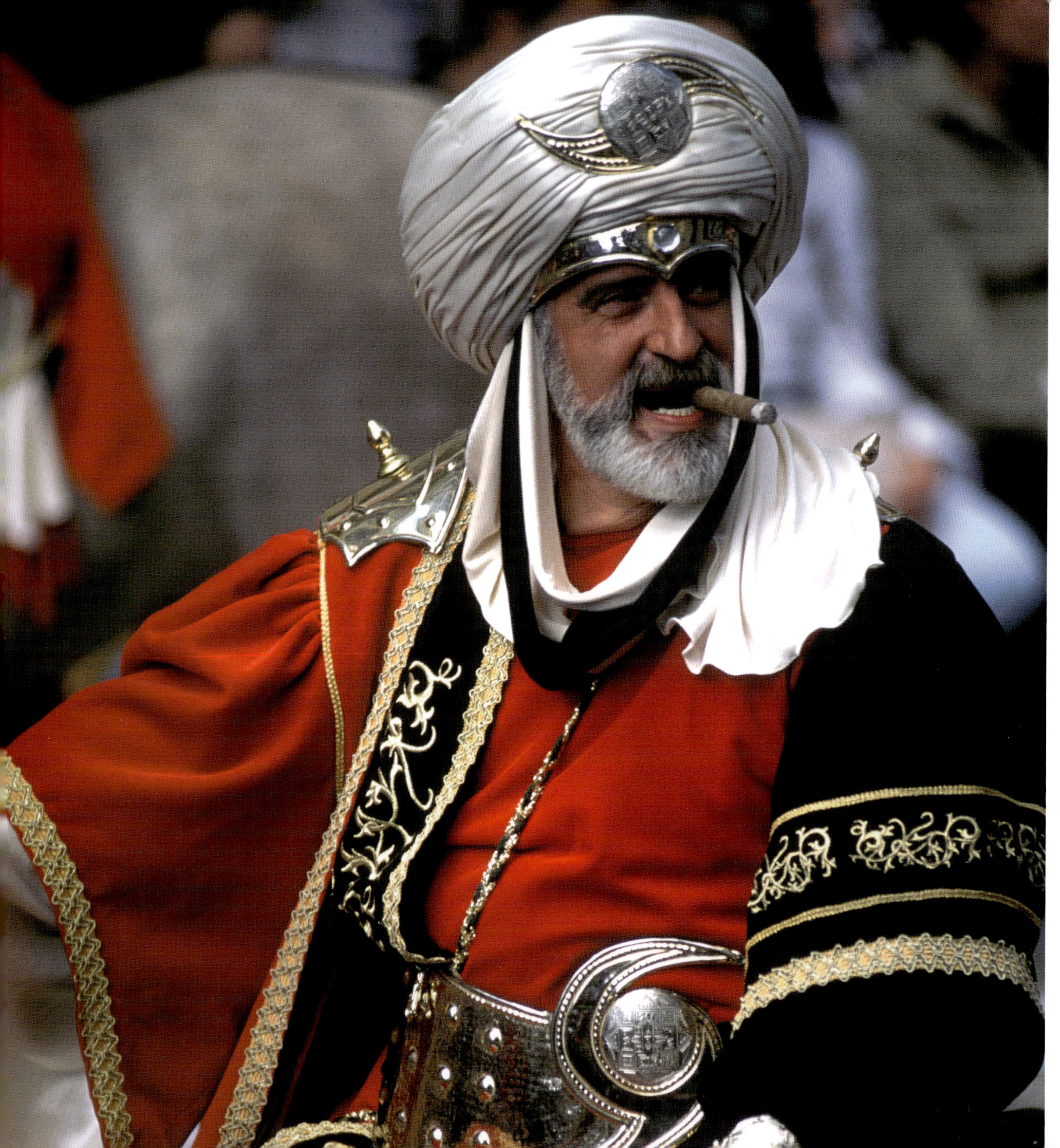

The inhabitants of Alcoy taking part in the local fiesta wear newly-sewn costumes every year – that's why the captains' elegant clothing is worth as much as a good-quality car.

A young woman in a brilliant red and gold dress participates in the festival at Alcoy.

By long tradition, there are 28 communities – or *filaes* – in the town, with 14 on each side (Moors and Christians), whose members spend all year preparing for the festival: sewing new costumes, manufacturing military accessories, attending meetings, banquets and rehearsals, discussing future performances. Taking part in these clubs requires not only a huge amount of time, but also a lot of money. Each year the festival becomes more luxurious, more sophisticated and more magnificent, forcing people to spend a fortune on kitting themselves out. For instance, the costume worn by a captain – that is, the head of a *filà* – costs as much as a good car. You will probably never see anything like this anywhere else in the world, either in terms of the scale of the event or the colourful nature of the action – or the heat of the passions it engenders. The atmosphere of the festival envelopes the audience too, so this festive event is fertile material for the photographer! You can just let yourself go, photographing the ranks of soldiers, the bright costumes and the faces lit with smiles.

To photograph holiday-makers, carnivals, processions and pilgrimages, when you have to run about from place to place to catch a shot, the ideal super-wide angle zoom has a focus distance of 16–35 mm. First of all, it has a big depth of focus – secondly, you are less likely to obtain smudged photos, and, the most important thing, you have the possibility of instantaneously changing from general view photos with a large number of people at a small distance to a close-up when you notice a particularly striking face or carnival costume in the crowd. You can get a lens like this from manufacturers of basic photographic equipment.

Each of the 28 *filaes* has one squadron in the parade at the start of the festival – a group of warriors, headed by a captain. And on the first day, these teams march through the streets of the town, in strictly regimented order, past a wooden fortress, erected on the cathedral square, which some of them will have to besiege, while others defend it. The crowds of yelling fans, friends and relatives who have come from other towns or are just tourists support their favourites from the balconies and rooftops, from the adjacent vantage points and alleyways. The procession goes on from eleven in the morning till dusk.

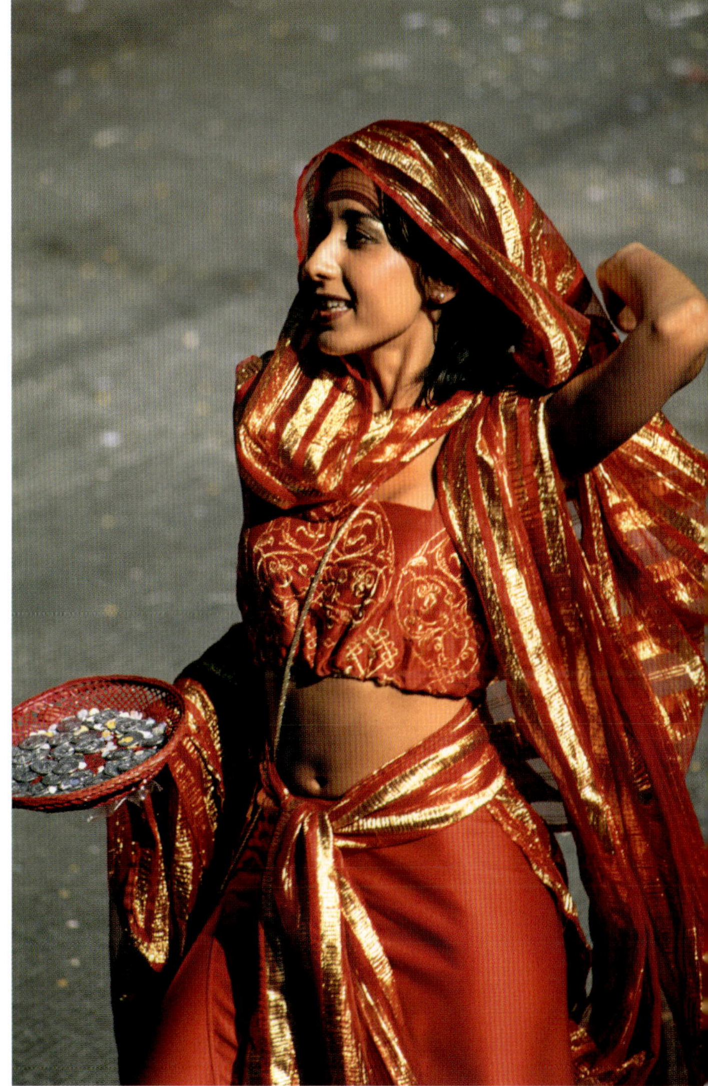

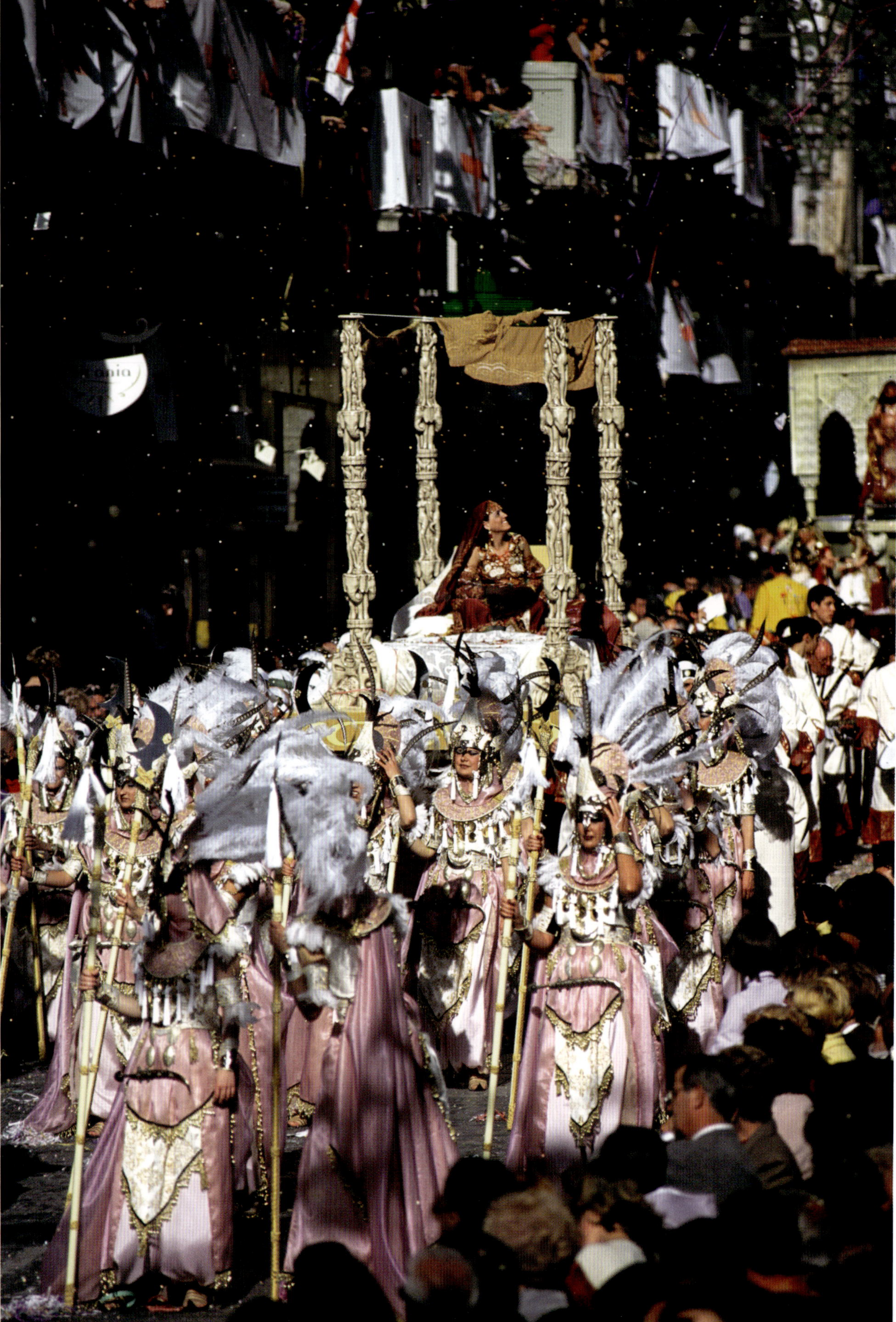

On the main street of Alcoy, under a hail of confetti, a body of Moors moves forward, defended by warlike types with halbards.

The second day is devoted to St. George, and a religious procession passes through the streets of the town. A service begins in the cathedral at noon, dedicated to the six heavenly guardians of the town. People distribute sweets and souvenirs in the streets. On this day it's the done thing to visit the hospitals and orphanages with gifts.

On the last day of the festival, the town is full of the thunder of firearms and gunpowder. All day, the Christians and Moors struggle for control of the fortress of Alcoy, with first one and then the other gaining the upper hand. People fire arrows from bows and shot from arquebuses, and the fifes and drums are never silent. The saintly cavalier appears at the decisive moment of the battle. The relics are returned to the churches, and fireworks explode over the town. People continue strolling through the bright, illuminated streets of Alcoy late into the night. It's time for photographers to get ready too, because there are so many peoples in the world, each with their own festivals.

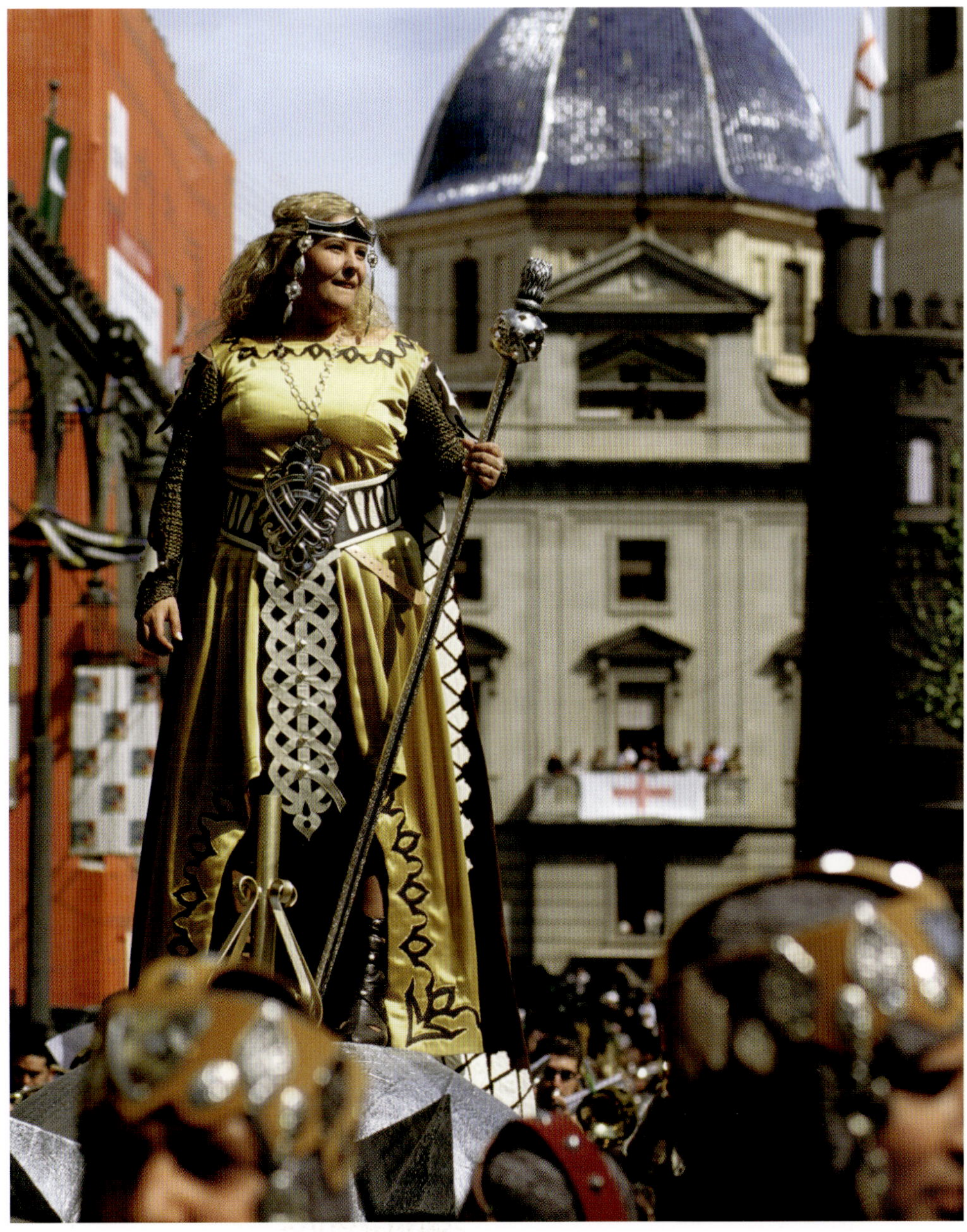

The central square of Alcoy, with the modern cathedral and the decorated fortress. The knights are attacking the Moors. And who wouldn't die for such a beautiful queen?

It's difficult to believe that the Arabs
went into battle with the knights with
such peacocks' crests on their heads
as we see here. But here they are
certain the costumes are absolutely
historically authentic .

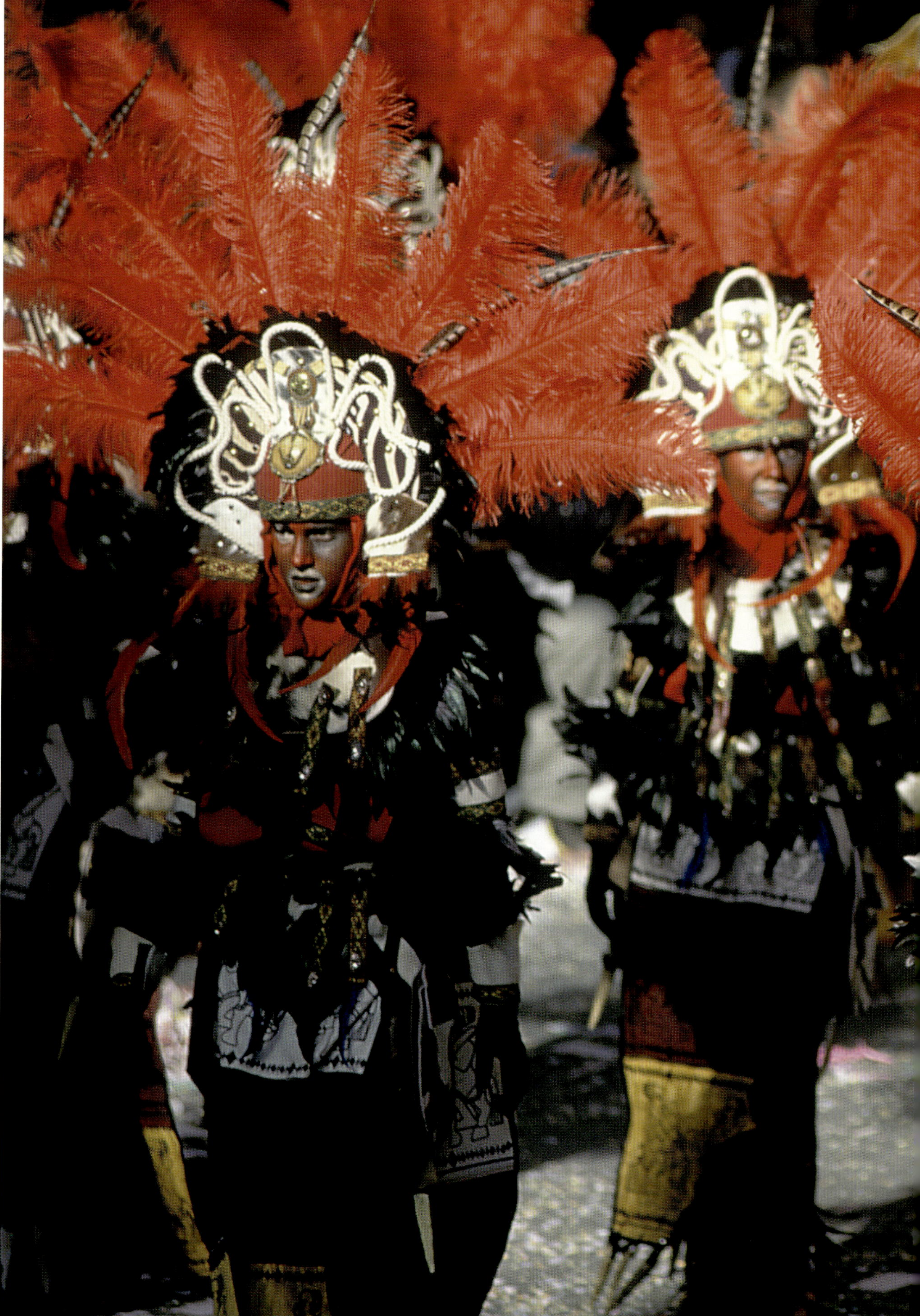

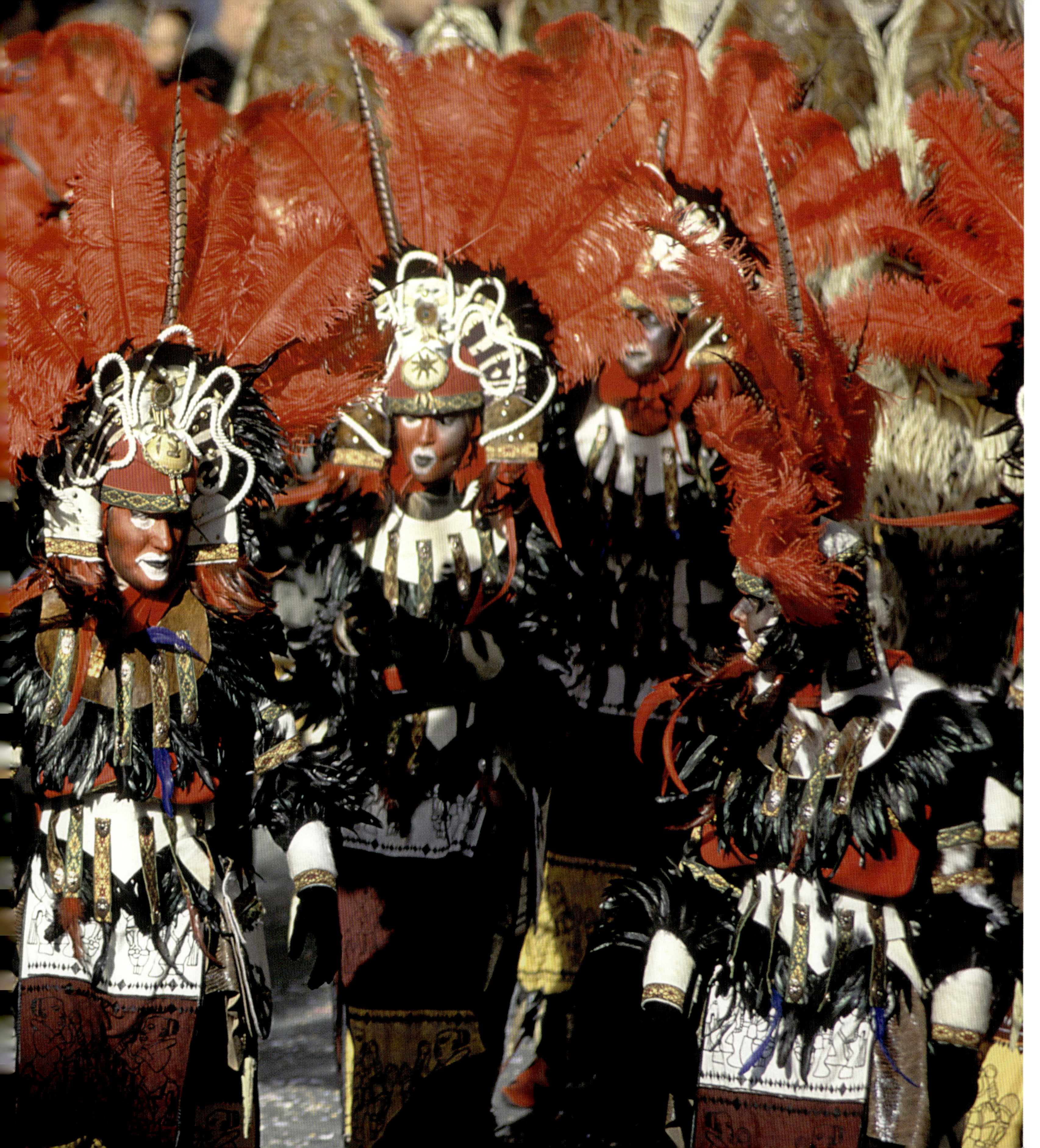

How can you photograph the Venus de Milo?

As a rule, photographing interiors and works of art in museums, art galleries, places of worship, palaces or even the metro requires exceptional resourcefulness and ingenuity. First of all, each of these places has its own rules about photography. A lot of museums have a sign at the entrance, showing a camera, a dog, a cigarette and a mobile phone, all crossed through with a thick red line. But if you cannot see any explicit prohibitions on photography – or you can see something that might be explaining such a ban, but in a language you don't know – then asking whether you can take pictures is the most ridiculous thing you can do. Much better to remember the pithy saying: 'everything that is not forbidden is permitted' and waste no time – keep shooting until somebody explains to you that it is not allowed. That's precisely how I managed to set up my tripod and very successfully photograph one of the best pictures in the National Gallery in Perugia for my photo-album on Italy. Then an attendant hurried up to me and tried to take my tripod away – apparently it was OK to take photos, just as long as you didn't use a tripod or a flash!

You will frequently have to take pictures without a tripod, with a fully open aperture and a shutter speed of $\frac{1}{8}$ of a second, using your arm or cheek to wedge the camera against your shoulder, and holding your breath. This approach is not recommended to the amateur. It is hardly likely that the resulting picture will be sharp. But there is no reason to curse the museum: its monopoly on professional photography enables it to earn a little money by putting out books, guides and postcards – you should be grateful it lets you in at all with a camera!

Where the photographer's way is barred by a big, bold 'no entry' sign, it's still worth asking whether photography is allowed by payment of a fee. This is the case in many places – and what's more, at very modest prices.

However, returning to the original question of how to photograph the Venus de Milo, perhaps we can look at this from a different angle: is it really necessary to photograph her at all? Maybe it would be better not to waste your time or your patience, you could buy a book instead or a postcard where she has been reproduced with a professional lighting set-up and a great deal of expression. On the other hand, we all know what the true travel photographer will say in answer to that – and there really isn't any argument. After all, he or she is the person for whom this book has been written.

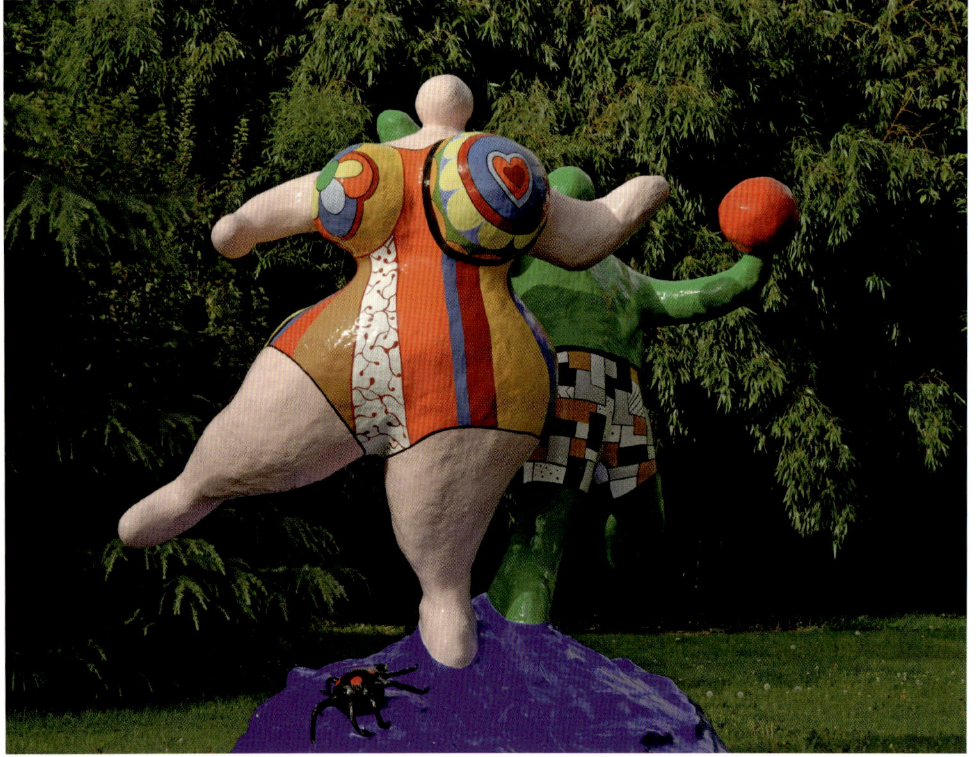

Martigny (Switzerland). 'The Bathing Beauties' (1984), a cult sculpture by Niki de Saint Phalle in the Pierre Gianadda Museum. Two thousand years after the creation of the great Aphrodite (the Venus de Milo), our ideas of what is beautiful have altered somewhat.

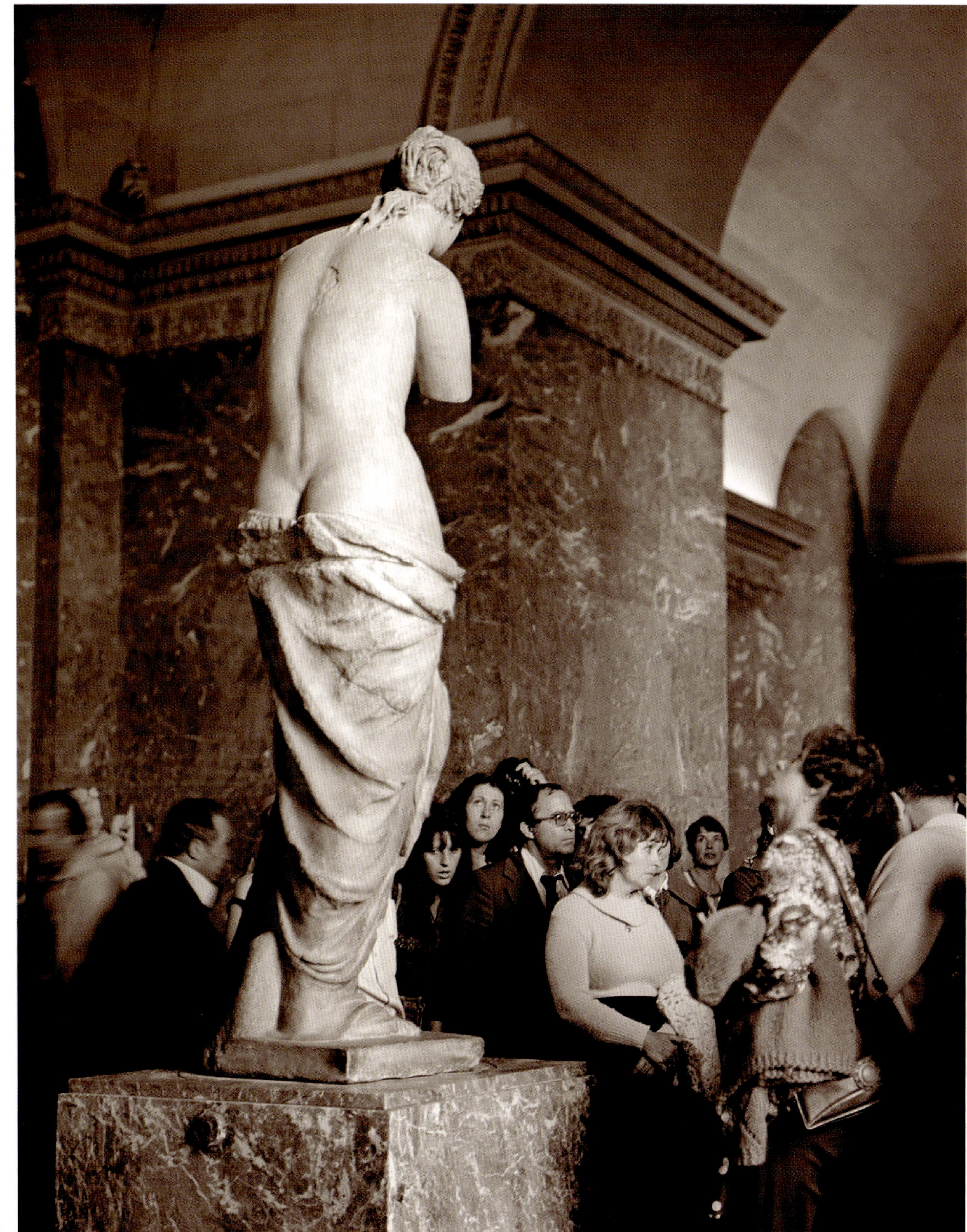

'Venus de Milo'. The Louvre, Paris, France. The most famous statue in the world is always surrounded by a mass of visitors. This photograph was taken on black-and-white film without any fill-in light using a professional twin-lens camera with a quiet central shutter and a right-angle viewfinder, allowing the photographer to shoot from waist level, unnoticed by people around him.

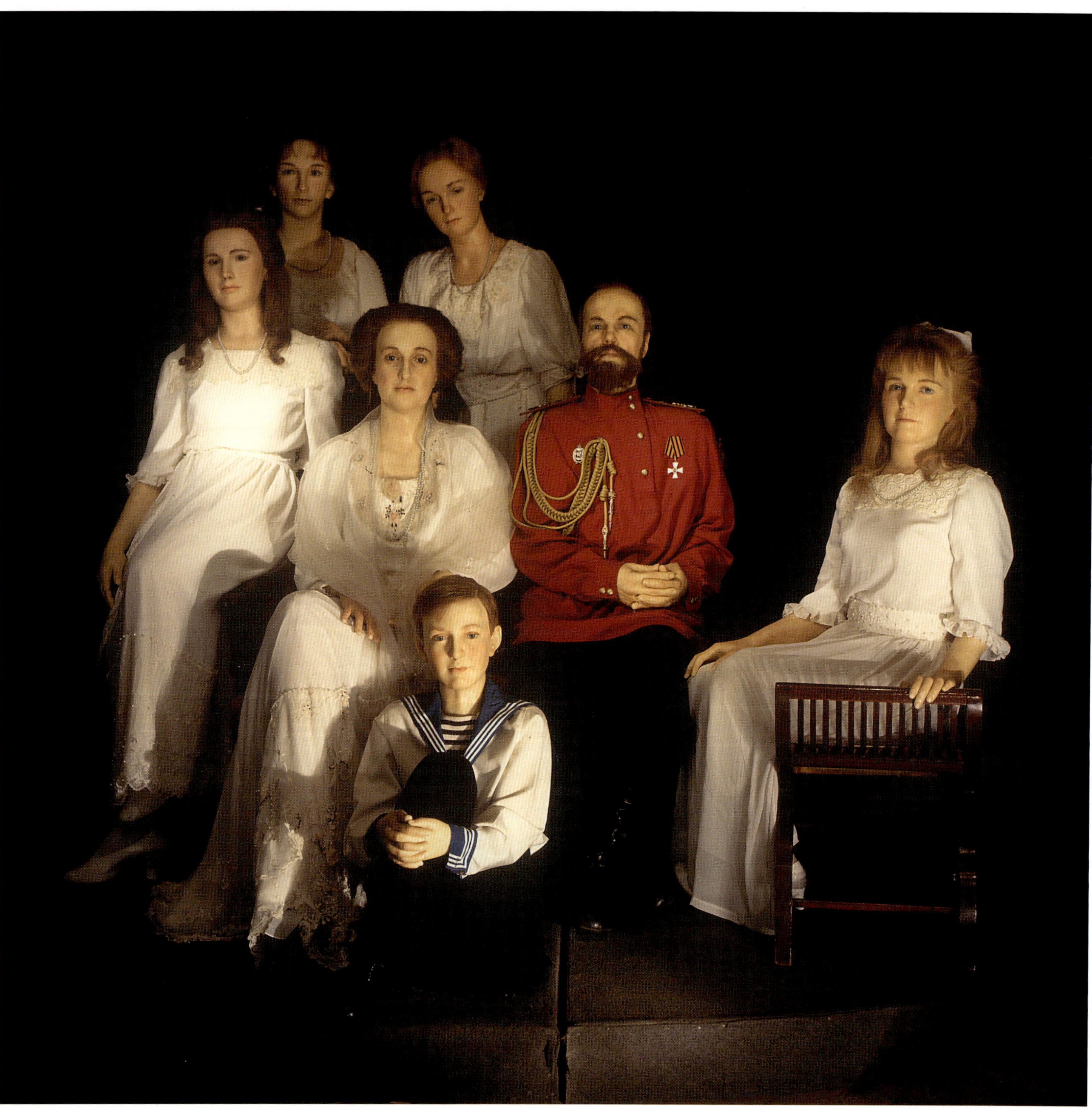

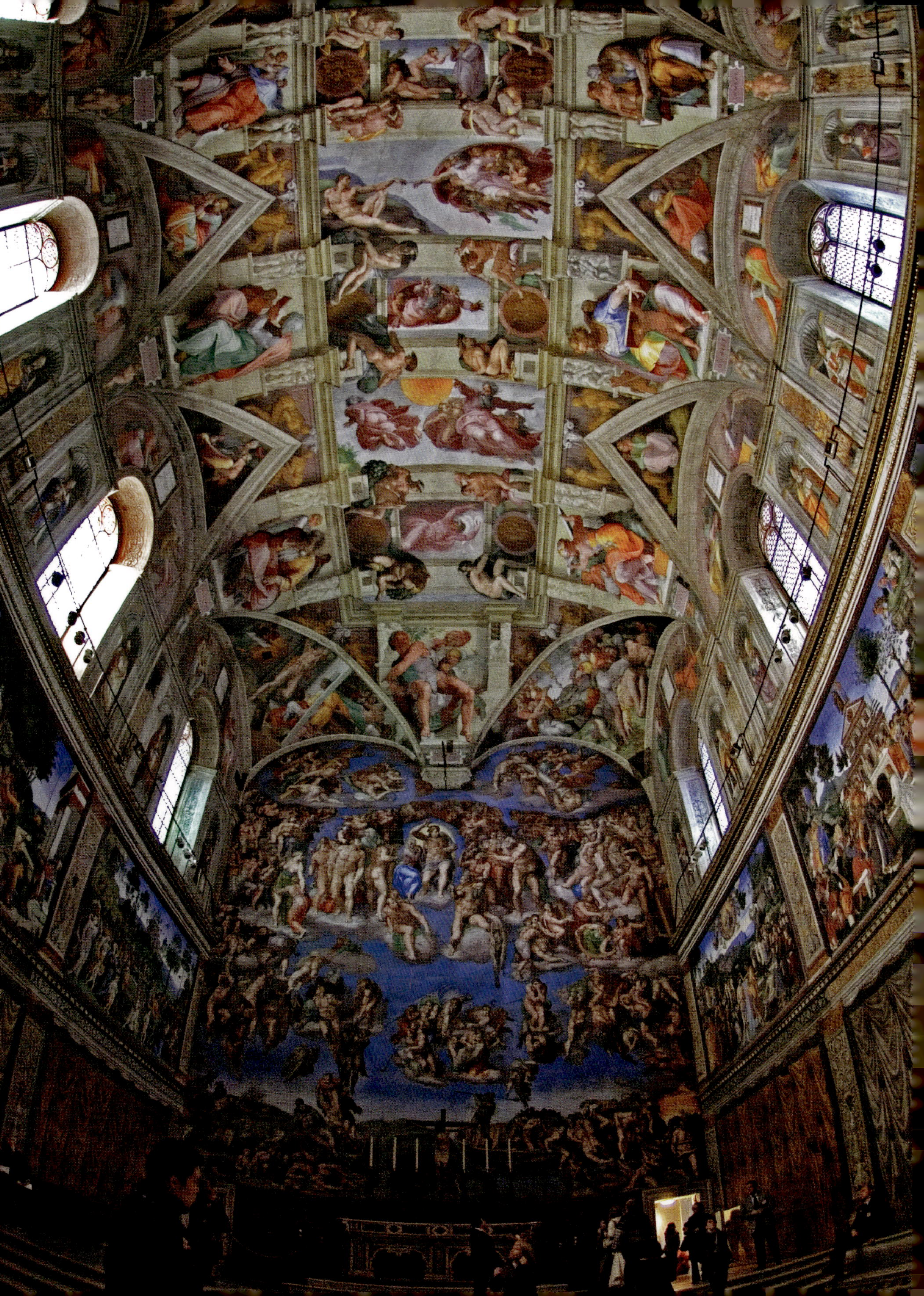

LEFT

Emperor Nicholas II and his family.
St Petersburg Waxworks Museum.
Russia. The photograph was taken
using film (6 x 6 cm format) and a
tripod, with fill-in light from the
right-hand side.

RIGHT

Vatican Museum. The Sistine chapel of
the great Michelangelo. Panel showing
the 'Day of Judgment'. Taken with a
fisheye lens with a sensitivity of
400 ASA.

The 64-gun flagship 'Vasa', decorated
in baroque style – one of the few fully
preserved old sailing ships. Stockholm,
Sweden. Her amazing state of
preservation is due to the fact that
she sank on her maiden voyage (in
1628) in cold waters and was found
by an enthusiast, Anders Franzén,
330 years later. The ship was carefully
lifted from the sea bottom and
painstakingly conserved (the whole
operation took almost 20 years).

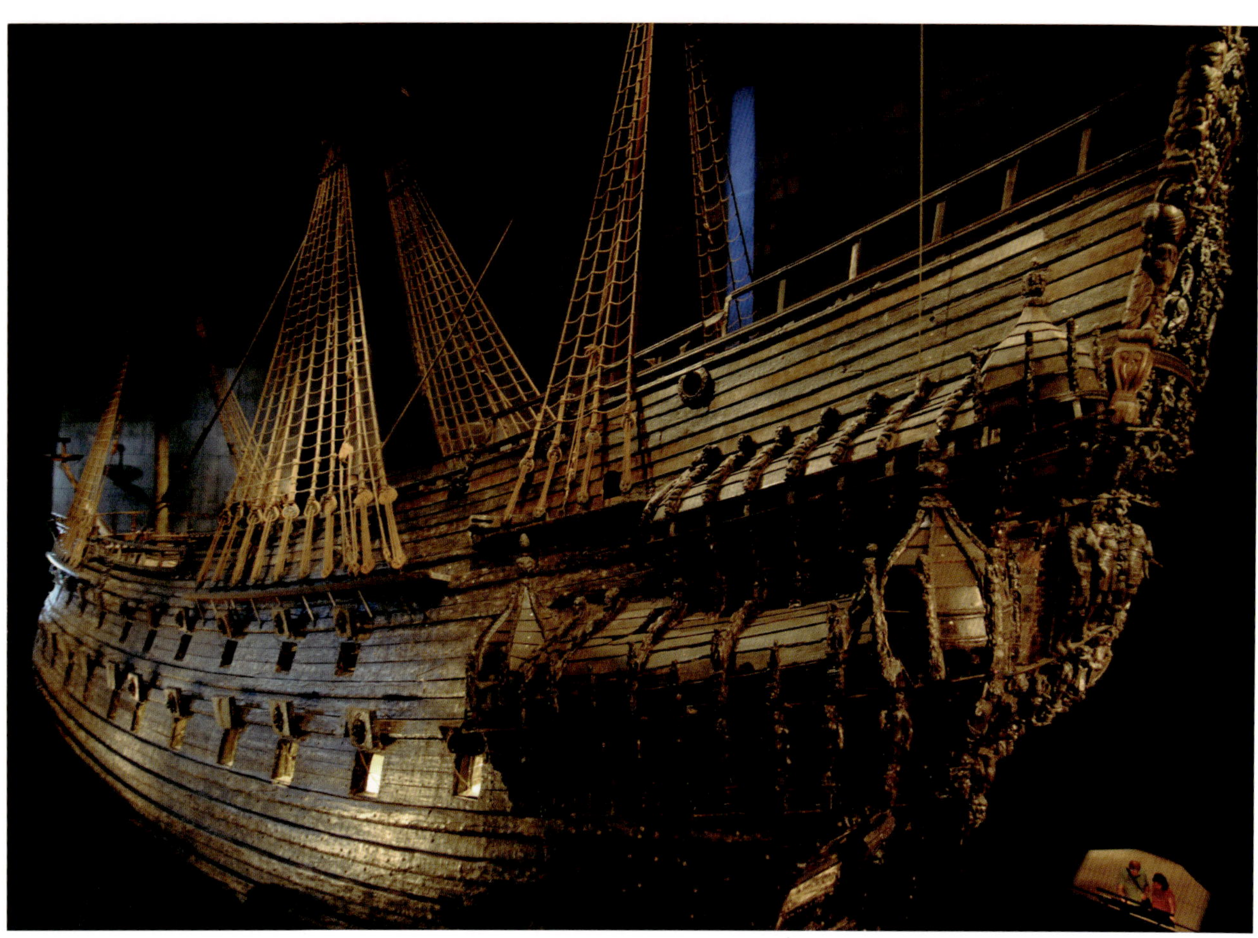

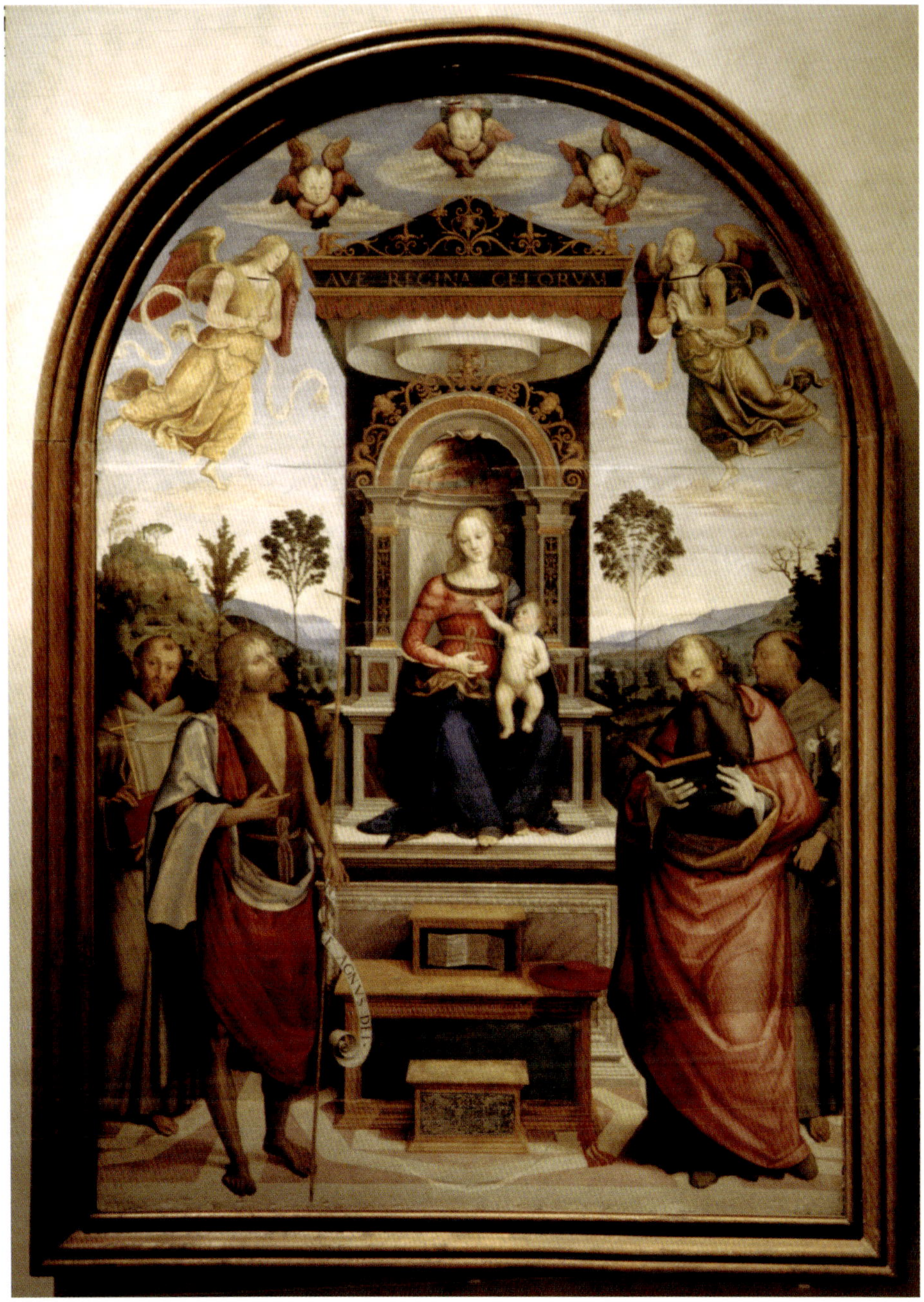

Pinturicchio. 'Madonna and Child'. National Gallery of Umbria, Perugia, Italy. Tripod photography is not permitted in the National Gallery in Perugia, but you can use a hand-held camera – a serious challenge for the photographer when indoors.

Ancient wooden idol in Viking Museum in Lofotre (Norway). Here on the Lofoten Islands the remains were discovered of the biggest Viking house in Scandinavia, and a museum was built on its foundations.

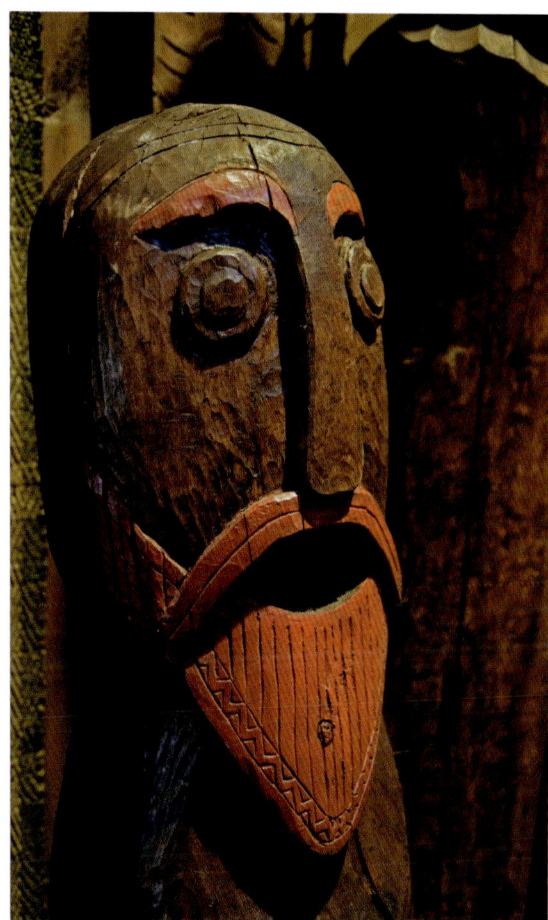

Open sesame!

With the advent of digital compact cameras, travel photography has become popular, and the saying 'When in Rome, do as the Romans do' is pertinent to photographers. Basically, the photographer doesn't need any explanation of 'what to do': just take pictures of everything that is interesting, beautiful or unusual – in short, everything that attracts the eye. The most beautiful things on Earth are the creations of nature, works of art made by people in a burst of creative inspiration and people themselves, especially in all the manifestations of spiritual life and love.

You'd think it was all plain sailing with natural and historical monuments, but there can be pitfalls waiting for you where you never expect them. I can still remember something that happened to me in my twenties, which could actually have turned out to be decidedly unpleasant for me. I was driving out of Santa Fe, New Mexico on my way to the Bandolero Canyon National Park, which I reckoned was about a hundred kilometres away, where there is one of the most interesting monuments left by an ancient Indian civilisation. It's a cave village from the twelfth century called White Cliff. I came upon a jeep at the side of the road in the middle of nowhere, with the bonnet open. A tall man in uniform was staring gloomily down at the engine which was giving trouble. I assumed he was one of the park rangers. I braked and offered to give him a lift to the nearest town. But the ranger replied that he couldn't leave his vehicle, as he had an automatic rifle in a special compartment in the car, and the guy who was due to relieve him had the only key that could unlock it. 'Ten miles from here' the ranger told me 'you'll see a gate, and he'll be standing there. Tell him to send out the technical assistance people'.

The gate appeared, large and solid, made of cast iron, with a big sign reading 'Los Alamos'. I realised as I read it that this was vaguely familiar, but I was in a hurry to get to White Cliff before sunset. So I jumped blithely out of the car and walked through the gates to explain to the guard what he had to do. And at that moment I realised what was familiar about the place: I was at the site of the ill-omened nuclear centre, at the birthplace of the bomb dropped on Hiroshima. I had a vivid memory of an American journalist, festooned in cameras with tele-zooms and speaking Russian (though with a pronounced accent). He'd penetrated by mistake into some site known as Arzamas-16 or Krasnoyarsk-26. It was too late to laugh or cry, so I just walked back towards my car, waiting to be challenged. However, no-one stopped me from going on my way.

There are no special problems with photographing nature, as long as you don't create them yourself; but when it comes to people's spiritual lives, architecture or art, things are less easy. It must be clearly understood that in churches,

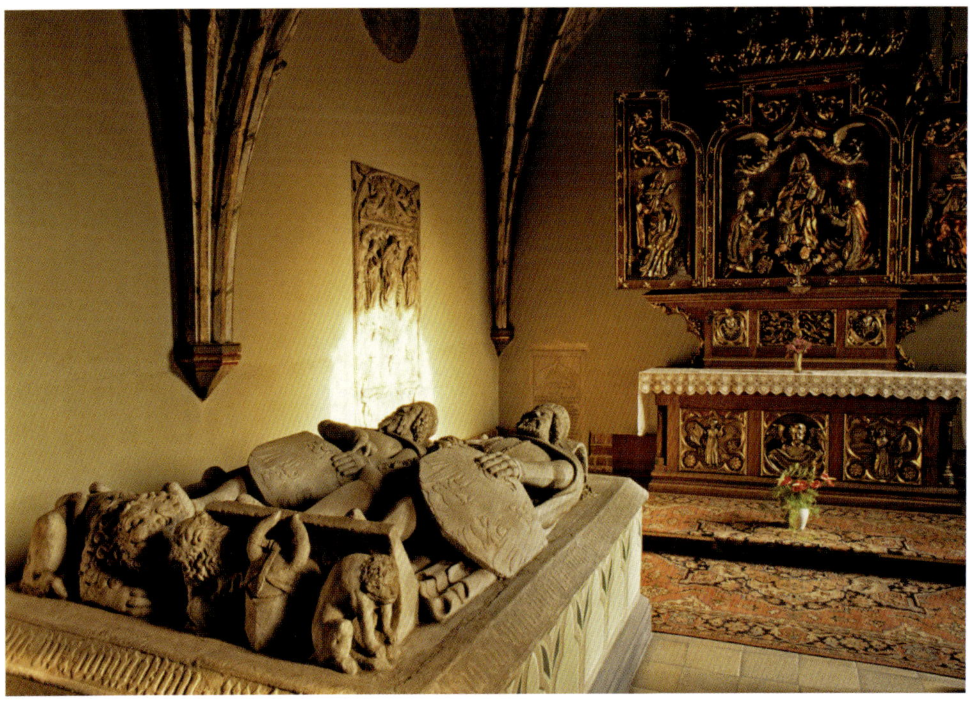

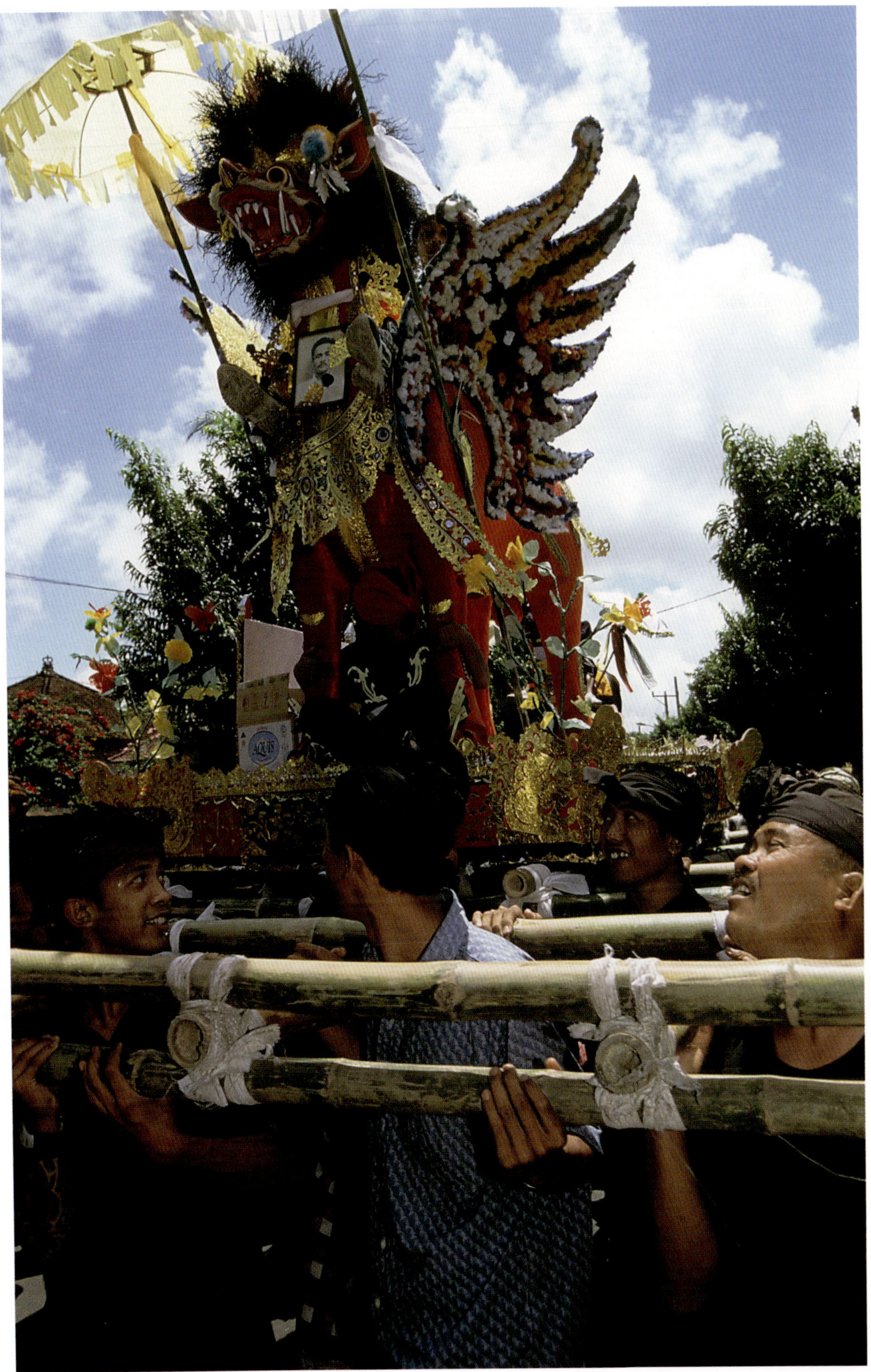

monasteries and sanctuaries – any sacred place, whether it is a Christian church of any denomination, a mosque, a synagogue, a Buddhist temple, a pagoda, an ashram, a monastery, a *kiva* or a ceremonial field of totem poles – a photographer with a camera displayed on his chest is not a welcome guest. If you start clicking away in a Buddhist temple, you'll be told in the nicest possible way that you shouldn't; in a Russian Orthodox church, old ladies will shush you and may show you the door. But be warned: don't use your flash to defile people at prayer in a mosque or indeed anywhere else in a Muslim fundamentalist country. You definitely should not try to take secret photos of a Native American or Australian Aboriginal initiation ceremony or some other kind of ritual that is absolutely closed to outside eyes. There you'll only escape by the skin of your teeth.

But the true photographer is the person who, when he or she mustn't, most wants to: And yes – sometimes sesame does open! But first you need pure thoughts, and to take a severe look at yourself and your appearance. Men – forget the shorts and sleeveless vest, women – forget the skin-tight trousers and bare shoulders. The only legal way – and the most correct one – to take photographs in a place of worship or a monastery is to get the blessing of the priest or prior, the imam or rabbi. One sign from him and, as if by magic, even the most zealous keepers of the faith and fanatics will simply take no notice of you. However, there must be very weighty reasons for such a request. Don't take it into your head to pose as a pilgrim – you will be unmasked in an instant. A polite request from a person who is respected there will give you the best chance – even better if it is somebody who knows the priest well. Your guide, who frequently goes into places of worship in the course of his or her job, may turn out to be just such a person.

Sometimes chance comes to your aid. I was travelling on the island of Bali in a chauffeur-driven car with a guide, on my way back from photographing a mountain temple. In one of the settlements out in the sticks, I saw a number of elegantly dressed women who appeared, one after another, carrying metre-high pyramids of artistically arranged fruit on their heads, together with some kind of confectionery. The guide explained that the women were taking offerings to the gods in the local temple (there are hundreds of such temples on Bali). In some queer way, Buddhism had been replaced by the ancient local superstitions there. There are huge numbers of gods, and they all have to be propitiated.

We slowed down and about half a kilometre later we'd driven through the village. We noticed that the women were turning off the highway down a side road. I asked the guide to come with me, and we spent twenty minutes walking along a forest path with the colourful procession, until we arrived at the gates of the temple. The guide went off to request

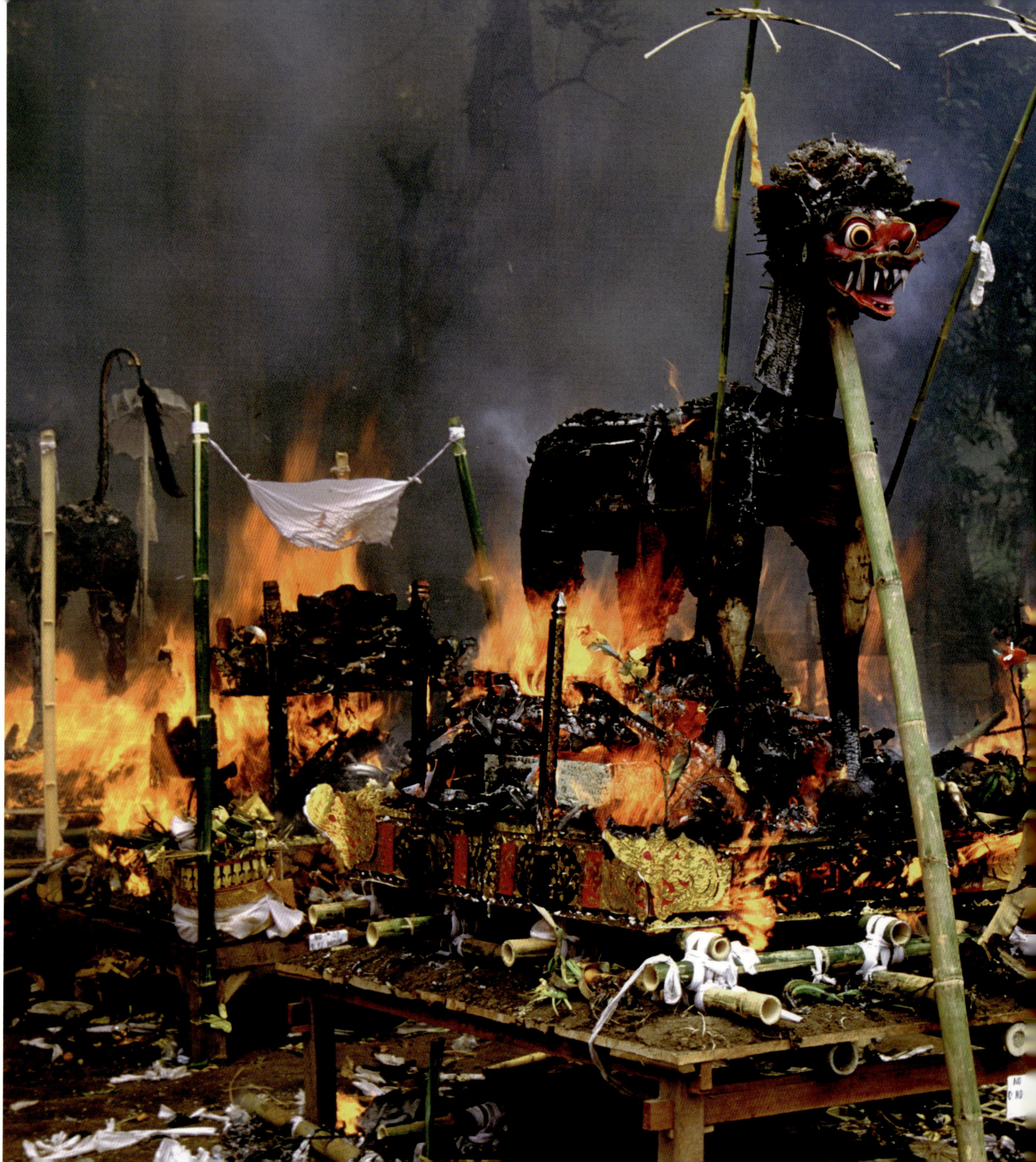

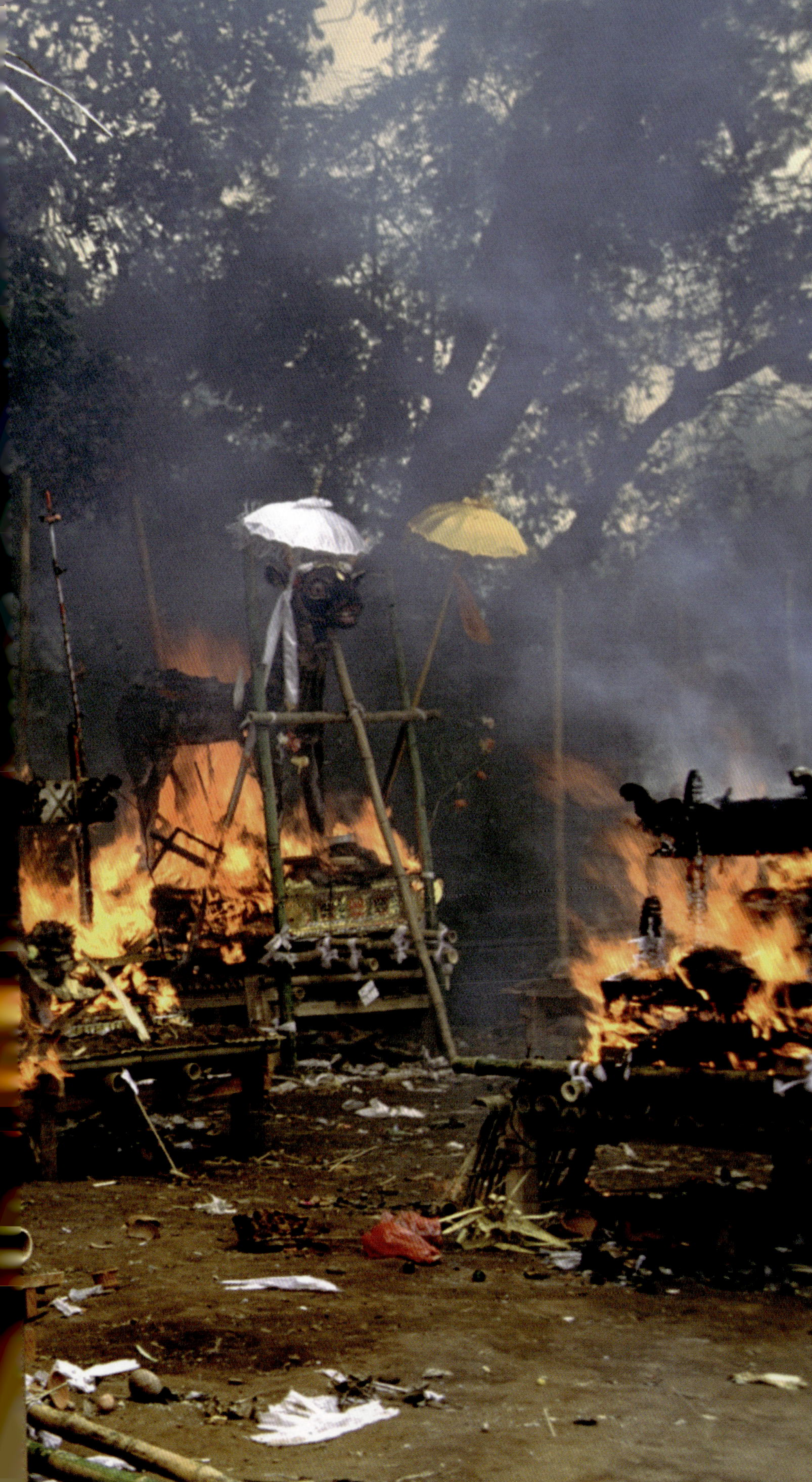

Cremation rites. Bali. This funeral ceremony can continue for many hours. Huge bulls, goats, elephants and monsters are placed at the edge of the forest on stands prepared earlier. People say goodbye to their long-dead kin, then the figures are surrounded with brushwood and turned into blazing, towering bonfires. And thus all the souls of the dead are set free.

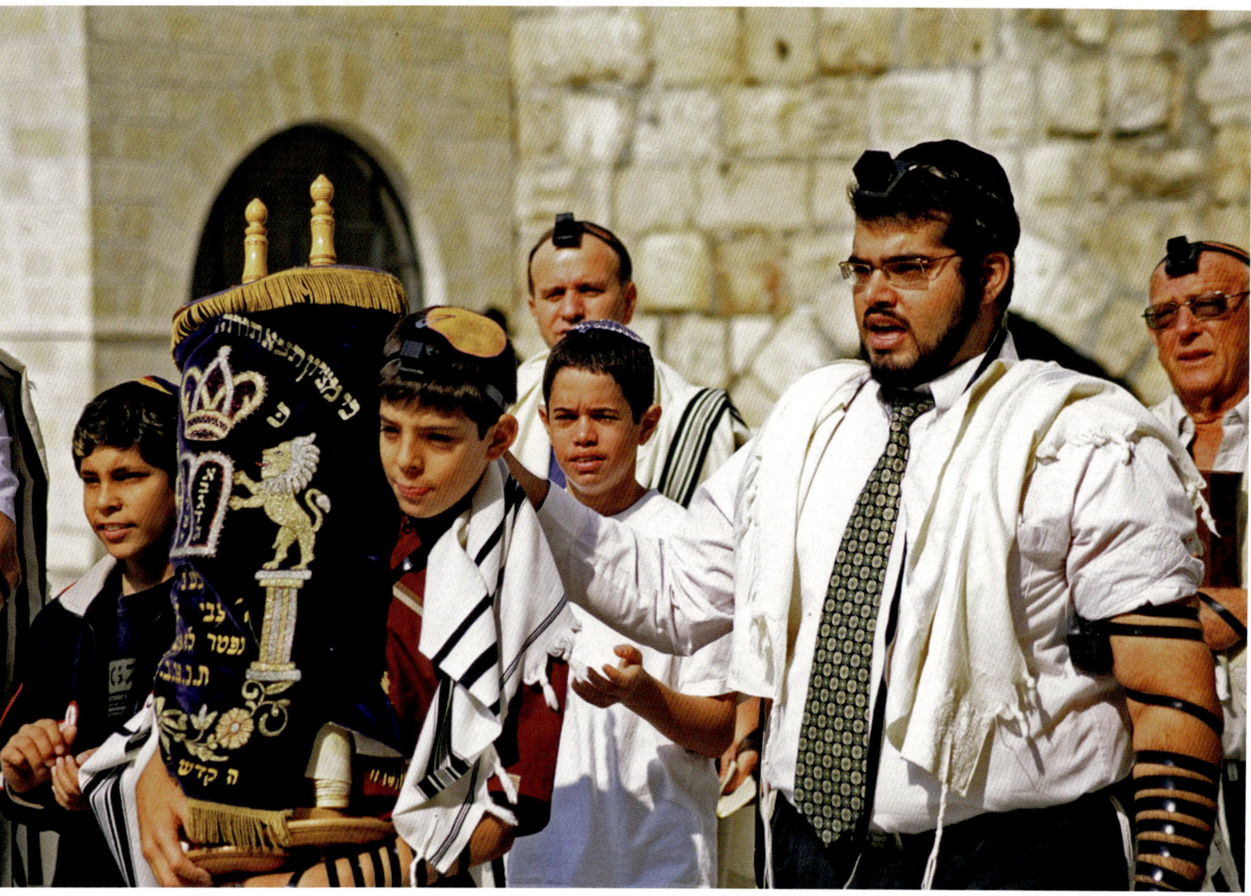

permission for me to take photographs, and he quickly returned
with the high priest. But he informed me that not only were
outsiders not allowed to take photographs but they weren't
allowed to cross the threshold of the temple. This had never
been permitted in the entire history of the temple. I spent
a long time trying to talk the old man round, hoping that he
might sympathise with a journalist from far-away Russia. But
he was immovable.

'You can not enter the temple precincts in any case – you
don't have a sarong'. This was his final word and concluded his
reply. And that's where he made his mistake. I sent the guide
off into the forest with instructions to buy me a sarong – no
haggling, never mind the price. Half an hour later, having paid
20 dollars, there I was clad in the national dress, which takes
the form of a large chunk of decorated material which you
wind around your waist like a long skirt. Soon I was standing
triumphantly before the cleric in my magnificent sarong, tied
up with a silken brocade belt. As it turned out, it suited me very
well. In the opinion of the local inhabitants, the blue-brown
colours of the fabric would somehow magically incite me to

noble thoughts and deeds! The inflexible old man gave in, and
allowed what may well have been the first foreign visitor to
enter his temple, where I spent an exotic three hours taking
photos. All the 'temple photos' from Bali which you normally
see in newspapers and guidebooks are taken in the temple
theatre of Batubulan or in a couple of other places where fancy
dress shows are put on especially for tourists - and for profit.

You sometimes have to resolve complicated ethical
questions. This happened to me in Pskov-Pecherski monastery,
where I was taking photographs at the celebration of the
Dormition of the Madonna, a very striking ceremony which
takes place at the end of August. I took some very successful
photos of the monks, the picturesque religious procession in
which the miracle-working icon of the Madonna is carried
around the monastery walls, and some colourful genre scenes.
And then, when twilight was already falling, I noticed, in
the monastery courtyard, the only remaining monk in the
monastery, Hrisana, who had taken the vows of schema (the
strictest vows in the Orthodox Church), and had deliberately
forsaken the world for an underground cavern cell, which

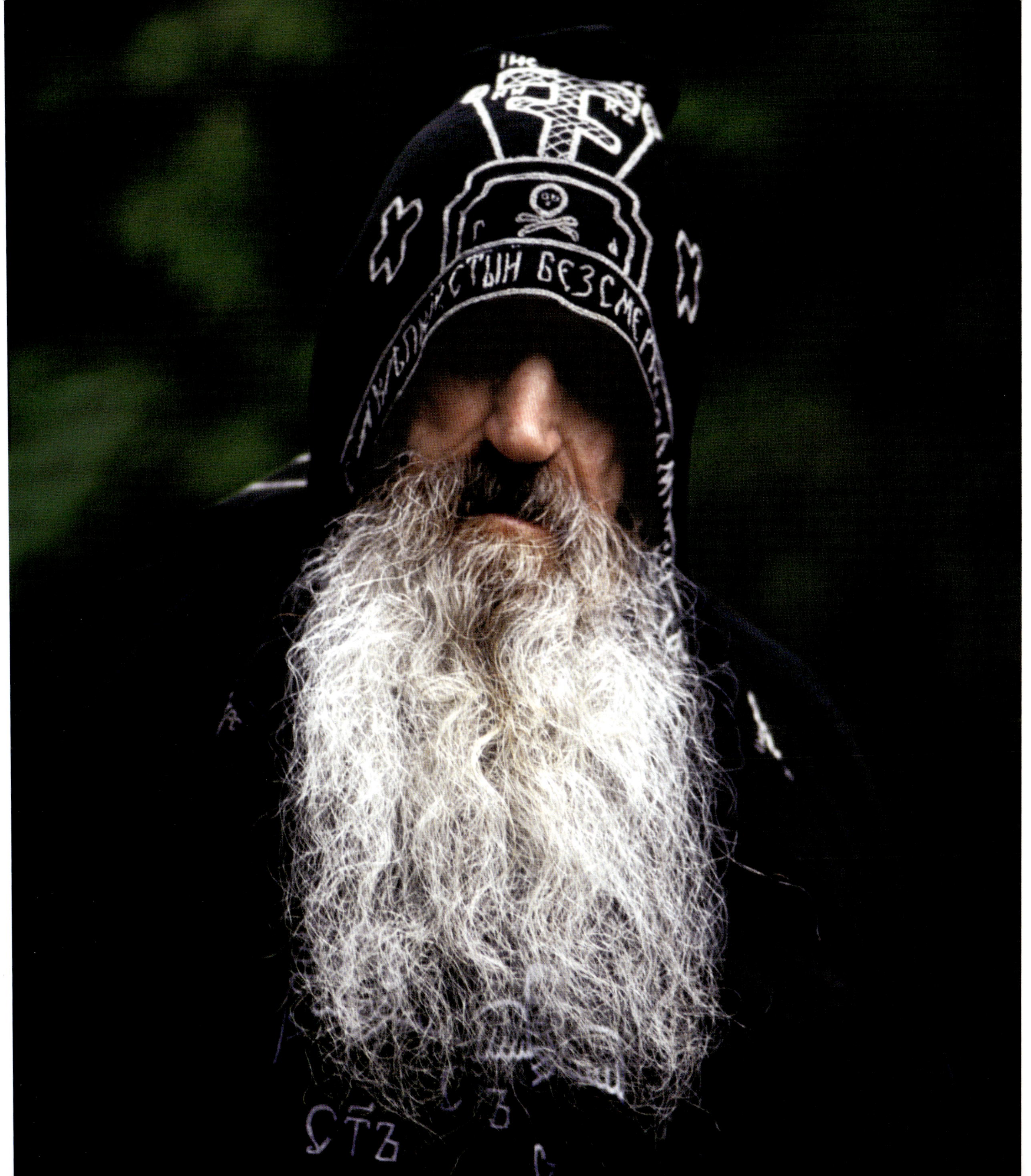
СТЫН БЕЗСМЕР
СТЪ

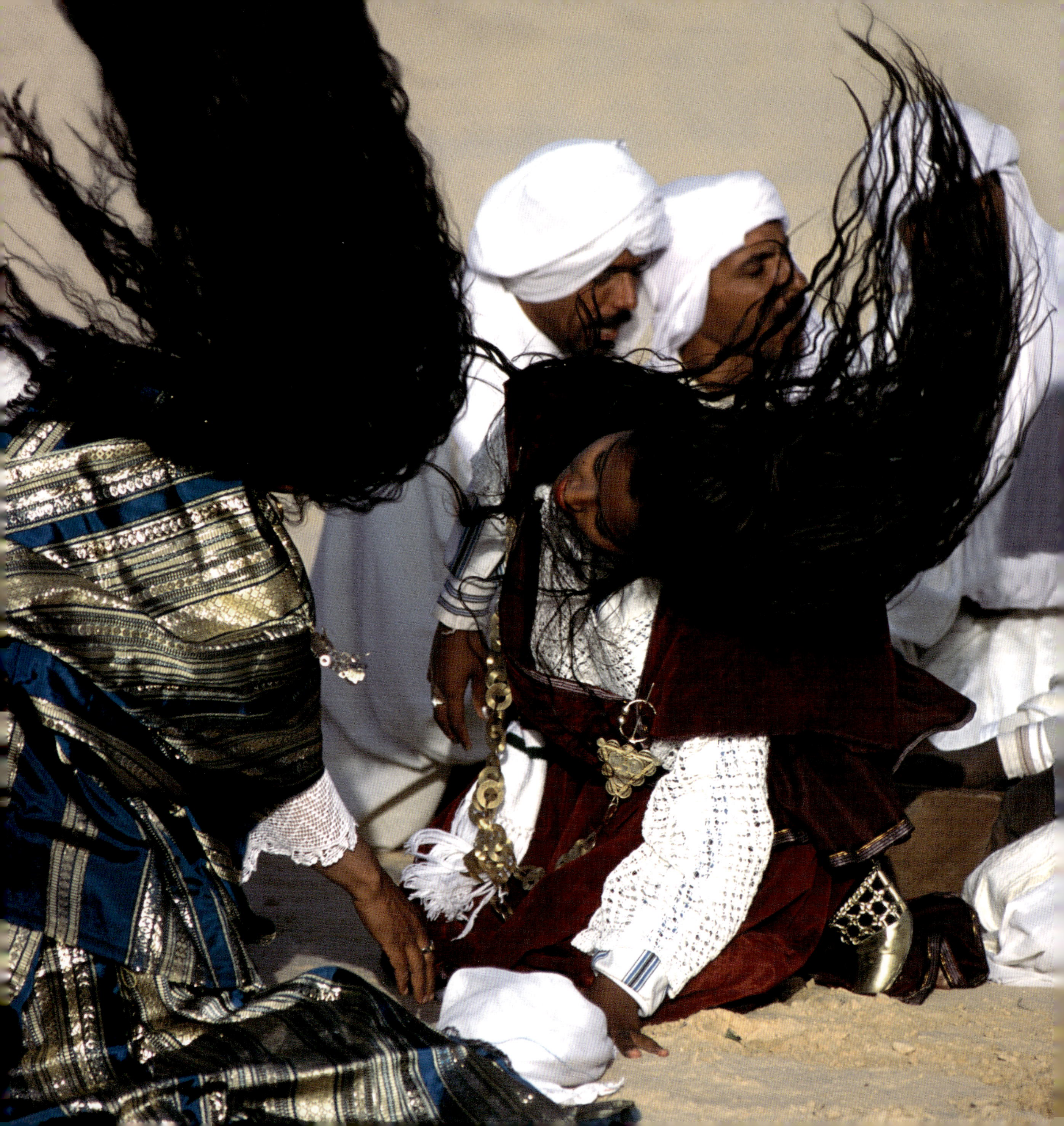

Wedding in the Sahara, Tunisia. In winter, the nomads of the Sahara come from all the countries of North Africa and gather at one of the oases for a celebration: competing in camel and horse races, choosing an intended bride. Swarthy beauties arrive at this bride-fair in special little cone-shaped 'houses' mounted on the backs of camels and, spreading their blue-black manes of hair, dance the dance of the brides.

Offerings to the gods. On the island of Bali, in one of the roadside villages, elegantly dressed women began to appear one after another with huge, metre-high pyramids of fruit and some kind of confectionery arranged artistically on their heads. Here there is a fantastical mixture of Buddhism and ancient beliefs.

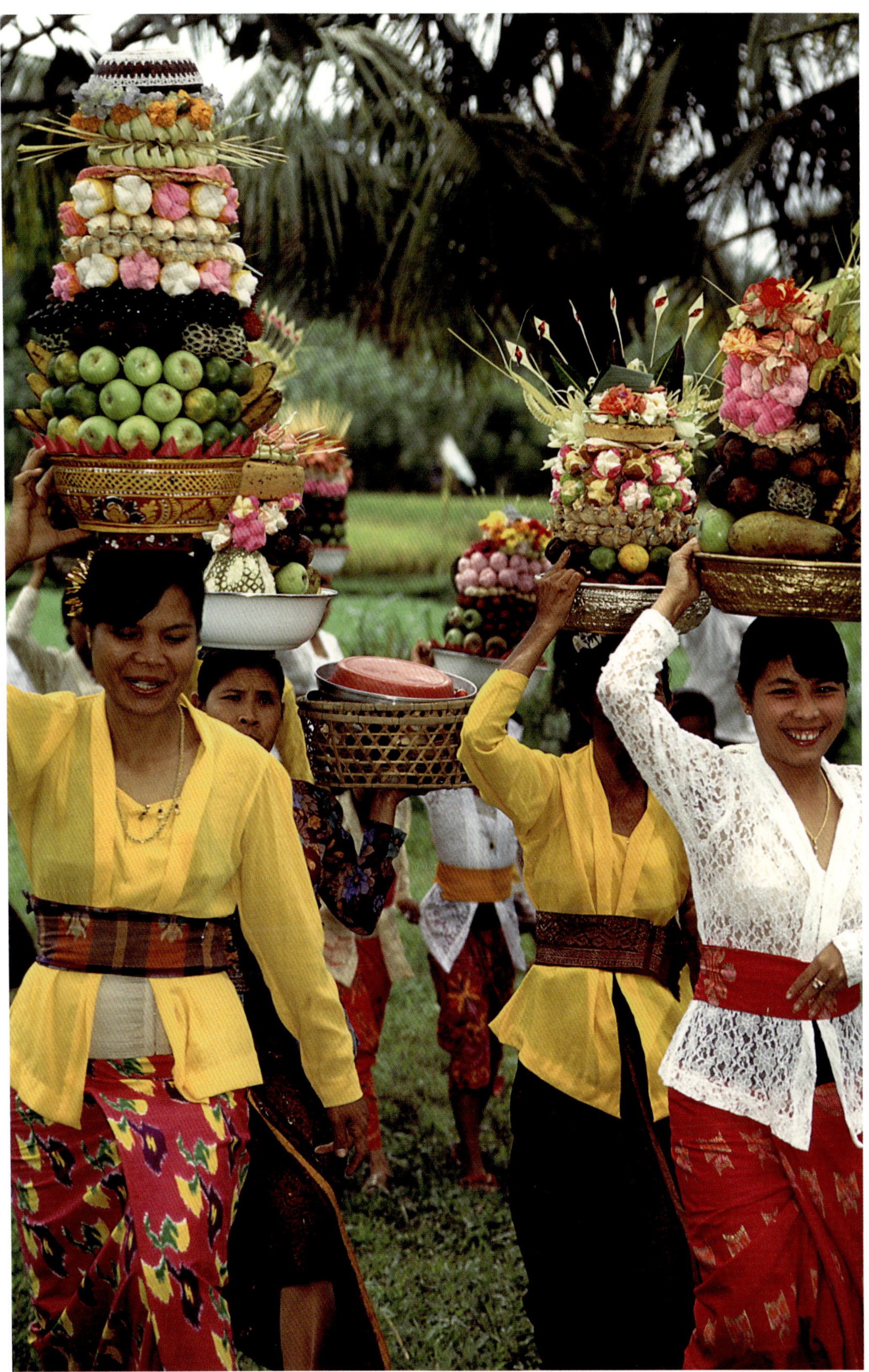

A cave under the Omar Mosque (Dome of the Rock) in Jerusalem, once the top of a hill from which the Muslims believe that Mohammed ascended to Paradise.

Optina Monastery, Russia. Using a wide-angled lens and with a correspondingly long exposure, it's possible to shoot only general views. But you can't take a close-up photograph of the most important thing – the inspired faces of those praying.

You need a telephoto lens. A 180/2.8 lens to photograph a face lit by candlelight – that's possible with an open aperture and a sensitivity of 1600 ASA, using an exposure of 1/60. You need a point of support for the camera or the lens.

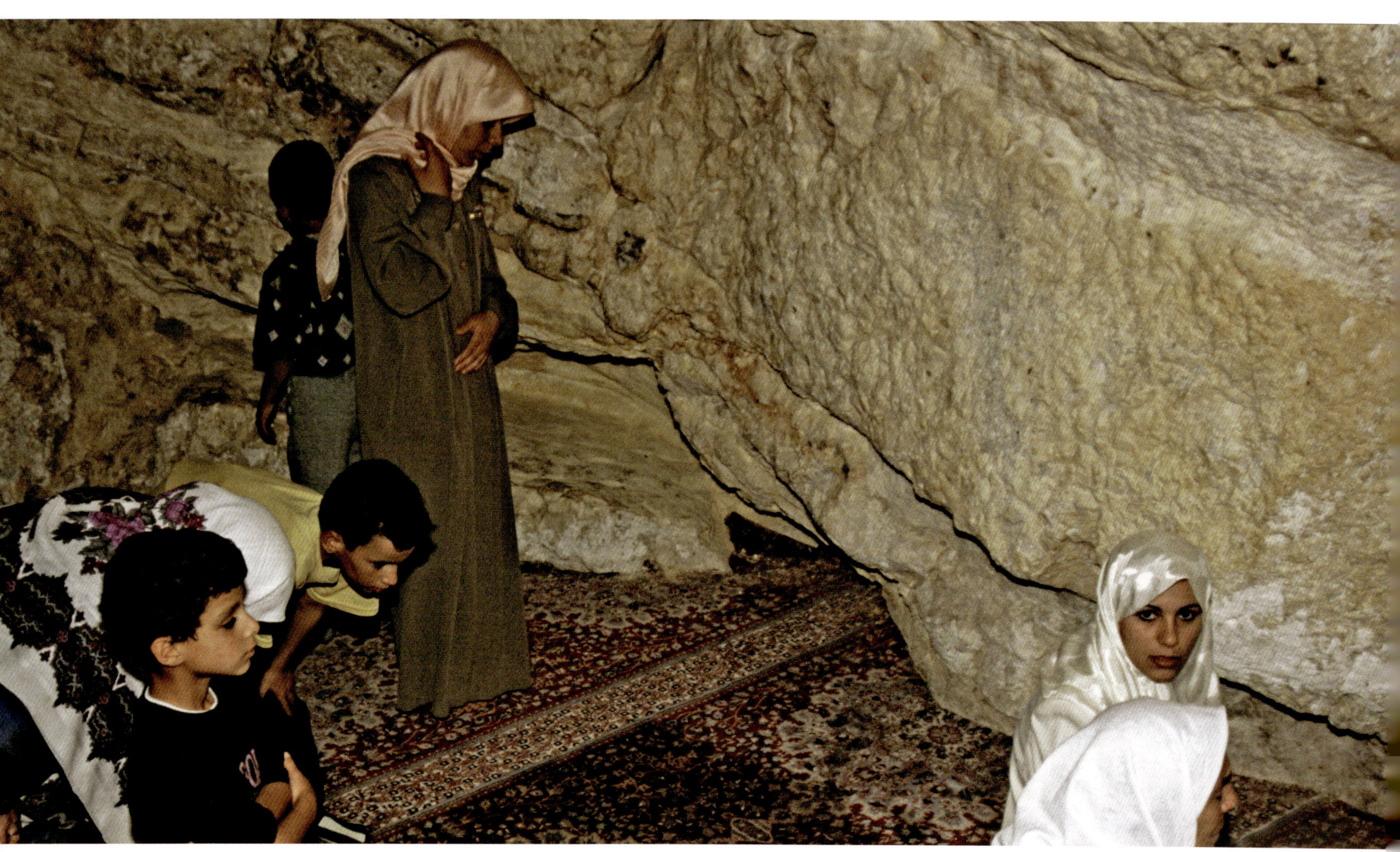

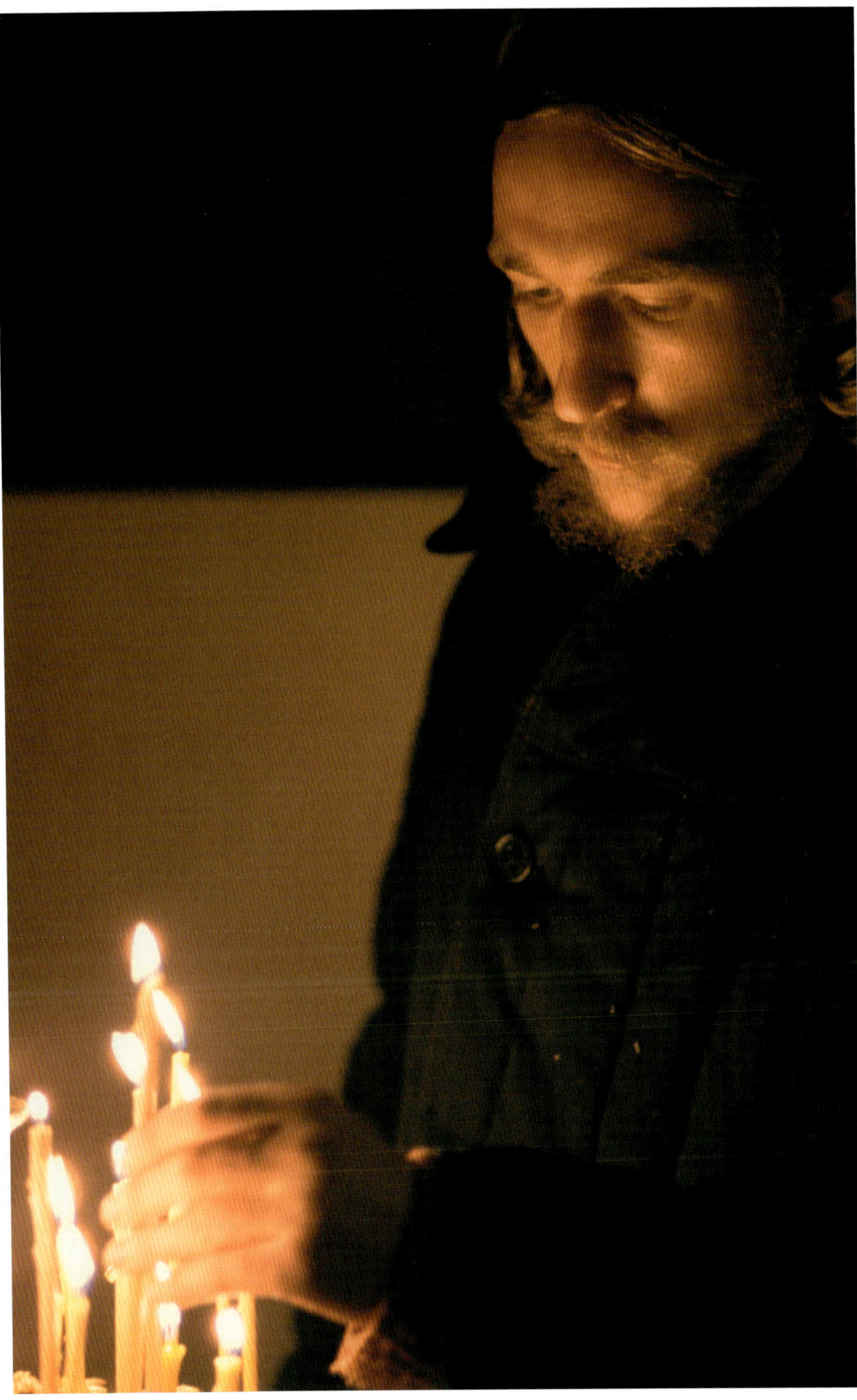

he left scarcely once a year, and then only for a short time. For this great monastery festival, the hood of his habit was moved onto his forehead, and his eyes were in deep shadow. I couldn't light up the eyes of a man living in the dark with a flash, even a weak one. The last hermit will remain like that for history – with shadows instead of eyes. Predicting when fate will smile on you and when you should take the photo you need, playing all the tricks in the book, is very difficult, but never miss a chance! His majesty fate can spring surprises which are sometimes difficult to believe - but a photo is a reliable witness. I am deeply convinced that here we are not talking about blind willpower, but about conformity to a law of some kind, a direct link with your energy and personality. For the very strictest of prohibitions can be overcome by these factors – in my many years of experience, I've seen amazing examples of this more than once.

However, so as not to tempt you to put your health or your life at risk, I reserve the right not to reveal how photos were taken of women with children, praying at one of the most sacred Islamic sites on Earth – the dark stone cave under the floor of the famous Omar mosque, the Dome of the Rock in Jerusalem, which was at one time the top of a temple from which, so the Muslims believe, Mohammed ascended – absolutely closed to unbelievers, not only for photographs, but also for access.

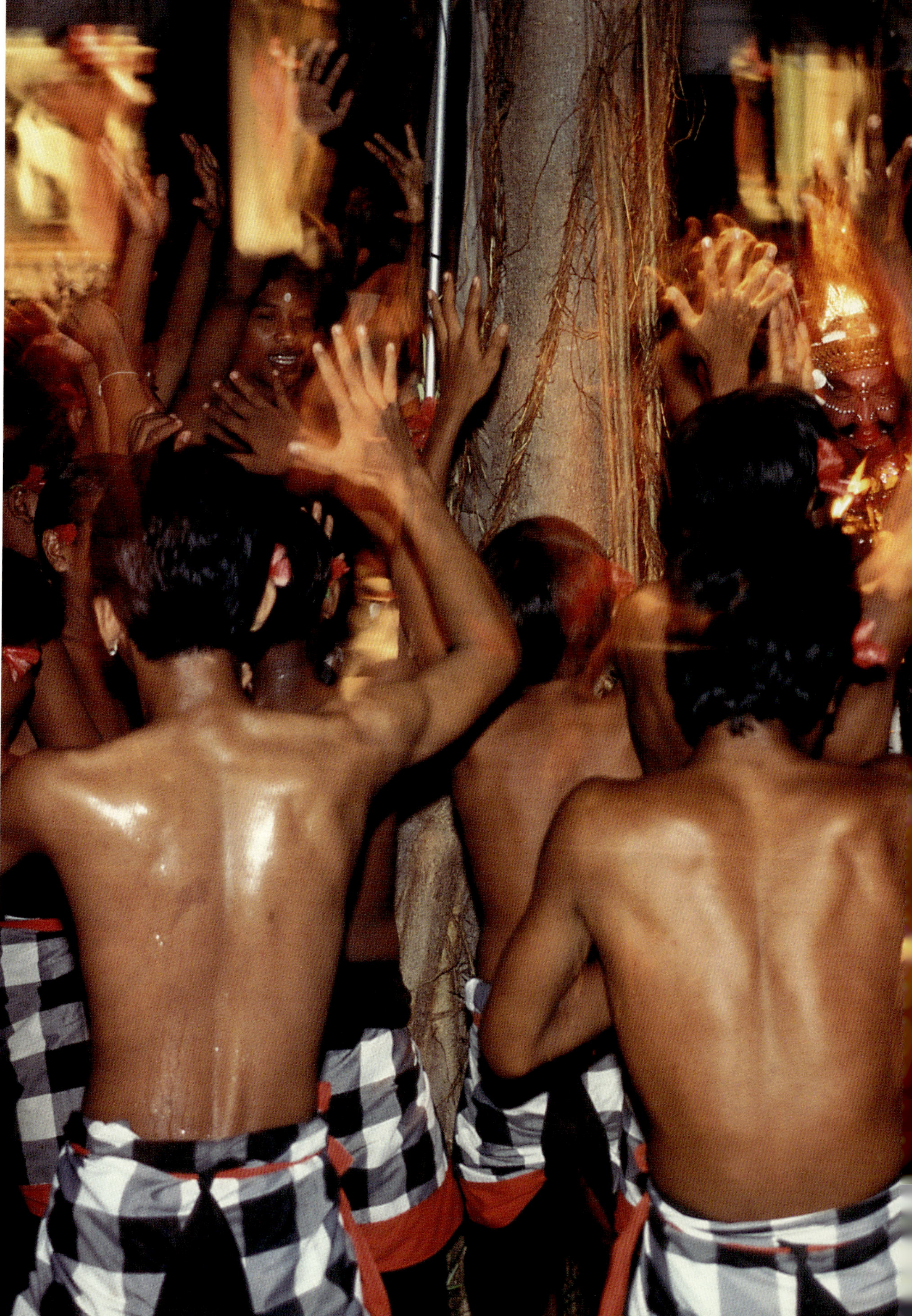

In Bali, the famous *kecak* trance dance is traditionally performed by men, naked to the waist. The synchronised rotation of their bodies, the snake-like gliding of their hands and the torches flaming in the dark enhance the mystical atmosphere of the action. The picture was taken with flash using rear curtain sync.

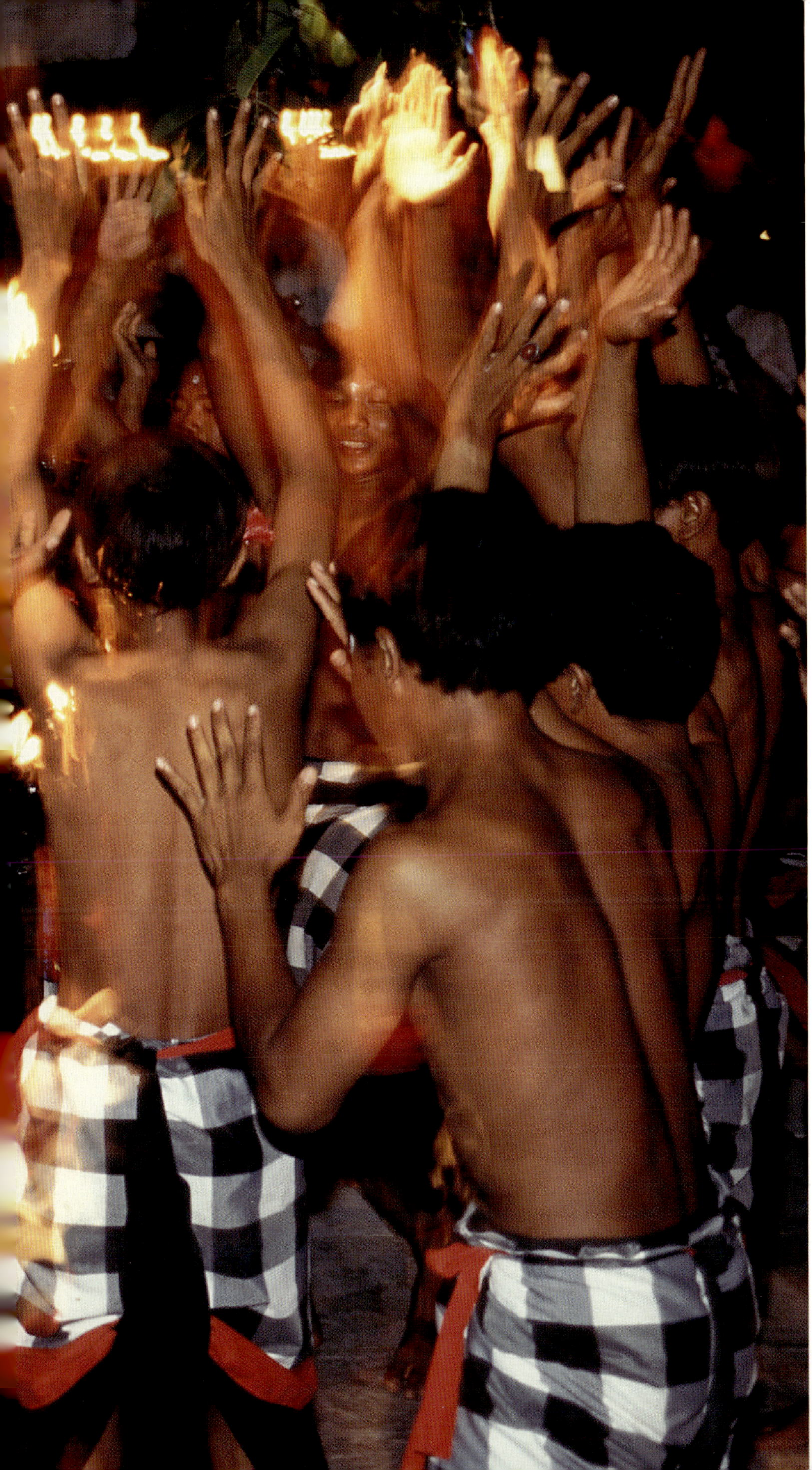

About the author

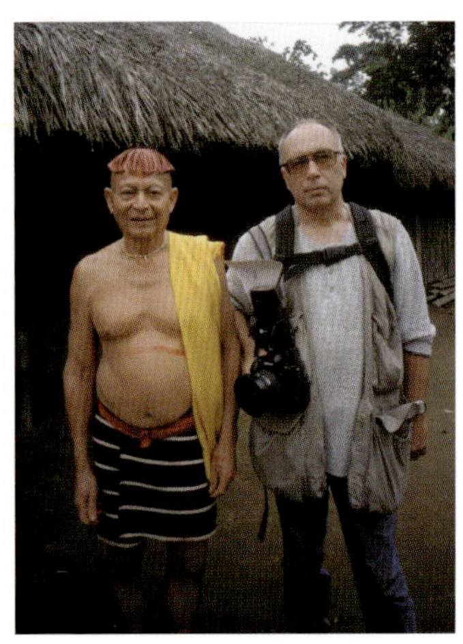

Alex Milovsky is a well-known travel photographer and journalist, a tireless traveller and discoverer, who has visited more than 80 countries. Thousands of his photos have been published in the magazines *GEO*, *Stern*, *Natural History*, *Vanity Fair*, *Vogue*, *GQ*, *Elle*, *Harper's Bazaar* and *Focus*, among others.

He has worked in the USA, Germany, the UK and Italy, with some of the best-known journalists and photographic agencies. Milovsky's work has also appeared in surveys of the best photographs in the world and is in the collections of various museums.